Victim Advocacy before the International Criminal Court

Elizabeth King • Rianne Letschert •
Sam Garkawe • Erin Pobjie
Editors

Victim Advocacy before the International Criminal Court

Springer

Editors
Elizabeth King
Member, List of Counsel
International Criminal Court
The Hague, The Netherlands

Victorian Bar
Greens List Barristers
Melbourne, VIC, Australia

Rianne Letschert
President of Maastricht University
Maastricht, The Netherlands

Sam Garkawe
School of Law and Justice
Southern Cross University
East Lismore, New South Wales, Australia

Erin Pobjie
International Law
University of Essex
Colchester, UK

ISBN 978-3-030-56731-6 ISBN 978-3-030-56733-0 (eBook)
https://doi.org/10.1007/978-3-030-56733-0

This Springer imprint is published by the registered company Springer Nature Switzerland AG.
The registered company address is: Gewerbestrasse 11, 6330 Cham, Switzerland

Acknowledgements

- *Prof. Esteban Peralta-Losilla*—Head of Counsel Support Section of the International Criminal Court (ICC), Professor at University of Zaragoza (Spain)
- *The Hon. Prof. George Hampel, AM QC*—Former Justice of the Supreme Court of Victoria (Australia), former Chairman and founder of the Australian Advocacy Institute (AAI)
- *Dr. Stephanie Fahey*—former deputy vice-chancellor of Global Engagement, Monash University (Australia), Chief Executive Officer at Austrade.
- *The Hon. Justice Ann Ainslie-Wallace*—Judge of the Appellate Division of the Family Court of Australia, Chairman of the Australian Advocacy Institute (AAI), Adjunct Professor of Law at UTS (Sydney, Australia), a fellow of the Australian Academy of Law, Council member of the Australian Institute of Judicial Administration
- *Her Hon. Judge Felicity Hampel SC*—member of the Board and Management Committee of the Australian Advocacy Institute, Advisory Board member of the Castan Centre for Human Rights, Steering Committee member of the International Institute for Forensic Studies.
- *Dr. Magda Karagiannakis*—Member of the List of Counsel of the International Criminal Court (ICC), Barrister of the Supreme Court of Victoria (Australia) and High Court of Australia, Associate Director International Criminal Law Advocacy and Research Centre (ICLRC), Lecturer La Trobe University (Melbourne, Australia)
- *Prof. Gideon Boas*—Barrister (Victorian Bar, Australia), Professor at the College of Arts, Social Sciences and Commerce at La Trobe University Law School (Melbourne, Australia)
- *Ms. Samira Hamzic*—Administrative Assistant and Secretariat of Disciplinary Organs for counsel at the International Criminal Court (ICC) (The Hague, The Netherlands)
- *Dr. Peter Groves*—Senior Lecturer in literary studies at the School of Languages, Literatures, Cultures and Linguistics, Monash University (Melbourne, Australia)

- *Ms. Elizabeth Brimer*—Barrister (Victorian Bar, Australia), Advocacy instructor at the Australian Advocacy Institute (AAI)
- *Mr. Randall Kune*—Barrister (Victorian Bar, Australia), Co-author of the *Advocacy Manual: The Complete Guide to Persuasive Advocacy* (published by the Australian Advocacy Institute), Senior Fellow at Monash University Law School (Melbourne, Australia)
- *Ms. Nina Massara*—Education Co-ordinator (Victorian Bar, Australia), Former Senior Business Development Officer (2015-17) at the Faculty of Law, Monash University (Melbourne, Australia)
- *Mr. Scott Wallace*—General Manager of the Australian Advocacy Institute (AAI)
- *Mr. David Sexton*—Barrister (Victorian Bar, Australia), Board Member of The International Criminal Law Advocacy and Research Institute (ICLAR).
- *Ms. Tiffanni Walton*—Editorial assistance
- *Ms. Eliza Sweeney*—French translation assistance
- *Ms. Kate Philips*—French translation assistance
- *International Criminal Court Bar Association (ICCBA)* https://www.iccba-abcpi.org (The Hague, The Netherlands)
- *International Victimology Institute Tilburg (INTERVICT)* Tilburg University https://www.tilburguniversity.edu/research/institutes-and-research-groups/intervict (Tilburg, The Netherlands)
- *World Society of Victimology (WSV)* http://www.worldsocietyofvictimology.org
- *Castan Centre for Human Rights Law*, Faculty of Law, Monash University monash.edu/law/castancentre (Melbourne, Australia)
- *International Criminal Law Advocacy and Research Centre (ICLAR)* (Australia)
- *The Australian Advocacy Institute (AAI)* http://www.advocacy.com.au/ (Australia)

. . .things standing thus unknown, shall live behind me!
If thou didst ever hold me in thy heart
Absent thee from felicity a while,
And in this harsh world draw thy breath in pain
To tell my story.—Hamlet (Act 5, Scene 2) by William Shakespeare

. . .si les choses restent ainsi inconnues, vivra après moi!
Si jamais tu m'as porté dans ton cœur,
absente-toi quelque temps encore de la félicité céleste,
et exhale ton souffle pénible dans ce monde rigoureux,
pour raconter mon histoire.—Hamlet (Scène 20) de William Shakespeare. Traduction de Victor Hugo[1]

My voice is heard in the court because my story will be read,
and will be known, and I will be represented.

Reflections of a Ugandan victim in an interview by Berkeley Law (CA, USA), discussing victim participation at the International Criminal Court[2]

Ma voix est entendue dans la cour parce que mon histoire sera lue et sera connue, et je serai représentée

Réflexions d'une victime ougandaise dans une interview de Berkeley Law (CA, USA), discutant de la participation des victimes à la Cour pénale internationale

[1] Hugo, François-Victor, (1865) *Le Deux Hamlet* (2e éd). Paris: France Pagnerre, p. 369.

[2] *The Victims' Court? A Study of 622 Victim Participants at the International Criminal Court* by Cody, S., Stover, E., Balthazard, M., Koenig, A., & Human Rights Center, University of California, Berkeley, School of Law. (2015:33). https://www.law.berkeley.edu/wp-content/uploads/2015/04/VP_report_2015_final_full2.pdf. Accessed 10 January 2020.

Contents

About the Editors

Elizabeth King is a member of the International Criminal Court's list of counsel and is a member of the Victorian Bar, Melbourne. Elizabeth is the prior recipient of the Gordon Lewis Speakers trophy (Law Institute of Victoria) and the John Phillips Advocacy Award, Monash University, Melbourne. Elizabeth conducts workshops in trial practice and advocacy with the Marsh Centre, Monash University, Melbourne.

Elizabeth formerly worked for the Australian Red Cross (Victoria Division) in International Humanitarian Law. She has previously taught on The Ethics of Global Conflict and Human Rights Theory in the School of Philosophical Enquiry (Monash University, Melbourne) and conducted post-graduate research on fair trial rights in International Humanitarian Law with the Castan Centre, Monash University.

Contact: liz_king33@iinet.net.au

Rianne Letschert studied International Law at Tilburg University, the University of Amsterdam and the University of Montpellier. She obtained her PhD from Tilburg University in 2005, with a thesis entitled *The impact of minority rights mechanisms*, exploring the competing international organisations that formulate policy and legislation on national minorities.

In March 2011, Letschert was appointed professor to the newly established chair in Victimology and International Law at Tilburg University. From April until August 2010, she was a visiting research fellow at the Lauterpacht Centre for International Law at the University of Cambridge as well as a research fellow at Clare College in Cambridge, where she is a lifelong member. In 2014, she also held a visiting professorship at the University of Barcelona. She has written and edited various books and published articles in national and international scholarly journals.

Professor Letschert received a Vidi grant from the Netherlands Organisation for Scientific Research (NWO) in May 2015 for her research on the impact of international tribunals on societies and people who are confronted with serious violations of human rights and international crime. She is an expert consultant on casualty cases to the Special Tribunal for Lebanon, and she previously also directed the International Victimology Institute Tilburg (INTERVICT). In 2012, she became a member of the

Young Academy of the Royal Netherlands Academy of Arts and Sciences (KNAW) and was appointed as its chair in April 2015.

Professor Letschert has been Rector Magnificus of Maastricht University since 1 September 2016.

Contact: r.letschert@maastrichtuniversity.nl

Sam Garkawe has been recently appointed as a Professor of Law at OP Jindal Global University, India, where he teaches a course on 'Crime Victims in National and International Justice: Protection, Participation and Reparation'. He is also an Adjunct Associate Professor at the School of Law and Justice at Southern Cross University, NSW, Australia. He has published widely in the field of victimology, concentrating on issues concerning the role of victims in both national and international justice, including their role in the International Criminal Court and the South African Truth and Reconciliation Commission. He taught victimology, human rights, criminal law and procedure and international criminal justice at Southern Cross University. He is a life member of the World Society of Victimology and was a member of its Executive from 2009 to 2015, and has been a continuous member of its United Nations Liaison Sub-committee since 2003.

Contact: sam.garkawe@scu.edu.au

Erin Pobjie is a Lecturer (Assistant Professor) in Law at the University of Essex and Senior Research Affiliate at the Max Planck Institute for Comparative Public Law and International Law. She is a member of the International Law Association's Committee on the Use of Force: Military Assistance on Request, and co-convener of the European Society of International Law's Interest Group on Peace and Security. Previously she has was visiting scholar at the Lauterpacht Centre for International Law at the University of Cambridge and served as a visiting professional at the International Criminal Court's Victims Participation and Reparations Section.

Contact: pobjie@mpil.de

Part I
Introduction of Legal Doctrine

Part I covers a number of preliminary matters for lawyers seeking to represent victims at the International Criminal Court (ICC). Solange Mouthaan's chapter: 'The Modalities of Victim Participation' provides an introduction to the ICC scheme for victim participation. While the provisions of the Statute of the ICC and its Rules of Procedure and Evidence provide a broad outline of the scheme, these provisions were drafted with a certain level of imprecision and vagueness, leaving ICC judges with considerable discretion in developing the victim participation scheme. To fully understand the scheme it is thus necessary to also study many ICC victim participation decisions, with the result that there is a level of uncertainty and complexity in the way the scheme has developed. This is not surprising given the reality that a case before the ICC could involve thousands and thousands of victims wishing to participate, with the consequential potential problems of how this might fit in with the need for efficient procedures and the preservation the rights of defendants to a fair trial. Mouthaan's chapter describes some key elements of the scheme—the application process, the criteria and procedure for a Pre-Trial Chamber to declare applicants as victims in the case, and the subsequent role and rights of victim lawyers at the various stages of a case. Overall this chapter makes it clear that despite the challenges, complexities and uncertainties of the scheme, the role of victims has progressed from their former role as mere witnesses in international criminal justice to potentially active participants in ICC cases. However, it is also important for lawyers to understand victims do not reach the status of parties to the case.

The other chapter in this Part by Sam Garkawe provides an outline for those appointed as victims' lawyers of three essential matters that are fundamental to most prosecutions before the ICC—the definitions of the international crimes that may be prosecuted at the ICC; the principles of criminal responsibility that might apply in cases where the defendant has not personally carried out any of the crimes; and defences that may be invoked by the defendant in order to escape criminal liability. The law relating to these three matters are important for victims' lawyers as in order to advise and present their clients 'views and concerns' they must be able to follow the prosecution and defence cases, especially given that ICC victim participation procedures allow victims certain rights at the various stages of cases. The chapter provides the relevant provisions of the ICC Statute in the three matters, together with further references that will assist victims' lawyers to find the law in the minority of cases where they might have to go beyond the plain meaning of the ICC Statute.

The Modalities of Victim Participation

Solange Mouthaan

1 Introduction

Numerous are the victims resulting from the great number of conflicts that have taken place or are taking place since World War II. These victims have suffered great harms from the commission of international crimes, yet victims' rights and interests have until recently been ignored.

Victims have only recently been given a significant place, in particular with the advent of the International Criminal Court (ICC). Indeed, the ICC is amongst the first international criminal tribunal to adopt a more victim-oriented approach. Victim participation is amongst a set of procedures formally recognising the interests of victims of international crime and to allow direct victim participation in the justice process. Victims have been given an unprecedented role. In particular, the ICC has established the Victims and Witnesses Unit (VWU) to provide protective measures, legal and socio-psychological support, and other supportive measures for victims and witnesses.[1] The Rome Statute allows the Court to award reparations to victims, because it is important for victims to be recognised and compensated for the harm they suffered.[2] Most importantly, the Rome Statute under article 68(3) provides the normative framework for victim participation and grants victims the right to

[1] Statute of the International Criminal Court (Rome Statute), July 17, 1998, 2187 U.N.T.S. 90 art. 43(6).

[2] Statute of the International Criminal Court (Rome Statute), July 17, 1998, 2187 U.N.T.S. 90 art. 75.

S. Mouthaan (✉)
School of Law, University of Warwick, Coventry, UK
e-mail: s.mouthaan@warwick.ac.uk

E. King et al. (eds.), *Victim Advocacy before the International Criminal Court*,
https://doi.org/10.1007/978-3-030-56733-0_1

participate in the justice process.[3] According to Article 68(3) of the Rome Statute, victims may present their views and concerns in proceedings when their personal interests are affected, as long as participation does not unduly prejudice the right of the defendant.[4]

A victim who has been given the right to participate is different to a witness who serves the interest of the Court. A witness is the person called by either the defence or prosecution to testify at a specific time about specific facts or events.[5] Victim participation refers to the system by which individuals are allowed access the judicial proceedings by becoming 'participants' (Van den Wyngaert, 2011, p. 483). Victims' experiences of the situation under investigation are not necessarily synonymous to the crimes prosecuted. Their stories could provide judges with useful insights into the situation under investigation; may contribute to the truth-finding process and add to the evidence presented by the Prosecutor. As a consequence, judges may grant participating victims appropriate sets of rights to enable them to participate in a meaningful manner at various stages of the proceedings. Compared to previous international criminal law tribunals, the Rome Statute has given participating victims a more prominent voice to 'tell their story' either by providing their personal testimony or other means of participation, such as the ability to attend hearings, provide and challenge evidence, and call and question witnesses and experts, as well as the accused (Van den Wyngaert, 2011, p. 476). However, as a consequence, participating victims may expose themselves to public scrutiny and to possible retaliation by the accused or those affiliated to the accused.

Victim participation is an important part of the international criminal justice process. The system of victim participation at the ICC has been hailed as one of the major successes, but as argued by Judge Christine van den Wijngaert, it is also a "controversial aspect of the ICC" (Van den Wyngaert, 2011, p. 476). Indeed, to give victims access to the justice process is one step in the right direction. Victims should be involved with the international criminal justice process in a meaningful manner to them: to be treated with respect, to be kept informed about their case and to be given the possibility for their voice to be heard. However victim participation also presents a number of challenges. Since its inception, the work of the ICC has evolved and its workload is growing due to the steady increase in the number of situations and cases

---

[3] *The Prosecutor* v. *Lubanga Dyilo*, Case No. 18 January 2008, ICC-01/04-01/06, Judgment on the Appeals of the Prosecutor and the Defence Against Trial Chamber I's Decision on Victims' Participation, para 94.

[4] Article 68(3): "Where the personal interests of the victims are affected, the Court shall permit their views and concerns to be presented and considered at stages of the proceedings determined to be appropriate by the Court and in a manner which is not prejudicial to or inconsistent with the rights of the accused and a fair and impartial trial. Such views and concerns may be presented by the legal representatives of the victims where the Court considers it appropriate, in accordance with the Rules of Procedure and Evidence".

[5] Booklet, Victims before the International Criminal Court – A Guide for the Participation of Victims in the Proceedings of the Court, p. 10. http://www.icc-cpi.int/NR/rdonlyres/C029F900-C529-46DB-9080-60D92B25F9D2/282477/160910VPRSBookletEnglish3.pdf. Accessed 10 January 2020.

under investigation. The corollary to this growing workload is a surge in the number of victims applying to participate in proceedings.

2 Victims of International Crimes: From Mere Witnesses to Participants

Since the 1940s, human rights law has steadily supported a greater role for victims "to participate in international human rights law mechanisms . . ." and has called upon States to grant a voice to victims and promote the rights and entitlements of victims (Schabas, 2007, p. 325; Trumbull, 2008, p. 777).[6] However, up until the Rome Statute, international criminal law generally has ignored victims.

In the 1980s, the United Nations' (UN) *Declaration of Basic Principles of Justice for Victims of Crime and Abuse of Power* called on states to recognise and to adopt basic rights for victims of crime, including victim acknowledgment, the right to access justice and right to fair treatment and the right to restitution.[7] In particular section 6(b) has inspired article 68(3) in that it invites Member States to allow:

> "the views and concerns of victims to be presented and considered at appropriate stages of the proceedings where their personal interests are affected, without prejudice to the accused and consistent with the relevant national criminal justice system".

The response to this declaration has been wide-ranging at the national level. Whereas many civil law jurisdictions already allowed for some form of victim participation, this was not the case for common law jurisdictions (McGonigle Leyh, 2011a, p. 70; Horovitz, 2013). Currently numerous major jurisdictions provide for victim participation to varying degrees, ranging from offering victims the possibility to make personal statements to presenting civil claims in criminal proceedings in the French criminal system (Stahn et al., 2006, p. 220; Wemmers, 2010, p. 633; McGonigle Leyh, 2011a, p. 65).

In contrast, the International Military tribunals of Nuremberg and Tokyo, the International Criminal Tribunal for Rwanda (ICTR) and the International Criminal

---

[6] For instance, access to justice is provided for in the International Covenant on Civil and Political Rights on 19 December 1966, the European Convention on Human Rights of 4 November 1950 or the UN Convention against Torture. *See* also Declaration of Basic Principles of Justice for Victims of Crime and Abuse of Power, G.A. Res. 40/34, U.N. Doc. A/RES/40/34 (Nov. 29, 1985); United Nations Convention Against Transnational Organized Crime, G.A. Res. 55/25, U.N. Doc. A/RES/55/25 (Jan. 8, 2001); Basic Principles and Guidelines on the Right to a Remedy and Reparation for Victims of Gross Violations of International Human Rights Law and Serious Violations of International Humanitarian Law, G.A. Res. 60/147, U.N. Doc. A/RES/60/147 (Mar. 21, 2006).

[7] General Assembly Resolution 40/34, 29 November 1985 available at: https://www.un.org/ruleoflaw/files/BASICP~4.PDF. Accessed 25 March 2020.

Tribunal for the former Yugoslavia (ICTY) largely ignored victims. The repression of the crimes that resulted in the victims' harms was the extent of consideration given to victims.

The role of victims in the *ad hoc* international tribunals is minimal, "limited to protection and the restitution of property" (Zappalà, 2010, p. 144) or as witnesses and thus few victims have been able to tell their stories. In fact, as the scholar Brianne McGonigle Leyh points out, the adversarial nature of trials before the *ad hoc* tribunals means that witnesses are not even given the opportunity to tell their experiences, but must instead endure "repetitive questioning" by the parties and ensure their answers do not digress from establishing the guilt or innocence of the accused (McGonigle Leyh, 2011a, p. 140).

The reluctance to grant victims a greater role is related to the potentially great numbers of victims who might have a stake in the judicial proceedings. In the Former Yugoslavia and Rwanda, the sheer numbers of victims of international crimes under the jurisdiction of the *ad hoc* tribunals necessarily would have meant that not all victims could be heard. This would have led to different categories of victims amongst whom only some would be given the opportunity to take part in the judicial proceedings. Instead both *ad hoc* tribunals only heard those victims that were called to testify as witnesses.

Furthermore, the potentially high numbers of victims seeking to participate before the *ad hoc* tribunals would have a negative impact on judicial proceedings (McGonigle Leyh, 2011a, p. 138). Judges of the ICTR stated that to incorporate victims' participation into international criminal proceedings "would not be efficacious, would severely hamper the everyday work of the Tribunal and would be highly destructive to the principal mandate of the Tribunal."[8] According to scholars Virginia Morris and Michael Scharf, the drafters of the ICTY and ICTR statutes considered the protection of the interests of the victims to be part of the interests of the community for which the prosecutor was responsible (Morris & Scharf, 1995, p. 167). Morris and Scharf argue that to allow counsel for victims to participate "could lead to interference with the case presented by the Prosecutor or divert the attention of the court from the relevant issues in the criminal proceeding thereby prolonging the trial." For both *ad hoc* tribunals, their principal mandate is the prosecution and punishment of the perpetrators, not the victims' interests.

---

[8] President of the ICTR, Letter dated Nov. 9, 2000 from the President of the International Criminal Tribunal for Rwanda addressed to the Secretary-General, *in* Letter dated Dec. 14, 2000 from the Secretary-General addressed to the President of the Security Council, Annex, para 4, U.N. Doc. S/2000/1198 (Dec. 15, 2000). Similar views were also expressed by Judges at the ICTY: *See* President of the Int'l Tribunal for the Former Yugoslavia, Letter dated Oct. 12, 2000 from the President of the International Tribunal for the Former Yugoslavia to the Secretary-General, Annex to a letter dated Nov. 2, 2000 from the Secretary-General to the President of the Security Council, U.N. Doc. A/60/706 (Nov. 2, 2000). *See* further: Judge Claude Jorda, speaking in Sarajevo on May 12, 2001. Press Release, Int'l Crim. Trib. for the Former Yugoslavia, The ICTY and the Truth and Reconciliation Commission in Bosnia and Herzegovina (May 17, 2001). http://www.icty.org/sid/7985. Accessed 10 January 2020.

Nonetheless, the ICC, by acknowledging victims, their interests and potential role, alleviates criticisms that the Court is too far removed from the victims themselves and addresses the lack of emphasis on restorative justice, which was perceived to be a concern in the *ad hoc* international criminal tribunals (Kamatali, 2006, p. 93). Indeed, as argued by Victims' Rights groups argued that there is an injustice in the fact that victims are those directly affected by the commission of international crimes, yet they have little power to participate in proceedings (Garkawe, 2008, p. 347; Morris & Scharf, 1995). As a consequence, the ICC is a more victim-oriented court. As will now be discussed, the Rome Statute includes a pioneering and gradually tested system of victim participation.

3 "Constructive Ambiguity" and Victim Participation[9]

Although victim participation has been widely discussed and addressed to varying degrees by both national and international criminal courts. The ICC defines victim participation in very broad terms. There is very little consistent practice for the ICC to fall back on for support or, as Jackson so eloquently put it, no "ready made garden to work from" (Jackson, 2008, p. 248). Furthermore, those involved in the creation and design of the ICC were influenced by their domestic systems and "[j]udges and other protagonists steeped in their own domestic culture still tend to view processes through adversarial and non-adversarial lenses" (Jackson, 2008, p. 238). The ICC combines features of adversarial and inquisitorial processes. The pre-trial procedure in particular is of an inquisitorial nature personified by the figure of the Prosecutor. The trial procedure is more akin to adversarial processes. Therefore the task given to the judges is not easily achievable, leaving it to them to create a system of victim participation that can be as restrictive or non-restrictive as decided by them. As a consequence, the judges have generally adopted a non-restrictive, victim-oriented approach. It is therefore not surprising that the system of victim participation is not always efficient or consistent.

3.1 Legal Foundation of Victim Participation

Article 68(3) of the ICC Statute, the key statutory provision, simply states the basic right of victims to present "their views and concerns when their personal interests are affected". Apart from a limited number of provisions in the Rules of Procedure and

[9] The expression "constructive ambiguity" as used by Phillippe Kirsch *in* Van den Wyngaert (2011), p. 478.

Evidence (RPE),[10] it has largely been left to the judges to prescribe the practical and procedural details of how victim participation will operate in their courtroom in a workable and meaningful manner.[11]

The wording used in Article 68(3) is sufficiently ambiguous for judges to have considerable leeway to explain and develop the content of victim participation. Article 68(3) leaves many issues to be determined at a later date, such as the various stages of the proceedings during which victim participation will be permitted and when exactly the Court will deem it 'appropriate' for the legal representatives of victims to present their views and concerns. Participating victims are given a voice, because they or their legal representatives are granted the right to present their "views and concerns,"[12] which is akin to the role that witnesses fulfil, albeit not at the behest of the parties.

Article 68(3) sits amongst an impressive number of victim-friendly provisions of the Rome Statute. The Court must pay particular attention to the safety, physical and psychological well-being, dignity and privacy of victims and witnesses.[13] Victims are also entitled to legal representation and common legal representatives represent victims in all current cases. Within the Registry three units: the VWU, the Victims Participation and Reparations Section (VPRS) and the Office of Public Counsel for Victims (OPCV) are devoted to a variety of needs of victims and witnesses. Finally, the Trust Fund for Victims gives general assistance to victims and their families and is responsible for the process of awarding reparations to victims after a conviction has been reached.

3.2 *Qualifying Victims*

Victims whose interests are affected may apply for participation during the trial stages.[14] The judges determine whether the applicant qualifies for victim

---

[10] Rules of Procedure and Evidence: Rule 89(1) permits the legal representative of victims to make opening and closing statements. Rule 91(2) enables the participation in hearing and the making of written or oral submissions during a hearing. Rule 91(3) allows the questioning of a witness, expert or the accused following an application to the Chamber. Rule 92(5) provides that the Registry notifies participating victims of hearings, decisions, and submissions or motions. Rule 121(10) and Rule 131(2) address the issue of access by the legal representative of victims to the record of proceedings.

[11] Rome Statute, article 68 (3). See *Prosecutor* v. *Katanga & Ngudjolo Chui*, 13 May 2008, ICC-01/04-01/07, Decision on the Set of Procedural Rights Attached to Procedural Status of Victim at the Pre-Trial Stage of the Case, paras 98–100.

[12] Statute of the International Criminal Court (Rome Statute), July 17, 1998, 2187 U.N.T.S. 90, art. 68(3).

[13] Statute of the International Criminal Court (Rome Statute), July 17, 1998, 2187 U.N.T.S. 90, art. 68(1).

[14] See *Prosecutor* v. *Lubanga Dyilo*, 19 December 2008, ICC-01/04-556, Judgment on Victim Participation in the Investigation Stage of the Proceedings in the Appeal of the OPCD Against the

participation. However the procedure to make this determination is very burdensome, in particular for the judges.

Rule 89(1) RPE requires that victims wishing to participate must file an application with the Registrar. Although the Registry has developed a seven-page application form to apply for victim participation and/or reparation, victims are not obliged to use this form, as long as they provide all the necessary information.[15] The Registrar transmits applications to the relevant Trial Chamber, Prosecution, and defense.[16] However, recent decisions saw the pre-trial chamber rationalise the application procedure to address the large numbers of victims seeking to participate.[17] Whilst victims who wish to appear individually before the ICC are still required to follow the procedure set out in Rule 89(1) RPE, victims who do not wish to appear individually can now apply to the Registry for their views and concerns to be represented as a group by their common legal representative. The application procedure is simplified and can be dealt with in a more expeditious manner. It enables the common legal representative to represent the individual views and concerns of a small number of victims whilst also representing the shared views of concerns of a greater group of victims.[18] This approach should also expedite the assessment procedure of application by the trial chambers.

As will be examined below, the application for grouped victims is far less onerous than for victims who want their individual concerns to be represented. The application for representation of shared views and concerns needs to contain the name of the victim, their contact details and information on the harm suffered.[19] The application as set out in Rule 89(1) serves the purpose of determining whether an applicant qualifies as a victim for the purpose of victim participation.[20] Consequently, it is essential that it contains the identity of the applicant; the date(s) of the crime(s); the location(s) of the crime(s); a description of the harm suffered by a crime that falls within the competence of the Court; proof of the applicant's identity and the applicant's signature or thumbprint "on the document and at the very least on the last page of the application".[21]

Decision of Pre-Trial Chamber I of 7 December 2007 and in the Appeals of the OPCD and the Prosecutor Against the Decision of Pre-Trial Chamber I of 24 December 2007, para 57.

[15] Forms are available at https://www.icc-cpi.int/itemsDocuments/palestine/Application-form-for-individuals-Eng.pdf, Accessed 25 March 2020.

[16] Rules of Procedure and Evidence, Rule 89(1).

[17] *The Prosecutor* v. *Uhuru Muigai Kenyatta,* ICC-01/09-01/11- 460; *The Prosecutor* v. *William Samoei Ruto and Joshua Arap Sang*, ICC-01/09-02/11-498; *The Prosecutor* v. *Laurent Gbagbo*.

[18] *The Prosecutor* v. *Uhuru Muigai Kenyatta,* ICC-01/09-01/11- 460, para 29; *The Prosecutor* v. *William Samoei Ruto and Joshua Arap Sang*, ICC-01/09-02/11-498, para 28.

[19] *The Prosecutor* v. *Uhuru Muigai Kenyatta,* ICC-01/09-01/11- 460, para 49; *The Prosecutor* v. *William Samoei Ruto and Joshua Arap Sang*, ICC-01/09-02/11-498, para 48.

[20] Rules of Procedure and Evidence, Rule 85(a): "Victims means natural persons who have suffered harm as a result of the commission of any crime within the jurisdiction of the Court".

[21] *The Prosecutor* v. *Germain Katanga and Mathieu Ngudjolo Chui*, 26 February 2009, ICC-01/04-01/07-933, para 28.

Where the application is made on behalf of the victim, the victim must give express consent and contain proof of kinship or legal guardianship.[22] In addition, Judge Politi clarified in the *Prosecutor* v. *Kony* case that "both the identity of the applicant and the identity of the person acting with his or her consent or on his or her behalf must be confirmed by one of the listed documents".[23] The judges are required to determine on a case-by-case basis whether each applicant meets the criteria of Rule 85 of the RPE and whether the applicant's interests are affected by the proceedings. To do so, judges will examine a number of requirements.

Firstly, the judge must determine whether applicant is a natural or legal person.[24] Due to the practical realities and consequences of armed conflict, proof of an applicant's identity is not always straightforward. Obstacles to communication and travel may make access to civil status records difficult, or these may not be available, too difficult or too expensive to obtain and thus applicants are not able to meet the requirements for proving their identity. It is therefore appropriate to adopt a flexible approach and to determine the acceptability of documents on a case-by-case basis.[25]

In the *Prosecutor* v. *Kony* case, Judge Politi agreed that the lack of proper identification documents for people in Northern Uganda necessitates that the requirement 'be lowered and adapted to the factual circumstances in the region'.[26] The Court established that it has the discretion to accept indirect proof as long as a recognised public authority issued the document which has a photograph of the applicant and states clearly the applicant's name and the date of birth.

Depending on the particular circumstances, the range of documents that in other circumstances would not be sufficient includes, amongst others, national identity cards; passports; short or long birth certificates; death and marriage certificates; family registration booklets; wills; driving licenses; cards from a humanitarian agency; voting cards; certificate of registration issued by the Electoral Commission; identity card issued by a workplace or an educational establishment; graduated tax ticket; letters from a local authority; camp registration cards; documents pertaining to medical treatment; employee identity cards; baptism cards; certificates attesting to loss of official documents; school documents; church membership cards; association and political membership cards; documents issued in rehabilitation centres for children associated with armed groups; certificates of nationality; and pension booklets; resident permit or card issued by a Local Council; letter issued by a leader of an Internally Displaced Persons (IDP) Camp; reunion letter issued by the Resident District Commissioner camp registration card or card issued by humanitarian relief

---

[22] *DRC* Situation, 19 December 2007, ICC-01/04 – 423, para 14.

[23] *The Prosecutor* v. *Joseph Kony et al.*, 14 March 2008, ICC-02/04 – 125, para 7.

[24] *The Prosecutor* v. *Thomas Lubanga Dyilo*, 18 January 2008, ICC-01/04-01/06 – 1119, paras 87–89.

[25] *See* for instance Judge Kaul, *The Prosecutor* v. *Jean Pierre Bemba Gombo*, Pre-Trial Chamber, 12 December 2008, ICC-01/05-01/08-320, para 34; *The Prosecutor* v. *Omar Hassan Ahmad Al'Bashir*, Pre-Trial Chamber, 10 December 2009, ICC-02/05-01/09-62, para 9.

[26] *The Prosecutor* v. *Joseph Kony et al.*, ICC 02/04 – 125, paras 4–6; ICC-02/04-01/05-371 OA2, para 16.

agencies, such as United Nations High Commissioner for Refugees or the World Food Program; baptism card; letter issued by a Rehabilitation Centre.[27]

The Court will also allow a statement signed by two witnesses attesting to the identity of the applicant or the relationship between the alleged victim and the person acting on his or her behalf, provided that there is consistency between the statement and the application. The statement should be accompanied by proof of identity of two credible witnesses who are persons of standing in the community.[28]

Secondly, it is the role of the judge to 'determine whether the alleged incidents described may be regarded as crimes within the jurisdiction of the Court'.[29] As previously discussed it is not sufficient for the applicant to show that they are victims of the three broad categories of crimes under the jurisdiction of the court, such as genocide, crimes against humanity and war crimes. The victims must demonstrate that they have suffered harm resulting from the crimes included in the indictment.

Thirdly, the judge must determine whether the applicant has suffered harm. Harm may be both individual and collective, as long as it is also personal to the individual victim.[30] The notion of harm necessarily implies the existence of personal harm suffered by the applicant even though it may have been suffered indirectly.[31] Harm is understood as a physical or mental injury, emotional suffering, economic loss, or substantial impairment of his or her fundamental rights.[32] For instance, in the *Prosecutor* v. *Lubanga* case, Thomas Lubanga Dyilo was the first person successfully prosecuted by the ICC for the war crimes of recruiting and using child soldiers. He was the leader of the *Union des Patriotes Congolais* (UPC), the rebel force that gained control of the town of Bunia in the Ituri region of the DRC. The UPC massacred civilians in the Bunia region and also recruited child soldiers. The Trial Chamber found that 'the harm suffered by these indirect victims may include the psychological suffering experienced as a result of the sudden loss of a family member or the material deprivation that accompanies the loss of his or her contributions'.[33]

Fourthly, for each category of victims the judge must determine whether a causal link exists between the crimes charged and the harm alleged.[34] In the *Prosecutor* v. *Lubanga* case, the court required that a 'causal link must exist between the crimes charged and the victim's harm: the injury, loss, or damage suffered by natural persons must be a result of the crimes confirmed against Thomas Lubanga

[27] *DRC* Situation, 19 December 2007, ICC-01/04 – 423, para 15.

[28] *DRC* Situation, 19 December 2007, ICC-01/04 – 423, para 15.

[29] *The Prosecutor* v. *Jean Pierre Bemba Gombo*, 12 December 2008, ICC-01/05-01/08-320, para 64; See also *CAR* Situation, Pre-Trial Chamber II, 11 November 2011, ICC-01/05-31, para 3.

[30] *The Prosecutor* v. *Thomas Lubanga Dyilo*, ICC-01/04-01/06 – 1432, para 35.

[31] *The Prosecutor* v. *Thomas Lubanga Dyilo*, 11 July 2008, ICC-01/04-01/06 – 1432, paras 32, 38 and 39.

[32] *The Prosecutor* v. *Thomas Lubanga Dyilo*, ICC-01/04-01/06 – 1119, paras 90–92.

[33] *The Prosecutor* v. *Thomas Lubanga Dyilo*, 8 April 2009, ICC-01/04-01/06-1813, para 50.

[34] *The Prosecutor* v. *Thomas Lubanga Dyilo*, 8 April 2009, ICC-01/04-01/06-1813, para 45.

Dyilo'.[35] On 29 June 2006, Pre-Trial Chamber 1 rejected a number of applicants, who had been beaten, tortured, raped and submitted to inhuman and degrading treatment and who were not granted the right to participate because their account does not mention the fact that they had been recruited and used as child soldiers.

Finally, as required by Article 68(3), the judge must be satisfied that the 'personal interests' of the applicant are affected.

On the whole, the process to decide whether an applicant should be granted the right to participate is burdensome for a number of reasons. Even if all relevant and necessary information is contained in the seven-page application form, supporting evidence will complement this form. The forms and supporting evidence may need to be translated and redacted of all identifying information. This involves the blackening out of names and any identifying passages in their stories that may lead to their identification. The application form and supporting evidence is then passed on to the Prosecutor and Defence teams for their observations before the judge decides. This is in itself a time-consuming process, in particular since the number of applying victims has noticeably increased. Furthermore, every time a victim applies at a different procedural stage, the victim has to make a written submission to the judge on which the Prosecutor and the Defence teams have the right to comment. Then the judge has to make an assessment whether their personal interest in the particular proceeding are affected.

In light of the growing number of victims applying to participate and the growing number of victims being granted the right to participate, it makes sense to have rationalised the application procedure and to differentiate between victims who want their individual views and concerns to be represented by the common legal representative and victims who want their common shared views and concerns to be represented by the common legal representative. The potential delays in the proceedings are not conducive to a proper and fair trial.

If the application is accepted judges then also determine and organise the extent of each victim's participation.[36] Consequently, judges are given a substantial amount of leeway to determine victim participation. Before discussing the variety of modalities of victim participation granted by judges, I would briefly like to clarify the categories of victims and appropriate proceedings for victim participation.

3.3 Categories of Victims

The Court has found that there are two categories of victims. Direct victims are 'those whose harm is the result of the commission of a crime within the jurisdiction

[35] *The Prosecutor* v. *Thomas Lubanga Dyilo*, 8 April 2009, ICC-01/04-01/06-1813, para 47.

[36] Rules of Procedure and Evidence, Rule 89(1).

of the Court' and indirect victims are 'those who suffer harm as a results of the harm suffered by direct victims.[37]

To be considered a direct victim, the Chamber must establish the harm suffered by the victim and thus will consider evidence that will demonstrate that the applicant suffered harm 'as a result of the commission of a crime within the jurisdiction of the Court'. In the *Prosecutor* v. *Lubanga* case the Trial Chamber has rejected an application from a woman whose husband and children were killed in an attack allegedly by the UPC. She was subsequently taken to a UPC camp and continually raped by the UPC militia for months. The application was rejected for lack of sufficient information to conclude that the applicant had suffered personal harm as a result of crimes included in the charges brought against the accused: the recruitment and use of child soldiers.

To be considered an indirect victim, the individual has suffered on the basis of harm suffered by another person who is the direct victim, such as a parent of a child who has been injured or killed as a result of the crimes under the jurisdiction of the Court.[38] In other words, it is important to establish the close relationship between the indirect and direct victim.[39] In the *Prosecutor* v. *Kony* case, the ICC is seeking to prosecute Joseph Kony as the alleged commander in chief of the Lords' Resistance Army (LRA) for crimes committed in Northern Uganda, including murdering, raping, maiming torturing, displacing civilians and recruiting and using child soldiers as crimes against humanity and/or war crimes. The Pre-Trial Chamber has granted victim status to four applicants who suffered emotional harm as a result of the death of their relatives due to crimes under the jurisdiction of the Court.[40] In the *Prosecutor* v. *Lubanga* case, the Trial Chamber allowed that, under certain circumstances, the loss, injury or damage suffered by a person intervening to prevent one of the crimes alleged against the accused may also serve as the basis for an application of an indirect victim, provided that the person's harm is sufficiently linked to the direct victim's harm. However, it specifically excludes individuals who suffered crimes committed by children who had been conscripted or enlisted whilst under the age of 15 or used to participate actively in hostilities as 'indirect victims'.[41] Instead, indirect victims 'are restricted to those whose harm is linked to the harm of the affected children when the confirmed offences were committed, not those whose harm is linked to any subsequent conduct by the children, criminal or otherwise'.[42] It

[37] *The Prosecutor* v. *Thomas Lubanga Dyilo*, 8 April 2009, ICC-01/04-01/06-1813, para 44.

[38] *The Prosecutor* v. *Thomas Lubanga Dyilo*, 8 April 2009, ICC-01/04-01/06-1813, para 49.

[39] *The Prosecutor* v. *Thomas Lubanga Dyilo*, 8 April 2009, ICC-01/04-01/06-1813, para 50 citing ICC-01/04-01/06-1432 OA9, para 32.

[40] *The Prosecutor* v. *Joseph Kony et al.*, 14 March 2008, ICC-02/04-125 and ICC-02/04-01/05-367, public redacted versions.

[41] *The Prosecutor* v. *Thomas Lubanga Dyilo*, Trial Chamber, 8 April 2009, ICC-01/04-01/06-1501-Conf-Exp, para 4 & ICC-01/04-01/06-1813, para 52.

[42] *The Prosecutor* v. *Thomas Lubanga Dyilo*, Trial Chamber, 8 April 2009, ICC-01/04-01/06-1813, para 52.

held that 'a causal link must exist between the crimes charged and the harm alleged both for direct and indirect victims'.[43]

3.4 What Type of Procedures?

From an early stage, the ICC had to determine whether the wording in article 68 (3) of the ICC Statute permits victims to participate at the investigative phase of a situation or whether this is not a judicial proceeding *per se* and thus participation can only be granted once the charges have been confirmed. Whereas the two Trial Chambers ruled that the investigative stage amounts to "proceedings", the Appeals Chamber decided that victims do not have a general right to participate at the investigation stage.

The Judges in the *DRC* situation and the *Darfur* situation decided that applicants' interests could be affected in the investigation stage and therefore victims should have the right to participate in order to express their views and concerns to the Chamber. The Judges reasoned that "the close link between the personal interests of the victims and the investigation is even more important in the regime established by the Rome Statute, given the effect that such an investigation can have on future orders for reparations pursuant to article 75 of the Statute."

However, the Appeals Chamber disagreed, because the subject matter of the proceedings for each case is defined by the crimes charged. As a consequence only victims of crimes charged will be able to demonstrate that their personal interests are affected by the trial proceedings.[44]

Additionally, the Appeals Chamber argued that article 68(3) quite clearly refers to the 'judicial proceedings', which is a "term denoting a judicial cause pending before a Chamber".[45] In contrast, the investigation is "an inquiry conducted by the Prosecutor into the commission of a crime with a view to bringing to justice those deemed responsible".[46] As a consequence, the investigative stage should be the sole remit of the Prosecutor.[47] The Appeals Chamber concluded that article 68(3) of the Rome Statute does not give victims a general right to participate at the investigation stage.

---

[43] *The Prosecutor* v. *Thomas Lubanga Dyilo*, Trial Chamber, 8 April 2009, ICC-01/04-01/06-1813, para 45.

[44] *The Prosecutor* v. *Thomas Lubanga Dyilo,* ICC-01/04-01/06 – 1432, para 62.

[45] For the victims' arguments, see Appeals Chambers decisions in the *DRC* and *Darfur, Sudan* situations: ICC-01/04-556 and ICC-02/05-177, para 32. For the Appeals Chambers' arguments, see Appeals Chambers decisions in the *DRC* and *Darfur, Sudan* situations: ICC-01/04-556 and ICC-02/05-177, para 45.

[46] Appeals Chambers decisions in the *DRC* and *Darfur, Sudan* situations: ICC-01/04-556 and ICC-02/05-177.

[47] Appeals Chambers decisions in the *DRC* and *Darfur, Sudan* situations: ICC-01/04-556 and ICC-02/05-177, paras 51–52.

Nonetheless, the Appeals Chamber did not dismiss completely the possibility for the Prosecutor to take into account the victims' views and concerns. It acknowledged that in some instances, victims might assist the Prosecutor by presenting information about the scope of his investigations.[48] In fact, the Appeals Chamber went further by preserving future possibilities for the Pre-Trial Chamber to grant participation to victims in the investigation phase if they can demonstrate that their "personal interests are affected by the issues arising for resolution".[49] In other words, victims may be allowed to participate in the investigative stage in the context of special judicial proceedings.[50] Therefore, on the whole victim participation is limited to judicial proceedings taking place after the confirmation of charges.

4 Identifying Modalities for Participation

Participation is a possibility, but it is not a general right As previously discussed, victims must file written applications describing how their personal interests are affected by each stage of the proceedings, and detailing their proposed intervention. The judges will use their discretionary powers to determine whether participation is granted and the extent of participation that would be appropriate and 'consistent with the rights of the defence to a fair and expeditious trial'.[51] Since 2010, a number of decisions from the Trial and Appeals Chambers enumerate the modalities of victim participation during the trial phase of cases before the ICC. Some modalities had already been established at the pre-trial phase and continued to be permitted during the trial phase of proceedings. Judges have granted the following rights.

4.1 Notification of Decisions That Affect the Interest of the Victims

In the first instance, participating victims will be kept informed of decisions that affect their interests in the case, and in particular, they have the right to be informed when the confirmation of charges against the accused will take place.[52]

---

[48] Appeals Chambers decisions in the *DRC* and *Darfur, Sudan* situations: ICC-01/04-556 and ICC-02/05-177, para 54.

[49] Appeals Chambers decisions in the *DRC* and *Darfur, Sudan* situations: ICC-01/04-556 and ICC-02/05-177, para 56.

[50] Appeals Chambers decisions in the *DRC* and *Darfur, Sudan* situations: ICC-01/04-556 and ICC-02/05-177, para 57.

[51] *The Prosecutor* v. *Thomas Lubanga Dyilo,* ICC-01/04-01/06 – 1119, paras 103–104.

[52] RPE, Rule 92, in particular Rule 92(3).

More generally, legal representatives of victims authorised to participate at the pre-trial stage of the case have the right to be notified of the decisions of the Chamber in the proceedings. On the same basis as the Prosecution and the Defence, they should also be notified of all public requests, submissions, motions, responses and other public procedural documents and public proceedings before the Court, including the date of hearings, any postponements, and the date of delivery of the decision, to have access to the transcripts of hearings contained in the record of the case, whether classified as public or confidential; all proceedings before the Court, including public and closed session hearings, as well as any postponement of those hearings, and the date of delivery of any decisions; to have access to the evidence proposed by the Prosecution and the Defence, and contained in the record of the case; to raise objections or make observations concerning issues related to the proper conduct of the proceedings prior to the confirmation hearing to attend all public and closed session hearings leading up to the confirmation hearing, as well as all public and closed sessions of the confirmation hearing itself; and, both in the lead up to and at the confirmation hearing, to participate by way of oral motions, responses and submissions, and to file written motions, responses and replies.[53]

4.2 Presence, Opening and Closing Statement

The pre-trial modalities tend to correspond closely to the forms of victim participation contemplated in the RPE. Firstly, on the basis of Rule 89(1) RPE, Pre-Trial Chambers have permitted victims' legal representative to make opening and closing statements and this has been confirmed by the Pre-Trial Chambers.[54] In the *Katanga* trial, victims have made opening statements and will be allowed to make closing statements after the Prosecution and before the Defence.[55]

Secondly, on the basis of Rule 91(2) RPE, Chambers have permitted legal representatives of victims to attend and participate in public and closed session hearings.[56]

Thirdly, the Trial Chambers in the *Prosecutor* v. *Lubanga* and *Prosecutor* v. *Katanga/Ngudjolo* cases approved the presence of victims' legal representative

[53] *The Prosecutor* v. *Germain Katanga & Mathieu Ngudjolo Chui*, 13 May 2008, ICC-01/04-01/07 – 474, paras 124–143.

[54] See for instance *The Prosecutor* v. *Bahar Idriss Abu Garda*, 19 October 2009, ICC-02/05-02/09-136, para 19; *The Prosecutor* v. *Jean Pierre Bemba Gombo,* 12 December 2008, ICC-01/05-01/08-320, para 102; *The Prosecutor* v. *Thomas Lubanga Dyilo*, 22 September 2006, ICC-01/04-01/-06-462-tEN, p. 6.

[55] *The Prosecutor* v. *Germain Katanga & Mathieu Ngudjolo Chui*, 22 January 2010, ICC-01/04-01/07-1788-tENG, para 68.

[56] See for instance *The Prosecutor* v. *Bahar Idriss Abu Garda,*19 October 2009, ICC-02/05-02/09-136, paras 17–18; *The Prosecutor* v. *Jean Pierre Bemba Gombo,* 12 December 2008, ICC-01/05-01/08-320, para 101.

in the witness familiarisation process, because at a later stage they may have the opportunity to question witnesses.[57] However, this does not mean that the legal representatives are permitted to speak to witnesses about the evidence. The modalities of their participation are regulated by a protocol established by the VWU.

4.3 Access to Public Documents and Decisions

Some modalities have been made more expansive at the trial phase than at the pre-trial phase. For example, at the pre-trial phase, the victims' legal representatives have been allowed to access the whole public case record at the pre-trial phase, including public filings such as transcripts of hearings, public evidence and public decisions,[58] whereas the Trial Chambers have all gone beyond and permitted the legal representative of victims to have access to confidential documents and evidence in the case record during the trial phase.[59] Access has been granted to victims' legal representatives only, but has not been granted to the victims themselves.[60] With respect to the evidence, the legal representatives are permitted to consult the evidence produced by the parties at least three days prior to the corresponding testimony.[61]

4.4 Witnesses

Most significant is that fact that the legal representative of victims can call victims or other witnesses to testify, independently from the Prosecutor or the Defence.[62] However, the need for a meaningful trial means that only a selection of victims

---

[57] *The Prosecutor* v. *Thomas Lubanga Dyilo*, 25 October 2010, ICC-01/04-01/06-1351, para 39; *The Prosecutor* v. *Germain Katanga & Mathieu Ngudjolo Chui*, 22 January 2010, ICC-01/04-01/07-1788-tENG, paras 79–80.

[58] See for instance *The Prosecutor* v. *Bahar Idriss Abu* Garda, ICC-02/05-02/09-136, para 13; *The Prosecutor* v. *Jean Pierre Bemba Gombo*, ICC-01/05-01/08-320, para 103 and ICC-01/05-01/08-807, para 47; *The Prosecutor* v. *Thomas Lubanga Dyilo*, ICC-01/04-01/-06-462-tEN, p. 6 and ICC-01/04-01/06-1119, para 106; *The Prosecutor* v. *Germain Katanga & Mathieu Ngudjolo Chui*, ICC-01/04-01/07-1788-tENG, paras 122–125 and ICC-01/04-01/07-1665, para 103 and ICC-01/04-01/07-T-86-Red-ENG, pp. 1–2.

[59] This was decided at a status conference on 1 October 2009, ICC-01/04-01/07-T-71-RED-FRA, pp. 5 and 6.

[60] *The Prosecutor* v. *Germain Katanga & Mathieu Ngudjolo Chui*, 22 January 2010, ICC-01/04-01/07-1788-tENG, paras 122–123.

[61] *The Prosecutor* v. *Germain Katanga & Mathieu Ngudjolo Chui*, 22 January 2010, ICC-01/04-01/07-1788-tENG, paras 121–122.

[62] *The Prosecutor* v. *Germain Katanga & Mathieu Ngudjolo Chui*, 22 January 2010, ICC-01/04-01/07-1788-tENG, paras 86–97.

will be able to testify: those that can effectively contribute to the establishment of the truth without duplication or hampering of the proceedings.[63]

If the judge grants such a right, this will take place at a separate stage in the proceedings. For instance in the *Prosecutor* v. *Katanga* trial, participating victims were heard after the case of the Prosecution and before the case of the Defence.

Trial Chamber II in the *Prosecutor* v. *Katanga* case found four female victims had the required personal interest and that their testimony would contribute to the truth seeking function of the Court. The four women were of Hema origin and lived in Bogoro at the time of the attack. Their testimony would clarify the social context, living conditions and atmosphere both before and after the Bogoro attack, the unfolding of the attack itself, the reasons for seeking refuge at the Bogoro Institute, the ethnic nature of the attack and the harm suffered.[64] The Chamber also found that the proposed testimony would cover the material and emotional consequences of the attack on civilians, detailed information on the unfolding of events at the Bogoro Institute preceding the attack, the action taken by the Red Cross after the attack, and the distinction made between Hemas and non-Hemas by the attackers. The Chamber found the proposed testimony of each witness to be relevant and thus they were authorised to appear as witnesses.[65]

Victims' legal representatives have also been granted the right to question witnesses, experts called by the Prosecutor or the Defence or the accused.[66] They must demonstrate that the personal interests of one or more victims were affected by the testimony. During the *Lubanga* trial the Trial Chamber clarified the manner in which witnesses could be questioned.[67] Victims' legal representatives are not parties, but participants in the proceedings and as a consequence the manner in which they question a witness should not necessarily be similar to the cross-examination of witnesses by the prosecution or the defence. Therefore, victims' legal representatives should follow a more neutral form of questioning unless it is necessary to press, challenge or discredit a witness by asking closed, leading or

---

[63] In practice, the Bemba case has shown that not all victims will be able to appear before the judges. See *Prosecutor v. Jean-Pierre Bemba Gombo*, 21 December 2011, ICC-01/05-01/08-2027, second order regarding the application of the legal representatives of victims to present evidence and the views and concerns of victims, para 12.

[64] *The Prosecutor* v. *Germain Katanga & Mathieu Ngudjolo Chui*, Trial Chamber II, 9 November 2010, ICC-01/04-01/07-2517.

[65] *The Prosecutor* v. *Germain Katanga & Mathieu Ngudjolo Chui*, Trial Chamber II, 9 November 2010, ICC-01/04-01/07-2602.

[66] See for instance *The Prosecutor* v. *Bahar Idriss Abu Garda*, ICC-02/05-02/09-136, paras 22–23. For the Trial Chamber in *The Prosecutor* v. *Thomas Lubanga Dyilo* see ICC-01/04-01/06-1119, paras 108, 113, 117; ICC-01/04-01/06-2127, paras 24–30; ICC-01/04-01/06-2340, paras 35–39. For the Trial Chamber in *The Prosecutor* v. *Germain Katanga & Mathieu Ngudjolo Chui* see ICC-01/04-01/07-1788-tENG, paras 68–78; ICC-01/04-01/07-1665, paras 14–48 and 90–91; For the Trial Chamber in *The Prosecutor* v. *Jean Pierre Bemba Gombo* see ICC-01/05-01/08-807, paras 38–40.

[67] *The Prosecutor* v. *Thomas Lubanga Dyilo*, 16 September 2010, ICC-01/04-01/06-2127.

challenging questions provided they make an oral request to the Bench beforehand.[68]

4.5 Evidence

The Trial Chambers in the *Prosecutor* v. *Lubanga* and *Prosecutor* v. *Katanga* cases have been most active in addressing the modalities of victim participation at trial, particularly in relation to evidence.

Firstly, both Trial Chambers in the *Prosecutor* v. *Lubanga* and *Prosecutor* v. *Katanga* cases have also permitted victims' legal representatives to lead evidence pertaining to the guilt or innocence of the accused and challenge the admissibility or relevance of evidence.[69] The Appeals Chamber in the *Prosecutor* v. *Lubanga* trial emphasised that victim participation in the proceedings must be meaningful and not merely symbolic. The Chamber noted that, without such modalities available to them, the right of victims to participate in the trial 'would potentially become ineffectual'.[70]

Secondly, legal representatives of victims are permitted to conduct investigations for the purpose of gathering information to establish the nature and extent of the harm suffered by their clients. However, they are not authorised to conduct investigations concerning the guilt of the accused as this would make them tantamount to assistant prosecutors, but they may conduct investigations into "the existence, nature and extent of the harm suffered by their clients".[71] Nonetheless, and despite some disagreement between Chambers, legal representatives might be allowed to submit evidence relating to the role of the accused in the crimes charged, if is necessary to determine the truth. If this is the case, the Trial Chamber may request that victims testify as long as it is satisfied that the right to a fair and impartial trial is respected.[72] Similarly, there may be circumstances where the Trial Chamber, having been made aware of the existence of exculpatory evidence and considering that it is necessary

---

[68] *The Prosecutor* v. *Thomas Lubanga Dyilo*, 16 September 2010, ICC-01/04-01/06-2127. para 28 & para 30.

[69] *The Prosecutor* v. *Thomas Lubanga Dyilo* ICC-01/04-01/06-1119, para.109 and *The Prosecutor* v. *Germain Katanga & Mathieu Ngudjolo Chui* ICC-01/04-01/07-1788-tENG, para 104.

[70] *The Prosecutor* v. *Thomas Lubanga Dyilo*, ICC-01/04-01/06 – 1432, para 97.

[71] *The Prosecutor* v. *Germain Katanga & Mathieu Ngudjolo Chui*, 22 January 2010, ICC-01/04-01/07-1788-tENG, paras 102–103.

[72] *The Prosecutor* v. *Germain Katanga & Mathieu Ngudjolo Chui*, 16 July 2010, ICC-01/04-01/07-2288, para 112. In *The Prosecutor* v. *Thomas Lubanga Dyilo*, ICC-01/04-01/06-1432, paras 93–99, the Appeals Chamber decided that victims did not have the right to present evidence on the guilt of the accused, but that the Trial Chamber may request the submission of all evidence which it considers necessary for the determination of the truth.

for the determination of the truth, will require victims to disclose the evidence it possesses.[73]

Finally, the most substantial advance in the modalities of victim participation relates to the submission of evidence. In the *Prosecutor* v. *Lubanga* case, the Trial Chamber ruled that victims participating in the proceedings have broad rights with respect to evidence before the Court, including the right to tender and examine evidence, 'if in the view of the Chamber it will assist in the determination of the truth', and the right to make submissions on matters of evidence.[74]

5 The ICC: A More Victim-Oriented Court?

During the negotiations of the Rome Statute, France and other civil law countries proposed a system very similar to that of the French *Partie Civile.* However, this was rejected. A number of states expressed their reluctance to an extended role for victims for fear that victim participation would have a detrimental effect on the rights of the defence (Funk, 2010, p. 86). In addition, the ICC cannot escape the issue of a high number of potential participating victims of international crimes under the jurisdiction of the ICC.

The Rome Statute protects trial fairness throughout the proceedings, but in particular genuinely places the rights of the defence alongside modalities of victim participation.[75] According to Article 68(3) judges may permit victims to present their views and concerns "in a manner which is not prejudicial or inconsistent with the rights of the accused and a fair and impartial trial". Judges thus, have to perform a balancing act between the interests of the victims in seeing the accused found guilty and convicted and the fair trial rights of the accused. As a consequence, participating victims and their legal representatives cannot be a third party to the proceedings or an additional Prosecutor. The defence does not have to face the accusations of the Prosecutor as well as those of the participating victims' legal team. It remains the duty of the Prosecutor to investigate crimes, formulate charges and decide what evidence to bring.[76] However, it is a difficult task to reconcile the disparate values and interests of the defence and participating victims in each individual case under investigation.

Furthermore, in determining the degree of participation for each victim, ICC judges have not resorted to a set of guidelines to help them adopt a consistent

[73] *The Prosecutor* v. *Germain Katanga & Mathieu Ngudjolo Chui*, 16 July 2010, ICC-01/04-01/07-2288, para 81.

[74] *The Prosecutor* v. *Thomas Lubanga Dyilo*, 18 January 2008, ICC-01/04-01/06 – 1119, paras 108–111.

[75] Rome Statute, Article 64(2): "The Trial Chamber shall ensure that a trial is fair and expeditious and is conducted with full respect for the rights of the accused and due regard for the protection of victims and witnesses."

[76] *The Prosecutor* v. *Thomas Lubanga Dyilo*, ICC-01/04-01/0601432, para 93.

approach. The scholar Brianne McGonigle Leyh, contrasting the *Prosecutor* v. *Katanga* case and the *Prosecutor* v. *Lubanga* case, highlights such differing approaches (McGonigle Leyh, 2011b, p. 510). In the *Prosecutor* v. *Katanga* case, the judge adopted a systematic approach whereby all victims who met the criteria of Rule 85 RPE had a right to participate and then granted each victim the same set of participatory rights.[77] In the *Prosecutor* v. *Lubanga* case, the Trial Chamber adopted a piecemeal approach, whereby victims had to demonstrate how their specific personal interests were affected by the case.[78] Thus, the ICC judges have different understandings of what victim participation entails, and this, together with their discretion in determining the modalities of victim participation, has led to a varied system in need of harmonization. For the sake of fairness, victims in each case must be treated similarly. In the determination of such a consistent approach, victim participation must be seen primarily as a contribution to truth-seeking justice process of the ICC.

In addition the ICC, as it becomes better known, has to deal with an increasing number of applying victims. In June 2103, figures showed that the ICC had received 12,998 applications.[79] It would be impossible for all victims to be given the opportunity to participate in the judicial proceedings and thus the organisation of victim participation will necessarily lead to inequality amongst victims from its situations and cases. A first selection amongst victims to identify those who may participate will be made on the basis of the indictment. The applicant is required to show the link between the incident causing him or her harm and the crimes allegedly committed in the case under examination.[80] As stated by Judge Kaul, 'it is those facts contained in the document containing the charges which define and delineate the scope of the present proceedings'.[81]

In the *Prosecutor* v. *Katanga* case, Germain Katanga and Mathieu Ngudjolo Chui are accused of having deliberately planned, orchestrated and ordered their respective troops to execute their plan to attack and wipe out the village of Bogoro, in the Ituri district of the DRC on February 24, 2004. Bogoro was a village controlled by the *Union des Patriotes Congolais* (UPC) led by Thomas Lubanga Dyilo, a rival of both the *Force de résistance patriotique en Ituri* (FRPI) led by Germain Katanga and the *Front des nationalistes et intégrationnistes* (FNI) led by Mathieu Ngudjolo Chui. It was considered strategic because it blocked the FRPI and FNI soldiers from the road leading to the key city of Bunia. Trial Chamber II established that only victims directly affected by the specific events covered by the indictment, namely the attack

[77] *The Prosecutor* v. *Thomas Lubanga Dyilo*, ICC-01/04-01/0601432, para 511–13. "'Victims' means natural persons who have suffered harm as a result of the commission of any crime within the jurisdiction of the Court." RPE, Rule 85(a).

[78] *The Prosecutor* v. *Thomas Lubanga Dyilo*, ICC-01/04-01/0601432, para 513–14.

[79] Women's Initiatives for Gender Justice, *Gender Report Card 2013*, p. 177.

[80] *The Prosecutor* v. *Jean Pierre Bemba Gombo*, 12 December 2008, ICC-01/05-01/08-320, para 61.

[81] *The Prosecutor* v. *Jean Pierre Bemba Gombo*, 12 December 2008, ICC-01/05-01/08-320, para 63.

on Bogoro on the 24 February 2003 and by the FNI and the FRPI, may be granted the status of participating victim or called to testify as a witness.[82]

Although there is a selection amongst victims to identify those who suffered harm from international crimes included in the indictment, the number of participating victims is still substantial. In June 2013, 6987 victims were granted the right to participate.[83] It is therefore important that victim participation does not detract from the judicial proceedings and that victims are coherently organised and represented.

So far, the judges have used arbitrary mechanisms to organize participating victims into groups, amongst other reasons, because of lack of time. In principle, victims may choose their own common legal representative.[84] In reality, judges have resorted to appointing common legal representatives for groups of victims, but this may at times seem arbitrary. In the Bemba case, in 2010, the Judge divided 1619 victims into two groups represented by a legal representative.[85] However, they were divided according to geographical location of the crimes rather than the communality of the harm they suffered. This trend has been confirmed subsequently.[86] Furthermore, in the *Prosecutor* v. *Gbagbo* case, in which the former president of Côte d'Ivoire stands trial for crimes against humanity, time constraints meant that the single judge appointed counsel from the Office of Public Counsel for Victims (OPCV) to represent the 139 victims, disregarding the recommendation the Registry arrived at in consultation with the victims.[87] The arbitrary nature of appointing a common legal representative may alienate victims from the proceedings.

Furthermore, the number of victims represented by each common legal representative does beg the question whether the common legal representative will be able to present the case for all the victims and thus whether victim participation can live up to the expectations of victims. If victims expect to be given the opportunity to express their grief, then this is unlikely to happen in international criminal law trials involving high numbers of victims. In addition, amongst the represented victims there may exist different theories and views of the case under investigation. It will be difficult for the common legal representative to do justice to all victims in equal measures. Furthermore, different views may not be conducive to establishing the truth and thus making the case more difficult for the judges. As mentioned above,

[82] *The Prosecutor* v. *Germain Katanga and Mathieu Ngudjolo*, 26 February 2009, ICC-01/04-01/07-933. *See* also Situation in DRC, 19 December 2008, ICC-01/04-556, 4; Situation in Darfur, 2 February 2009, ICC-02/05-177, Situation in the Republic of Kenya, 3 November 2010, ICC-01/09-24, 16.

[83] Women's Initiatives for Gender Justice, *Gender Report Card 2013,* p. 181.

[84] RPE, Rule 90(2) and Rule 90(3).

[85] *The Prosecutor* v. *Jean-Pierre Bemba Gombo*, 10 November 2010, ICC-01/05-01/08-1005, Decision on Common Legal Representation of Victims for the Purpose of Trial.

[86] *The Prosecutor* v. *Uhuru Muigai Kenyatta,* ICC-01/09-01/11- 460 at para 60; *The Prosecutor* v. *William Samoei Ruto and Joshua Arap Sang*, ICC-01/09-02/11-498 at para 59.

[87] *The Prosecutor* v. *Laurent Gbagbo*, 4 June 2012, ICC-01/09-01/11-138, Decision on Victims Participation and Victims' Common Legal Representation at the Confirmation of Charges Hearing and in the Related Proceedings, para 42.

decisions on the rationalization of victim representation and participation have started to address these concerns. In the *Prosecutor* v. *Uhuru Muigai Kenyatta* and the *Prosecutor v. William Samoei Ruto and Joshua Arap Sang*, the judges carved out a differentiated application procedure for victims who were happy to be represented as a group with common views and concerns.[88] It also confirmed that the appointment of common legal representatives should be guided by geographical proximity, because the common legal representative is the point of contact between victims and the ICC. Finally, the decisions also adopted a division of labor between the common legal representative and the OPVC. These measures were all taken to improve the efficiency of victim participation. Hopefully, this will not unduly minimize the role that victims can play in the proceedings.

6 Conclusion

With this complex and extensive range of modalities for victim participation, the judges at the ICC have developed and continue to develop an innovative system for victim participation at the trial stage, where the victims are more than mere witnesses called by the prosecutor. If the victims desire, they can form an integral part of the criminal prosecution process by taking an active role alongside the prosecutor and the defense. Victims do not achieve the complete status of party to the proceedings, because victim participation is not automatic and their participatory rights will be limited compared to those of the prosecution or the defense.

It is questionable whether this complex and at times inconsistent system of victim participation will remain a meaningful and workable system when the increase in participating victims tests its limited resources. Interventions by victims and/or their legal representatives will need to be managed strictly to preserve the effectiveness of the trial.

References

Funk, T. M. (2010). *Victims' rights and advocacy at the International Criminal Court*. OUP.

Garkawe, S. (2008). Victims and the International Criminal Court: Three major issues. *ICLR, 3*.

Horovitz, S. (2013). The role of victims. In L. Carter & F. Pocar (Eds.), *International criminal procedure: The interface of civil law and common law*. Elgar Publishing Ltd.

Jackson, J. (2008). Faces of transnational justice: Two attempts to build common standards beyond national boundaries. In J. Jackson, M. Langer, & P. Tillers (Eds.), *Crime, procedure and evidence in a comparative and international context*. Hart Publishers.

Kamatali, J.-M. (2006). From ICTR to ICC: Learning from the ICTR experience in bringing justice to Rwandans. *New England Journal of International Law and Comparative Law, 12*(1).

[88] *The Prosecutor* v. *Uhuru Muigai Kenyatta*, ICC-01/09-01/11- 460; *The Prosecutor* v. *William Samoei Ruto and Joshua Arap Sang*, ICC-01/09-02/11-498.

McGonigle Leyh, B. (2011a). *Procedural justice? Victim participation in international criminal proceedings*. Intersentia.
McGonigle Leyh, B. (2011b). Victim participation and the International Criminal Court. In R. Letschert, R. Haveman, A.-M. De Brouwer, & A. Pemberton (Eds.), *Victimological approaches to international crimes: Africa*. Intersentia.
Morris, V., & Scharf, P. (1995). *An insider's guide to the international criminal tribunal for the former Yugoslavia*. Transnational Publishers Inc..
Schabas, W. A. (2007). *An introduction to the International Criminal Court* (3rd ed.). University Press, Cambridge.
Stahn, C., Olásolo, H., & Gibson, K. (2006). *Journal of International Criminal Justice, 4*(2), 219–238.
Trumbull, C. P., IV. (2008). The victims of victim participation in international criminal proceedings. *Michigan Journal of International Law, 29*(4), 777.
Van den Wyngaert, C. (2011). Victims before international criminal courts: Some views and concerns of an ICC trial judge. *Case Western Reserve Journal of International Law, 44*(1–2), 483.
Wemmers, J.-A. (2010). Victims' rights and the International Criminal Court: Perceptions within the court regarding the victims' right to participate. *Leiden Journal of International Law, 23*(3), 633.
Zappalà, S. (2010). The rights of victims v. the rights of the accused. *Journal of International Criminal Justice, 8*(1), 144.

Solange Mouthaan is an Associate Professor at the University of Warwick, School of Law. Her research interests focus on two defined fields related to the protection of people under international law: first, the legal protection of minorities, particularly linguistic minorities, and, second, the effective protection of individuals through the International Criminal Law. Her current research project falls in the realm of international criminal law with especial reference to the notion of gender, children and gendered aspects of armed conflict. She examines the developments of international criminal law through the workings of the ICC regarding the protection, voice and role given during the trials to victims of gender-based crimes, such as children. Her recent publications include 'Barefoot, pregnant and in the kitchen: am I a child soldier too?' Women's Studies International Forum, 51, 2015 and 'The ICC and victim participation for victims of gender-based crimes - a conflict of interest?' Cardozo Journal of International and Comparative Law, 21 (3) 2013. She obtained her degrees at the Université de Paris.

A Brief Overview of the Crimes Prosecuted by the ICC, Defences to These Crimes, and the Scope of Liability for These Crimes

Sam Garkawe

1 Introduction

Lawyers who act for victims during ICC proceedings should have a good working knowledge of the definitions of the crimes that the defendant is charged with, and how those definitions might be interpreted. Furthermore, many cases in international criminal law are decided not so much on whether the defendant's behaviour fulfilled the definition of the crime involved (this is often obvious or admitted to by the defendant), but upon whether that defendant can satisfactorily plead a defence to the crimes or upon whether the defendant has individual criminal responsibility for international crimes committed by others. It is thus also important that a victims' advocate has knowledge of both defences and the principles of the scope of liability.

One may well question why this is the case, given that generally victims' advocates will not be a major decision maker on any of the above issues. It is the prosecutor who will set the parameters for the prosecution case against the defendant by deciding which crimes to prosecute,[1] and in situations where the defendant has not personally committed the crime themselves, which principles of criminal liability to utilise to successfully prosecute the defendant. Furthermore, it will be the defence lawyer who will normally decide upon which defences their client will raise, and good prosecutors will be aware of what evidence and arguments they will need to rebut these defences. The reasons why victims' advocates still need a good working knowledge of these matters are varied, but one overarching reason is, once appointed under article 68(3) of the Rome Statute of the ICC (1998), victim advocates have a duty to represent the views and concerns of their clients at all appropriate stages of

[1] Although ultimately it is the Pre-Trial Chamber that will approve the final charges to be laid at the confirmation of charges hearing. See Article 61 of the Rome Statute of the ICC (1998).

S. Garkawe (✉)
School of Law and Justice, Southern Cross University, East Lismore, NSW, Australia
e-mail: sam.garkawe@scu.edu.au

E. King et al. (eds.), *Victim Advocacy before the International Criminal Court*,
https://doi.org/10.1007/978-3-030-56733-0_2

the proceedings and arguably they cannot do so adequately without such knowledge. Other reasons very much depend upon which stage of the proceedings the case is up to. Although the ICC Appeals Chamber in the *Lubanga* case[2] seemed to imply that victims do not have a general right to participate at the investigation stage of proceedings, it did acknowledge that victims may assist the Prosecutor by presenting information on the scope of investigations.[3] Such information could be vital in ensuring the Prosecutor does not omit or neglect important issues for victims whose knowledge of events may well reveal that further or different charges to what the Prosecutor proposes should be pursued.[4] In circumstances where the victims' advocate cannot convince the Prosecutor to add or amend the charges, they may well have an important role at the confirmation of charges hearing by making arguments that extra charges should be laid against the accused.[5] At the trial stage of proceedings the victims advocate must be able to follow the case as it will be important that the advocate knows what both the prosecution and defence are attempting to achieve so that they understand the context of the case, its future likely course, and most importantly, what gaps there might be in the prosecutor's case that their client could fill. At the sentencing stage of proceedings victims may be able to present a statement to the court of how the crime affected them, but this can only be in respect of crimes for which the defendant has been convicted.[6] It is thus important that victims' advocates are aware of the scope of these crimes when advising and/or assisting their clients in the preparation of their statements. This is particularly significant as ICC Chambers do have the power to change the legal characterisation of the facts at some later stage of the proceedings,[7] which may affect victims' sense of justice. Finally, with respect to reparations hearings, victims' advocates generally have greater rights than they might have during other proceedings.[8] Given victims may generally only receive individual reparations for suffering harm from crimes

---

[2] See *The Prosecutor v Thomas Lubanga Dyilo*, ICC-01/04-01/06 – 1432, Decision of 11.7.2008, Judgment on the Appeals of the Prosecutor and Defence against Trial Chamber I's Decision on Victims' Participation of 18.1.2008.

[3] See discussion in this volume, S. Mouthaan, 'The Modalities of Victim Participation'.

[4] This was particularly a major issue for many victim advocates in the *Lubanga* trial. The confirmed charges concerned the conscription, enlistment and use of child soldiers, but not any charges relating to sexual offenses. Not surprisingly: '. . . victims' advocates protested that rape and other sexual crimes should have been included.' (Leyh, 2011, pp. 294–295).

[5] See the discussion in this volume, S. Mouthaan, 'The Modalities of Victim Participation'. It is unclear whether Pre-Trial Chambers will allow victims' advocates to be heard at confirmation of charges hearings. Both Article 61 (confirmation of the charges before trial) of the Rome Statute of the ICC (1998) and Rule 121 of the Rules of Procedure and Evidence of the ICC (2002) are silent on whether victims are able to have an input into this proceeding.

[6] Allowing such a statement would be subject to the Court's discretion, but it seems clear to the writer that this statement would be directly relevant to the victims 'personal interests' being affected and constitute their 'views and concerns' as is required for victim participation, pursuant to article 68(3) of the Rome Statute of the ICC (1998).

[7] See Regulation 55 of the Regulations of the ICC (2004).

[8] See Rule 91(4) of the Rules of Procedure and Evidence of the ICC (2002).

that the defendant was convicted of,[9] this implies that victims' advocates need to be aware of the scope of these crimes when representing their clients at such proceedings.

2 Sources of Law for the ICC Crimes, Defences and the Principles of Criminal Responsibility

Article 21 (applicable law) of the Rome Statute of the ICC (1998) establishes a three tiered hierarchy for the sources of law the ICC must draw from in order to ascertain the law with respect to the criminal liability of defendants coming before the court. The first tier is that the Court shall apply: '(a) ... this Statute, Elements of Crimes and its Rules of Procedure and Evidence'.

Although it appears from this sub-section that these three sources of law are equal, it is clear and not surprising that by far the most important source is the Rome Statute of the ICC Statute (1998) itself. For example, with respect to the definitions of the ICC crimes, at first instance the plain meaning of the definitions of the crimes found in the articles of the Statute (see below) clearly constitutes by far the most significant source of law and should be the starting point for advocates in comprehending the law. Most of the time this will provide the answer as to whether the defendant's behaviour falls within the relevant definition, and it is only in a minority of cases where lawyers may have to look towards the other sources of the law. The other source particularly relevant to the definitions of crimes is found in the later document: Elements of Crimes, ICC (2002),[10] which is intended to clarify and further articulate these definitions. This source is clearly subservient to the Statute itself, as shown by article 9 (3) of the Rome Statute of the ICC Statute (1998) which states that: 'The Elements of Crimes and amendments thereto shall be consistent with this Statute'.[11]

The second tier in the hierarchy of sources is Article 21 (b): (the Court shall apply) ... 'where appropriate, applicable treaties and the principles and rules of international law, including the established principles of the international law of armed conflict;' This possible source of law (which probably includes customary

---

[9] 'The Appeals Chamber notes that only victims ... who suffered harm as a result of the commission of the crimes of which Mr Lubanga was found guilty, may claim reparations against Mr Lubanga'. *The Prosecutor v Lubanga* No. ICC-01/04-01/06 – 3129, Decision of 3 March 2015, judgment on the appeals against the "Decision establishing the principles and procedures to be applied to reparations" of 7 August 2012, at para 211. While individual reparations are likely to be so limited, this may not be true for collective reparations.

[10] This document was drafted by Preparatory Committee sessions in 1999 & 2000, and confirmed by the Assembly of State Parties in September 2002.

[11] Article 51(5) of the Rome Statute of the ICC (1998) also makes it clear that in any conflict between the Statute and the other document referred to in article 21 (a) of the Rules of Procedure and Evidence of the ICC (2002), the Statute will prevail.

international law[12]) is only relevant where an issue cannot be resolved by examining the Rome Statute of the ICC (1998) itself, or the Rules of Procedure and Evidence of the ICC (2002) and Elements of Crimes, ICC (2002) documents.

The third tier in the hierarchy of sources applies in cases where the first two sources cannot resolve the issue:

> Article 21 (c) . . . 'general principles of law derived by the Court from national laws of legal systems of the world including, as appropriate, the national laws of States that would normally exercise jurisdiction over the crime, provided that those principles are not inconsistent with this Statute and with international law and internationally recognized norms and standards.'

This brings in elements of comparative criminal law, although: 'the Court has been quite resistant to arguments based upon national practice as a source of general principles' (Schabas, 2017, p. 194).

The three tiered hierarchy does not mention expressly previous case law. Many lawyers will be aware that previous court decisions are likely to be influential in later cases, however international law generally does not have a formal doctrine of *stare decisis*. Article 21 (2) of the Rome Statute of the ICC (1998) states simply that: 'The Court may apply principles and rules of law as interpreted in its previous decisions.' Clearly this refers to ICC decisions, which will be of the most significance. However, the reasoning used in decisions from other courts, particularly international criminal courts such as the ICTY and ICTR, may also be utilised (although caution must be exercised[13]) where it is relevant to an issue the ICC is dealing with. Finally, although not mentioned in article 21, lawyers new to the field in particular may find very useful textbooks and other academic writings on international criminal law to obtain both an overview of the law in the area relevant to their case, and to also follow the arguments and controversies in the minority of cases where the law may be unclear.

With these introductory remarks in mind, we now move to briefly examine in turn the three areas of ICC law victim advocates should be aware of—the definitions of the crimes; possible defences to the crimes; and the principles of individual criminal responsibility. By far the most important source of law will be the Rome Statute of the ICC (1998) itself, and thus most questions advocates may have will be resolved by examining the words of the Statute, and for this reason this Chapter concentrates almost solely on this document. There are now numerous publications and much case law on many aspects of the laws where the words of the Statute do not resolve an issue, and it is thus beyond the scope of this Chapter to delve into these matters.

---

[12] See Schabas (2017, p. 191).

[13] See Schabas (2017, p. 193), who quotes a passage from the Court's decision in *Situation in Uganda* decided on 28/10/05: 'judges of the International Criminal Court have cautioned against mechanistic application of the case law of the *ad hoc* tribunals'.

The intention of this Chapter is to provide enough information so that the basics can be understood, and the Chapter will also point to a few selected examples in the literature as a guide to victim advocates who need to learn more about an aspect of the law in order to prepare themselves properly to represent their clients.

3 The Definitions of the ICC Crimes

The primary source of the definitions of the four ICC crimes, as stated above, is the Rome Statute of the ICC (1998) itself. The definitions of crimes are set out in article 6 (genocide), article 7 (crimes against humanity), article 8 (war crimes) and article 8*bis* (aggression).

These crimes outlined below must be read in conjunction with the important article 30 of the Rome Statute of the ICC (1998) below, which specifies that the mental element of each crime is either 'intent' or 'knowledge', both terms which are further defined in the article.

Article 30 Mental Element

1. Unless otherwise provided, a person shall be criminally responsible and liable for punishment for a crime within the jurisdiction of the Court only if the material elements are committed with intent and knowledge.
2. For the purposes of this article, a person has intent where:
   (a) In relation to conduct, that person means to engage in the conduct;
   (b) In relation to a consequence, that person means to cause that consequence or is aware that it will occur in the ordinary course of events.
3. For the purposes of this article, "knowledge" means awareness that a circumstance exists or a consequence will occur in the ordinary course of events. "Know" and "knowingly" shall be construed accordingly.

Note that the phrase 'unless otherwise provided' precedes the rest of the article, so it possible for a crime in the ICC Statute to have a different mental element requirement, in particular a lower standard than 'intent' or 'knowledge'.[14]

3.1 Genocide

The first ICC crime to be considered is sometimes referred to as 'the crime of crimes' and the most odious of all crimes—genocide. The legal definition of genocide was

[14] For example, article 28 of the Rome Statute of the ICC (1998) sets only a negligence standard for guilt due to command responsibility.

first articulated in Article 2 of the Genocide Convention (1948), and this is exactly the same definition found as in the Rome Statute of the ICC (1998) and in other international legal instruments. This shows that the crime of 'genocide' has had a very stable definition for over 50 years now, and this is unlikely to change in the future, and it is part of customary international law. Of course, this does not mean that the *interpretation* of the definition has not been without change or controversy. The definition found in the article 6 of the Rome Statute of the ICC (1998) is as follows:

> **Article 6**
> "genocide" means any of the following acts committed with intent to destroy, in whole or in part, a national, ethnical, racial or religious group, as such:
>
> (a) Killing members of the group;
> (b) Causing serious bodily or mental harm to members of the group;
> (c) Deliberately inflicting on the group conditions of life calculated to bring about its physical destruction in whole or in part;
> (d) Imposing measures intended to prevent births within the group;
> (e) Forcibly transferring children of the group to another group.

There are three distinct elements of this crime that a prosecutor must prove. First, the defendant must have committed one or more of the enumerated acts found in (a) to (e) of the definition. These are supplemented by the further definitions found in the Elements of Crimes, ICC (2002) document. This is generally considered to be the *actus reus* or the 'physical' or 'external' element of the crime. Secondly, one or more of these acts must be directed at least at one of the defined groups—national, ethnical, racial or religious. Thirdly, the prosecution must prove that the defendant had the *intent* to destroy the group 'in whole or in part'. This is probably the hardest element to prove, and as a result it is not uncommon for prosecutors to prefer to press charges of crimes against humanity as this crime covers a broader spectrum of prohibited activities, and does not require the prosecution to prove this specific intent element. The latter two elements would be considered the *mens rea* or the mental element of the offence.

Further resources for the definition of genocide under international law:

- Schabas (2009)
- Cryer et al. (2019), Chapter 10, 'Genocide', pp. 205–226
- Ratner et al. (2009), Chapter 2, 'Genocide and the Imperfections of Codification'
- Schabas (2017), Genocide discussed at pp. 86–94
- Niemann (2014), Genocide discussed at [6.38]–[6.57] & [8.65]–[8.83]

3.2 Crimes Against Humanity

Unlike the crime of genocide, the definition of crimes against humanity has evolved in the modern era. Article 7 of the Rome Statute of the ICC Statute (1998) is now the relevant definition for prosecutions at the ICC. To understand this definition it must be recognised that for a finding of a crime against humanity the prosecution must be able to prove two distinct matters in what is a two-step process. The first and foremost step for the prosecution to satisfy is found in the introductory paragraph or *chapeau* of article 7 that states:

> For the purpose of this Statute, "crime against humanity" means any of the following acts when committed as part of a widespread or systematic attack directed against any civilian population, with knowledge of the attack:

This paragraph embodies the key requirements that elevate prohibited behaviour to the level of a crime against humanity as an international crime, and distinguishes it from behaviour that might only amount to a domestic crime. One very important element is the *mens rea* or mental element of the crime—the defendant must have 'knowledge of the attack'. The other key element that the prosecution must prove is that there must have been 'a widespread or systematic attack directed against any civilian population'. The words 'widespread' and 'systematic' are not further defined in the Statute, but it is important that they are alternative words; only one must be present in the relevant situation. This might seem to suggest that an attack could be a singular event (albeit a widespread one), but there is a later definition in article 7 of the phrase 'attack directed against any civilian population' that would make it unlikely that a single attack could be a crime against humanity. This definition is found in paragraph two of article 7:

> (a) "Attack directed against any civilian population" means a course of conduct involving the multiple commission of acts referred to in paragraph 1 against any civilian population, pursuant to or in furtherance of a State or organizational policy to commit such attack;

One controversy arising from this definition is the requirement that the attack must originate from 'a State or organisational policy'—the question of whether an attack can be carried out by non-state actors, and what exactly is meant by the word 'policy', is beyond the scope of this Chapter.[15]

The second step in the process is that this 'widespread or systematic attack' as referred to above must then result in one or more of a list of eleven different acts or groups of acts that are found in the continuation of paragraph one. Many of these acts, such as murder and rape, might be well-known crimes to a lawyer working in a domestic legal system. Others such as torture, persecution, apartheid and enforced disappearance are more the product of modern developments in international criminal law. These are listed in the continuation of paragraph one as follows:

[15] See the detailed discussion in Schabas (2017, pp. 97–101).

Article 7 Paragraph 1

(a) Murder;
(b) Extermination;
(c) Enslavement;
(d) Deportation or forcible transfer of population;
(e) Imprisonment or other severe deprivation of physical liberty in violation of fundamental rules of international law;
(f) Torture;
(g) Rape, sexual slavery, enforced prostitution, forced pregnancy, enforced sterilization, or any other form of sexual violence of comparable gravity;
(h) Persecution against any identifiable group or collectivity on political, racial, national, ethnic, cultural, religious, gender as defined in paragraph 3, or other grounds that are universally recognized as impermissible under international law, in connection with any act referred to in this paragraph or any crime within the jurisdiction of the Court;
(i) Enforced disappearance of persons;
(j) The crime of apartheid;
(k) Other inhumane acts of a similar character intentionally causing great suffering, or serious injury to body or to mental or physical health.

With the notable exception of murder, paragraph 2 of article 7 then proceeds to provide further amplification of most of these acts or groups of acts:

Aticle 7 Paragraph 2

2. For the purpose of paragraph 1:

(b) "Extermination" includes the intentional infliction of conditions of life, inter alia the deprivation of access to food and medicine, calculated to bring about the destruction of part of a population;
(c) "Enslavement" means the exercise of any or all of the powers attaching to the right of ownership over a person and includes the exercise of such power in the course of trafficking in persons, in particular women and children;
(d) "Deportation or forcible transfer of population" means forced displacement of the persons concerned by expulsion or other coercive acts from the area in which they are lawfully present, without grounds permitted under international law;
(e) "Torture" means the intentional infliction of severe pain or suffering, whether physical or mental, upon a person in the custody or under the control of the accused; except that torture shall not include pain or suffering arising only from, inherent in or incidental to, lawful sanctions;
(f) "Forced pregnancy" means the unlawful confinement, of a woman forcibly made pregnant, with the intent of affecting the ethnic composition of any population or carrying out other grave violations of international law. This definition shall not in any way be interpreted as affecting national laws relating to pregnancy;

(g) "Persecution" means the intentional and severe deprivation of fundamental rights contrary to international law by reason of the identity of the group or collectivity;
(h) "The crime of apartheid" means inhumane acts of a character similar to those referred to in paragraph 1, committed in the context of an institutionalized regime of systematic oppression and domination by one racial group over any other racial group or groups and committed with the intention of maintaining that regime;
(i) "Enforced disappearance of persons" means the arrest, detention or abduction of persons by, or with the authorization, support or acquiescence of, a State or a political organization, followed by a refusal to acknowledge that deprivation of freedom or to give information on the fate or whereabouts of those persons, with the intention of removing them from the protection of the law for a prolonged period of time.

Where the Rome Statute of the ICC (1998) does not provide a clear answer to an issue a lawyer might have, they can resort to the supplementary definitions found in the Elements of Crimes, ICC (2002) document, and the other sources of international criminal law as discussed above.

Further resources for the definition of crimes against humanity under the ICC Statute:

- Ratner et al. (2009), Chapter 3, 'Crimes Against Humanity and the Inexactitude of Custom'
- Cryer et al. (2019), Chapter 11, 'Crimes against Humanity', pp. 227-258
- Schabas (2017), Crimes Against Humanity discussed at pp. 94–109
- Niemann (2014), Crimes Against Humanity discussed at [6.11]–[6.21] & [8.2]–[8.64]

3.3 War Crimes

Before examining the definition of the set of international crimes under the rubric of 'war crimes', it is important to point out that there are three threshold issues to be resolved before there can be a conviction for a war crime. The first is that whereas both genocide and crimes against humanity can be committed under the Rome Statute of the ICC (1998) in either times of peace or in times of armed conflict, a defendant can only be convicted for a war crime where there is an ongoing armed conflict or where the context of the actions of the defendant arose because of an armed conflict. The law relating to this threshold issue can be complex and is thus beyond this Chapter's scope, but in most situations it will be obvious that an armed conflict is occurring.

The second threshold question that needs resolution is whether the actions of the defendant have taken place in the context of an *international* armed conflict or a *non-international* armed conflict. Once more the law relating to this issue can be complex, and increasingly in modern warfare today it will not be obvious which of the two is occurring. The reason why this is an important legal distinction is that different crimes apply depending upon whether the situation is classified as one of international armed conflict or of non-international armed conflict, with a broader array of crimes applying to the former for historical reasons. The war crimes related to international armed conflict are set out in article 8 (2) (a) and (b) below, and war crimes related to non-international armed conflict are set out in article 8 (2) (c) and (e) below. Note that in accordance with the first threshold issue above, article 8 (2) (d) and (f) makes clear that neither sets of war crimes will apply 'to situations of internal disturbances and tensions, such as riots, isolated and sporadic acts of violence or other acts of a similar nature.' Furthermore, article 8 (2) (f) specifies a further restriction on crimes found in article 8 (2) (e)—namely, that they only apply 'to armed conflicts that take place in the territory of a State when there is protracted armed conflict between governmental authorities and organized armed groups or between such groups.'

The final threshold issue is that found in article 8 (1) of the Rome Statute of the ICC (1998) which states: 'The Court shall have jurisdiction in respect of war crimes in particular when committed as a part of a plan or policy or as part of a large-scale commission of such crimes.' Whether this subsection limits the jurisdiction of the ICC to more than mere isolated acts committed during armed conflict is not clear; one can say however that this section seems to favour a viewpoint whereby only something more than isolated acts should be the subject of ICC prosecution.

Article 8 War Crimes

2. For the purpose of this Statute, "war crimes" means:

(a) Grave breaches of the Geneva Conventions of 12 August 1949, namely, any of the following acts against persons or property protected under the provisions of the relevant Geneva Convention:

(i) Wilful killing;
(ii) Torture or inhuman treatment, including biological experiments;
(iii) Wilfully causing great suffering, or serious injury to body or health;
(iv) Extensive destruction and appropriation of property, not justified by military necessity and carried out unlawfully and wantonly;
(v) Compelling a prisoner of war or other protected person to serve in the forces of a hostile Power;
(vi) Wilfully depriving a prisoner of war or other protected person of the rights of fair and regular trial;
(vii) Unlawful deportation or transfer or unlawful confinement;
(viii) Taking of hostages.

(b) Other serious violations of the laws and customs applicable in international armed conflict, within the established framework of international law, namely, any of the following acts:

(i) Intentionally directing attacks against the civilian population as such or against individual civilians not taking direct part in hostilities;
(ii) Intentionally directing attacks against civilian objects, that is, objects which are not military objectives;
(iii) Intentionally directing attacks against personnel, installations, material, units or vehicles involved in a humanitarian assistance or peacekeeping mission in accordance with the Charter of the United Nations, as long as they are entitled to the protection given to civilians or civilian objects under the international law of armed conflict;
(iv) Intentionally launching an attack in the knowledge that such attack will cause incidental loss of life or injury to civilians or damage to civilian objects or widespread, long-term and severe damage to the natural environment which would be clearly excessive in relation to the concrete and direct overall military advantage anticipated;
(v) Attacking or bombarding, by whatever means, towns, villages, dwellings or buildings which are undefended and which are not military objectives;
(vi) Killing or wounding a combatant who, having laid down his arms or having no longer means of defence, has surrendered at discretion;
(vii) Making improper use of a flag of truce, of the flag or of the military insignia and uniform of the enemy or of the United Nations, as well as of the distinctive emblems of the Geneva Conventions, resulting in death or serious personal injury;
(viii) The transfer, directly or indirectly, by the Occupying Power of parts of its own civilian population into the territory it occupies, or the deportation or transfer of all or parts of the population of the occupied territory within or outside this territory;
(ix) Intentionally directing attacks against buildings dedicated to religion, education, art, science or charitable purposes, historic monuments, hospitals and places where the sick and wounded are collected, provided they are not military objectives;
(x) Subjecting persons who are in the power of an adverse party to physical mutilation or to medical or scientific experiments of any kind which are neither justified by the medical, dental or hospital treatment of the person concerned nor carried out in his or her interest, and which cause death to or seriously endanger the health of such person or persons;
(xi) Killing or wounding treacherously individuals belonging to the hostile nation or army;
(xii) Declaring that no quarter will be given;
(xiii) Destroying or seizing the enemy's property unless such destruction or seizure be imperatively demanded by the necessities of war;
(xiv) Declaring abolished, suspended or inadmissible in a court of law the rights and actions of the nationals of the hostile party;
(xv) Compelling the nationals of the hostile party to take part in the operations of war directed against their own country, even if they were in the belligerent's service before the commencement of the war;

(xvi) Pillaging a town or place, even when taken by assault;
(xvii) Employing poison or poisoned weapons;
(xviii) Employing asphyxiating, poisonous or other gases, and all analogous liquids, materials or devices;
(xix) Employing bullets which expand or flatten easily in the human body, such as bullets with a hard envelope which does not entirely cover the core or is pierced with incisions;
(xx) Employing weapons, projectiles and material and methods of warfare which are of a nature to cause superfluous injury or unnecessary suffering or which are inherently indiscriminate in violation of the international law of armed conflict, provided that such weapons, projectiles and material and methods of warfare are the subject of a comprehensive prohibition and are included in an annex to this Statute, by an amendment in accordance with the relevant provisions set forth in articles 121 and 123;
(xxi) Committing outrages upon personal dignity, in particular humiliating and degrading treatment;
(xxii) Committing rape, sexual slavery, enforced prostitution, forced pregnancy, as defined in article 7, paragraph 2 (f), enforced sterilization, or any other form of sexual violence also constituting a grave breach of the Geneva Conventions;
(xxiii) Utilizing the presence of a civilian or other protected person to render certain points, areas or military forces immune from military operations;
(xxiv) Intentionally directing attacks against buildings, material, medical units and transport, and personnel using the distinctive emblems of the Geneva Conventions in conformity with international law;
(xxv) Intentionally using starvation of civilians as a method of warfare by depriving them of objects indispensable to their survival, including wilfully impeding relief supplies as provided for under the Geneva Conventions;
(xxvi) Conscripting or enlisting children under the age of fifteen years into the national armed forces or using them to participate actively in hostilities.

(c) In the case of an armed conflict not of an international character, serious violations of article 3 common to the four Geneva Conventions of 12 August 1949, namely, any of the following acts committed against persons taking no active part in the hostilities, including members of armed forces who have laid down their arms and those placed hors de combat by sickness, wounds, detention or any other cause:

(i) Violence to life and person, in particular murder of all kinds, mutilation, cruel treatment and torture;
(ii) Committing outrages upon personal dignity, in particular humiliating and degrading treatment;
(iii) Taking of hostages;

(iv) The passing of sentences and the carrying out of executions without previous judgement pronounced by a regularly constituted court, affording all judicial guarantees which are generally recognized as indispensable.

(e) Other serious violations of the laws and customs applicable in armed conflicts not of an international character, within the established framework of international law, namely, any of the following acts:

(i) Intentionally directing attacks against the civilian population as such or against individual civilians not taking direct part in hostilities;
(ii) Intentionally directing attacks against buildings, material, medical units and transport, and personnel using the distinctive emblems of the Geneva Conventions in conformity with international law;
(iii) Intentionally directing attacks against personnel, installations, material, units or vehicles involved in a humanitarian assistance or peacekeeping mission in accordance with the Charter of the United Nations, as long as they are entitled to the protection given to civilians or civilian objects under the law of armed conflict;
(iv) Intentionally directing attacks against buildings dedicated to religion, education, art, science or charitable purposes, historic monuments, hospitals and places where the sick and wounded are collected, provided they are not military objectives;
(v) Pillaging a town or place, even when taken by assault;
(vi) Committing rape, sexual slavery, enforced prostitution, forced pregnancy, as defined in article 7, paragraph 2 (f), enforced sterilization, and any other form of sexual violence also constituting a serious violation of article 3 common to the four Geneva Conventions;
(vii) Conscripting or enlisting children under the age of fifteen years into armed forces or groups or using them to participate actively in hostilities;
(viii) Ordering the displacement of the civilian population for reasons related to the conflict, unless the security of the civilians involved or imperative military reasons so demand;
(ix) Killing or wounding treacherously a combatant adversary;
(x) Declaring that no quarter will be given;
(xi) Subjecting persons who are in the power of another party to the conflict to physical mutilation or to medical or scientific experiments of any kind which are neither justified by the medical, dental or hospital treatment of the person concerned nor carried out in his or her interest, and which cause death to or seriously endanger the health of such person or persons;
(xii) Destroying or seizing the property of an adversary unless such destruction or seizure be imperatively demanded by the necessities of the conflict;

Further resources for the definition of war crimes under the ICC Statute:

- Ratner et al. (2009), Chapter 4, 'War Crimes and the Limitations of Accountability for Acts in Armed Conflict'
- Cryer et al. (2019), Chapter 12, 'War Crimes', pp. 259–296
- Schabas (2017), War Crimes discussed at pp. 110–131
- Niemann (2014), War Crimes discussed at [6.2]–[6.10] & in Chapter 7 'Elements of War Crimes'

3.4 Aggression

Although the crime of 'aggression'[16] was included in the original Rome Statute of the ICC (1998), no definition was provided. A definition was only agreed to at the 2010 ICC Review Conference, and this crime could not be actionable until at least 2017.[17] There is some doubt as to whether individuals can be considered victims of this crime.[18] Furthermore, even if one can identify individuals as victims, given the fact that the nature of this crime is that it only concerns major decisions by key leaders in a State, it would seem that there would be a low probability that any such individuals might have been witnesses to the key decision-making processes leading to the crime of aggression, and thus be of use to the prosecution as witnesses.

Article 8*bis* Crime of Aggression

1. For the purpose of this Statute, "crime of aggression" means the planning, preparation, initiation or execution, by a person in a position effectively to exercise control over or to direct the political or military action of a State, of an act of aggression which, by its character, gravity and scale, constitutes a manifest violation of the Charter of the United Nations.
2. For the purpose of paragraph 1, "act of aggression" means the use of armed force by a State against the sovereignty, territorial integrity or political independence of another State, or in any other manner inconsistent with the Charter of the United Nations. Any of the following acts, regardless of a declaration of war, shall, in accordance with United Nations General Assembly resolution 3314 (XXIX) of 14 December 1974, qualify as an act of aggression:

   (a) The invasion or attack by the armed forces of a State of the territory of another State, or any military occupation, however temporary, resulting from such invasion or attack, or any annexation by the use of force of the territory of another State or part thereof;

[16] This was prosecuted in the past as 'crimes against the peace' and this term should be regarded as interchangeable with 'aggression'.

[17] See articles 15*bis* and 15*ter* of the Rome Statute of the ICC (1998) as to the circumstances when this crime might become actionable.

[18] For a detailed analysis of this issue from both legal and policy perspectives see Pobjie (2017).

(b) Bombardment by the armed forces of a State against the territory of another State or the use of any weapons by a State against the territory of another State;
(c) The blockade of the ports or coasts of a State by the armed forces of another State;
(d) An attack by the armed forces of a State on the land, sea or air forces, or marine and air fleets of another State;
(e) The use of armed forces of one State which are within the territory of another State with the agreement of the receiving State, in contravention of the conditions provided for in the agreement or any extension of their presence in such territory beyond the termination of the agreement;
(f) The action of a State in allowing its territory, which it has placed at the disposal of another State, to be used by that other State for perpetrating an act of aggression against a third State;
(g) The sending by or on behalf of a State of armed bands, groups, irregulars or mercenaries, which carry out acts of armed force against another State of such gravity as to amount to the acts listed above, or its substantial involvement therein.

Further resources for the definition of aggression under the ICC Statute:

- Cryer et al. (2019), Chapter 13, 'Aggression', pp. 297–318
- Schabas (2017), Aggression discussed at pp. 131–139
- Niemann (2014), Aggression discussed at [6.58]–[6.68] & [8.84]–[8.88]
- Kreß and Holtzendorff (2010)
- Barriga and Kreß (2015)

4 Defences to the ICC Crimes

As stated in the Introduction, in certain circumstances an ICC trial will be more about whether the defendant can argue a recognised defence than any issues on the definition of the crime(s); and thus it is also important for victim advocates to have a basic knowledge of the key defences. Again, the Rome Statute of the ICC (1998) will be the most important source of the law relating to defences, although note that apart from the defences specifically mentioned in the Statute, it might also be possible for a defendant to argue another defence based upon either customary international law or a defence used in a particular domestic legal system. Article 31 (3) of the Rome Statute of the ICC (1998) seems to imply this—it states: 'At trial, the Court may consider a ground for excluding criminal responsibility other than those referred to in paragraph 1 (see below) where such a ground is derived from applicable law as set forth in article 21.' As referred to above, article 21, in listing possible sources of the law for the ICC, does mention treaties, general principles of law and comparative criminal law.

Some defences that are normally able to be utilised under international law have been ruled out altogether. For example:

Article 27 Irrelevance of Official Capacity

1. This Statute shall apply equally to all persons without any distinction based on official capacity. In particular, official capacity as a Head of State or Government, a member of a Government or parliament, an elected representative or a government official shall in no case exempt a person from criminal responsibility under this Statute, nor shall it, in and of itself, constitute a ground for reduction of sentence.
2. Immunities or special procedural rules which may attach to the official capacity of a person, whether under national or international law, shall not bar the Court from exercising its jurisdiction over such a person.

The key defences are found in articles 31, 32 and 33 as follows:

Article 31 Grounds for Excluding Criminal Responsibility

1. In addition to other grounds for excluding criminal responsibility provided for in this Statute, a person shall not be criminally responsible if, at the time of that person's conduct:
   (a) The person suffers from a mental disease or defect that destroys that person's capacity to appreciate the unlawfulness or nature of his or her conduct, or capacity to control his or her conduct to conform to the requirements of law;
   (b) The person is in a state of intoxication that destroys that person's capacity to appreciate the unlawfulness or nature of his or her conduct, or capacity to control his or her conduct to conform to the requirements of law, unless the person has become voluntarily intoxicated under such circumstances that the person knew, or disregarded the risk, that, as a result of the intoxication, he or she was likely to engage in conduct constituting a crime within the jurisdiction of the Court;
   (c) The person acts reasonably to defend himself or herself or another person or, in the case of war crimes, property which is essential for the survival of the person or another person or property which is essential for accomplishing a military mission, against an imminent and unlawful use of force in a manner proportionate to the degree of danger to the person or the other person or property protected. The fact that the person was involved in a defensive operation conducted by forces shall not in itself constitute a ground for excluding criminal responsibility under this subparagraph;
   (d) The conduct which is alleged to constitute a crime within the jurisdiction of the Court has been caused by duress resulting from a threat of imminent death or of continuing or imminent serious bodily harm against that person or another person, and the person acts necessarily and reasonably to avoid this threat, provided that the person does not intend to cause a greater harm than the one sought to be avoided. Such a threat may either be: (i) Made by other persons; or (ii) Constituted by other circumstances beyond that person's control.

2. The Court shall determine the applicability of the grounds for excluding criminal responsibility provided for in this Statute to the case before it.

Article 32 Mistake of Fact or Mistake of Law

1. A mistake of fact shall be a ground for excluding criminal responsibility only if it negates the mental element required by the crime.
2. A mistake of law as to whether a particular type of conduct is a crime within the jurisdiction of the Court shall not be a ground for excluding criminal responsibility. A mistake of law may, however, be a ground for excluding criminal responsibility if it negates the mental element required by such a crime, or as provided for in article 33.

Article 33 Superior Orders and Prescription of Law

1. The fact that a crime within the jurisdiction of the Court has been committed by a person pursuant to an order of a Government or of a superior, whether military or civilian, shall not relieve that person of criminal responsibility unless:

   (a) The person was under a legal obligation to obey orders of the Government or the superior in question;
   (b) The person did not know that the order was unlawful; and
   (c) The order was not manifestly unlawful.

2. For the purposes of this article, orders to commit genocide or crimes against humanity are manifestly unlawful.

Further resources for the definition of the defences under the ICC Statute:

- Ratner et al. (2009), see pp. 150–161, 'Defenses under International Law & Statutes of Limitations'
- Cryer et al. (2019), Chapter 16, 'Defences/Grounds for Excluding Criminal Responsibility', pp. 380–402
- Schabas (2017), Defences discussed at pp. 224–230, and with respect to issues concerning possible immunity from prosecution of certain persons, see pp. 61–66.
- Niemann (2014), Defences discussed at [9.67]–[9.82]

5 Principles of Individual Criminal Responsibility

There are two key separate and distinct situations where a defendant, who did not actually commit the prohibited act themselves, may still be found liable for that act under the Rome Statute of the ICC (1998). Such cases are particularly prominent because the ICC is only intended to prosecute the 'most serious crimes of concern to the international community' and thus generally speaking, only defendants in very high up positions in the chain of command or leaders of governments are targeted for prosecution by the ICC Prosecutor.

The first situation is where defendants, while not carrying out the crime themselves, are complicit through positive measures they have undertaken and/or supported as part of the completion of the relevant crimes. This may involve a number of concepts, all found in article 25 (3) of the Rome Statute of the ICC (1998). These include committing a crime jointly with another or through another (see article 25 (3)(a) below); ordering, soliciting, inducing, aiding and/or abetting a crime (see article 25 (3)(b)&(c) below); the common purpose or joint criminal enterprise doctrines (see article 25 (3)(d) below); and where a defendant attempts an ICC crime but the crime is not completed (see article 25 (3)(f) below). Another such concept is incitement, but this only applies to the crime of genocide (see article 25 (3) (e) below). The law is laid down in the following article:

> **Article 25 Individual Criminal Responsibility**
> 3. In accordance with this Statute, a person shall be criminally responsible and liable for punishment for a crime within the jurisdiction of the Court if that person:
>
> (a) Commits such a crime, whether as an individual, jointly with another or through another person, regardless of whether that other person is criminally responsible;
> (b) Orders, solicits or induces the commission of such a crime which in fact occurs or is attempted;
> (c) For the purpose of facilitating the commission of such a crime, aids, abets or otherwise assists in its commission or its attempted commission, including providing the means for its commission;
> (d) In any other way contributes to the commission or attempted commission of such a crime by a group of persons acting with a common purpose. Such contribution shall be intentional and shall either:
>
> (i) Be made with the aim of furthering the criminal activity or criminal purpose of the group, where such activity or purpose involves the commission of a crime within the jurisdiction of the Court; or
> (ii) Be made in the knowledge of the intention of the group to commit the crime;
>
> (e) In respect of the crime of genocide, directly and publicly incites others to commit genocide;
> (f) Attempts to commit such a crime by taking action that commences its execution by means of a substantial step, but the crime does not occur because of circumstances independent of the person's intentions. However, a person who abandons the effort to commit the crime or otherwise prevents the completion of the crime shall not be liable for punishment under this Statute for the attempt to commit that crime if that person completely and voluntarily gave up the criminal purpose.

The second situation is where a defendant, while again not carrying out the crime themselves, does not prevent people under their command from carrying out the crime. Rather than the defendant taking positive action as in the first situation mentioned already, this second situation concerns individual international criminal liability for an *omission* to act. The key question that article 28 attempts to answer is—when can a commander be criminally liable for the actions of those under their command? The law is laid down in article 28 as follows:

Article 28 Responsibility of commanders and Other Superiors

In addition to other grounds of criminal responsibility under this Statute for crimes within the jurisdiction of the Court:

(a) A military commander or person effectively acting as a military commander shall be criminally responsible for crimes within the jurisdiction of the Court committed by forces under his or her effective command and control, or effective authority and control as the case may be, as a result of his or her failure to exercise control properly over such forces, where:

(i) That military commander or person either knew or, owing to the circumstances at the time, should have known that the forces were committing or about to commit such crimes; and (ii) That military commander or person failed to take all necessary and reasonable measures within his or her power to prevent or repress their commission or to submit the matter to the competent authorities for investigation and prosecution.

(b) With respect to superior and subordinate relationships not described in paragraph (a), a superior shall be criminally responsible for crimes within the jurisdiction of the Court committed by subordinates under his or her effective authority and control, as a result of his or her failure to exercise control properly over such subordinates, where:

(i) The superior either knew, or consciously disregarded information which clearly indicated, that the subordinates were committing or about to commit such crimes; (ii) The crimes concerned activities that were within the effective responsibility and control of the superior; and (iii) The superior failed to take all necessary and reasonable measures within his or her power to prevent or repress their commission or to submit the matter to the competent authorities for investigation and prosecution.

Further resources for the principles of individual criminal responsibility under the ICC Statute:

- Ratner et al. (2009), see 'Forms of Individual Criminal Responsibility', found at pp. 141–150
- Cryer et al. (2019), Chapter 15, 'General Principles of Liability', pp. 341–379
- Schabas (2017), Individual criminal responsibility and Responsibility of commanders is discussed at pp. 211–221
- Niemann (2014), Principles of individual criminal responsibility, joint criminal enterprise and command or superior responsibility are discussed at [9.14]–[9.25]

6 Conclusion

The above represents a brief account of the law in relation to the definitions of the four ICC crimes, possible defences to these crimes and the principles of individual criminal liability. Advocates for victims that may have to deal with, or at least have some knowledge of these issues, directly or indirectly, should not be daunted by the potential volume and complexity of law in this field. As stated above, for most issues the answers can be found in the plain meaning of the Rome Statute of the ICC (1998) which governs the law in each area.

References

Barriga, S., & Kreß, C. (Eds.). (2015). *Commentary on the crime of aggression*. Cambridge University Press.

Cryer, R., Robinson, D., & Vasilliev, S. (2019). *An introduction to international criminal law and procedure* (4th ed.). Cambridge University Press.

Elements of Crimes, ICC. (2002). Assembly of States Parties to the Rome Statute of the International Criminal Court, First Session, Official Records, Part II (B), UN Doc. ICC-ASP/1/3.

Genocide Convention. (1948). *Convention on the Prevention and Punishment of the Crime of Genocide*. 9 December 1948, 78 UNTS 277.

Kreß, C., & Holtzendorff, L. (2010). The Kampala compromise on the crime of aggression. *Journal of International Criminal Justice, 8*(5), 1179–1217.

Leyh, B. M. (2011). *Procedural justice? Victim participation in international criminal proceedings*. Intersentia.

Niemann, G. (2014). *Foundations of international criminal law*. LexisNexis Butterworths.

Pobjie, E. (2017). Victims of the crime of aggression. In S. Barriga & C. Kreß (Eds.), *The crime of aggression: A commentary*. Cambridge University Press.

Ratner, S. R., Abrams, J. S., & Bischoff, J. L. (2009). *Accountability for human rights atrocities in international law: Beyond the Nuremberg Legacy* (3rd ed.). Oxford University Press.

Regulations of the ICC. (2004). May 26, 2004, No. ICC-BD/01-01-004.

Rome Statute of the ICC. (1998). July 17, 1998, UN Doc. A/CONF. 183/9, 2187 U.N.T.S., 90.

Rules of Procedure and Evidence of the ICC. (2002). Sept. 3-10, 2002, No. ICC-ASP/1/3

Schabas, W. (2009). *Genocide in international law: The crime of crimes* (2nd ed.). Cambridge University Press.

Schabas, W. (2017). *An introduction to the international criminal court* (5th ed.). Cambridge University Press.

Sam Garkawe has been recently appointed as a Professor of Law at OP Jindal Global University, India, where he teaches a course on 'Crime Victims in National and International Justice: Protection, Participation and Reparation'. He is also an Adjunct Associate Professor at the School of Law and Justice at Southern Cross University, NSW, Australia. He has published widely in the field of victimology, concentrating on issues concerning the role of victims in both national and international justice, including their role in the International Criminal Court and the South African Truth and Reconciliation Commission. He taught victimology, human rights, criminal law and procedure, and international criminal justice at Southern Cross University. He is a life member of the World Society of Victimology, and was a member of its Executive from 2009 to 2015, and has been a continuous member of its United Nations Liaison Sub-committee since 2003.

Part II
Essential Advocacy Techniques; Advocacy Skills for the Victim Advocate

Part II gives the advocate practical advice on how to represent a victim in a court setting, with the contained chapters focusing on how to prepare for a case, compose an opening address, develop a legal argument, effectively communicate in the court room, lead evidence in chief, conduct a cross-examination, and effectively deal with expert evidence.

At the conclusion of this Part the reader is invited to practice the skills discussed with Appendices 1 and 2 containing several exercises, wherein the advocate is given an opportunity to prepare necessary notes for a fictional case.

The material contained within this Part has been methodically extrapolated from the Australian Advocacy Institutes' "Advocacy Manual: the complete guide to persuasive advocacy" written by the Hon. George Hampel AM QC and associates. With permission from the authors the material featuring in these subsequent chapters has been edited accordingly to ensure that the information is relevant to the context of *this* book and its readers.

For more information on preparing to represent a client, see resources listed in Ronda Cress' chapter in this volume, "Ensuring that Your Client Receives Adequate Non-legal Professional Support Before, During and After the Court Process", which equips the victim's advocate with a compilation of comprehensive, practical and easily accessible information on the issues most likely to be encountered by the advocate.

Understanding Your Role and Responsibilities as Counsel for the Victim

George Hampel

1 Duties to the Court

The paramount duty of an advocate is to the court.

There is sometimes tension between this duty and the advocate's other most important duty, that is, to the client. The resolution of any tension or conflict must always be in favour of the duty to the court. Duties to the court include

- duty to maintain the dignity of the court;
- duty of candour, which encompasses the duty not to mislead the court;
- duty of fairness; and
- duty of cooperation, consistent with the client's legitimate interest.

1.1 Other Duties

There are a number of other ethical obligations, which include:

- Duty of competence and diligence:
  - acquiring and maintaining a level of professional competence,
  - competently informing and advising the client,

Text within this chapter has been directly extracted, with authors permission, from Hampel, G., Brimer, E., & Kune, R. (2016). *Advocacy manual: The complete guide to persuasive advocacy*. Melbourne Australian Advocacy Institute.

G. Hampel (✉)
Faculty of Law, Monash University, Melbourne, VIC, Australia
e-mail: george.hampel@monash.edu

E. King et al. (eds.), *Victim Advocacy before the International Criminal Court*,
https://doi.org/10.1007/978-3-030-56733-0_3

  - competently preparing to present the case in court, and
  - competently presenting the client's case in court.

- Duty to act on instructions.
- Duty of confidentiality:

  - not breaching the client's confidence, and
  - not using confidential information to the detriment of the client.

- Duty of loyalty, that is, having no other interest than that of the client.
- Duty of advocates to each other:

  - ensuring that 'your word is your bond',
  - cooperating with each other, and
  - not interfering with opponents' ability to perform their task.

An ethical advocate will have a good reputation. Such a reputation takes time, effort and vigilance to acquire—but is easily lost.

2 Mindfulness of the Role of the Bench and the Other Professionals in the International Criminal Court Judicial Process

2.1 Conduct and Etiquette

Ethical conduct by advocates, in and out of court, is of first importance, but observing the rules of etiquette is also important.

Observing the rules of etiquette will

- ensure that court proceedings are dignified, orderly and respected;
- preserve courteous professional relations with the Bench;
- enhance confidence in and out of court;
- enhance the advocate's standing; and
- gain the respect of clients, opponents, and the courts.

The International Criminal Court (ICC) has a Professional Code of Coduct for Counsel. It can be accessed online via their website[1] under Resources/Legal Professionals.

[1] International Criminal Court—https://www.icc-cpi.int/. Accessed 15 May 2020.

2.2 *Language*

Courteous and respectful language does not detract from frank and courageous conduct by counsel, it enhances it.

- Language in court should be clear and simple.
- Language should not be flowery, flamboyant or unnecessarily formal.
- In argument counsel 'submit'; they do not 'think' or 'believe'.
- The plural 'we submit' should be used only when there are two or more counsel.
- The term 'with respect' should be used economically and not in a way that converts the opposite.

In taking issue with the court in argument, examples of correct form are

- 'in my submission Viro's case does not support that proposition',
- 'with respect, that is not the evidence given by Mr Smith', and
- 'I submit that the evidence does not support such an inference'.

3 Contribution to Your Victim Client's Experience of the Investigative, Trial and Reparations Process

3.1 *Making and Answering Objections*

- Objections should be formally made and answered.
- Only one counsel should be standing and speaking at any one time.

3.2 *Preserving Decorum*

Advocates' conduct must be appropriate to the solemnity of the proceedings and sensitive to opponents, clients, witnesses and court staff.

Courageous, effective advocacy does not require rudeness, unnecessary aggression or insensitivity.

The following behaviour is unacceptable and counter-productive to good advocacy:

- Interrupting or speaking over the judge/s.
- Interrupting or speaking over the opponent (except for formal objections).
- Interrupting a judge in the course of a ruling or judgement (except to correct an obvious slip or error).
- Continuing to argue after a ruling has been made.
- Bickering between counsel at the bar table.
- Yelling at the opponent or the judge.

- By comments or body language, demonstrating disapproval of the opponent's argument or the opponent's way of dealing with evidence and rulings by the judge.
- Making personal attacks on opponents.
- Frivolous, intensive and disruptive behaviour which is incompatible with the solemnity of the occasion.

Humour by advocates has a limited place in the courtroom because

- the issues and consequences are grave,
- the proceedings are solemn and formal, and
- people are under stress.

Some humour may be used sensitively to relieve tension, but not at others' expenses.

Apart from those basic rules, courtroom etiquette is all about respect, consideration and sensitivity.

George Hampel AM QC was a Justice of the Supreme Court of Victoria from 1983 to 2000, having previously practised as a barrister since 1958.

Hampel has held numerous positions in the legal profession, such as Vice-President of the Law Council of Australia, Vice-Chairman of the Victorian Bar Institute and Chairman of the Constitution Commission of Victoria.

For over 40 years, George developed advocacy teaching methods, case studies and the training of advocacy instructors in Australia and abroad. Since 2000, he has been Professor of Trial Practice and Advocacy at Monash University. His training experience of professional advocates extends internationally to USA, UK, Scotland, New Zealand, Hong Kong, Singapore, South Africa, and war crime prosecutors at The Hague.

George was the Founding Chairman of the Australian Advocacy Institute in 1991 and over the following 24 years continued to develop its teaching methodology and workshop programs. He is the principal author of the two editions of the Australian Advocacy Manual, which is now required reading for the Victorian Bar Readers Course and is used as a reference work in most common law jurisdictions. George has developed workshops for training of members of other professions including forensic accountants, doctors, engineers and computer experts in their roles as expert witnesses.

As a result of his contribution in these areas, George was made a Member of the General Division of the Order of Australia (2006), received the Centenary of Federation Medal, and a Monash University Teaching Award.

Case Preparation and Analysis

George Hampel

1 Introduction

Competent advocacy requires a combination of conceptual thinking and performance skills.

It is helpful to adopt the following method of preparation, which is both effective and efficient.

There are four components of, or steps in, preparation:

1. Thorough knowledge of case materials.
2. Knowledge of current relevant law, evidence and procedure.
3. Analysis to develop a case theory (what to do).
4. Performance preparation (how to do it).

Preparation is best approached in this way because these steps follow a logical order.

Analysis is not possible without knowledge of all available relevant materials from all parties and the current relevant law.

Performance preparation is not possible without a developed case theory, because the performance would lack direction and could even be counter-productive.

Although it is useful to approach preparation under these four steps, you will need to return to earlier steps to reassess the materials as you progress in preparation, refine the case theory and prepare for performance.

Text within this chapter has been directly extracted, with authors permission, from Hampel, G., Brimer, E., & Kune, R. (2016). *Advocacy manual: The complete guide to persuasive advocacy.* Melbourne Australian Advocacy Institute.

G. Hampel (✉)
Faculty of Law, Monash University, Melbourne, VIC, Australia
e-mail: george.hampel@monash.edu

E. King et al. (eds.), *Victim Advocacy before the International Criminal Court*,
https://doi.org/10.1007/978-3-030-56733-0_4

2 Knowledge of Case Materials

Become thoroughly familiar with all available and potentially relevant factual materials in your case, and the available and anticipated material in the opponent's case.

Examples *may* include

- witness statements,
- recorded interviews,
- depositions,
- exhibits,
- expert reports,
- results of tests,
- telephone intercepts,
- documents and records in the possession of the prosecution,
- documents and records in the possession of third parties,
- pre-trial proceedings and conferences,
- pleadings,
- further and better particulars,
- discovered and subpoenaed documents,
- witness statements or affidavits,
- expert witness reports, or
- pre-trial decisions, directions and orders.

It is important to assess the quality of the evidence in your case, by

- conferring with witnesses,
- examining all original documents and other real evidence, and
- visiting relevant sites where possible.

2.1 Conferring with Witnesses and Victim Clients

Confer with the victim client and witnesses well before the hearing. This will give you the opportunity to shape your case and to obtain further evidence if necessary.

Use the opportunity to correct and clarify your impressions from the instructions or written material.

In conference with each victim client or witness, explore

- the victim clients/witness's personal background (if relevant);
- his or her full version of events, particularly in light of other versions and obvious gaps;
- the victim clients/witness's explanations or reasons for his or her behavior;

- the victim clients/witness's instructions about documents that he or she prepared or can identify; and
- further information to assist in cross-examination.

Have the victim client/or witness prepare any visual aids like plans, diagrams, charts or graphics to explain his or her version of events.

2.2 Examining All Original Documents and Other Real Evidence

It is important to examine original documents and read evidence where possible because

- copies of documents can obscure important annotations, and
- photographs or descriptions of real evidence can mislead.

2.3 Visiting Relevant Sites

Where possible, visit in conditions similar to this described by witnesses, such as

- same time of day,
- similar weather conditions, and
- similar light conditions.

Bring witnesses who can help you better to understand the scene and the events. Take measurements to check relevant distances.

At the scene, consider whether the various versions of events are realistic based on the features of the scene and the locations of the parties or witnesses at the time.

2.4 Organising the Material

This can be done in a number of different ways, for example, arranging information according to

- events, by preparing chronologies,
- sources of evidence, such as witnesses or documents,
- particular scenarios,
- factual issues, or
- legal issues.

3 Knowledge of Relevant Law, Evidence and Procedure

Become familiar with the relevant current law applicable to the issues in the case.

You should identify and consider any evidentiary issues that may arise. It is important to understand the principles behind the rules of evidence.

4 Analysis to Develop a Case Theory

The case theory will be the foundation for the performance of all advocacy tasks. In an attempt to define or describe what a case theory is different expressions have been used such as 'theme', 'guide', 'road map', 'strategy' or 'concept'. All these terms describe some characteristic of what the case theory is but they do not define it.

The preferred descriptor of the case theory is as a 'constructed pathway' through all the factual and legal issues of a case leading the way towards a planned outcome. Unlike the Zen concept with its focus on the journey, the conceptual part of preparation in advocacy is focused on the end result and the way of getting to it.

4.1 Characteristics of a Good Case Theory

A good case theory should

- make sense in the light of human knowledge and experience:
  - being realistic and not fanciful; based on evidence and rational inferences, not on mere supposition or speculation.
  - being consistent with as much evidence as possible; where it is inconsistent, the inconsistencies are explicable.
  - having an appropriate emotional quality and is empathetic.
- be directed to the desired outcome.

4.2 A Positive Construct

A construct is a conceptual synthesis, or the drawing together of the various circumstances into an overall thesis. A positive construct has the following features:

- it is a positive *explanation* of the circumstances,
- it is expressed in propositional form,

- it is not simply the proposition (for example - the defendant did or did not commit the crime, or that the prosecutions has not proved its case to the relevant standard, or that the victim client suffered harm.), and
- it is not simply a narrative of the circumstances or a summary of the arguments.

4.3 Developing the Case Theory or Theories

The development of a case theory is a continuing process. From the first impressions of your brief, a possible case theory or theories may emerge. The final case theory, however, will emerge only after thorough analysis and consideration of possible alternatives.

Ultimately the chosen case theory should be one that provides the easiest pathway through the factual and legal issues in the case.

It will become the guide to the way the evidence of all witnesses is treated.

For instance, where a witness gives evidence that does not support your case, one part of the case theory may be that the witness is mistaken about what he or she perceived. This would be simpler and easier for the decision-maker to accept than a case theory that the witness is lying. This is so unless there is a basis to support the conclusion that the witness is lying.

If several theories are potentially available, then you may use them provided they are consistent with each other. To be consistent, the factual foundation for one must not be incompatible with or destructive of the factual foundation of the other.

4.4 Suggested Steps in Developing a Case Theory

These steps are intended to provide a methodology for progressing through your preparation effectively and efficiently, from the time you receive your brief to the time you can say to yourself 'I am ready to perform'.

The order in which these steps are taken may vary and will depend on the particular case and the nature of the evidence.

- Read and analyse the charge or claim.
- Consider what elements must be established.
- Read the prosecution brief and consider all material and exhibits.
- Visit the places where the events in the case occurred.
- Attempt to visualise the events described by the witnesses and/or your victim client.
- Ensure that you understand the narrative on both sides.
- Prepare a chronology of events from the perspective of all witnesses.
- Analyse your instructions and the narrative of which they rely; they are the anchors of your case theory.

- Identify the differences between your instructions and other accounts.
- Consider what you may use or must undermine to support your instructions.
- Identify the general case theory upon which you may rely, based upon your first intuitive impressions, which help in deciding whether your theory is likely to be realistic.
- Now refine that case theory by a rational assessment and comparison of all the information.

One method is to set out in table form all available facts, and classify them into what appear to be 'good', 'bad', and 'neutral' facts from the perspective of your case and your general theory.

Once the possible case theories have been identified, go back to the table, where the facts have been categorised into 'good', 'bad' and 'neutral', re-evaluate them and select the best case theory.

The best case theory will often be one that applies the principle of Ockham's Razor, the principle of 'economy of hypothesis'. That is, the correct explanation of any problem is usually the one that makes the simplest use of all available information. This will help to avoid unnecessary confrontation.

Before selecting your final case theory or theories consider the likely case theory on the other side. How will your opponent best put their case? What are the strengths and weaknesses of the case against you? How does your case theory sit with the opponent's theory? How can you develop your case theory to conflict with the opposing theory as little as possible?

Almost invariably, there will be gaps in the information available. The process of analysis will help to identify where those gaps are and will often also suggest to you the lines of further inquiry that are required. Before finally deciding on your case theory or theories, you may be assisted by further conferences.

Your chosen case theory MUST be consistent with your instructions and

- contain a higher proportion of 'good' or 'neutral' facts,
- sit most comfortably with your opponent's case theory,
- have fewer witnesses to contradict, and
- allow any remaining 'bad' facts to be explained credibly and realistically or to be weakened or destroyed in cross-examination.

5 Performance Preparation

Knowing what to achieve in your case does not prepare you for how to achieve it during the hearing. Performance skills and techniques require performance preparation. After preparing a case theory, you will know *what* you need to achieve in the case. Then you should prepare *how* you will achieve this during your performance, consistently with your case theory.

A trial will have four main stages, which are performed in this order:

1. Opening address
2. Examination in Chief
3. Cross-examination, possibly followed by re-examination (secondary questioning)
4. Final address

In preparation for performance, these four stages must be prepared in a different order. The starting point must be the final address.

The most useful order of preparation for performance is:

1. Final address
2. Examination in chief
3. Cross-examination
4. Opening address

The final address must be prepared first because

- when prepared first, argument as to facts and law, based on your case theory, will give you the direction needed for the other steps in the trial;
- it will serve as a guide to what needs to be done in order to support your case theory, on which the result will depend. This is like an architect preparing final plans before the building starts; and
- this approach will enable you to focus and organise your case in chief, to identify what needs to be done in cross-examination, and to decide on the most effective opening address.

Examination in chief is prepared next because

- it usually provides the foundation for your final factual argument, and
- your case theory and final argument are usually based on your client's instructions and evidence to support the desired outcome.

Cross-examination is prepared next because:

- the need to cross-examine and the nature and scope of cross-examination of the other side's witnesses will be dictated by the argument prepared first in support of your case theory; and
- having prepared your final address, you will know what you need to add or weaken by cross-examination.

The opening address is prepared last because in preparation, the trial is not shaped by the opening address. The opening address is shared by the way you will conduct the trial.

Note that re-examination cannot fully be prepared effectively in advance as

- it is limited to matters arising from cross-examination.
- it can be prepared only during cross-examination of your witnesses.

However, it is possible to consider in advance the likely line of cross-examination and therefore the evidence that may have to be dealt with in re-examination. This is so particularly with expert witnesses.

Having chosen your case theory and prepared the final address by setting out all the available arguments in support of your case, and identifying all the facts that support each argument, you are now in the best position to order and prepare:

- the evidence in chief to support your arguments;
- the cross-examination:
  - to elicit further facts or add emphasis to support your arguments
  - to discredit evidence that contradicts your case and argument;
- an opening that will persuasively introduce your case, limit the scope of the disputed issues, and defuse the opponent's case; and
- argument about evidentiary issues.

5.1 The Physical Process of Performance Preparation

The method of performance preparation will differ from person to person. Some people will write out what they intend to perform; others will make brief notes, use diagrams, highlight passages of text, or use other methods.

The important point to remember is that you prepare to perform; you do not preparation your preparation. You perform *on the basis of* your preparation.

5.2 Preparing and Using Notes

During the early steps of preparation and in the process of preparing your case theory, you will produce notes such as chronologies, lists and propositions in argument.

These are not the notes that will assist you during your performance in the court, because the court performance is not a presentation of your preparation.

Notes must be prepared as triggers to assist you during your performance.

They must be

- brief,
- clearly set out,
- easily referred to at a glance, and should
- include clearly identified references to documents or other matters to be referred to during performance.

Use of notes during the performance should be minimal and they should be used only as a prompt when necessary. There should be no reading of notes, although in a complex case, notes may be necessary for details such as figures, tests or dates. Performance without notes is best, particularly when dealing with the basic story of your case and the main arguments that you wish to advance.

5.3 Organising Your Material

At trail you must have all of your materials well organised and readily accessible. This may be done by preparing a trial notebook or folder, clearly indexed and tabbed with headings such as

- indictment (or statement of claim),
- particulars (or pleadings),
- exhibit lists,
- list of authorities,
- chronology, or
- performance notes for each stage of the trial.

Such notebook should be kept separately from other materials, especially if the materials are voluminous, as in a complex case.

Thorough preparation, as described, will help you to

- significantly reduce performance anxiety,
- present with confidence,
- be more creative in your style because you know what to do,
- communicate more effectively,
- gain the respect and confidence of the judge and jury,
- be a more credible advocate, and
- impress your clients and those who brief you.

The importance of preparation and the amount of time that must be devoted to it are encapsulated in an American advocacy teacher's comment: *'One hour of preparation for every minute on your feet.'*

George Hampel AM QC was a Justice of the Supreme Court of Victoria from 1983 to 2000, having previously practised as a barrister since 1958.

Hampel has held numerous positions in the legal profession, such as Vice-President of the Law Council of Australia, Vice-Chairman of the Victorian Bar Institute and Chairman of the Constitution Commission of Victoria.

For over 40 years, George developed advocacy teaching methods, case studies and the training of advocacy instructors in Australia and abroad. Since 2000, he has been Professor of Trial Practice and Advocacy at Monash University. His training experience of professional advocates extends internationally to USA, UK, Scotland, New Zealand, Hong Kong, Singapore, South Africa, and war crime prosecutors at The Hague.

George was the Founding Chairman of the Australian Advocacy Institute in 1991 and over the following 24 years continued to develop its teaching methodology and workshop programs. He is the principal author of the two editions of the Australian Advocacy Manual, which is now required reading for the Victorian Bar Readers Course and is used as a reference work in most common law jurisdictions. George has developed workshops for training of members of other professions including forensic accountants, doctors, engineers and computer experts in their roles as expert witnesses.

As a result of his contribution in these areas, George was made a Member of the General Division of the Order of Australia (2006), received the Centenary of Federation Medal, and a Monash University Teaching Award.

Developing Legal Argument

George Hampel

1 Introduction

Any argument made to a court should be

- a series of structured propositions,
- supported by reasons,
- to persuade the tribunal,
- to conclusions of fact and/or law, and
- towards the desired result.

Argument must be based on evidence and legal principle, consistent with your case theory, and consistent with the onus of proof.

General principles of effective argument apply no matter what type of argument is presented, including

- argument in interlocutory applications,
- argument about evidentiary issues before or at trial,
- final address to a jury or to a judge alone,
- plea in mitigation of sentence, and
- an appellate argument.

Text within this chapter has been directly extracted, with authors permission, from Hampel, G., Brimer, E., & Kune, R. (2016). *Advocacy manual: The complete guide to persuasive advocacy.* Melbourne Australian Advocacy Institute.

G. Hampel (✉)
Faculty of Law, Monash University, Melbourne, VIC, Australia
e-mail: george.hampel@monash.edu

E. King et al. (eds.), *Victim Advocacy before the International Criminal Court*,
https://doi.org/10.1007/978-3-030-56733-0_5

These principles apply whatever the nature of the argument, whether it is

- purely legal argument, for instance the interpretation of a statute or the applicability of some legal principle or authority;
- factual argument, for instance about the credibility of witnesses; or
- mixed factual and legal argument, for instance final address in a civil or criminal trial about the factual conclusions and the legal consequences that flow from them.

2 Potential Areas of Legal Argument for the Victim Advocate

2.1 Preparation of Argument

The structure and focus of argument will depend on the jurisdiction in which it is performed and the purpose it seeks to achieve. However, as noted above, there are generic principles that apply to all argument.

The key to effective argument is that is it designed to persuade. In the words of Justice A.F Mason (1984):

> Too often counsels forget that advocacy is an exercise in persuasion rather than a defence or statement of a position. Persuasion calls not only for mastery of the materials, but also for an element of constructive imagination and boldness of approach.

A persuasive argument is neither a list of facts nor merely a series of assertions.

So what constitutes a persuasive argument? The answer to this question emerges from the writings of the Greek philosopher Aristotle over two thousand years ago. There has been no significant improvement on his approach since then.

What emerges from Aristotle's work is that for an argument to be persuasive, it must have the following characteristics:

- *logos* (or logic)
- *ethos* (or ethics)
- *pathos* (or empathy)

2.1.1 Logos

A persuasive argument should be logical in its reasoning and its structure. The various parts of the argument must cohere.

Logical Reasoning To construct an effective argument, you must demonstrate the logical strengths of your case, and the logical weaknesses of your opponent's case.

An argument is designed to persuade the court to adopt a reasoning process that leads logically to the ultimate conclusion for which you contend. The argument must demonstrate that reasoning process, leading from the evidence to the desired legal outcome.

It will be useful in the preparation of argument to apply the 'because' test: that is, follow each statement or assertion you make with the reasons that support its correctness.

Logical Structure A logical argument is a conclusion supported by the evidence. In the context of advocacy, it usually consists of a number of conclusions, which are supported by the reasoning process based on the evidence and legal principle.

A structure that first informs the decision-maker of the conclusions helps the decision-maker to evaluate the reasoning process. This is because the supporting facts and principles are understood in the context of the stated conclusions.

If, on the contrary, the argument begins with a statement of facts without the context of the conclusions, then the decision-maker may find it difficult to evaluate and appreciate the force of the reasoning process.

Usually, the ultimate conclusion should be stated first, followed by the other conclusions and supporting facts that lead to it. In some pleas in mitigation in which the ultimate conclusion is the identification of the sentence contended for, it may not be appropriate to state that conclusion.

The benefits of this structure are

- it is easy to understand,
- it enables the judge (or jury) to evaluate the supporting propositions when the conclusion is first stated,
- it encourages conversation with the judge, and
- this enables the advocate to develop the argument further.

2.1.2 Ethos

Ethos refers to credibility. It is about correctness in the light of human experience and knowledge, not necessarily having any relation to logical validity. It has two aspects:

1. the credibility of the argument, and
2. the credibility of the person presenting the argument.

It is also about the character and reputation.

Credible argument For an argument to be credible, it must be realistic and balanced.

To be realistic, it must be consistent with the understanding of ordinary people about human conduct and the way the world works. It must be sensible in the light of human knowledge and experience.

In terms of the defence case theory, it is the 'R' in RAT: Realistic Alternative Theory. It must not be fanciful or ridiculous. To be persuasive, the defence theory and the evidence that supports it must be reasonable and realistic.

So, a convincing argument may be credible yet not strictly logical. An argument which is logical but lacks *ethos* will rarely persuade.

Your argument must be realistic and balanced.

To be balanced, an argument must deal with its weaknesses in a realistic way, and not simple ignore them. It must also grapple with the strengths of the opponent's case. A balanced argument is effective because

- it shows that you have analysed and considered all the issues from both perspectives;
- it helps the decision-maker, who has to consider the issues from both points of view, not each side's argument in isolation; and
- it anticipates the opponent's arguments and thereby takes the wind out of the opponent's sails, and removes the opponent's advantage of the element of novelty and surprise.

Credible arguer The second aspect of *ethos* is the credibility and trustworthiness of the arguer. As an arguer, you should be trusted by the decision-maker and have their confidence. This entails being respectful and tactful in dealing with the court and your opponent.

A credible arguer adds value to the argument.

The following may detract from the credibility of the arguer:

- lack of preparation,
- misstatement of the evidence or law,
- lack of cohesive structure,
- overstating the argument,
- unbalanced or unrealistic argument, or
- pursuing unsupportable or untenable arguments instead of making appropriate concessions.

It is better to volunteer concessions than to be forced into making them by questions and comments from the judge. Conceding at the outset shows that you have analysed the case, selected realistic arguments and abandoned untenable ones. The jury will also appreciate a focus on realistic arguments, and will be impressed by your forthrightness in making concessions.

As a professional, you must also comply with ethical obligations in argument—for example, citing of relevant authorities contrary to your argument, or in an *ex parte* application disclosing relevant information adverse to your case.

2.1.3 Pathos

Another characteristic of persuasive argument is what Aristotle called *pathos*. A persuasive argument must be empathetic.

This is a more elusive concept, but it is very important. It involves making a realistic connection with the thinking and the feeling of the decision-maker.

Empathy can also be expressed as 'making a connection', 'getting through', and 'being in touch'.

Pathos is also about commitment to the argument and passion for it.

It embraces the idea of mutual understanding, and maintaining empathy with the decision-maker, which is a relationship most conducive to persuasion. The advocate who understands the emotions and is able to put the listener into a receptive frame of mind has a decided advantage in the courtroom.

2.2 *Structure*

A well-structured argument will have the following characteristics:

- It will utilise the Principle of Primacy;[1] it should start with something that will engage the listener's attention and interest.
- It will avoid repetition of the opponent's argument, it is more effective to reframe the issues or at least put the respondent's argument positively, not defensively.
- It will avoid repetition of the opponent's argument when attacking it. This unnecessary repetition may clarify and reinforce the opponent's argument.
- It will acknowledge and deal with weaknesses and make appropriate concessions.

2.3 *Burden of Proof*

The argument must be framed and presented in a way that is consistent with the burden and standard of proof.

Example

Say in a defence argument 'Witness A did not know that Defendant was intoxicated because...' is a positive assertion that is inconsistent with the onus of proof. The correct formulation is 'There is a real possibility that Witness A did not realise that the Defendant was intoxicated because...'.

In an appellate context, if you simply assert that 'the judge below misunderstood the effect of the decision of the High Court in X v Y', such an assertion is formulated in a way that does not recognise the role of the appellate court. A more accurate formulation would be: 'The judge below erred by applying a test which is inconsistent with the test formulated in the binding authority of X v Y.'

[1] When teaching appellate advocacy for the Australian Advocacy Institute, David Bennett QC, former Solicitor-General of Australia, says that to be most persuasive, the advocate should aim to capture the decision-maker's attention and interest in the first 20 seconds of the presentation. It is known as the Principle of Primacy.

3 Performance of Argument

3.1 Addressing the Bench

The question is often asked whether there is a difference between argument directed to judges and argument directed to juries. The answer is yes and no. Legal argument before a judge is different because there is a common understanding of legal principles. Therefore, the language can be that used between professional people of the same discipline.

When addressing a jury and referring to the legal principles that must underlie its decision, different language must be used to ensure lay understanding of the applicable legal principles.

However, when it comes to argument about the evidence, we think it better to approach the judge as another juror. This is because when it comes to making findings of fact, and decisions about the credibility of witnesses, there is a respectable view that a judge is no better equipped than the jury to make those decisions.

3.2 Presentation

The following techniques will assist in effective presentation of your argument:

- Structure your argument so as to inform the decision-maker progressively.
- Treat the tribunal as a 'first-time listener' to your argument. Although a jury has no previous knowledge of your argument, whereas an appellate court usually does, they are both 'first-time listeners' to the way you develop your argument.
- Reduce difficult factual argument and legal concepts to simple propositions.
- Do not restate the opponent's argument in order to put yours, as this may explain and reinforce the opposing argument. Go to your own first.
- State the proposition before the reasoning that supports it. This encourages the listener to consider the reasoning process in the light of the conclusion for which you contend.
- Encourage conversation with the bench, welcoming questions and responding.
- Listen carefully to questions and consider your answer. Do not rush in.
- Answer questions when asked. Saying 'I will deal with this later' results in a break in communication because while you are developing your point, the judge may still be thinking of the question and why you have not answered it. The better approach is to say 'The answer is . . .; may I develop this later?' If the judge says 'No, tell me now', you must do so.
- It is therefore necessary in preparation of argument to prepare for questions likely to be asked, and either deal with them in advance as part of a balanced argument, or be ready to answer them.
- Avoid lecturing or oratorical style.

- Pose rhetorical questions and answer them to help explain your reasoning process.
- Adjust you pace and timing so that the decision-maker can absorb the argument as well as hear it. The aim is to persuade as you go.
- When using authorities, state the principles for which they stand rather than reading slabs of judgments.
- Use materials such as notes, affidavits and exhibits, transcripts or evidence, but not by simply reading the text aloud.
- Avoid unnecessary formality. The overuse of formal phrases such as 'May it please the court', 'In my submission', 'With respect', even 'Your Honour' interrupts the flow of conversational argument and is a distraction.
- Avoid meaningless clichés such as 'Your Honour, the balance of convenience is clearly in my client's favour'. Instead, refer to those matters that show that the balance of convenience favours your side.

3.3 Outlining the Argument

When presenting oral argument without a written outline, avoid outlining the argument at the beginning. Avoid the 'road map' approach typical in debating.

For example, if the judge is told that there are five reasons why an expert witness should not be accepted, and the reasons are briefly identified at the beginning as a road map, there is a risk that while you are developing you first or second point, the judge may be thinking about the flagged fourth point. It detracts from the attention you are able to command.

A different and often better approach is to say 'There are five reasons why the expert witness should not be accepted. The first is...', and develop that point fully before moving to the next. This is more likely to keep the judge's attention on the part of your arguement while it is being delivered.

This approach is controversial, and some advocates take the view that the fuller road map is appropriate. Judges prefer the full road map so that they can move the argument along. It is our view that it is appropriate in some cases, such as when written outlines are required. However, in pure oral argument, we think the approach that focuses the mind of the judge on one thing at a time is better advocacy.

3.4 Speaking to Written Submissions

When the court has a written outline of your submissions, whether you were required to provide them or chose to do so, you must consider the best way to present your oral submissions to the court.

In oral presentation, do not simply read the submissions, use different language to develop and illustrate the submissions. Relate the submissions to your outline as you develop them. This provides the opportunity to explain your argument differently and provides variety for the listener. In some cases you may consider adopting a different structure from your outline if it provides a better opportunity to tell a story and better illustrates your argument.

A similar approach is often adopted by good appellate advocates when speaking to the grounds of appeal. Rather than organising and delivering the argument by direct reference to each ground, it is often better to tell a story that supports the specific grounds. This story will give a context to the formal grounds of appeal.

References

Mason, A. F. (1984). The role of counsel and appellate advocacy. *Australian Law Journal, 58*, 537.

George Hampel AM QC was a Justice of the Supreme Court of Victoria from 1983 to 2000, having previously practised as a barrister since 1958.

Hampel has held numerous positions in the legal profession, such as Vice-President of the Law Council of Australia, Vice-Chairman of the Victorian Bar Institute and Chairman of the Constitution Commission of Victoria.

For over 40 years, George developed advocacy teaching methods, case studies and the training of advocacy instructors in Australia and abroad. Since 2000, he has been Professor of Trial Practice and Advocacy at Monash University. His training experience of professional advocates extends internationally to USA, UK, Scotland, New Zealand, Hong Kong, Singapore, South Africa, and war crime prosecutors at The Hague.

George was the Founding Chairman of the Australian Advocacy Institute in 1991 and over the following 24 years continued to develop its teaching methodology and workshop programs. He is the principal author of the two editions of the Australian Advocacy Manual, which is now required reading for the Victorian Bar Readers Course and is used as a reference work in most common law jurisdictions. George has developed workshops for training of members of other professions including forensic accountants, doctors, engineers and computer experts in their roles as expert witnesses.

As a result of his contribution in these areas, George was made a Member of the General Division of the Order of Australia (2006), received the Centenary of Federation Medal, and a Monash University Teaching Award.

Written Advocacy

George Hampel

1 Introduction

The opportunity for advocacy in writing arises when an advocate drafts or settles

- a pleading,
- a witness statement,
- an affidavit, or
- a written submission.

Oral advocacy is the most persuasive form of advocacy because of the immediacy of communication and exchange of ideas between the advocate and the decision-maker. In the 'conversation' with the court, the advocate can 'read' the court's reactions and react by varying and reshaping the argument. There is also the force of personality and body language.

The advocate can engage the judge by understanding and 'speaking to' that judge's particular characteristics. In an appellate argument, the advocate can engage each judge differently.

Questions from the bench, which should be encouraged, can provide a means of emphasising or reframing the argument.

Written advocacy also has an important role, and can be a powerful, persuasive tool.

Written submissions can stand alone, but can also be used in combination with oral argument.

Text within this chapter has been directly extracted, with authors permission, from Hampel, G., Brimer, E., & Kune, R. (2016). *Advocacy manual: The complete guide to persuasive advocacy*. Melbourne Australian Advocacy Institute.

G. Hampel (✉)
Faculty of Law, Monash University, Melbourne, VIC, Australia
e-mail: george.hampel@monash.edu

E. King et al. (eds.), *Victim Advocacy before the International Criminal Court*,
https://doi.org/10.1007/978-3-030-56733-0_6

It is important to check the rules of the relevant court when preparing pleadings, witness statements, affidavits or submissions, in order to comply with requirements as to form and substance. These requirements will vary between jurisdictions.

2 Form of a Document

The way in which a document is set out is important. Set it out so that it will be easy to follow. It is useful for the reader to have space provided in the document to make notes. This is particularly helpful in submissions.

Use short, numbered paragraphs, one for each part of the evidence, topic or event. The numbering system in a complex document should also be simple. It is best to number paragraphs consecutively in a simple form, and to avoid complex and confusing numbering such as '3.4.1(a)(iii)'.

Each paragraph should deal with only one subject matter.

In more complex documents, headings are useful to identify the subject matter with which the paragraphs that follow deal.

2.1 Pleadings

A detailed discussion of the finer points of pleadings is beyond the scope of this chapter. However, when considering how to make a pleading the most persuasive tool that it can be, it is important to keep in mind the purpose of pleadings. Pleadings are documents designed to ensure that all material facts and questions of law in dispute between the parties are stated clearly for the court's determination (Britts, 1994).

The pleadings are the first documents to which a decision-maker will refer. First impressions will be formed on a reading of the pleadings. Therefore, where there is scope in a pleading to organise and present the facts in such a way as to lead to the conclusion for which you contend, that opportunity should not be lost.

An advocate should consider:

- what facts should be pleaded,
- what level of detail should be pleaded, and
- in what order the facts should be pleaded with a view to maximising the document's persuasive qualities.

2.2 Witness Statements

In many civil jurisdictions, witness statements or affidavits contain factual material which, when tendered, becomes the evidence upon which the court relies. Once tendered, the factual material takes the place of the evidence in chief of each witness.

A good witness statement is

- the detailed story of part of the case,
- told by the witness,
- based on relevant and admissible evidence, and
- persuasively written.

2.2.1 A Detailed Story of Part of the Case

In many civil cases, the story told by the witness in his or her statement is treated as the evidence in chief of the witness. No oral evidence is adduced, although leave may be granted to give additional oral evidence in certain circumstances.

The witness whose statement is tendered can be cross-examined and re-examined.

A witness statement is usually prepared by a lawyer taking instructions from the witness in conference. In order for the lawyer to arrive at a final narrative text of the story as told by the witness, he or she requires an understanding of the principles of preparation of evidence in chief.

Although the witness statement is arrived at as a result of questions in conference, it is ultimately presented in the form of a narrative.

Before taking instructions from a witness for the purpose of preparing a witness statement, the advocate must identify the purpose of that witness's evidence, its relevance and admissibility. Where does it fit into the advocate's case theory?

The advocate should revisit the pleadings in the case to ensure that the issues in dispute are at the forefront of his or her mind. What is it that this particular witness's evidence will prove?

2.2.2 Told by the Witness

When taking instructions for a witness statement, the lawyer should

- let the witness tell the story, using his or her own words and expressions;
- enquire by non-leading questions: 'what', 'when', 'where', 'how', and 'why';
- avoid ambiguity and generalities in question;
- explore details by probing questions;
- get facts not conclusions;
- ask for explanations of inconsistencies;
- explore the peripheries of the story; and
- get the specific language of conversations, not a summary, the effect of or a conclusion about what the conversation meant.

It is important to follow up if information is incomplete, and to persist in getting answers to difficult questions. If information that is unhelpful to the case is going to emerge, it is best that it emerges in conference rather than in the witness box.

Although it is accepted that it is the lawyers who prepare the witness statements in the form in which they are used in court, the witness statement should use the language and expression of the witness, as closely as possible. This will help to prevent the other side, in cross-examination, from suggesting that

- the story is in the language of the lawyer, not the witness; and
- the lawyer has influenced the witness by suggesting answers or asking leading questions.

2.2.3 A Witness Statement Based on Relevant and Admissibly Evidence

The evidence must

- be relevant;
- be admissible;
- contain statements of facts, not opinion (other than the opinions of expert witnesses); and
- comply with rules of the relevant court.

The statement should be the witness's recollection of personal experiences, of what he or she perceived.

During the conference with the witness, the lawyer should focus the witness's attention on the relevant issues. The client's perception of what is relevant and important may not relate to the real issues in the case. It is for the lawyer to retain control of the conference, and therefore the way in which the story is told in the witness statement.

Include all of the detail to tell the full story:

- If describing an event, include the time, the place, and then the action.
- If describing a conversation, include the time, place, who was present, and the actual words spoken by each party in the conversation.

Example

'I said to the builder, "I am not happy about this three-month delay", not 'I related my concern about the delay to the builder'.

Such detail helps to make the story, the characters and the action come alive. Words that conjure up images in the mind of the reader make the story more memorable and credible.

Use visual aids and exhibits:

- Refer to plans, diagrams, charts, or graphs to set the scene or explain different concepts.
- Refer to relevant exhibits.
- Attach the visual material to the witness statement.

2.2.4 Persuasively Written

The witness statement should be structured as a narrative told by the witness.

A good written story, like good evidence in chief:

- will be logical;
- will be structured in a way that is easy to understand and recall;
- will interest the listener by bringing people, places and events to life;
- will be simply told; and
- will not be repetitive.

Consider how the story will best be received by the court. Ask yourself how it will be most persuasively told, by reference to the follow considerations:

- How will the decision-maker best understand the story?
- How will the decision-maker's interest be maintained?

The following techniques are useful:

- Evidence should follow a chronological or other logical order.
- To avoid being vague, the story must have sufficient detail to be credible.

2.3 Affidavits

An affidavit is another way in which evidence may be adduced in writing. The same principles that apply to the drafting of a good witness statement apply to the drafting of a good affidavit.

An affidavit should

- be a persuasive account of the facts relevant to that particular witness;
- contain only relevant and admissible evidence;
- be expressed in simple, clear and concise language;
- be set out in numbered paragraphs; and
- comply with the relevant rules of the court.

An affidavit should not:

- be argumentative,
- contain legal submissions or evidence of opinion (unless the witness is an expert),
- use phrases such as 'I verily believe…', or
- begin each paragraph with the word 'That'.

Where affidavits are used in interlocutory proceedings, a deponent may state a proposition of fact on the basis of information and belief, but the source of the information and the reasons for the belief must be identified.

2.4 Written Submissions

The fundamental characteristics of persuasive oral argument apply equally to persuasive written argument. If the written argument has to be submitted in advance of the hearing, it can be a golden opportunity to make a favourable impression on the decision-maker before the oral presentation. It can also save time, by helping the decision-maker to focus on the real issues.

Depending on the circumstances and jurisdiction, the advocate may need to prepare full written submissions, or alternatively an outline of submissions. The relevant rules of court often set out what is required.

2.4.1 Criteria for Persuasive Written Submissions

In order to enhance oral argument, persuasive written submissions should be informed by the question, 'What is the author trying to do?'

To achieve their purpose, written submissions must be useful to the decision-maker, both in substance and in form. In other words, they must help the decision-maker to understand what has to be decided. They should mould the decision-maker's thinking so that he or she arrives at the conclusion for which the advocate contends.

Written submissions can serve this function only if they are

- clear.

  To be clear, the advocate should

  - identify the party for whom he or she is acting;
  - explain at the earliest stage what decision that party wants the court to make and why;
  - formulate each proposition of fact and law followed by the supporting material;
  - organise the issues in a logical sequence;
  - use clear, simple language;
  - use short sentences;
  - use numbered paragraphs;
  - use appropriate headings;
  - use appropriate definitions;
  - ensure that the submissions are well set out, providing space for the decision-maker to make notes; and
  - include cross-references to key documents where appropriate.

- cogent.

  If the written submission is not concise, it is more difficult for the reader to maintain focus. Too much detail that is not central to the argument can distract the reader from the main thesis of the submissions.

- accurate.

  If the written submissions are not accurate, or present an argument unfairly, the decision-maker is more likely to put them aside in favour of the opponent's submissions. Furthermore, an oral presentation based on inaccurate written submissions lacks credibility.
- comprehensive.

  Submissions that miss important detail or are inappropriately selective undermine the credibility of the advocate and of the argument. Address all of the issues as briefly as seems appropriate.

Other considerations when writing a writing submission:

- Do not overload the document with unnecessary case references or lengthy quotations. Pick the best authority and cite the key passage, or if it is too long, append a photocopy and highlight it.
- Try to pick the three strongest arguments in your favour on each issue. Avoid long lists.
- Use few adverbs as possible.
- Use short sentences and paragraphs.
- Think of the document as a springboard for oral submission. The advocate should leave himself or herself something to say when developing the case orally.

  If time allows, put the first draft away for at least a few hours and then read through it afresh as if you were the decision-maker. Exercise or shorten any passage or sentence that appears overlong or unnecessary.

2.4.2 Outline of Written Submissions

The outline of submissions provides the foundation from which the oral argument proceeds. It should identify and encapsulate the very essence of the issues and of the submissions to be made.

Provisions of a well-structured and concisely articulated outline of submissions presents an opportunity to develop a clear and principled approach to the questions in dispute and to make a strong initial impression on the members of the court (Sackville, 1996–1997). It allows the advocate to set the stage for oral persuasion.

As a concise summary of the argument, the outline of submissions may be used as a road map. As such, an outline should

- give an immediate overview of the entire presentation; and
- provide a structure for the decision-maker to follow so that at any given point, he or she knows what point is being argued in the overall context of the matter.

The aim of the advocate when drafting an outline should be the same as when drafting more detailed written submissions. The same objectives apply, but the outline is in summary form.

At the end of oral argument, the outline of submissions will continue to provide an important reference point for the judge evaluating the competing arguments. In some cases it can also be used as the basis for more detailed written submissions, which contain cross-references to the evidence or which deal with new arguments that may have arisen in the course of the hearing.

When citing authorities in full written submissions or summaries, reference should be made to the principle for which it is contended the case stands.

Although reference should be made to place where relevant passages can be found, transcribing passages from judgments should be avoided.

A simple, brief and concise statement of the argument can be a powerful and persuasive starting point for the reader and for the advocate. It takes considerable discipline to reduce an argument to its essence.

When you are finished with the writing of submissions it is useful to put them away, then reread them one more time, placing yourself in the position of the person to whom they are addressed.

Then ask

- Is it realistic?
- Does it have a chance of succeeding?
- Do I need to do more or less?
- Is it easy to follow?
- Does it read well?

Whether written or oral, as Justice Kirby (1995) has said, 'In the end, the object of advocacy is, by communication, to persuade.'

References

Britts, M. G. (1994). *Pleading Precendents*. Law Book Company.
Kirby, M. (1995). *Ten Rules of Appellate Advocacy*. Speech. Retrieved May 16, 2020, from http://www.lawfoundation.net.au/ljf/app/&id=50F875B247E96DD4CA2571A8007DBAE3
Sackville, R. (1997). Appellate advocacy. *Australian Bar Review, 15*(2), 99–108.

George Hampel AM QC was a Justice of the Supreme Court of Victoria from 1983 to 2000, having previously practised as a barrister since 1958.

Hampel has held numerous positions in the legal profession, such as Vice-President of the Law Council of Australia, Vice-Chairman of the Victorian Bar Institute and Chairman of the Constitution Commission of Victoria.

For over 40 years, George developed advocacy teaching methods, case studies and the training of advocacy instructors in Australia and abroad. Since 2000, he has been Professor of Trial Practice and Advocacy at Monash University. His training experience of professional advocates extends internationally to USA, UK, Scotland, New Zealand, Hong Kong, Singapore, South Africa, and war crime prosecutors at The Hague.

George was the Founding Chairman of the Australian Advocacy Institute in 1991 and over the following 24 years continued to develop its teaching methodology and workshop programs. He is the principal author of the two editions of the Australian Advocacy Manual, which is now required reading for the Victorian Bar Readers Course and is used as a reference work in most common law jurisdictions. George has developed workshops for training of members of other professions including forensic accountants, doctors, engineers and computer experts in their roles as expert witnesses.

As a result of his contribution in these areas, George was made a Member of the General Division of the Order of Australia (2006), received the Centenary of Federation Medal, and a Monash University Teaching Award.

Effective Court Room Communication

George Hampel

1 The Importance of Communication in Advocacy

Advocacy is the art of persuasion.

The word 'persuasion' is from the Latin *persuadere.* In the forensic context it means to prevail by reasoned argument and communication of information and feeling, by both verbal and non-verbal means.

Effective communication is essential to persuasion. The origin of the word 'communication' is from the Latin *communicare*, meaning 'to share'. It involves the conveying and sharing of information, ideas and emotion, by both verbal and non-verbal means.

For an advocate, communication is the building of a relationship between the advocate and the decision-maker. Persuasion involves affecting the decision-maker's intellectual and emotional responses towards a desired end by

- engaging the interest of the decision-maker, and
- making the desired impression during argument and the evidence of witnesses in order to:
  - build a relationship conducive to persuasion,
  - create new perceptions in the mind of the decision-maker, and/or
  - change perceptions already held.

Text within this chapter has been directly extracted, with authors permission, from Hampel, G., Brimer, E., & Kune, R. (2016). *Advocacy manual: The complete guide to persuasive advocacy.* Melbourne Australian Advocacy Institute.

G. Hampel (✉)
Faculty of Law, Monash University, Melbourne, VIC, Australia
e-mail: george.hampel@monash.edu

E. King et al. (eds.), *Victim Advocacy before the International Criminal Court*,
https://doi.org/10.1007/978-3-030-56733-0_7

The first stage in the building of a relationship with the decision-maker is active listening. This applies to

- what the advocate's opponent is saying,
- what the judge is saying, and
- what the witnesses are saying.

Active listening involves

- being in a position to look at the speaker and maintain appropriate eye contact,
- taking in what is being said,
- taking in how it is being said, and
- not interrupting.

As an advocate, you will be better able to listen actively if you are

- not tied to notes; and
- sufficiently prepared, so that you can focus on what the speaker is saying rather than thinking about what you want to say next.

Active listening is essential to

- understanding and absorbing,
- being able to respond appropriately,
- giving the speaker the confidence that you are listening and interested, and
- avoiding being at cross-purposes.

It is important to 'listen before you speak'.

The test of effective communication is the message that the decision-maker receives. Building a relationship allows the advocate's message to be understood, accepted and acted upon.

The content of the message must be good, but that in itself may not be sufficient. To be effective it must be communicated persuasively.

Therefore, effective communication is the most significant quality of good advocacy.

2 Advocacy Skills for Effective Communication

To communicate effectively, the advocate must first

- be thoroughly prepared.

This involves:

- complete familiarity with factual material;
- knowledge of relevant law, rules of evidence and procedure;
- analysis of the materials and development of a case theory; and
- preparation for performance.

- have developed specific advocacy disciplines and techniques. and
- have knowledge of the characteristic of the decision-maker.

It is then necessary to

- understand the characteristics of effective communication,
- understand the obstacles to effective communication,
- find a means of overcoming the obstacles to effective communication,
- identify personal strengths and weaknesses, and
- consciously develop communication techniques through critical self-appraisal and practice.

As an advocate you bring to your task your own personality and experience of life. It is important to remember to be yourself. You will communicate more effectively if you use what comes naturally.

You may admire other advocates and their particular styles but you should not try to emulate their style in precisely the same way. Attempts to do so will invariably appear contrived and artificial. Nevertheless, we can learn from other advocates by adapting their techniques to suit our own.

Communication skills, like those of advocacy, are best taught and developed by the workshop method. (See Appendix 1 and 2 within this Part for practical exercises to improve advocacy skills).

3 Aspects of Effective Communication

Effective communication is manifested in an advocate's performance when that performance employs

- appropriate language,
- appropriate body language,
- clarity,
- brevity,
- simplicity,
- timing,
- pace,
- voice control, and
- appropriate eye contact.

Other skills that will be evident include

- command of materials—the ability to use relevant materials and control their presentation;
- precision or accuracy in the content of what is presented, either orally or in written form;
- organisation;
- active listening;
- reason and logic—the conclusions argued for are validly drawn from the supporting information provided;

- empathy—the ability to identify with a person;
- sensitivity and responsiveness;
- balance; and
- control—the power to hold people's attention and influence their behaviour.

These characteristics, in combination, exemplify good communication in advocacy. An observer can discern a good advocate by what he or she is doing. However, seeing what is done does not necessarily disclose the skills and techniques used to perform what is manifestly good advocacy.

For example, seeing a good cross-examiner control a witness or a good advocate exhibiting 'presence' in court does not teach how those qualities are achieved.

Before considering the specific skills and techniques involved in effective communication, it is useful to identify the obstacles to effective communication.

4 Obstacles to Effective Communication

There are two categories of obstacles to effective communication: functional and psychological.

A lack of specific advocacy skills in handling witnesses or presenting argument is a functional obstacle. The psychological obstacles are generally produced by performance anxiety.

By the time people become advocates they are generally good communicators in ordinary day-to-day situations. In everyday communication there are no barriers of the kind that affect communication in the courtroom, such as

- hierarchical relationships;
- formality of proceedings;
- the layout of the courtroom;
- the requirement to comply with the rules of ethics, evidence and etiquette;
- the pressure of skilled performance;
- competitive pressure in the adversary system; a
- pressure of responsibility for the client.

To gain understanding of what interferes with effective communication in the courtroom, it is useful to ask:

- What is the psychological impediment to effective communication?
- What can be done to minimise it?

The psychological impediment to effective communication is performance anxiety, caused by any of a number of factors.

A degree of nervousness or anxiety is to be expected before and during any performance. For an advocate, performance anxiety is increased by worries about

- insufficient familiarity with the materials,
- insufficient familiarity with the court process and environment,

- insufficient familiarity with the characteristics of the decision-maker,
- inadequate legal knowledge and skills level,
- making mistakes,
- looking foolish,
- failure to do the best for the client, and
- professional failure.

It is natural for advocates to have critical, destructive thoughts as a result of those fears. Such thoughts ('I am not really up to it'; 'I am going to look stupid', 'I am going to fail') are sometimes referred to as 'the second voice'. If not dealt with, it undermines one's ability to perform.

This 'second voice' is something that develops and intensifies as we grow up. A toddler learning to walk does not, when falling over for the first, second or even third time, say to him- or herself, *'That's it, I give up, I'm never going to learn to walk. What will people think of me!'*. A toddler will keep standing up, and falling down, until he or she has learned to walk. Skills are best learned when people are young, before they develop inhibitions and defences and their thoughts become critical and unhelpful.

Human thinking follows a pattern of asking and answering questions or dealing with propositions. For example, the questions 'What sort of day is it? What will I wear?' may be answered by, 'Its cool; wear a jumper.'

Positive questions or propositions can help to encourage constructive, positive thinking and actions. For example: 'I have to be at court by 9.00am; how do I get there on time? What time do I have to leave to make sure I'm on time?' In this example, the positive question will lead to looking in the street directory to find the best way to that court, and checking train schedules for relevant departure and arrival times.

If the 'second voice' asks a negative question or puts a negative proposition—for example, 'I don't know how to get to Court; I'm going to be late'—the answer will be an unhelpful response that will increase anxiety.

Example
The 'second voice' undermines confidence:

Q Why didn't I put that argument?
A You're incompetent.

Q Why didn't I ask the right questions?
A You're lazy, you did not do enough preparation.

4.1 Overcoming Obstacles to Effective Communication

In the above Example, the obstacle can be minimised by understanding that positive thinking and asking positive questions will produce more useful responses leading to positive action.

For example, ask 'How can I improve my questioning?'; 'How can I better analyse and prepare my case?'

Performance anxiety can also be minimised by

- consciously developing performance skills;
- improving knowledge and preparation;
- becoming more familiar with the court and the decision-maker. By knowing the decision-maker and his or her approach, the advocate can better anticipate issues that may arise;
- analysing one's own performance and assessing it critically but positively;
- organising the materials for easy identification and access;
- using relaxation techniques such as deep breathing and slowing down;
- focusing on and visualising the performance; and
- being realistic about what can be achieved in the available time and circumstances.

It is important that expectations are commensurate with the advocate's level of experience, skill and ability. For example, it is unrealistic for a junior barrister to expect to achieve what a senior barrister could achieve in a short space of time. What is realistic is a positive commitment to preparation, and performance to the highest standard possible within the available time and level of ability.

5 Communication Skills and Techniques for Persuasive Advocacy

5.1 Organisation

An advocate must structure the evidence, cross-examination or argument to support the case theory in a way that is most likely to persuade the decision-maker.

To be most persuasive, the advocate should aim to capture the decision-maker's attention and interest in the first 20 s of the presentation.[1]

The advocate should use this opportunity to:

[1] This is a view expressed by David Bennett QC, former Solicitor-General of Australia, when teaching appellate advocacy for the Australian Advocacy Institute. It is known as the Principle of Primacy.

- focus the attention of the bench on the most significant issue;
- encapsulate the case in a concise by interesting way; and
- eliminate unnecessary introductory padding.

The advocate should also provide the decision-maker with sufficient information, in progressive sequence, so that each point will be understood in the light of the previous information. This overcomes the problem of the advocate assuming that the decision-maker has the same knowledge of the facts as the advocate does, which may not be a justified assumption.

Finally, the advocate should ensure that the decision-maker is ready to absorb and respond favourably to each stage of the evidence or argument. The advocate must work out the most advantageous time to make the request, state the desired conclusion or make the best point.

It must not be:

- too soon, when the listener is not ready and therefore may misunderstand or have a negative reaction; or
- too late, when the decision-maker may have formed a different or adverse state of mind.

The most persuasive style of argument in court is conversational, not oratorical. This helps to build the relationship between the arguer and the decision-maker.

A good structure should:

- reflect the Principle of Primacy;
- provide a clear introduction, development and conclusion;
- capture and maintain interest; and
- control the listener's reasoning process so as to persuade 'as you go'.

5.2 Telling a Story

People are conditioned from childhood to hear and respond to stories.

We see and experience life as a set of stories and associated feelings. Most cases are based on events, which constitute a story. In most cases there are competing or different stories based on people's differing perceptions, recollections and honesty.

Storytelling is important in the courtroom in:

- the presentation of an interesting opening address;
- the leading of evidence;
- describing the factual foundation for an argument; and
- setting the scene in an application, a plea in mitigation, or an appeal.

A good, persuasive story will

- have a structure that is easy to follow;
- maintain interest;

- be simple;
- use words to create images in the mind of the listener;
- engage other senses as well as hearing, by the use of visual aids and exhibits;
- be directed towards an objective; and/or
- have appropriate, emotive content.

It is much easier to communicate a scene or event to a listener if the advocate has first visualised the scene for him- or herself.

In order to tell a persuasive story, advocates should, from the material available to them, be able to visualise the scene. Going to the actual scene to view it, if possible, can be of enormous assistance.

Effective use of visual aids such as diagrams, photographs, charts, etc, is a powerful communication tool. Even where visual aids are not available, the advocate should help the listener to visualise the scene. This can be done only if the advocate has visualised the scene first.

The events and action that take place in a particular setting are much better understood when the listener understands the scene. Once the advocate has visualised the scene, it is easier to introduce action by reference to the scene.

The action should be visualised in the course of preparation. Where witnesses differ in their accounts of the action, it is useful in preparation to visualise the action from the perspective of each witness. This will help you deal with each witness's account.

5.3 Lines of Communication in the Courtroom

Communication lines in the courtroom are unnatural and can be difficult. Normally, when a person is asked a question, the communication is between the questioner and the person answering.

It is natural for the answer to be directed back to the questioner, particularly if the questioner shows interest and actively listens.

However, in the courtroom, the information, and therefore the impact of the story, should be directed to the decision-maker and not to the questioner. Witnesses find this difficult.

It is important that the advocate 'directs' the communication in the courtroom. In evidence in chief, the advocate asks questions of a witness. The witness's answers should be directed to the judge and/or the jury, depending on the case. An advocate can help the witness to direct his or her answers to the judge or jury by using a number of techniques:

- saying to the witness 'Tell the jury what Mr X did after leaving the bottle shop';
- using hand gestures to indicate that the witness should direct his or her answers to the jury; or
- moving eye contact from the witness to the jury towards the end of the question.

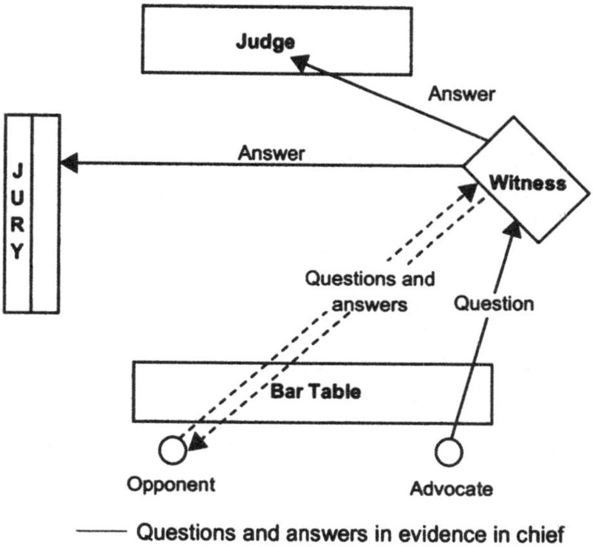

Fig. 1 The appropriate lines of communication in a cross-examination (Reproduced from Hampel et al., 2016 © Australian Advocacy Institute)

Overuse of any of these is distracting; however, a combination of these techniques will keep the line of communication between the witness and the judge or jury.

In cross-examination, directing communication in the courtroom is more complex. In order to control the witness it is useful to maintain eye contact and occupy the attention of the witness, so that his or her answers are directed to you.

Figure 1 clearly illustrates the appropriate lines of communication.

5.4 *Including All Decision-makers*

Whether it be an appellate bench of three or five judges, or a jury of twelve, it is critical that the advocate involve all decision-makers.

This will mean considering not only how to address the bench or jury as a group, but also how to attend to the needs of each member of the bench or jury as an individual.

For example, in the case of an appeal, it may be apparent that one of the judges is having trouble accepting the advocate's proposition, as revealed by the judge's facial expression. The advocate should take the time to address that judge and reframe the proposition, beginning with 'Perhaps, Your Honour, I can put this another way.'

Making every decision-maker feel involved and valued is an important part of effective communication.

5.5 The Art of Simple Expression

Simple language is powerful. It is expressive and easy to understand. Simple words and sentences help to communicate and persuade. It also helps to create images (word pictures) and provide emotive content.

This applies to both speech and writing. For advocates it applies to questioning and arguing.

Obstacles to simple expression include

- unclear thinking,
- fear of commitment to a clear idea,
- fear of making mistakes, or
- fear of appearing unprofessional.

Listening, noticing and practising will help to develop the art of simple expression.

6 The Principles of Clear Expression

> Write to express, not impress. (Trout & Rivkin, 2001)

> I like short words... (Churchill, 1953)

> Empty your knapsack of all adjectives, adverbs and clauses that slow your stride and weaken you pace. Travel light. Remember the most memorable sentences in the English language are also the shortest: 'The King is dead' and 'Jesus wept'. (Moyers quoted in Trout & Rivkin, 2001, p. 17)

When speaking and writing:

- use short and simple words.
- use familiar, expressive words.
- don't be pretentious by using Latin terms unnecessarily, such as *per coram, contra,* etc.
- avoid clichés (trite stereotypical expressions).
- avoid jargon (language particular to a profession or group). This particularly applies when leading evidence from an expert witness. It is essential to ensure that the witness explains any technical terms.
- use direct expression.
  E.g. 'If the prosecution withdraws count 1, my client will plead guilty'
  not
  'If the prosecution considers an appropriate step in relation to the first count my client will take a certain course.'
- use identifying names and humanising expressions, not depersonalising terms.
  E.g. 'Daniel Jones' *not* 'my client'

- use correct grammar and syntax.
- use descriptive language to create word pictures.
- avoid standard expressions or 'fillers'.
- use short sentences.
- use the active voice.
- use rhetorical questions to 'involve' the audience.
- use metaphors.
- use appropriately emotive language.

Example
Examples of simpler words and expressions.

in the event that	if
at the present point in time	now
for the reason that	because
reside	live
utilise	use
commence	start
endeavour	try
be desirous of	want
make reference to	refer
proceed	go
subsequent	later
prior to	before
alighted from	go out

Example
Examples of more effective sentences.

Instead of:	'The Defendant was arrested by Constable X' or 'Constable X was responsible for the Defendants arrest' (passive voice)
use:	'Constable X arrested the Defendant' (active voice)
Instead of:	'Section 5 of the Public Order Act was breached by the defendant when the bottle of alcohol was provided by the defendant to Witness A' (complex passive voice)
use:	'Defendant breached section 5 of the Public Order Act by supplying the bottle of alcohol to Witness A' (simple active voice)

(continued)

Instead of:	'By reason of the fact that Witness A was released from the police station and can no longer be located he is unavailable to appear as a witness' (padding)
use:	'Witness A cannot be called to give evidence because he cannot be found' (simple positive)
Instead of:	'A barrister must do his best for his client' (sexist language)
use:	'Barristers must do their best for their clients'

Inaccurate phrases such as 'I seek to tender this document as an exhibit' should be avoided. When a document is proved, the advocate should simply say 'I tender the document'.

In examination in chief, you should avoid questions in the following form:

- Are you able to remember who was in the room when you walked in?
- Do you recall what she was wearing?
- Can you describe what she did?

There are two problems with such questions. The first is that the strictly accurate answer to each is 'yes' or 'no' and the advocate must then ask the real question.

The second and more significant is that by introducing the idea of possible difficulties in recalling or describing, you are calling into question the witness's capacity to recall or describe.

Better and simpler questions are

- Who was in the room when you walked in?
- What was she wearing?
- What did she do?

7 Non-verbal Communication

Appropriate body language helps the advocate to create the desired effect and atmosphere, and to convey appropriate emotional messages and seriousness of purpose.

Where there is a conflict between what is said and the advocate's body language, it is the advocate's body language that will leave the greater impression.

Body language that enhances communication includes

- stance or posture that conveys confidence and can be either receptive or commanding,
- movement designed to have an impact or create a change of mood,
- gesticulation used for emphasis,
- mannerisms that are natural but not distracting,
- facial expressions that are appropriate to the subject matter and atmosphere, and

- eye contact that creates a rapport.

  Eye contact can be sympathetic and inquiring, or hard and glaring.

  Eye contact, together with facial expressions, should be appropriate to the occasion and to the witness or decision-maker.

It is difficult for advocates to change their natural mannerisms. A person who tends to move and use his or her hands would find it difficult to remain very still. It is important for an advocate to remain natural, but aim to ensure that his or her mannerisms do not detract from effective communication.

Some mannerisms that detract from effective communication include:

- unconscious, continuous hand movements;
- playing with a pen;
- flicking or twisting hair;
- constantly shifting weight from one foot to another; and
- shuffling of papers.

8 Delivery

Effective delivery involves:

- timing and use of pauses;
- pace, to enable the decision-maker to absorb the information;
- intonation for emphasis, change of meaning, or emotive quality;
- volume, to make listening easier;
- enunciation, for clarity; and
- minimal use of notes, to enhance the relationship with the listener.

8.1 Use of Notes

In performing all advocacy tasks, an advocate who is tied to his or her notes creates a number of communication problems, including:

- lack of appropriate eye contact.

  If the advocate is reading notes, he or she is not looking at the decision-maker. The advocate cannot monitor the decision-maker's responses, nor build a relationship with the decision-maker. The advocate may miss an opportunity to reframe a proposition so that it is accepted by the decision-maker.
- inappropriate pace.

  Most people read more quickly than they would speak. It is very difficult for a decision-maker to hear what is being said, consider it and evaluate it if the advocate is going at 'reading pace'.
- wasted opportunities for emphasis.

An advocate who is reading is less likely to pause for emphasis, or to use tone and volume for particular effect.
- inappropriate stance.
  If notes are on a table or lectern, then the temptation will be to lean forward and look down, rather than standing upright with shoulders back. An advocate who is standing upright and looking at the decision-maker not only appears more confident, but compels the decision-maker to pay attention.

It is unrealistic, however to expect an advocate to run an entire trial or lengthy matter without a note. The key to using notes so that they do not interfere with effective communication is to ensure that they

- prompt the advocate's thoughts, and
- do not constitute the substance of what the advocate will say.

When the advocate has finished a particular topic, he or she may look down at the notes to be prompted about the next topic. There is nothing wrong with the advocate pausing to look down to read the prompt, then looking up again and continuing on with the next topic. The decision-maker will most likely be grateful for the pause, which is opportunity to consider what has just been said.

The key to effective communication in this context is to avoid talking and looking down at the notes at the same time.

Useful notes will often be dot points: simple propositions written as a list. They should not be in narrative form. It is also helpful to break the subject matter down into topics, highlighting topic headings.

These useful notes can be produced only after all of the preparation and analysis of the case has been finished. They are part of the performance preparation phase. It is only at this stage of the preparation that the advocate will know what is the substance behind the prompt.

Remember that you prepare to perform. You do not perform your preparation.

References

Churchill, W. (1953). Speech: Margate, 10 Oct '53. In Czamomski (Ed.), *The Wisdom of Winston Churchill*. Allen & Unwin, 1956.

Hampel, G., Brimer, E., & Kune, R. (2016). *Advocacy manual: The complete guide to persuasive advocacy*. Melbourne Australian Advocacy Institute.

Trout, J., & Rivkin, S. (2001). *The power of simplicity: A management guide to cutting through the nonsense and doing things right*. McGraw-Hill.

George Hampel AM QC was a Justice of the Supreme Court of Victoria from 1983 to 2000, having previously practised as a barrister since 1958.

Hampel has held numerous positions in the legal profession, such as Vice-President of the Law Council of Australia, Vice-Chairman of the Victorian Bar Institute and Chairman of the Constitution Commission of Victoria.

For over 40 years, George developed advocacy teaching methods, case studies and the training of advocacy instructors in Australia and abroad. Since 2000, he has been Professor of Trial Practice and Advocacy at Monash University. His training experience of professional advocates extends internationally to USA, UK, Scotland, New Zealand, Hong Kong, Singapore, South Africa, and war crime prosecutors at The Hague.

George was the Founding Chairman of the Australian Advocacy Institute in 1991 and over the following 24 years continued to develop its teaching methodology and workshop programs. He is the principal author of the two editions of the Australian Advocacy Manual, which is now required reading for the Victorian Bar Readers Course and is used as a reference work in most common law jurisdictions. George has developed workshops for training of members of other professions including forensic accountants, doctors, engineers and computer experts in their roles as expert witnesses.

As a result of his contribution in these areas, George was made a Member of the General Division of the Order of Australia (2006), received the Centenary of Federation Medal, and a Monash University Teaching Award.

Making an Opening Address

George Hampel

1 Introduction

An opening address is:

- a simple, narrative outline of your case;
- consistent with your case theory;
- told as a persuasive story;
- directed to a specific legal result; and
- without argument.

An opening is a powerful forensic tool because it is the first presentation of your case to the decision-maker.

You should use an opening address whenever possible, whether appearing for the party that bears the onus of proof—that is, prosecution or plaintiff—or for the defendant.

Traditionally in criminal cases, the defence opened its own case at the close of the prosecution case. Since the 1990s, the practice has developed of allowing the defence to open its case at the end of the prosecution opening.

The law and practice vary from state to state, so it is important for the advocate to check this before the trial.

It is essential for the defence counsel to avail themselves of the opportunity to use this powerful forensic tool, and to open before the prosecution begins its examination in chief.

Text within this chapter has been directly extracted, with authors permission, from Hampel, G., Brimer, E., & Kune, R. (2016). *Advocacy manual: The complete guide to persuasive advocacy.* Melbourne Australian Advocacy Institute.

G. Hampel (✉)
Faculty of Law, Monash University, Melbourne, VIC, Australia
e-mail: george.hampel@monash.edu

E. King et al. (eds.), *Victim Advocacy before the International Criminal Court*,
https://doi.org/10.1007/978-3-030-56733-0_8

This will

- allow the jury's attention to be refocused to the defence case before the prosecution evidence is led, and
- avoid having to regain lost ground.

Knowing the defence case also helps the judge to make evidentiary and other rulings in the trial. In civil cases, the defence position is better known from pleadings. Nevertheless, it is an advantage to open immediately after the plaintiff's opening, for the same reasons as in a criminal case.

2 Outline Your Case

The opening must be a relatively brief and concise outline of your case. It should identify the essential facts of the story.

An opening by the party going first is different from an opening by the defence.

A defendant's advocate should not repeat the uncontested facts in the prosecution's or plaintiff's opening, which the court will have just heard.

The defence opening is better made as a positive story, based on the defence's realistic alternative theory focusing on the facts that support it.

In a criminal case, it is useful to bring out the good character of the accused as early as possible.

The opening may include a brief summary of your position in relation to the issues in the case; for example, it may be appropriate for the defence to indicate that it does not contest one of the elements of the offence.

It is not appropriate for the defence to make positive assertions that are inconsistent with the client's instructions.

2.1 Told as a Persuasive Story

An opening is an exercise in storytelling. A good story will

- be well-structured;
- engage the interest of the listener by bringing people, places and events to life;
- be told simply;
- be communicated clearly;
- be realistic and not overstated; and
- make appropriate use of visual aids.

The opening delivered to a judge alone may differ from an opening delivered to a jury. The differences may be about legal principles or issues, but as a fact-finder the judge is 'just another juror'.

2.1.1 The Story Will Be Well-Structured

To be persuasive, the opening should be structured so that the story can be easily understood and remembered by the decision-maker.

A structured narrative of events is much easier to understand and remember than a list of facts, or merely a summary of each witness's statement.

The structure of your opening address must

- apply the Principle of Primacy,[1] and
- relate to the legal framework of the case.

Start your opening with the story of what happened. That is what the judge or jury wants to hear first. Do not start discussing legal principles or issues in a vacuum.

How the story is organised and told is ultimately a matter for you to choose in each case. There is no right way to do it, but it would be wrong not to consider how to do it in the most effective way possible.

In a complex case, in which many factual and legal issues must be communicated in an opening address, the advocate must be conscious of the 'communication bottleneck', where the quantity and density of information make it difficult to be absorbed and processed by the decision-maker.

This bottleneck occurs because lawyers have had the advantage of thorough preparation, which the judge or the jury does not have. They are truly the 'first time listeners'. The risk for the advocate who delivers the opening address lies in attempting to provide too much complex information to the decision-maker too quickly. As a result, it can be difficult for the decision-maker to absorb and understand the opening.

The approach sometimes adopted of presenting the judge with a densely written opening accompanied by materials is undesirable.

While the fundamental principles of good storytelling still apply, care must be taken in complex cases to ensure that the simple signification narrative of the case is told first, before providing more detail. In this way, the judge or jury will hear and absorb the story progressively, adding the more complex elements to the simple story that has already been told, understood and remembered.

Especially in complex cases, much of the detail is not necessary in the opening; it is more important first to capture the story of the case as a whole. How much detail has to be included is a matter for the advocate's judgment.

A useful exercise is for the advocate to consider how to outline the case generally to a lay person in a few minutes. Such an exercise might start with the advocate formulating the initial simple story by beginning, 'This case is about...'

To gain the impact of immediacy, avoid introductory formality and padding.

---

[1] The Principle of Primacy is a term used by David Bennett QC, former Solicitor-General of Australia. He believes that to be the most persuasive, the advocate should aim to capture the decision-maker's attention and interest in the first 20 seconds of the presentation.

Example
These types of introductory formalities should be avoided in your opening.

'Good Morning, members of the jury.'
'The accused is charged with...'
'It is my function to open the case for the prosecution.'
'I will outline the facts but it is the witnesses' evidence that matters.'
'As a matter of law, the elements of the offence are...'
'What I say is subject to Her Honour's directions on the law.'

Where it is appropriate to identify the details of the charge, or the role of the jury, these are better left until later in the opening, so that they can be understood in the context of the story. The legal issues in the case will make better sense once the narrative has been told.

It is unnecessary to refer to the elements of the offence before a judge, unless the offence is an unusual one.

In a criminal trial, the judge will probably have explained the jury's role to them.

2.1.2 The Story Will Engage the Interest of the Listener

The listener should be able to visualise the events as the story is being told. To bring the people, places and events to life, the advocate must first visualise the story.

A good story will answer the questions

- Who was involved?
- What happened?
- Where and when did it happen?
- Why did it happen?

You should always personalise your client and witnesses, referring to them by their names. You should refer to opposing witnesses in a more objective way.

Example
Personalise your client.
For the prosecution, you would refer to 'Constable X', not 'the police'.
For the defence, you would refer to 'Daniel Jones', not 'the defendant'.

2.1.3 The Story Will Be Told Simply

To make the story simple, include the important facts but do not give the whole detail of the case in the opening.

Your opening address is designed to work with evidence in chief, during which you will lead all the detail of your story from the witnesses.

By leaving out some details from your opening, and then leading them in evidence in chief, you are progressively informing the listener. This will have the effect of

- maintaining the interest of the listener in the story during evidence in chief, and
- creating the impression of corroborating your opening address, as each witness gives evidence in chief in detail, which fits the more general story told in the opening.

Limiting the detail in your opening will also have the benefit of avoiding potential discrepancies between what is said in opening and the evidence given during examination in chief.

2.1.4 The Story Will Be Communicated Clearly

For maximum effect, your opening should be a good piece of communication. That is, it should cater to the needs of the listener.

It must be presented in a manner and at a pace that enables the listener to hear, understand and absorb the story.

You should be sufficiently familiar with the story to present it without notes, or with limited use of notes, so that you can engage the listeners when you speak by talking to them instead of reading.

You should use simple language. Simple words and phrases have an immediate impact on the listener because they make it easy for the listener to understand, visualise and remember the story. Simple language is effective in creating 'word pictures'.

2.1.5 The Story Will Be Realistic and Not Overstated

Another factor in the power of the opening narrative is that the listener tends to measure other versions of the story against the one first heard.

A realistic story clearly told leaves a strong impression on the listener.

Avoid overstating or exaggerating the evidence that will be given. This may damage your credibility because the detail in the evidence, once given by the witness, will not permit overstatement or exaggeration. An understatement is often more effective, as it emphasises the strength of the evidence.

2.1.6 The Story Will Be Enhanced by Visual Aids

A picture is worth a thousand words. Use plans, diagrams, exhibits and other visual aids during the opening to explain events.

Relevant documents and other physical evidence can be used in an opening address with your opponent's consent or by leave of the court. You must be able to prove the documents or exhibits in evidence.

Take time to show and explain the visual aid to the listener before describing the action in your narrative.

Example

Using and/or tendering an exhibit in opening address.

Prosecution: Your Honour, with my learned friend's consent, may I use (or tender) a plan of the hotel and surrounding streets?

Judge: Does the defence consent to that?

Defence: Yes, Your Honour, the defence consents to the document being used (or tendered).

[Prosecution hands up the plan to the court officer, and a copy to opponent.]

Judge: That will be Exhibit 1, plan of Royal Oak Hotel.

Prosecution: Could the jury be given copies of Exhibit 1?

[Prosecution hands copies to the court officer, to distribute to the jury.]

Prosecution: *[Holding up the plan to jury and indicating locations]* You can see the intersection of Wide Street and Jackson Avenue with the Royal Oak Hotel and its bottle shop in the corner. There is the counter. There is the door. The police car was parked here. The police could see into the bottle shop through a plate glass window that was partly covered by advertising etc...

2.1.7 Directed to a Specific Legal Result

The story should be organised and told in a way that supports the conclusions relating to the elements of the offence.

It is not enough to state that a witness will give evidence to establish an element of an offence or claim. Let the narrative do the work.

2.1.8 Not Argumentative

The only rule of law that applies to openings is that argument is not permitted. This is because there is no point in argument before the evidence is heard.

If told as a good story, an opening can be persuasive without being argumentative. It is permissible and desirable at the end of the opening for the prosecutor to identify the elements of the offence intended to be proved by the facts outlined. It will be desirable for the defence to identify the inadequacy of the prosecution case. Both of these things must be done without argument.

You descend into argument when you give reasons as to

- why one witness is preferable to another,
- why one version of events is preferable to another, and
- what conclusions should be drawn from the evidence and why.

The opening is a powerful forensic tool because it provides an opportunity to anticipate and defuse the opposing case theory. That is not the same as presenting an argument.

A well-prepared and skilfully delivered opening by the prosecution or the plaintiff creates a positive, powerful story and impressions at the outset. It is the first telling of a story to a 'first-time listener'.

A good opening by the defence, delivered at the beginning of the trial, is effective in introducing parts of the story important to the defence and in refocusing the decision-maker's attention to aspects that will help the defence case.

The requirement to open is an opportunity that should never be wasted.

George Hampel AM QC was a Justice of the Supreme Court of Victoria from 1983 to 2000, having previously practised as a barrister since 1958.

Hampel has held numerous positions in the legal profession, such as Vice-President of the Law Council of Australia, Vice-Chairman of the Victorian Bar Institute and Chairman of the Constitution Commission of Victoria.

For over 40 years, George developed advocacy teaching methods, case studies and the training of advocacy instructors in Australia and abroad. Since 2000, he has been Professor of Trial Practice and Advocacy at Monash University. His training experience of professional advocates extends internationally to USA, UK, Scotland, New Zealand, Hong Kong, Singapore, South Africa, and war crime prosecutors at The Hague.

George was the Founding Chairman of the Australian Advocacy Institute in 1991 and over the following 24 years continued to develop its teaching methodology and workshop programs. He is the principal author of the two editions of the Australian Advocacy Manual, which is now required reading for the Victorian Bar Readers Course and is used as a reference work in most common law jurisdictions. George has developed workshops for training of members of other professions including forensic accountants, doctors, engineers and computer experts in their roles as expert witnesses.

As a result of his contribution in these areas, George was made a Member of the General Division of the Order of Australia (2006), received the Centenary of Federation Medal, and a Monash University Teaching Award.

Leading Evidence in Chief

George Hampel

1 Rules of Evidence

To be effective as an advocate both in preparation and in court, you must know the rules of evidence relevant to your jurisdiction. Some evidentiary issues can be anticipated in preparation, but others can arise quickly, when there is no opportunity to research and prepare.

You must distinguish between admissibility of evidence and the weight of evidence. Court will not consider evidence that is found to be inadmissible. However, once evidence is admitted, the court will consider its weight or probative value, that is, whether the court should rely on the evidence.

During preparation you must

- consider evidentiary issues apparent from the materials,
- assess the admissibility of potential evidence on both sides,
- prepare to argue about the admissibility of evidence, and
- consider which evidentiary issues should be dealt with before trial.

Evidentiary issues typically arise in relation to

- relevance,
- admissibility,

Text within this chapter has been directly extracted, with authors permission, from Hampel, G., Brimer, E., & Kune, R. (2016). *Advocacy manual: The complete guide to persuasive advocacy.* Melbourne Australian Advocacy Institute.

G. Hampel (✉)
Faculty of Law, Monash University, Melbourne, VIC, Australia
e-mail: george.hampel@monash.edu

E. King et al. (eds.), *Victim Advocacy before the International Criminal Court*,
https://doi.org/10.1007/978-3-030-56733-0_9

- form of questions, or
- fairness.

Common admissibility issues include

- hearsay and its exceptions in jurisdictions where the proposed uniform evidence legislation does not apply,
- opinion evidence,
- privilege,
- confessions,
- identification evidence,
- similar fact evidence,
- propensity evidence,
- *res gestae,*[1]
- discretionary exclusions,
- statuatory exclusions, or
- evidence that can be adduced only with leave of the court.

You might make submissions about the admissibility of such evidence

- on a *voir dire* in which there are evidentiary and legal issues before or during trial, or
- by making or answering objections during the course of a trial.

A question may be objectionable if the form of the question is

- leading,
- argumentative,
- compound or multiple, and/or
- a comment or statement.

A question may also be objectionable as unfair if it is

- misleading, ambiguous, confusing, or unintelligible;
- harassing, intimidating or oppressive;
- repeated if it has already been asked and answered;
- an inappropriate conclusion from evidence already given;
- vague or lacking content about the subject matter;
- a misstatement of evidence already given;
- asking for speculation or a guess; and/or
- hypothetical, except in the case of experts.

Some further common evidentiary issues include

- dealing with a hostile witness,
- refreshing a witness's memory,

[1] *Res gestae* are the events, circumstances, remarks, etc. which are related to a particular case, especially constituting admissible evidence in a court of law.

- impeaching the credibility of a witness,
- dealing with prior inconsistent statements,
- using the principle of judicial notice,
- tendering documents or other exhibits, and
- complying with the rule in *Browne v Dunn.*[2]

2 The Cycle of Evidence

The system of calling evidence used in court is intended to create a complete and orderly but fair cycle, to ensure that each party has every opportunity to bring out the relevant and admissible evidence it wishes to rely on.

The process cannot be a free-for-all where witnesses are at liberty to say whatever they want to say, whenever they want to say it. The system requires a disciplined and controlled process. The court relies on the advocates' knowledge of what is relevant and admissible. The advocates are therefore expected to exercise control over what is adduced in evidence.

The cycle of evidence is designed to ensure that

- during evidence in chief, all relevant and admissible evidence is given;
- during cross-examination, the witness and his or her evidence can be discredited or accredited, or additional evidence adduced under the control of the cross-examiner by leading questions. The cross-examiner is entitled to confine the witness to answers to specific questions. (For more information on cross-examination, see the discussion in this volume, George Hampel, 'Conducting Cross-examination')
- during re-examination, material raised in cross-examination can be clarified, completed or explained. Because leading questions are permitted in cross-examination, and the witness is confined to answering only the questions that are put, the process would not be fair without the opportunity to re-examine. Evidence sought to be adduced in re-examination must be relevant and admissible.

With leave, further examination in chief of a witness can be permitted and the cycle of evidence begins again with respect to that further evidence.

[2] The rule of *Browne v Dunn* is a rule of evidentiary fairness named after the British case of the same name (*Browne v Dunn*, 6 R. 67 (1893, House of Lords)). If you intend to later impeach a witness with contradictory evidence, that evidence ought to be put to the witness. On the parallel issue of procedural fairness and principles of evidentiary fairness in International Criminal Law, advocates are encouraged to access the ICC's Legal Tools database, see the Part IV Resources in this work. https://www.legal-tools.org/.

3 Evidentiary Issues Involving Questions of Law

It is important to understand the principles behind the rules of evidence, and the application of the rules, even when appearing before tribunals which are not bound by the rules of evidence. Such understanding enables you to argue about the admissibility and weight of evidence in court, and about the weight of evidence in the tribunal.

3.1 Relevance

The court will consider evidence only if it is relevant. Relevance is a matter of law, which is decided by the court.

Evidence is admissible if it is relevant to

- the issues in dispute, such as the elements of the offence or claim, or
- a fact relevant to a fact in issue in dispute, or
- the credibility of a witness,

and if it is not excluded in the judge's exercise of discretion.

3.2 Hearsay and Its Exceptions

At common law, an out-of-court statement is excluded as hearsay if it is tendered to prove the truth of the facts contained in it. This is because the source of the information cannot be tested.

The continuing legislative trend is to abolish the strict exclusionary rule and allow the admission of hearsay if the source is sufficiently reliable.

In jurisdictions where the common law rule remains in force, there are many exceptions, such as admissions against interest.[3]

Self-serving statements, such as 'I told my neighbours that I didn't set fire to my car', are inadmissible, if the issue is whether the witness set fire to his car. However, statements made by a person under questions which are part admissions and part self-serving statement or denials, in response to allegations, are admissible as part of the narrative and in the interest of fairness.

For example, a person being questioned about an assault could say that he was present on the occasion and that he struck the victim. Those are admissions. It would be unfair to exclude the next statement, that the striking was in self-defence, and so that statement, which is self-serving, would be admissible as part of the narrative.

[3] See the chapters on exceptions to hearsay evidence in Heydon (2004), and Gans and Palmer (2004).

3.3 *Opinion Evidence*

Lay witnesses are permitted to give evidence of facts in their direct knowledge, based on the perception of their senses. For example: 'I saw a blue motor car enter the intersection against the red light'; 'I heard the screech of brakes'; 'I smelt the burning rubber'.

Lay people are not permitted to give opinion evidence because it is the function of the court, not the witness, to draw relevant inferences or reach conclusions based on the witness's observations. For example, it is the court's role to decide why the accident occurred or who was at fault.

In some circumstances, lay witnesses may be allowed to give limited opinions about matters of common understanding, knowledge and experience, such as assessing speed or intoxication, or identifying people. Such statements are more impressions than they are opinions of the kind given by an expert witness. (For more information on expert witnesses, please see in this volume George Hampel, "Dealing with Expert Evidence")

3.4 *Privilege*

3.4.1 Privilege Against Self-incrimination

The common law privilege against self-incrimination allows a witness or party to a criminal or civil case to refuse to answer questions or produce documents that tend to incriminate them, that is, to expose them to criminal conviction or other penalty.

The witness or party must establish some reasonable grounds for the claim of privilege.

The privilege has been modified by statute in most jurisdictions, not in courts but in proceedings such as Royal Comminions and inquiries. In such cases, a witness can be compelled to answer questions, but usually those answers cannot be used in criminal proceedings if the witness relies on the cover of privilege.

3.4.2 Legal Professional Privilege

Confidential communications between a lawyer and client which have been created for the dominant purpose of legal advice, or actual or contemplated legal proceedings, are protected by the client's legal professional privilege. This privilege is that of the client, not the lawyer, and may be waived by the client.

This extends to documents exchanged between either the lawyer or the client and third parties for the purpose of actual or contemplated litigation.

There are several exceptions to the privilege and many instances where it will be deemed to have been waived.

3.5 Confessions

Admissions or confessions made out of court are admissible under an exception to the rule against hearsay, as admissions against interest. However, in criminal proceedings, courts will exclude admissions and confessions from evidence if they are involuntarily made, for instance as a result of inducement or oppression.

Courts also have a discretion to exclude confessions or admissions made in circumstances where it would be unfair to the accused or against public policy for them to be admitted. For example, where a confession is obtained during unlawful detention, or some other unlawful or unfair means, it could be excluded.

Some statutes also require certain procedural steps, such as recordings, to have been taken at or after the time of admission before any confession can be admitted.

3.6 Identification

In criminal proceedings, identification evidence can be excluded if the evidence is so inherently unreliable that its prejudicial effect outweighs its probative value. Once identification evidence is admitted, its weaknesses must be considered by a judge sitting alone, and must be highlighted to the jury.

Various principles have developed to exclude identification based, for example, on a single photograph shown to the identifying witness, or an identification in court, known as a 'dock' identification.

3.7 Similar Fact Evidence

Similar fact evidence is generally used to identify a person as the same actor on different occasions. This frequently occurs where an accused is alleged to have used the same specific technique on different occasions.

For example, if a person can be shown to have unlawfully entered a house by a specific pretext and method, the evidence of the use of the same or a similar method can be used to identify that person as the actor on other occasions.

3.8 Propensity Evidence

Propensity evidence involves the attempt to prove that a person acted in some way on a previous occasion, from which the court may infer that he or she acted in the same way on the occasion in question at the trial.

The potential overlap between similar fact evidence and propensity evidence, and the purposes for which they can be used, can pose difficult questions requiring careful analysis of the evidence and current law.

3.9 Res Gestae

The doctrine of *res gestae* is used to characterise evidence which becomes admissible because it forms 'part of the story' needed to understand other parts of the evidence.

The doctrine is chiefly used as an exception to the rule against hearsay, on the basis that the evidence sought to be admitted is reliable, as it was made proximate in time to the events, and its purpose is to explain those events.

3.10 Character Evidence

Character evidence may be given and used in two different ways in the course of a trial:

- to support the evidence of the accused that he or she did not commit the offence, and
- to support his or her credibility.

In a criminal trial, character evidence is limited to evidence:

- that the accused has no prior convictions (usually asked of the police and/or given by the accused);
- that the accused had a good general reputation; and
- of the witness's knowledge of the good reputation of the accused in the relevant community, for example as to honesty.

3.11 Discretionary Exclusions

Courts in criminal proceedings have the discretion to exclude evidence on the basis of unfairness if

- the evidence has been illegally or improperly obtained, or
- the prejudicial effect of the evidence on the accused would outweigh its probative value.

3.12 Evidence Excluded by Statute

Some evidence is excluded specifically by statute.

For instance, in all jurisdictions, the prior criminal history of the accused in a a criminal proceeding is inadmissible, unless character is put in issue by the accused, or an attack is made on the character of a prosecution witness which has no connection to the issues in the case.

3.13 Evidence That Can Be Adduced Only with Leave of the Court

In some situations, statutes require a party to obtain leave before leading evidence relevant to particular issues. For instance, this applies to the prior sexual history of the complainant in sexual offences, under *Evidence Act 1958* (VIC, Australia) s 37A.

4 Making Submissions About Admissibility

Good advocates will anticipate issues, and deal with them before or at the start of any trial. This will help the efficient running of the trial. It is helpful to prepare a written summary of all objections before the hearing, identifying

- the evidence that you will argue is inadmissible, and
- the legal basis for your objections.

This can be given to your opponent and to the court before the hearing, and provides an efficient structure to help the court consider the arguments.

5 Arguing for or Against the Admissibility of Evidence on a *Voir Dire*

A *voir dire* is a procedure for determining the admissibility of evidence (Stephen, 1997). *Voir Dire* is a procedure

- performed before or during a trial;
- to enable a ruling to be made; and
- to discover whether evidence is admissible, and if admissible, whether it should be excluded in the exercise of discretion.

The party who seeks to exclude evidence has carriage of the proceeding on a *voir dire*. Generally, the onus is on the party who seeks to exclude the evidence to establish that it is not admissible.

In criminal cases where a confession is challenged, and the question of the voluntariness is raised, the prosecution must establish that the confession was voluntary. In such a case, the prosecution has carriage of that issue. If the confession is shown to be voluntary, it is for the accused to show that it should nevertheless be excluded in the exercise of discretion.

Both parties can call evidence and make submissions.

5.1 Voir Dire on the Admissibility of Expert Evidence

The admissibility of proposed expert evidence can be challenged on the grounds that

- there is not an accepted field of expertise relevant to the opinion;
- the witness does not have the necessary training, skill or experience to give expert evidence; or
- the evidence is within common knowledge.

In a *voir dire* where the expertise of the witness is challenged, the following background information about the proposed expert witness may be relevant:

- occupation and length of time in occupation,
- place of employment and current title,
- current duties,
- areas of specialisation,
- academic qualifications and research,
- professional licence or certification,
- past relevant work experience,
- publications and teaching,
- membership of professional societies and organisations, or
- awards or other recognition received.

These questions remain relevant to the weight of the evidence once it is admitted, particularly where there are conflicting expert opinions. For more information about expert evidence and expert witnesses see in this volume, George Hampel, "Dealing with Expert Evidence".

6 Examination in Chief

Examination in chief should be structured by the advocate to allow the witness to tell a persuasive story. You should ask yourself

- How will the witness best recall events?
- How will the decision-maker best understand the story?
- How will the decision-maker best remember the story?
- How will the decision-maker's interest be maintained?

To achieve these purposes, you should use the following techniques:

- Evidence should follow a chronological or other logical order.
- The story should progressively inform the listener.
- Where more than one witness tells the same story or part of it, decide the order of witnesses—usually strongest and most detailed witness first.

The story must have sufficient detail to be credible and persuasive. A detailed story is more realistic and persuasive than a vague and generalised one, and a logical structure also tends to allow the witness to see where you are going.

Avoid merely following the structure in a written statement prepared by someone else, because this may not have been done with a view to the order in which the story should be told in court.

7 Preparation for Examination in Chief

When preparing for performance, you should

- decide on the order in which you will call witnesses;
- break down the story into individual, single facts; and
- list those facts in the order you would like them to be told.

This creates a checklist, which helps to ensure that no facts are left out by the witness during evidence in chief.

Writing out questions is not helpful because if the witness does not give you the full answer you want, your next prepared question may be irrelevant or objectionable.

Consider the questions that would elicit those specific facts as answers, and ensure that your checklist includes only facts, not opinions, arguments or other inadmissible material.

Example
Below is a sample list of facts to be elicited from witness Betty Smith.

Fact	Question	Answer
In bottle shop	Where were you on 24 December last year at about 8.45 p.m.?	I was in the bottle shop.
Royal Oak Hotel	Where was the bottle shop?	In the Royal Oak Hotel.
selecting wine	What were you doing there?	I was trying to find a nice bottle of wine.
from specials stand	Where were you selecting wine from?	From the specials stand.
near the window	Where is the specials stand located?	Near the window.
saw man enter shop	While you were selecting wine, did you see anyone in the shop in relation to this case?	Yes, I saw a man come into the bottle shop.
bumped into me	What did he do when he entered the shop?	He bumped into me.
didn't apologise	Was anything said?	No. He didn't apologise, which I thought was very rude.
strong smell of alcohol	As he bumped into you, did you notice anything about him?	Yes. He had a strong smell of alcohol.
He approached the counter	After he bumped into you, did he go anywhere?	He went to the counter.
had a conversation	What did he do when he approached the counter?	He had a conversation with the barman.
with Daniel Jones	Who was the barman?	Daniel Jones.

Note: this is a fictional case.

7.1 Getting the Complete Story from the Witness

Ensure that the witness gives a complete account of his or her version of events. If you don't get all of the evidence out, then

- you will weaken your case or fail to prove an element of your case, and
- the cross-examiner may use omitted evidence effectively as a surprise or use its omission to attack the honesty or accuracy of the witness.

Example

Ensure that during the examination in chief of Constable X you lead the fact that Constable X saw Watkins pause for a few moments before entering the store, even if this evidence does not help the prosecution case.

Q What happened after he crossed the road?
A He stumbled and almost fell at the southern kerb of Wide Street.
Q And then?
A He walked into the bottle shop.
Q Did he do anything before he walked in?
A He paused at the door.
Q How long did he pause for?
A For a few moments.

Note: this is a fictional case.

7.2 *Conferences*

The purpose of the conference is to learn, to teach and to build confidence in both yourself and the witness.

At a conference you should

- clarify ambiguities or inconsistencies in instructions or accounts of events,
- explain to the witness:
  - the questioning process for examination in chief
  - the prohibition on leading questions
  - the need to address answers to the decision-maker
  - the process of re-examination
  - the prohibition against discussion when the witness is under cross-examination
  - behaviour in court, and form of address for judge, jury and counsel,
- understand and rehearse any demonstrations you may ask the witness to give,
- explain the structure that you will adopt in leading the evidence, and
- explain to character witnesses the nature and limitations of character evidence at trial.

8 Performing Examination in Chief

When you are performing examination in chief, you should

- focus on the witness, and let him or her tell a story—without relinquishing control of the process;

- although you know the story, ask questions with the curiosity of someone who wants to know. This avoids flatness and will encourage the listener's attention;
- use simple language;
- ask short, one-proposition questions;
- focus on facts, not on conclusions; and
- be aware of the decision-maker, and of how the decision-maker is responding to the evidence.

8.1 Describing the Scene and Events

Describe the scene of an event, preferably by using visual aids, before describing the action.

Use a plan by proving it through the witness.

Example

Evidence in chief of Constable X.

Q On the evening of 24 December last year, where were you?
A I was on duty.
Q Where were you on duty?
A In a police car, parked on Jackson Avenue, near Wide Street.
Q Was there anyone else in the police car?
A Yes, I was with Constable Y.
Q Please look at this document.

[Hand plan to the Associate/Clerk to be given to the witness.]

Q Could you identify this document?
A That is a plan of the street where we were parked.
Q Who prepared that plan?
A I did.
Q When did you do that?
A On 25 December last year.
Q What do you say about its accuracy?
A It is not to scale but it shows the streets and other features in the right proportions.
Q I tender that, Your Honour.
Court: That will be Exhibit 1, plan of Jackson Avenue and Wide Street.

Note: this is a fictional case.

When describing the scene, ensure that the witness describes and shows the relevant features such as

- the place,
- the time,
- the layout,
- who was present and their positions,
- distances (if necessary), and
- other relevant structures.

It is helpful to have enlarged copies of plans or other diagrams so that they can be seen by others when the witness is using them.

Example

Continued examination in chief of Constable X.

Q Do you have the plan in front of you?
A Yes.
Q I will take you through that plan and ask you to describe the features marked on it. Please hold the plan up for His Honour and the jury to see and indicate.
A Yes.
Q Where was your police car?
A It was parked here on Jackson Avenue. [Indicating]
Q How far was it from Wide Street?
A It was about 10 to 12 metres from the corner.
Q How wide is Wide Street?
A It is about 6 to 8 metres across.
Q Where were you in the car?
A Sitting in the driver's seat.
Q As you sat in the car, which way were you facing?
A South, down Jackson Avenue.
Q What was the state of the natural light?
A There was little natural light.
Q What was the state of any artificial light?
A There were two streetlights here and here, which gave us a clear view of the street. There were also traffic lights on each corner of Wide Street and Jackson Avenue.
Q Using the plan, would you describe for His Honour the layout of the bottle shop?
A Through the door of the bottle shop there were wine racks left and right followed by the counter. On the counter was a cash register and brown paper bags. Behind the counter were the fortified wines. The bar and lounge are located here.

(continued)

Q What was your view of the bottle shop from the police car?
A I could see into the bottle shop through the plate glass widow, which made up most of the eastern wall.
Q How much could you see through the plate glass window?
A I could see people's heads and shoulders inside the bottle shop above the displays and advertising on the window.
Q From where you were sitting in the police car, how far was it to the counter of the bottle shop?
A It was about 8 to 10 metres.

Note: this is a fictional case.

Once the plan has been tendered and the scene described, the action, which took place, is easier to understand.

Example
Continued examination in chief of Constable X.

Q As you sat in the car, did you see anyone in relation to this case?
A Yes.
Q Who did you see?
A I saw Walter Watkins.
Q How did you first see him?
A I first saw him through the rear view mirror.
Q Where was he when you first saw him?
A He was standing on the north kerb of Wide Street.
Q Would you use the plan to show the court where he was?
A Yes, he was here. [Indicating]
Q What did you see him do?
A He started walking across Wide Street.
Q How was he walking?
A He was staggering and had great difficulty making it to the other side.
Q How were you looking at him at this time?
A I had turned around and I was looking at him through the rear window of the police car.
Q What happened after he crossed the road?
A He stumbled and almost fell at the southern kerb of Wide Street.

Note: this is a fictional case.

8.2 Describing Conversations

When you want a witness to recount a conversation, set the scene by having the witness describe the place, the time, the circumstances and who was present.

Ensure that the conversation is recounted in detail by having the witness use the actual words of it, and not a summary of the meaning of the conversation. If a witness does not recall the precise words, then you should

- seek permission to refresh the witness's memory, or
- have a witness give the substance of the conversation.

Example
Examination in chief of witness, Betty Smith.

Q When the police left the bottle shop, where were you standing?
A I was standing near the door of the bottle shop.
Q Immediately after they left, did you go anywhere?
A I walked over to the bar.
Q What did you do at the bar?
A I spoke to the Jake Welsh.
Q What was said?
A Well, we spoke about the police arresting the old drunk, and Mr Welsh told me how sorry he felt for the old drunk.
Q Ms Smith, I want to take you through that conversation in detail. Who spoke first?
A I did.
Q What did you say?
A I said to him, 'Just as well the police arrested that old drunk; I wonder what they will do with the bottle they took from him—probably drink it for Christmas'.
Q What did he say?
A He said, 'The poor old bugger. I suppose I shouldn't have sold him the grog if he was so drunk.'
Q Was anything else said?

Note: this is a fictional case.

8.3 Piggyback Questions

It is permissible to use part of a witness's answer to provide focus for the next question by reference to time, place or action.

The 'piggyback question' repeats in the new question useful facts already stated by the witness. This connects the facts between the prior answer and the current question, and further reinforces the story. An effective 'piggyback question' does not simply repeat facts.

Example
Evidence in chief of witness, Betty Smith.

Q What were you doing in the bottle shop?
A I was selecting wine.
Q While you were selection wine, did you see anyone in relation to this case?
A Yes, the man who bumped into me.
Q As he bumped into you, did you notice anything about him?

This technique not only reinforces the fact of the bump, but also emphasises Smith's opportunity of noticing something about Watkins while in close proximity to him.

Note: this is a fictional case.

8.4 *Commenting on Answers*

It is inappropriate to comment on a witness's answers using words such as 'okay', 'right', or 'I see'. This is usually done from force of habit, rather than as an intentional comment, but it is nevertheless objectionable. Some advocates have even commented 'great' or 'fantastic'.

Nor is it appropriate to thank witnesses for their answers.

Avoid commentary will also help with the flow and continuity of the story in evidence.

8.5 *Involve the Listener*

It is natural for a witness to answer the person who is asking the question. You will need to get the witness to direct his or her answers to the decision-maker. This can be achieved through the form of question, and also through your body language.

Example
To involve the listener, you could turn or gesture with your hands towards the listener, to show the witness where to direct his or her answer.

When leading evidence from the police ask:

- Tell Her Honour (or the jury) what you saw in the shop?

Do not ask:

- Tell me what you saw in the shop?

Note: this is a fictional case.

8.6 Focused Questions

Remain in control by using focused questions, but allow the witness to tell the story. Do not interrupt the witness's evidence if he or she continues with the account beyond your specific question. Using the checklist, make sure that the witness does not leave out significant detail.

If the witness is reliable and impressive, and you want to display this to the judge or jury, you may ask for a general description first without asking questions about each fact.

However, use questions such as 'What happened next?' sparingly.

8.7 Getting the Entire Story

Listen to the answers, and check off answers on your checklist. Ensure that each fact on your checklist has been stated by the witness. With a vague witness, it may take several questions to do so. If the witness gets ahead of you by providing more information that asked, then allow him or her to finish, provided the evidence is relevant and helpful.

Then return to your checklist to check what points the witness has covered ahead of you, and whether necessary evidence has been left out. Where evidence has been left out by the witness, take the witness back over the evidence and elicit those further facts.

Example
Continued examination in chief of Constable X.

Q When Watkins entered the shop, what did you see him do?
A I saw Watkins approach the counter and have a short conversation with the barman, who I know now to be Jake Welsh. I didn't lose sight of either of them while Watkins was in the bottle shop. A short time later I saw Watkins emerge from the door of the bottle shop.
Q Let me take you back to what you saw in the bottle shop. How much of Watkins and Welsh could you see when Watkins approached the counter?
A I could see Watkins' and Whelsh's heads and shoulders above the displays and advertising in the bottle shop window.

Note: this is a fictional case.

If the witness cannot recall a fact you need, go back into a sequence which may help to prompt the witness's recollection of detail.

Example
Continued evidence in chief of Betty Smith.

Q After he bumped into you, did he go anywhere?
A Yes, I saw him leave the shop.
Q Let me take you back to the time when he bumped into you, and the time you saw him leave the shop. Did you see him do anything else?
A Oh yes. I saw him approach the counter and have a conversation with Jake Welsh.

Note: this is a fictional case.

Avoid unnecessarily complex and counter-productive questions.

Example
Evidence in chief of Constable X.

Ask questions in the most direct way:

- Describe where the advertising was on the bottle shop window?
- Where did Watkins go after he left the bottle shop?

Do not ask

- Can you describe whether there was anything on the bottle shop window?
- Are you able to recall where Watkins went after he left the bottle shop?

Note: this is a fictional case.

The complex questions should be avoided for two reasons:

- The correct answer to a question that begins with 'Are you able to recall…' is 'Yes' or 'No'. A pedantic witness may do that.
- The question that begins by asking whether a witness is able to recall or describe a fact suggests to the listener that the witness' recollection or ability to describe is an issue. That is counter-productive.

8.8 Headlining

The use of headlining or topic phrases is helpful, particularly in the case of a lengthy story, in order to organise the story and concentrate the attention of the witness and the listener.

Example
Examination in chief of Constable X.

Q I want to take you back to what happened to Watkins after you spoke to him?
A I arrested him for being drunk and disorderly.
Q When you arrested him, where did you go?
A To the police station, where I lodged him in the cells.
Q After you lodged him in the cells, did you go anywhere?
A Yes, I returned to the Royal Oak Hotel.

Note: this is a fictional case.

Use evidence already given by other witnesses, if your witness was present in court, to direct the witness to a specific matter.

When leading evidence to contradict another witness, be specific and accurate about what the other witness said, then ask your witness to respond to that.

Example
Examination in chief Jake Welsh.

Q You have heard Betty Smith give evidence that when Watkins entered the bottle shop, he bumped into her. What do you say about that?
A No. I saw her bump into Watkins.

Note: this is a fictional case.

Have the witness use visual aids, such as plans or other exhibits, when describing events. Ensure that the witness is familiar with the document before you begin asking questions about it.

If the witness is not familiar with the document, ensure that he or she is given an opportunity to read it in the witness box and understand all its features before you ask questions about it and its contents.

Example
Examination in chief of witness, Betty Smith.

Q Could the witness be shown Exhibit 1, the plan of the area and the bottle shop?
[Clerk/associate hands Exhibit 1 to witness.]

(continued)

Q Ms Smith, are you familiar with that document?
A I have seen it once, yes.
Q Could you hold up the plan and show the jury where you were standing when Mr Watkins entered the bottle shop?

Where the witness has not seen it:

Q Ms Smith, are you familiar with this document?
A No.
Q This is a plan of the area and the bottle shop. Do you understand it?
A Yes.
Q Please take a moment to familiarise yourself with it?

Note: this is a fictional case.

9 Proving Documents and Tendering Exhibits Through the Witness

It is wise to show your opponent any document you propose to tender. This will allow you to resolve any possible objection before evidence is given.

Provide enough copies for your opponent and the court, judge and jury, to be handed out when the exhibit is marked.

To prove a document through a witness, you must

- show the document to the witness;
- ask the witness to identify the document, its author, and when and how it was prepared, and if possible confirm its accuracy; and
- tender the document.

Once a document is tendered, you may question the witness about it and have the witness use it during evidence.

10 Evidence by Witness Statements or Affidavit

In some courts, particularly in the civil jurisdictions, evidence in chief can be received by affidavit or witness statements.

Provide the witness with the statement or affidavit in the witness box. Have the witness confirm that it is accurate, or make any corrections.

Direct the witness's attention to parts of the document and ask him or her to explain if necessary. If you need the witness to make major changes or expand on the material in the statement or affidavit, you must seek leave of the court to adduce this further evidence.

Notice of significant further evidence should be given to your opponent, as he or she may be entitled to more time to prepare cross-examination.

References

Gans, J., & Palmer, A. (2004). *Australian principles of evidence*. Cavendish Pub.
Heydon, J. D. (2004). *Cross on evidence*. LexisNexis Butterworths & CCH Australia.
Stephen, K. D. (1997). *Voir Dire Law*. Criminal Law Publications Pty Ltd.

George Hampel AM QC was a Justice of the Supreme Court of Victoria from 1983 to 2000, having previously practised as a barrister since 1958.

Hampel has held numerous positions in the legal profession, such as Vice-President of the Law Council of Australia, Vice-Chairman of the Victorian Bar Institute and Chairman of the Constitution Commission of Victoria.

For over 40 years, George developed advocacy teaching methods, case studies and the training of advocacy instructors in Australia and abroad. Since 2000, he has been Professor of Trial Practice and Advocacy at Monash University. His training experience of professional advocates extends internationally to USA, UK, Scotland, New Zealand, Hong Kong, Singapore, South Africa, and war crime prosecutors at The Hague.

George was the Founding Chairman of the Australian Advocacy Institute in 1991 and over the following 24 years continued to develop its teaching methodology and workshop programs. He is the principal author of the two editions of the Australian Advocacy Manual, which is now required reading for the Victorian Bar Readers Course and is used as a reference work in most common law jurisdictions. George has developed workshops for training of members of other professions including forensic accountants, doctors, engineers and computer experts in their roles as expert witnesses.

As a result of his contribution in these areas, George was made a Member of the General Division of the Order of Australia (2006), received the Centenary of Federation Medal, and a Monash University Teaching Award.

Conducting Cross-Examination

George Hampel

1 Purpose and Scope of Cross-Examination

Your aim in cross-examination is to lay a foundation for your final argument by demonstrating something about the evidence or the witness.

The purposes of cross-examination are to

- elicit new favourable evidence to support your case,
- accredit a helpful witness or evidence,
- discredit an unfavourable witness or evidence, and/or
- emphasise or place a different complexion on existing evidence.

Counsel's right to cross-examine includes the right to use leading, pressing and persistent questions or propositions provided they are

- relevant to an issue or to credibility, and
- not limited or prohibited by law.

Within those limits, the subject matter of cross-examination, its extent, its form and manner are matters for counsel, not for the judge.

The judge, however, has discretion to curtail cross-examination if it is

- unfair, such as unnecessarily repetitive, or based on misrepresenting what the witness has said;

Text within this chapter has been directly extracted, with authors permission, from Hampel, G., Brimer, E., & Kune, R. (2016). *Advocacy manual: The complete guide to persuasive advocacy*. Melbourne Australian Advocacy Institute.

G. Hampel (✉)
Faculty of Law, Monash University, Melbourne, VIC, Australia
e-mail: george.hampel@monash.edu

E. King et al. (eds.), *Victim Advocacy before the International Criminal Court*,
https://doi.org/10.1007/978-3-030-56733-0_10

- scandalous, insulting or offensive; or
- designed to intimidate the witness.

These common law rules are now being reinforced and enshrined in legislation.

2 Consistency with Your Case Theory

Because the purpose of cross-examination is to lay a foundation for your final address, cross-examination must be directly related to your case theory and to your arguments in support of your case theory in the final address.

Before you cross-examine a witness, you must know what your arguments will be, about the credibility of the witness and about the weight the court should place on the witness's evidence.

Do not cross-examine for the sake of it just because you may see a potential weakness in the evidence; mere 'point scoring' is unnecessary and may be counter-productive to your case.

Do not cross-examine simply to please your client.

3 Form of Questions in Cross-Examination

In cross-examination, the rules of evidence permit leading questions.

We distinguish three forms of questions:

1. non-leading questions,
2. leading questions, and
3. leading propositional questions.

Example

Non-leading question	Where were you seated?
Leading question	Were you seated in the front seat?
Leading propositional question	You were sitting in the front seat, weren't you?

While questions in evidence in chief and re-examination should be truly interrogative, questions in cross-examination should generally be leading and propositional.

3.1 Leading and Non-leading Questions

Leading questions about contested facts are not permitted. Their use also constitutes ineffective advocacy, because the answers lack probative value when given as a result of suggestions by the advocate.

A leading question is one that either

- directly or by selection of subject matter suggests the answer, or
- assumes a fact not yet established.

Advocates are able to ask leading questions because they know the answers. It would be impossible to ask leading questions and get the correct answers without that knowledge.

To avoid asking leading questions

- use inquiring words such as 'when, 'where', 'what', 'why' and 'how'; and
- avoid words that require you to state the subject matter, such as 'did', 'was' and 'is'.

One exception may be if the question is general, for example 'Did you go *anywhere*?' or 'Was there *anyone* in the room?', provided those questions do not touch the real issue in the case.

To identify the contested facts:

- First, examine the pleadings or elements and particulars of the offence.
- Next, examine and compare witness statements and other accounts (including affidavits, records of interview, depositions, etc.).
- Consider what issues will be contested and what the opposing case theories may be.
- If necessary, talk to your opponent to clarify what may or may not be an issue.

Some non-leading questions may be useful even in the non-contentious areas, in order to

- Enable the story to flow more smoothly from the non-contentious into the contentious areas, so the transition is not sudden; and
- Prepare the witness for the non-leading form of questions in contested areas.

Leading questions are permitted to get your witness to deny specific allegations or to contradict other evidence.

This should be done early, particularly in the evidence in chief of an accused, as it allows the listener to appreciate the story in light of the denials.

3.2 Propositional Questions

Your propositional questions should

- be expressed simply,
- deal with only one factual proposition, and
- clearly be capable of being answered with 'Yes' or 'No'.

It is important to be prepared for cross-examination so as to be able to maintain a flow of questions. Pausing to think about the next question is likely to enable the witness to go on beyond the answer to your propositional question.

This form of question is vital to the cross-examiner's ability to control the witness. If your leading questions are expressed in such a form, you are entitled to limit the witness to the answer.

If the witness does not respond to a simple propositional question, you may repeat the question and insist on an answer.

The principles of advocacy dictate that you must put only leading propositional questions to the witness in cross-examination, unless there is a good reason not to do so.

It is rarely good advocacy to ask non-leading questions in cross-examination, such as 'Why didn't you contact the police?' or 'What were you doing on the morning of the 1 June?'

It may be appropriate to ask such an open-ended question if there is a specific justifiable purpose for doing so. One such purpose might be if there is reason to believe that the witness will give an explanation that can be shown to be wrong—for example, if there is some independent evidence contrary to what the witness said. This may be a useful method of attacking the witness's credibility. It can be used, for instance, where a witness gives as an alibi an account of having been at a function, and you can show that the function did not take place.

In order to phrase propositions as leading propositional questions, they either should be asked in an interrogative voice indicating that you want a response, or you may add a phrase such as 'wasn't it?' or 'weren't you?' to the end of the proposition.

Witnesses often want to go on after answering the propositional question. While the cross-examiner has a right to confine the witness to the answer to a propositional question, a tactical decision should be made whether to do so. This is because confining the witness may look as if you are withholding information, and if done in an aggressive manner, it may look as if you are bullying the witness. In any event, once the topic has been raised in cross-examination, the witness will be permitted to explain and clarify in re-examination.

4 Structuring Your Cross-Examination

The structure will depend on the purpose of your cross-examination.

4.1 Accrediting a Witness

Cross-examination can be used to accredit a witness and the evidence given. You may wish to accredit a witness in cross-examination when the evidence in chief of the witness supports your case theory.

This can be done by expanding upon and emphasising the witness's evidence to support the account the witness gave, to make it more clearly consistent with your case theory. This is different from merely restating the evidence in chief before asking a question in cross-examination.

4.2 Discrediting the Witness

In a well-known lecture, Professor Irving Younger, an early advocacy teacher with the National Institute for Trial Advocacy in the United States, sets out what he calls the 'Nine Pigeonholes of Impeachment'. These are the nine categories of impeachment (or attacks on credibility) of a witness, which cover the field of possible impeachment.

Professor Younger refers to the nine pigeonholes as the technology of cross-examination, or the 'what to do' of cross-examination.[1]

The nine pigeonholes are separated into two groups of 4 and 1. The first four pigeonholes relate to the competency of the witness. To be competent, a witness must have the

1. ability to take an *oath* or affirmation (except, for example, in the case of a child),
2. ability to *perceive* the events (record sense data) about which he or she gives evidence,
3. ability to *recall* those events, and
4. ability to rationally *communicate* his or her perception to the court.

If any of these four elements is missing, a lay witness is not competent to give evidence, and therefore the evidence is inadmissible.

Competence and admissibility are matters of law for the judge to determine. This is usually considered on *voir dire*[2] before or during a trial.

Where the witness is ruled competent and his or her evidence is admissible, you may use these four pigeonholes as a basis to impeach the witness's credibility. You can direct your cross-examination during the trial to reduce the weight the court will give the evidence. Irving Younger calls this 'the reverse use of the principles of competence'.

For example, you may show that the witness

---

[1] To find out more information on Irving Younger's technology of cross-examination and his explanation of the nine pigeonholes visit https://youtu.be/m5JkPpB2bv8. Accessed 16 May 2020.

[2] *Voir Dire* is a preliminary examination to determine the competency of a witness or juror.

- has problems of perception, for example poor vision, poor visibility in the conditions, or other difficulties in identifying the relevant events;
- has a problem with memory, or has reconstructed the events in his or her mind in a way that does not match reality;
- cannot rationally communicate what happened, in that he or she is using another's words without understanding them; or
- is lying.

The next four pigeonholes relate to areas of impeachment and require a 'good-faith basis': in other words, some basis in either evidence or instructions to justify making the allegation during cross-examination. You may impeach a witness by alleging that

5. the witness is *biased* (in favour of a party), *prejudiced* (against a party), has an *interest* (in the outcome of proceedings), or is *corrupt*. You will be permitted to lead evidence to prove these allegations if the witness denies them.
6. the witness has *prior criminal convictions*. If a witness is the defendant in criminal proceedings, the use of this basis for impeachment is subject to the common law or statutory shield against cross-examination based on prior convictions, unless the accused opens the issue of his own character, or the defence is conducted in such a way as to open the issue of his credibility. Subject to the proviso, you will be permitted to lead evidence to prove the convictions if the witness denies them.
7. the witness has *committed prior bad acts* (acts of an immoral, criminal or vicious nature), even if those acts have not been the subject of a conviction or an adverse finding.
8. the witness has demonstrated an *inconsistency in their statement or testimony.*

The final pigeonhole relates to affirmative evidence attacking the credibility of the witness.

9. *Reputation testimony*, demonstrating the witness has a poor reputation for truth or veracity.

Generally, in such an attack on credibility, you are bound by the witness's answers and you cannot go on to prove the truth of the allegations if the witness denies them.

It is unethical to allege fraud without proper foundation. If the witness has made a prior inconsistent statement, this prior statement can be proved as part of the impeachment of the witness if the material in the prior statement goes to a fact in issue, or a fact relevant to a fact in issue.

It is important to note that not all jurisdictions and courtrooms permit all nine pigeonholes to be utilised.

4.3 *Cross-Examination to Discredit Another Witness*

It is not permissible to cross-examine a witness in order to discredit another witness.

There are some exceptions, such as where the cross-examiner seeks to prove previous convictions or bias.

5 The Ten Commandments of Cross-Examination

These 'Ten Commandments' are the subject of another seminal lecture by Professor Irving Younger, on the 'art of cross-examination' or 'how to do it'.[3] They are a mix of what to do and what not to do.

1. *Be brief.* You need to be selective in cross-examination and to cross-examine only towards an identifiable case theory and arguments to support it. You should not be repetitive or cross-examine at large.
2. *Use short questions and plain words.* Ensure that your questions deal with one subject matter only, so that they can be answered simply. Propositions can be agreed with or denied by the witness, but not explained. Plain, simple words provide clarity, both for the witness and for the decision-maker.
3. *Ask only leading questions.* Although Professor Younger calls them leading questions, we prefer to call them 'leading propositional questions'.
4. *Be prepared.* Don't ask a question you do not know the answer to. This commandment is based on the principle that cross-examination is designed to support your prepared final argument. In both cross-examination to obtain further evidence, and cross-examination to discredit, it is important that the cross-examiner knows what the witness will say.[4] Cross-examination at trial is not an inquiry, an opportunity to investigate, or a 'fishing expedition'. If you have no material to contradict a witness's negative response, such as a prior inconsistent statement, or evidence of bias, you may wish to leave it to your closing address to argue that the witness's answer is improbable. The aim of the cross-examiner is to gain ground or at least remain in no worse a position than that already conveyed by the witness in evidence in chief. A bad answer should not be risked on important issues. As a general rule, a beginner at cross-examination should take the most conservative approach.
5. *Listen* to the witness's answers. This commandment serves to remind the cross-examiner that cross-examination must be prepared in advance, and no questions

[3] To find out more information on Younger's Ten Commandments and a detailed explanation of the art cross-examination visit https://youtu.be/dBP2if0l-a8. Accessed on 17 May 2020.

[4] This fourth commandment can be supplemented by the phrase 'unless you can contradict the witness if he or she gives an unhelpful answer, or you can live with an unfavourable answer'. In other words, you can ask a question to which you don't know the answer provided you have some material with which to contradict an answer that does not support your case.

or propositions should be dreamt up during the performance. If you are not sufficiently prepared and try to construct the cross-examination on the run, you will not be concentrating on the answers given by the witness, and useful information will be missed. The commandment also emphasises the need to pay close attention to the words, the nuance of the answers, and the witness's demeanour, rather than focusing on the next question.

6. *Do not argue* with the witness. The aim of cross-examination is not to persuade the witness of anything, but to lay the foundation for your final argument and/or demonstrate something about the witness to the decision-maker. If you take up an argument with the witness, you risk the witness giving information, which will enable him or her to win that argument. You will get into an argument with the witness by putting a conclusion to the witness with which the witness disagrees, and then using such material as you have to try to contradict the witness's answer. For example, you start your cross-examination by suggesting to the witness that he could not have seen what he claims he saw, which the witness denies, and then you put to the witness that it was a foggy night and the witness didn't have his glasses. The better approach is the 'gate-closing' technique (discussed in more detail below).
7. *Avoid repetition.* Do not allow the witness to repeat his or her evidence in chief. Although when accrediting a witness, some selective repetition may be necessary, the danger of repeating the evidence in chief by asking whether it was given may reinforce the evidence. It will also give the witness an opportunity to change or add to what was said in chief. There is no need to repeat evidence already given in order to come to the propositions relevant to the point in cross-examination. The seventh commandment is often broken by questions which start with 'You told the Court that…' or 'In your evidence in chief you said…'. Instead, you should go directly to your propositions.
8. *Disallow witness explanation.* Leading propositional questions give the cross-examiner control over the witness, by forcing an answer of 'Yes', 'No', or 'I don't know/can't remember'. If the witness is asked for explanations, then that control is lost. This commandment is frequently broken by the use of inquiring phrases such as 'How could you have seen that?', 'What do you mean by…?', and 'How can you explain this if…?'
9. *Limit questioning.* There is no need to go beyond the questions that are necessary to support your final argument. The 'one question too many' is usually an attempt to get the witness to agree with the conclusions you want, and this may develop into an argument with the witness.
10. *Save the final point for your closing address.* These last two commandments reinforce commandment number six. The cross-examiner should go only as far as is necessary to obtain answers that support the final argument, and not put to the witness the conclusions from the evidence. Cross-examination questions that begin with words such as 'Therefore…' or 'So…' or 'But…' are likely to be argumentative.

6 Performance Preparation of Cross-Examination

6.1 Risk Management

In performance preparation, you must consider the possible reactions of the witness and be prepared to deal with them. If you ask simple, leading propositional questions, possible answers should be

- Yes,
- No, or
- I don't know/don't remember

As a cross-examiner, you cannot be optimistic about what answer will be given. You must be prepared for the witness to give the least helpful response and consider how you can deal with such a response.

Cross-examination can require you to take measured risks in your questioning. See, for instance, our discussion of the fourth of Younger's Ten Commandments of Cross-examination above.

To cross-examine merely for emphasis or about a minor issue can be risky, as you might allow the witness to retell the story in his own way, or explain other inconsistencies in the process, and so your case may come out worse than if you had not cross-examined the witness at all.

It is counter-productive to cross-examine to discredit a witness when doing so is not necessary to your case theory, even if an opportunity to do so arises, and particularly if the witness's evidence is otherwise helpful to your case.

If you need to discredit a witness, it may be more difficult to rely on those parts of the witness's evidence that help you. If this has to be done, get any helpful information first, before discrediting the witness or his or her evidence.

Cross-examination opens the gates to re-examination. If you conduct an unnecessary cross-examination which introduces new evidence or issues, you may indirectly damage your case, by giving your opponent the opportunity to re-examine the witness.

How much you are prepared to risk must depend on

- the value to your case of the answer sought. It is a benefit/detriment analysis asking whether the risk is worth taking in the context of the case as a whole.
- your experience. A beginner at cross-examination should be conservative. An experienced cross-examiner is able to make a better assessment of the witness during cross-examination to determine whether the witness is likely to be cooperative, and is more likely to be able to get out of trouble by dealing with difficult situations if they arise.

6.2 Manor and Demeanour of the Cross-Examiner

To maintain the flow of the cross-examination, you must be thoroughly prepared, so that you do not allow the witness time to supplement his or her answers while you are thinking about the next questions to ask.

Generally, it is best to assume a demeanour in cross-examination which is conversational, not aggressive or confrontational.

Consider the following case study in relation to the manner and approach appropriate for cross-examination of an expert witness.

Example

In a case where the issue was whether a fire was deliberately lit or started accidentally, Expert A was consulted on the morning after the fire. He examined the scene and took photographs. In his opinion, the fire was intentionally lit with the use of accelerants.

The other party called Expert B, who was consulted one year after the fire. She had available Expert A's report and the photographs. The scene of the fire was no longer available. In her opinion the fire was probably accidental as a results of a fault electric blanket.

Cross-examination of Expert B

The aim of this cross-examination is to lay the foundation for the argument that Expert B is disadvantaged by not having had the opportunity to inspect the scene, particularly if Expert A can give evidence of some advantage of having examined the scene.

There is no point in cross-examining Expert B in a confrontational manner about her not having gone to the scene, because she could not have done so. A question such as 'You didn't go the scene of the fire?' asked in an aggressive, critical, confrontational manner will elicit the right answer. However, it will also alienate the decision-maker, because it is unfair to criticise the witness when she could not have gone to the scene.

The better approach would be to get the same answer and also useful concessions from the witness without confrontation.

For example:

Q You were consulted about 12 months after the fire?
A Yes.
Q You were provided with the photographs and report of Expert A?
A Yes.
Q You didn't have the opportunity to attend the scene of the fire?
A No, I didn't.
Q Sometimes going to the scene may be helpful, mightn't it?
A Yes, it might.

(continued)

Q Such as the smell of some substance or the feel of some object?
A Yes, that's right.
Q If you'd had the opportunity to attend the scene, you would no doubt have taken it?
A Yes, that's right.

It would be dangerous and unnecessary to go on and put the argumentative proposition, 'So you are at a disadvantage by not going to the scene?', because the witness may disagree and explain why not in re-examination.

The witness is most likely to agree with the last few propositions, but if she does not, then you could argue in your final address that her answers were unreasonable.

Note: this is a fictional case.

It is also counter-productive to preface your questions with often-used phrases such as 'It's true that…', 'Isn't it the case…', 'Isn't it a fact…'. 'You would agree that…', etc. These phrases send a negative message to witnesses being cross-examined, and as a result they may feel that they are under siege and thus are not likely to want to agree with you.

While you should not get 'cross' in cross-examination, you may need to appear to be firm or confronting when that is appropriate to the cross-examination. For instance, you cannot pleasantly and conversationally suggest to a police officer that he assaulted your client or fabricated evidence. Your manner must be consistent with the subject matter of the cross-examination.

You should ensure that your manner of questioning, and your questions, are fair to the witness. This is particularly important for a prosecutor.

As a matter of evidence law, your questions are not the evidence: only the witness's answers are. Nevertheless, your attitude, manner and body language communicate messages to the decision-maker.

6.3 The Gate-Closing Technique

As previously stated, your aim in cross-examination is to lay a foundation for your final argument. When organising the structure of cross-examination, you should

- build the facts to support your argument, and
- avoid putting the argument or conclusions to the witness.

This process is known as 'gate-closing'. It can be described also as closing off avenues for the witness to escape, argue or explain away his or her position in a way that supports the witness's case, and not yours.

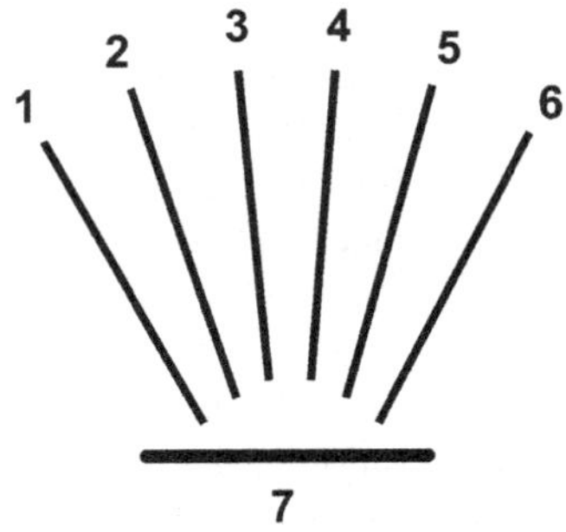

Fig. 1 Preparing to perform "gate-closing" technique (Reproduced from Hampel et al., 2016 © Australian Advocacy Institute)

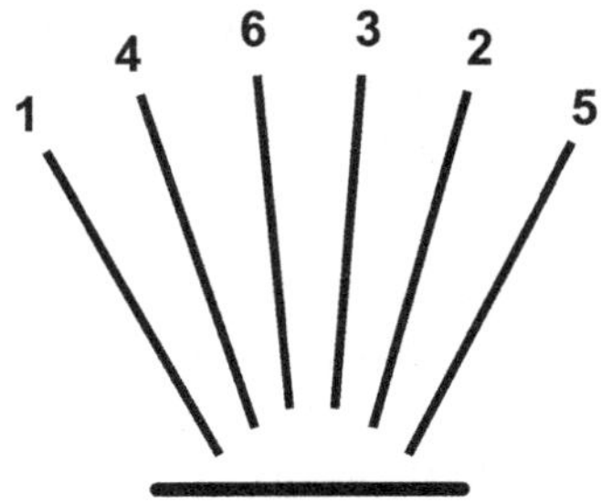

Fig. 2 Alternate order of 'gate-closing' (Reproduced from Hampel et al., 2016 © Australian Advocacy Institute)

Preparation of the order of cross-examination is essential to effective cross-examination. If you start your cross-examination with the conclusion and the witness disagrees with you, then cross-examination tends to become argumentative.

Often you may have recourse during the 'gate-closing' process to other evidence which the witness could not deny (such as comments made in a police interview or written down by the witness), before moving to the more difficult 'gates' or to the conclusion.

Each advocate may have a different method of preparing to perform a gate-closing cross-examination. It is not a good idea to write out questions. One method is to use a diagram which readily suggests the substance and order of gate-closing cross-examination. In Fig. 1 numbers 1–6 represent certain aspects of the case that you need to "close off" and number 7 is the final proposition: 'These are your words, are they not?' The answer does not really matter.

Despite the benefits of a logical structure, for some witnesses it may be better to use a structure that appears more jumbled, which does not so obviously lead a witness to identify where you are headed. This can be achieved by using a mix of questions about a number of different issues. Such cross-examination will be more difficult for the decision-maker to follow and understand at the time, but you can put it all together in the final address. This technique is also less likely to produce an argument from the witness. A similar diagram (Fig. 2) can be used to show what propositions can be put to the witness and where the cross-examination should stop, leaving the conclusion until the final address. It also shows the jumbling of the order of questions.

7 Specific Aspects of Cross-Examination

7.1 Cross-Examination on Prior Inconsistent Statements or Evidence

Prior inconsistent statements can be oral or in writing, and either can be used to discredit the witness.

Before you confront the witness with the prior inconsistent statement, you must first direct the witness's attention to the occasion or writing of the prior statement.

If the material in the prior statement is what Professor Younger calls 'important'—that is, sufficiently connected to the issues in the case—and is consistent with your case theory, then you can go on to prove the making of the prior inconsistent statement. If the impeaching information relates merely to credibility, you may not go beyond the answer.

The prior inconsistent statement is not the evidence. The evidence is what the witness says in the witness box when confronted with the prior inconsistent statement. If the witness accepts having made it, you may argue that he had changed his story and hence lacks credibility. If he denies have made it, your argument is about his dishonesty in denying it.

7.2 Cross-Examination on Documents

When cross-examining by reference to the contents of documents not already tendered in evidence, your opponent can demand that you tender them through the witness. Despite this rule, the court has a discretion in criminal trials not to enforce the tender.

7.3 Applying for Leave to Recall or Further Examine a Witness

The method of preparing and leading evidence in chief (which is discussed in detail in this volume, George Hampel, "Leading Evidence in Chief") should ensure that you adduce all relevant and admissible evidence.

However, if you have completed your cross-examination of a witness, and you realise that there is further evidence you need to lead from the witness, then you should apply to the judge

- to ask further questions of the witness in evidence in chief, where the witness is still in the witness box; or
- to recall the witness, if the witness has been excused.

You should make such applications promptly, as soon as you realise that there is a need to do so.

The court will usually ask for an explanation of why the omission occurred, and require you to state what evidence is sought to be led, and satisfy the court of its significance.

The court will usually allow further cross-examination following further evidence in chief.

In a criminal case, if the evidence left out by the prosecution is significant, and the defence has not had notice of it, the court may require formal notice of the content of the evidence, to allow the defence to consider it before cross-examination.

8 Re-examination of Right of Reply

Re-examination is permitted only in relation to matters which

- arise out of cross-examination, and
- require relevant clarification or explanation.

It is not permitted merely to add new evidence, which should have been led in evidence in chief; that can only be done by applying for leave to recall or further examine a witness.

Example
Examination in chief of Jake Welsh.

Q What was the condition of the bottle shop that evening?
A It was busy.

Cross-examination of Jake Welsh.

Q I suggest to you that most of the people on the premises that night were in the lounge.
A Not really.

Re-examination of Jake Welsh.

Q Approximately how many people were in the bottle shop when you saw the customer bump into Watkins?
A There would have been four or five people in there at that time.

This re-examination would not be allowed if there had been no cross-examination on the question of how many people were in the bottle shop or lounge area of the hotel.

(continued)

Note: this is a fictional case.

Example
Cross-examination of Constable X.

Q You were watching Watkins and Mr Welsh through the window of the bottle shop?
A Yes.
Q That window contains displays and advertising material, doesn't it?
A Yes.
Q So you could not see all of Watkins while he was at the counter?
A No.
Q Nor could you see all of Mr Welsh while he was at the counter?
A No.
Q Your view of them was obstructed by the displays and advertising material?
A Yes.

Re-examination of Constable X.

Q During cross-examination, you agreed that your view of Watkins and the defendant at the counter of the bottle shop was obstructed. What part of your view was obstructed?
A I could only see their heads and shoulders above the display and advertising material on the window.

Here we assume that no questions were asked of Constable X in examination in chief as to whether his view was obstructed. This re-examination would not be allowed if there had been no cross-examination on the question of whether the police view was obstructed.

Note: this is a fictional case.

Both of the above Examples show how re-examination is used to clarify matters raised in cross-examination, not simply to repeat matters already dealt with in examination in chief or to add new evidence.

The rule prohibiting leading questions in evidence in chief is strictly enforced in re-examination. Answers to leading questions in re-examination have little probative value.

It is permitted in re-examination to refer to the subject matter raised in cross-examination as part of the question.

Well-prepared and presented evidence in chief directed to your case theory, and effective re-examination, are important foundations of your case.

Reference

Hampel, G., Brimer, E., & Kune, R. (2016). *Advocacy manual: The complete guide to persuasive advocacy*. Melbourne Australian Advocacy Institute.

Dealing with Expert Evidence

George Hampel

1 Expert Evidence

If a person has specialised knowledge based on their training, study or experience, that person can express an opinion in court if it is wholly or substantially based on that knowledge or experience.

This exception to the general rule that opinion evidence is not admissible allows expert witnesses to assist the Court to find facts and conclusions in areas in which it has no expertise. Such evidence becomes part of the evidence, which the court considers in reaching its conclusions.

The court can accept or reject the evidence, but because of the expert nature of the evidence, the court cannot substitute its own opinion. By definition it cannot have an 'expert' opinion, it must evaluate the evidence and consider the extent to which it will rely on that evidence.

1.1 Framework for Expert Evidence

Expert evidence, like any other evidence, must be relevant and admissible. In summary, for expert opinion evidence to be admissible

Text within this chapter has been directly extracted, with authors permission, from Hampel, G., Brimer, E., & Kune, R. (2016). *Advocacy manual: The complete guide to persuasive advocacy.* Melbourne Australian Advocacy Institute.

G. Hampel (✉)
Faculty of Law, Monash University, Melbourne, VIC, Australia
e-mail: george.hampel@monash.edu

E. King et al. (eds.), *Victim Advocacy before the International Criminal Court*,
https://doi.org/10.1007/978-3-030-56733-0_11

- the court must accept that the field in which the opinion is expressed is an identified field of specialised knowledge; it is outside the ambit of normal human knowledge and experience;
- the witness must be an expert in that field of specialised knowledge by reason of specified training, study or experience; and/or
- the opinion must be wholly or substantially based on the witness's expert knowledge and not, for example, a purely factual analysis

Court rules and practice notes in respect of expert evidence in the various jurisdictions interact with the requirements of the Evidence Act (Cth), the Uniform Evidence Acts and other State legislation. Each set of rules is different and must be known both by experts and advocates in the relevant jurisdiction.

In general terms, however, the rules

- stipulate that the experts' primary responsibility is to the Court; they are not advocates for the party calling them;
- determine the structure, content and timing of the service or exchange of expert reports;
- require the expert to identify the assumptions of fact upon which the opinion is based and the reasons why the assumptions have been made;
- provide requirement for the structure and presentation of expert evidence; and
- are designed to narrow the expert issues in dispute, to promote settlement and therefore to reduce the costs of litigation.

A common element of the rules is the mechanism by which the issues between experts are narrowed; joint expert conferences and the production of joint expert reports. In general terms and depending on the complexity of the case, experts

- exchange expert reports (depending on the circumstances, a report in reply may be filed). This is to ensure that each party understands the other party's case where the expert evidence is concerned. Timely exchange of reports facilitates this understanding;
- participate in a joint expert conference. Sometimes questions are framed for the experts to answer;
- prepare a joint expert report which identifies what the experts agree on and what is in dispute; and
- participate in concurrent evidence sessions. The way in which the sessions are conducted will likely depend on the court and the judge.

Courts require compliance with the rules in relation to expert reports and expert evidence. They are designed to enable the Court to run more efficiently and better assess the expert evidence.

The parties assist the court in that process. However, decisions in relation to what expert evidence is to be called and how it is to be presented and tested remains in the hands of the parties.

1.2 Assessing Expert Evidence

Factors the Court likely will consider include:

What are the expert's qualifications?

Education.
Practical experience.
Knowledge in a specific area of the general discipline.
Experience in evaluation issues in that field.
Research, publications, teaching.
Seniority and standing in the profession.

What was the opinion sought?

What instructions were given?
How the instructions we given?

What information was available to the expert?

History and background provided
Documents provided.
Anything else provided.

What did the expert assume?

Reasonableness of assumptions on the available information.
Appropriateness of assumptions on the information available.
Whether there was a gap in the assumptions.
Whether the assumptions originally made are still valid and should be acted upon.
Whether the assumption is factually correct on the evidence and should be acted on.

What did the expert do?

Investigations.
Tests.
Inspections.

What methodology did the expert use?

Whether there were multiple methodologies available.
Why one methodology was chosen.
Limitations of that and other methodologies.

How did the expert reason?

From the information available
From the assumptions made.
From his or her expert knowledge and experience.
Whether there are any gaps in the reasoning process.

What is the expert's opinion?

Clarity of communication and authority of the opinion.
Whether it follows logically from information and the expert's reasoning process.

How does it compare with the opposing opinion?

Whether the basis of the opinion and reasoning is sound compared with the opposing experts.
Its reasonableness in light of all of the other evidence.

How professional is the expert?

Whether the expert has demonstrated his or her understanding of the expert's duties to the court.
Whether the expert and his or her report complied with professional protocols and court rules/guidelines.
Has the expert acted diligently and has demonstrated accuracy?

Should the evidence be acted on?

Whether the expert is impartial and trustworthy.
Whether the expert's opinion is unbiased and trustworthy.

1.3 Choice of Expert

It is important task of choosing an appropriate expert, the following should be considered:

- What aspect of the case requires expert opinion? It is important to identify with some precision the area of expertise required. Resolution of one issue may involve more than one discipline. It may be that, for example, both a metallurgist and an engineer are required to consider two aspects of the one problem.
- Consider whether the expert has the specialised knowledge in his or her own discipline to express that opinion, based on his or her training, study or experience.
- The quality of the specialised knowledge is important as it relates to the issue involved in the case. If the issue concerns experimental science, for example, then an expert who is experienced in carrying out experiments would likely be preferable to an expert with predominantly theoretical background.
- Whether the expert is independent, open-minded and credible. The mere fact that an expert is employed by or is connected to an organisation who has engaged the expert, does not of itself diminish the expert's independence. For example, a pathologist employed by a government agency giving evidence called by the Office of Public Prosecutions (OPP).
- Whether the expert is of good standing among his or her colleagues, lawyers and judges. Interaction between experts in a concurrent evidence session reveals

much about how they view each other. The credibility of one expert may be undermined if the court perceives that another, impressive expert does not regard your expert well.

- How thorough and well-prepared the expert will be. If your expert has given expert opinion evidence before, you should check whether the matter went to judgment and whether any comments were made about that expert's evidence and level of preparation.
- How the expert's qualifications, experience and opinion will compare with those of any opposing expert.
- How the expert will present and communicate as a witness. Will the expert be able to communicate in such a way as to be an effective witness, and to explain technical concepts to a lay audience?
- How experienced the expert is in giving evidence in court and does the expert have a good reputation for independence with the profession and the courts.
- How the expert will withstand cross-examination.

1.4 Preliminary Instructions

To prepare expert evidence effectively, depending on the nature and complexity of the case involved, you should

- Inform the expert of the issue about which the expert opinion is sought. Depending on the nature of the issue involved, and whether definition of the issue is readily apparent, it may be prudent to provide the chosen expert with documents for their consideration before any instructions or questions are formulated. Discussion in conference with the expert could then assist in the formulation of the question/s, which require the expert's further consideration.
- Consider whether it is prudent to engage a 'shadow' expert to assist in clarifying the issue to be framed for the consultant expert who will provide the report, if definition of the issue is particularly complex. This will assist to preserve the independence of the reporting expert and avoid any suggestion that the expert is too close to the litigation strategy.
- Ensure that the expert is instructed in a way that does not affect the expert's objectivity. This is an important question to consider well before the expert is provided with any documents.
- Ensure that each document is provided to the expert, and that each instruction and question framed for the expert to answer be assessed for the potential impact of perception of the expert's objectivity.
- Provide all relevant material to the expert. Consider critically whether the withholding of a particular document may give rise to a question of whether the expert had all the necessary information before him or her in order to properly consider their opinion.

- Give the expert sufficient time to conduct a comprehensive assessment of the material provided to them.
- Determine whether the expert will be instructed to prepare a report for the purpose of giving evidence in the proceeding. The stage at which this occurs may vary depending on the complexity of the case. It may be that the decision is not made until after a conference is held with the expert to better inform the decision whether or not to engage the expert to prepare a report for the purpose of giving evidence in the proceeding.

  Once the decision is made to instruct the expert to prepare a report, inform the expert of the rules of court or practice notes which may dictate what form the report is to take and the content required in order for the report to be admissible.
- Ensure that all instructions, assumptions or information upon which the expert is to rely is provided to the expert in writing. If the expert's opinion is based on something said to the expert by you, you risk becoming a witness.
- Review the experts report. There is no rule against counsel's involvement in reviewing an expert report to ensure that it is in admissible form; being well, clearly structured and complete. However, care must be taken that the substance of what is presented is the evidence of the expert.
- Continue communication with your expert witness. If there is a significant gap in time between production of the expert's report and the trial, make sure you have a further conference with the expert before the trial reconvenes. If there has been a shift in the expert's position since the preparation of the report, any inconsistency should be picked up during the conference and not come to light for the first time while the expert is in the witness box.
- At all stages of the preparation process, consider the implications for legal professional privilege of the steps that you take in relation to the instruction of and conferencing with experts. In general terms

  - ensure that no documents over which a claim for privilege exists are provided to the expert (unless the client has instructed you that they are prepared to waive their claim for privilege);
  - avoid the preparation of draft reports. They are fertile ground for a cross examiner to exploit any change in position, view or shift in the expert's thinking. Conferencing with the experts before the preparation of any report ought to minimise the opportunity for misunderstandings to occur; and
  - assume that letters of instruction, correspondence between expert and lawyers, working papers, draft reports, copies of documents retained by the experts, and documents recording communications between the expert and third parties will have to be produced.

1.5 Conferences

Timely pre-trial conferences with experts are essential. This is particularly so in cases where you have not been briefed early and have had no previous involvement in the case. A pre-trial conference should be held as early as possible to

- Enable you to become familiar with the expert's qualifications, research or experience (or lack of it) and how this supports or diminishes his or her opinion.
- Promote a better understanding of the expert's opinion and the reasoning that supports it.
- Enable the expert to help you ascertain the strengths and weaknesses of his or her opinion. This may be necessary particularly if your expert is participating in a concurrent evidence session in a more complex case. Once in the concurrent evidence session, your expert may be asked questions by the judge, the opposing party or other experts about matters within their area of expertise, even though these matters may be outside the scope of their retainer and upon which the expert did not opine in their report.
- Enable the expert to help you ascertain the strengths and possible weaknesses of the opposing expert/s opinion including to inform decisions as to whether objection ought be taken to any parts of another expert's report.
- To equip you to cross-examine the opposing expert.
- Give the expert the time to develop confidence in the barrister and the barrister's ability to recognise where something needs to be dealt with in re-examination and thus to help the expert feel confident that the barrister will do all that is necessary to support the expert's opinion.
- Enable further enquiry or work to be done if necessary.

During the conference you will

- Inform the expert of his or her role; to assist the court. The expert must not advocate the parties' cause. To do so creates a perception of bias and adversely affects the expert's credibility.
- Take the expert through the relevant expert witness code/s of conduct and request that they re-read the code/s before giving evidence.
- Review with the expert how you will elicit his or her qualifications. The extent to which qualifications may be elicited orally may depend on orders made by the particular judge.
- Prepare the expert for examination in chief by you and cross-examination by your opponent and the possibility of re-examination by you.
- Tell the expert to listen to the questions both in examination in chief and cross-examination, and answer them directly.
- Identify weaknesses in the opinion of any opposing expert.
- Instruct the expert in the need to
  - answer the questions responsively and cooperatively both in examination and cross-examination and to ensure that their demeanour remains the same in cross-examination as in examination in chief;
  - make concessions where reasonable and appropriate; the expert is there to assist the court, not as an advocate for the party calling the expert;
  - decline to answer a question which calls on the expert to go beyond his or her area of expertise;

  - use as little technical language as possible. Be prepared to explain technical terms and concepts; and
  - have all relevant materials available in court, organised and ready to produce if required.
- If the expert is not experienced, inform the expert of relevant legal terminology, procedure and the manner in which the expert will give evidence.
- Explain that the expert is limited to answering the questions asked in cross-examination, but that you may re-examine if necessary and appropriate.
- Ensure that you see the original working notes, lab records, interview schedules or any other data or reports.
- Ensure that the expert prepares any helpful visual aids, such as graphs, charts or simple illustrations of technical concepts, in a way that clearly communicates the point to be made.
- Ensure that the expert reviews any notes or reports before giving evidence.
- Ensure that the expert has checked whether there have been any developments or new work done in the relevant field of expertise of which the expert ought to be aware before giving evidence.

1.6 Presentation of Expert Evidence

Expert evidence may be adduced in a number of ways, depending on the rules and practice of the jurisdiction:

- In criminal trials before a jury, the expert will give oral evidence in chief, although he or she would usually be able to refer to the report and other notes.
- In a plea in mitigation, you can rely on the expert's report but your opponent may well want the witness called to be cross-examined.
- In non jury trials, and in most civil cases, the expert's report is usually used as evidence in chief.
- If the report is used as evidence in chief, there may still be oral evidence to supplement or explain the report, or, by leave of the judge, to give further evidence and the expert can be required for cross-examination.

1.7 Joint Expert Conferences

The purpose of the joint expert conference is to identify, between the experts, which areas or issues are agreed and which remain in dispute. Issues may arise in the joint expert conference as a consequence of the

- different framing of instructions by the different parties,
- the adoption of different methodologies or different assumptions, or
- the provision of different background materials.

The outcome of the joint expert conference may involve

- further work being done by some or all of the experts involved;
- a further joint conference;
- provision of additional material to some or all of the experts; or
- additional questions being asked of experts, not contemplated by the party instructing the expert at the outset.

At the conclusion of the joint expert conference/s, a joint report will be produced identifying what issues were agreed upon and which are in dispute.

2 Examination in Chief of Expert Witnesses

Generally, the same principles about leading evidence in chief will apply to the examination of an expert witness (see chapter, George Hampel, "Leading Evidence in Chief"). However, the evidence in chief of an expert also includes the following:

- the witness's qualifications, experience, and special expertise. Particular focus should be on qualifications and experience relevant to the issues in the case;
- Information provided to the expert on which the expert's opinion is based;
- methodology used by the expert;
- the process of reasoning leading to the opinion; and
- reasons why the opposing opinion is incorrect.

3 Expert Reports

In preparing to lead evidence in chief from an expert witness, you must consider:

- Whether the written report will be tendered instead of evidence in chief;

  In criminal cases, particularly jury trials, the expert will not be permitted to present a report but will instead be required to give oral evidence of his or her opinion. In civil cases before a judge alone, the report is usually tendered, and sometimes stands in place of evidence in chief, with further oral evidence permitted only to correct, explain or supplement the report.
- Whether you will anticipate problems to be raised in cross-examination and elicit them during evidence in chief.
- Whether visual aids may enhance communication.
- Encouraging experts to use aids of communication with which they are most at ease.

To enable the decision-maker to understand and accept the expert evidence, it is necessary to inform and educate the decision-maker, and therefore the structure of the evidence should be such as to help in that process.

Example

Qualifying an expert witness.

When qualifying a witness as an expert, you might ask questions during evidence in chief such as:

- 'What is your occupation?'
- 'How long have you been an accountant?'
- 'What educational qualifications do you have?'
- 'What areas of accounting do you practise in?'
- 'What have you published in that area?'

Example

Tendering and supplementing an expert report in a civil case.

When tendering an expert report in a civil case, you may need to allow the witness to supplement or correct the report. For example, you may ask?

- 'Is there anything you wish to correct in the report?'

Alternatively, if no changes are needed, you might ask 'Is that document true and correct?'

- 'I want to take you to some parts of your report...'
- 'Look at paragraph 10. What do you mean by these words...?
- 'In paragraph 12 you refer to a valuation method you used. What is involved in that method?'
- 'You have seen that in Mr Smith's report, he chose a different method. Why should the method you chose be appropriate in this case?'

The expert in the witness box must also be a good communicator, although he or she is not the persuader. It is your role to ensure that the expert communicates his or her evidence effectively to the court. Effective communication by the expert witness involves

- use of simple non-technical language;
- the ability to explain technical terms, methodology and ideas to lay people;
- good eye contact and delivery;
- answering questions directly, simply and clearly; and
- not being defensive in cross-examination.

Example

Example of Expert Report

Dr Jules Berne

Clinical and Forensic Psychologist

(continued)

Psy.D., New York, MA (Clin.Psych), London, Ass.Dip. (Behavioural Sciences)

At your request, I saw and tested Ms. X on two occasions last week, once in the presence of her father.

Ms. X is suffering from long-standing and serious depression. The symptoms of this include chronic poor self-esteem, depressed mood, repeated suicidal ideas, difficulty with sleep and appetite, and feelings of hopelessness about the future. In addition, she shows a clear disturbance in judgment, difficulty in establishing satisfying relationships with other people, and considerable immaturity.

This woman also has a four-year history of heroin abuse and is currently using marijuana and alcohol excessively. In all likelihood, she is addicted to one or both of these substances. It is noteworthy that these offences occurred while she was taking Valium.

Ms. X requires consistent and ongoing psychiatric treatment. This can be arranged through her local doctor. If Ms. X cannot be weaned away from the abuse of alcohol and marijuana through the treatment outlined above, on an out-patient basis, she may need a period of in-patient treatment in a drug and alcohol facility.

It is likely that her current drug abuse represents her own meagre attempts at medicating herself for depression.

The overall prognosis for Ms. X is guardedly optimistic. She expresses some remorse and guilt about her recent behaviour and in looking back at the last few years, she is clearly aware of the difficulty she has caused herself and her parents. She is apparently been able to stay off heroin since her release from prison last year. If this is correct, it shows great determination.

It is noteworthy that she did not have any difficulty with the law prior to her involvement with drugs.

Her relationship with her biological father is very new, but promising. He is supportive of her and clearly has both emotional and financial resources which he is eager and willing to make available to his daughter.

Yours sincerely,

Dr Jules Berne

Note: this is a fictional case.

4 Cross-Examination of Expert Witnesses

The same advocacy principles apply to the cross-examination of expert witnesses. Further considerations apply given the nature of expert evidence as opinion evidence.

Cross-examination as to the *admissibility* of expert evidence may be

- that the claimed area of expertise is not a sufficiently recognised field of specialist knowledge;
- that the area of expertise claimed is within common knowledge and so not appropriate for the reception of expert evidence; or
- that the witness does not have the training, qualifications or experience necessary to be classified as an expert witness.

Cross-examination as to the *weight* to be given to expert evidence will usually be directed to one or more of the following areas:

- qualifications or experience;
- correctness of the facts upon which the opinion is based;
- correctness and accuracy of the methodology used, and its appropriateness to the circumstances;
- gaps in tests or investigations conducted;
- the degree to which any assumptions were reasonable at the time they were made;
- ultimate correctness of the assumptions;
- the reasoning process leading to the opinion;
- comparison between the opinion and other expert opinions; or
- bias.

It is permissible to cross-examine an expert by questions that appear to be hypothetical but in fact are designed to lay the foundation for new information, about which the expert witness did not know or which contradict the assumptions made. For example, you might ask of a medical practitioner consulted by a claimant: 'If you knew that the person you examined had made prior claims, you would have taken that into account in determining whether he was a malingerer?'

The potential to cross-examine about bias must be thoroughly considered. Bias may fall into three categories:

1. The degree of independence from the issues. For example, is the expert involved in a generally connected cause?
2. The objectivity of the expert's approach. For example, does the expert start out to prove a fact in an issue such as 'This writing is a forgery'? Or does the expert have an ideological stance, perhaps reflected in his or her professional writing or opinions in prior cases?
3. The expert's professional independence. For example, does the expert's income depend on a conclusion favourable to the income provider? If an expert's main income is from an insurance company, you might consider how often this witness has given similar evidence, and her prior stance on similar issues.

By conferring with your own expert witness or a consultant, you should learn about the subject matter in dispute. It is unlikely, however, that you would develop a greater knowledge than the expert to be cross-examined. For this reason, you should avoid arguing about information within the expert's area of knowledge unless there is a sound basis for doing so. The expert will usually know more.

Similarly, lengthy cross-examination along the lines of the expert's theory or methodology can be counter-productive and should rarely be attempted. At most, you should focus on the plausibility of other theories or methodologies consistent with your client's case.

For examples of cross-examination of the expert witness, see Freckelton and Selby's *Expert Evidence: Law, Practice, Procedure and Advocacy* (3rd ed), Law Book Company, Sydney, 2005.

4.1 Advocacy Hints for Court

- Use every opportunity to elicit evidence from your expert about their qualifications and experience. It is good advocacy and an important part of persuading the decision maker that your expert ought to be accepted.
- Eliciting the expert's qualifications and experience at the beginning of evidence in chief allows the witness an opportunity to settle comfortably into the witness box.
- Consider in advance that the judge or the jury may ask questions themselves. Listen carefully to the questions and answers and pick up on any matters raised in the expert's answer, which need further elucidation or clarification.
- When cross-examining the expert for the other side, be respectful and avoid being unnecessarily confrontational. Ensure that your manner is consistent with the point to be made about the expert evidence.

Example

In an arson case, two experts are called. The prosecution expert (Expert A) is the fire investigator called to the scene after the fire. He is a fire investigator with 6 years experience and has attended approximately 200 fire scenes in that time. He inspected the scene and conducted a number of tests. He concluded the fire was deliberately lit.

The defence expert is a highly qualified and well regarded consultant expert with about 25 years experience; 15 years as a fire investigator, and about 10 years solely as a consultant expert (Expert B). She was engaged months after the fire and the property, the subject of the fire, had been demolished. She was provided with photographs and other documentary material upon which she was asked to opine as to the cause of the fire. She concluded that the fire was started by a faulty electric blanket.

The prosecutions case theory in relation to the expert evidence is that the opinion of Expert A ought be preferred as he had the benefit of going to the scene. First hand observations made by him, including of colours and smells,

(continued)

were critical to the formation of his opinion. Expert B was at a significant disadvantage because she did not have that opportunity.

Cross-examination of Expert B in an aggressive manner with questions formulated in a challenging way would be counter-productive, such as:

- "The only task you performed was to look at documents including photographs?"
- "You didn't even go to the scene of this fire?"

Cross-examination to that effect is likely to alienate counsel from the jury and engender feelings of empathy, possibly even support for Expert B as it is clear that as a consultant, she would never have had an opportunity to go to the scene; it was not something that she 'failed' to do. Such a cross-examination is unfair.

A better approach to the cross-examination would be as follows:

- "During your career you would have attended the scenes of many fires?"
- "Attendance at the scene allowed you to take in not just what you could see, but also what you could smell?"
- "It also enabled you to see colours first hand?"
- "During the time that you worked as a fire investigator, if you had a choice you would choose to attend the scene if you could?"
- "To ensure that you had the maximum opportunity to form the most accurate and thorough opinion possible"
- "As a consultant, the opportunity was not available to you in this case"
- "Had it been, you would have taken it"

Note: this is a fictional case.

George Hampel AM QC was a Justice of the Supreme Court of Victoria from 1983 to 2000, having previously practised as a barrister since 1958.

Hampel has held numerous positions in the legal profession, such as Vice-President of the Law Council of Australia, Vice-Chairman of the Victorian Bar Institute and Chairman of the Constitution Commission of Victoria.

For over 40 years, George developed advocacy teaching methods, case studies and the training of advocacy instructors in Australia and abroad. Since 2000, he has been Professor of Trial Practice and Advocacy at Monash University. His training experience of professional advocates extends internationally to USA, UK, Scotland, New Zealand, Hong Kong, Singapore, South Africa, and war crime prosecutors at The Hague.

George was the Founding Chairman of the Australian Advocacy Institute in 1991 and over the following 24 years continued to develop its teaching methodology and workshop programs. He is the principal author of the two editions of the Australian Advocacy Manual, which is now required reading for the Victorian Bar Readers Course and is used as a reference work in most common law jurisdictions. George has developed workshops for training of members of other professions including forensic accountants, doctors, engineers and computer experts in their roles as expert witnesses.

As a result of his contribution in these areas, George was made a Member of the General Division of the Order of Australia (2006), received the Centenary of Federation Medal, and a Monash University Teaching Award.

Part III
Interdisciplinary Considerations

This Part contains chapters on interdisciplinary considerations that victim advocates face in their work representing victims before the International Criminal Court. Experts provide insights into and practical advice on representing victims with specific needs, namely, those who have suffered crimes of sexual violence, victims who are children, victims who are women, and victims of mass trauma and violence. The chapter by Solange Mouthaan, Representing Victims Who Have Been Subject to Violent Sexual or Reproductive Crimes, provides a guide to legal representatives of victims of these specific crimes and is intended to complement the ICC's Manual for Legal Representatives of Victims. Francesca Capone's chapter, Representing Victims Who Are Children, introduces and discusses the main challenges of representing children in international criminal proceedings. The interview with Melinda McPherson discusses considerations of gender in representing victims before the International Criminal Court. Legal representatives of victims before the International Criminal Court work with clients who have suffered harm resulting from grave international crimes, often in the context of armed conflict and mass atrocity. The chapter Post-Conflict Mental Health and the Role of Transitional Justice, by Alvin Kuowei Tay and Zachary Steele, examines the effects of mass trauma and violence and subsequent transitional justice programs on the mental health of the individual as well as on the family and community. Tay and Steele then provide a set of concrete recommendations for victims' legal representatives to recognise these effects, address the challenges that they raise for victims providing testimonial evidence, and provide support for victims appearing before the International Criminal Court. Another key interdisciplinary consideration for legal representatives of victims before the International Criminal Court is working with interpreters in multilingual court proceedings. The chapter by Andrew Constable, Effective Communication in Multilingual Judicial Proceedings, explains the processes involved in simultaneous interpretation, common problems that arise, and provides examples of best practice and specific recommendations for Counsel on working with interpreters to communicate effectively in the courtroom.

Representing Victims Who Have Been Subject to Violent Sexual or Reproductive Crimes

Solange Mouthaan

1 Introduction

> Sexual violence in war is a complex issue involving wartime political and military structures and peacetime inequalities and ideologies (Boesten & Fisher, 2012)

Invaluable progress was made when the ICC Statute expressed a clear commitment to addressing violent sexual or reproductive crimes by criminalising a number of crimes of sexual or reproductive violence as international crimes, including genocide, crimes against humanity and war crimes. However, the criminalisation of these crimes is not, in itself, enough to prevent these crimes from taking place. A 2013 United Nations Security Council (UNSC) Resolution recognises that prosecution is a necessary step to deter and prevent violent sexual crimes.[1]

International criminal justice is one way to redress the suffering of victims of violent sexual or reproductive crimes. Prosecutions confirm the rule of law and intolerance of such crimes. However, for victims of violent sexual or reproductive crimes, to seek justice can be a personal and social struggle, which requires that they confront severe trauma, most often alone, whilst encountering significant stigmatisation within their communities. Victims will thus have specific physical and emotional needs, but may also face security issues. Thus, the decision to participate in the judicial proceedings in order to seek some degree of justice is a personal challenge. In addition, the International Criminal Court (ICC) is situated in The Hague, The Netherlands, far away from the victims and the events that have taken place. These are but some of the concerns to take into account when representing victims who have been subject to violent sexual or reproductive crimes.

[1] UNSC Resolution S/C/2106, 24 June 2013, p. 1.

S. Mouthaan (✉)
School of Law, University of Warwick, Coventry, UK
e-mail: s.mouthaan@warwick.ac.uk

E. King et al. (eds.), *Victim Advocacy before the International Criminal Court*,
https://doi.org/10.1007/978-3-030-56733-0_12

Once victims of violent sexual or reproductive crimes have been granted the right to participate in the judicial proceedings before the ICC, a legal representative will be appointed. Their role is to guide them through the judicial proceedings, to represent the 'views and concerns' of the victims during the judicial proceedings, to persuade the court that victims' experiences can add to establishing the truth and therefore that they should be allowed to participate to the judicial proceedings.[2] As a corollary, legal representatives should manage victims' expectations of what the judicial process may be able to achieve for them.

The challenge for legal representatives is to acknowledge the specificity of this category of victims, but also their bravery and resilience in coming forward. The ICC has produced a manual for legal representatives which aims "at providing some guidance on the main issues related to victims' participation in the proceedings and therefore helping legal representatives in their daily work, representing the views and concerns of victims in the proceedings".[3] Although the manual provides essential information to assist legal representatives, it is not aimed at representing a particularly vulnerable group of victims of violent sexual and reproductive crimes. Effective legal representation must therefore understand the suffering of victims in order to devise the best way to represent them. It should be developed around the victims' security, and their emotional and physical needs. To do so in a meaningful manner raises significant difficulties.

This chapter will serve as a guide to legal representation of victims of violent sexual or reproductive crimes to complement the ICC's legal manual. The chapter will commence by addressing the distinctive nature of violent and reproductive crimes in order to highlight the specific needs of victims. It will then discuss the move towards a common legal representative and the challenges of group representation of victims of violent sexual or reproductive crimes. Subsequently it will address the gathering of information about the victims' experiences, the identification of the link between the victims' experiences and victims' contributions to judicial proceedings.

---

[2] Statute of the International Criminal Court (Rome Statute), July 17, 1998, 2187 U.N.T.S, Article 68(3): "[w]here the personal interests of victims are affected, the Court shall permit their views and concerns to be presented and considered at stages of the proceedings determined to be appropriate by the Court and in a manner which is not prejudicial to or inconsistent with the rights of the accused and a fair and impartial trial".

[3] The Office of Public Counsel for Victims, *Representing Victims before the International Criminal Court – A Manual for Legal Representatives*, 5th edition, 2019. https://www.icc-cpi.int/Pages/item.aspx?name=pr1447. Accessed 25 March 2020.

2 Legal Representation of Violent Sexual or Reproductive Crimes

Before addressing challenges related to legal representation of victims of violent sexual and reproductive crimes, it is useful to characterise the complex distinctiveness of the crimes suffered.

2.1 *Complex Crimes*

There is no simple or single explanation for the occurrence of large-scale violent crimes of sexual or reproductive violence. Feminist writers and NGO reports often argue that pre-conflict subordination may explain the prevalence of violent sexual or reproductive crimes during war.

Violent sexual or reproductive crimes cannot be understood as isolated crimes and are distinct from their domestic counterpart. They take place on a large-scale and in a variety of contexts, such as in armed conflict, social or political unrest or extreme organised collective violence. The crimes involve a variety of acts, motivations, meanings, perpetrators and victims. These crimes are committed against an individual who is one victim amongst many other victims of different genders and ages. The individual may be targeted because they belong to a specific group, including ethnic, racial or religious groups. Accordingly, such crimes lead to mass prosecutions against multiple perpetrators who were organised in a variety of groupings, such as state armies, para-military groups or local police units. Additionally, these crimes are different to peacetime sexual violence, because they are committed in multiple locations, involving numerous perpetrators, with large numbers of potential witnesses and substantial documentary and other physical evidence. Moreover, the acts of sexual or reproductive violence are part of a larger set of harms inflicted upon the targeted population such as the destruction of property and murders. They not only impact on the individual victim, but also on the group or community they belong to.

However, such crimes are a frequent occurrence in conflict situations and may be part of a widespread and systematic campaign to brutalize and destroy targeted groups. The UNSC has more than once highlighted the plight of civilians subjected to these crimes. In particular UNSC Resolution 1820 acknowledged that "women and girls are particularly targeted by the use of sexual violence, including as a tactic of war to humiliate, dominate, instil fear in, disperse and/or forcibly relocate civilian members of a community or ethnic group." This does not preclude the fact that men and boys may also suffer these crimes, and therefore it is important to recognise that some of the participating victims of violent sexual or reproductive crimes may be men or boys.[4] The scale at which these crimes occur has led to the recognition that

[4] UNSC Resolution S/C/2106, 24 June 2013.

they constitute international crimes worthy of prosecution. At the time of writing the International Criminal Court has brought charges of violent sexual crimes in a number of cases: *The Prosecutor* v. *Simone Gbagbo,*[5] *The Prosecutor* v. *Charles Blé Goudé,*[6] *The Prosecutor* v. *Laurent Gbagbo,*[7] *The Prosecutor* v. *Abdel Raheem Muhammad Hussein,*[8] *The Prosecutor* v. *Omar Hassan Ahmad Al Bashir,*[9] *The Prosecutor* v. *Ahmad Muhammad Harun and Ali Muhammad Ali Abd-Al-Rahman,*[10] *The Prosecutor* v. *Joseph Kony and Vincent Otti,*[11] *The Prosecutor* v. *Jean-Pierre Bemba Gombo,*[12] *The Prosecutor* v. *Matthieu Ngudjolo Chui,*[13] *The Prosecutor* v. *Sylvestre Mudacumura,*[14] *The Prosecutor* v. *Calixte Mbarushimana,*[15] *The Prosecutor* v. *Bosco Ntaganda.*[16] It is thus likely for legal representatives in these particular cases that the participating victims they represent have suffered violent sexual and reproductive crimes. However, even in cases in which none of the charges include violent sexual or reproductive crimes, participating victims may have suffered such crimes. It is thus important for legal representatives to understand the distinctive and complex nature of these crimes, because it produces important practical differences in the formulation of a strategy for participation in the judicial proceedings that represents the views of the victims and persuades the judges of the legitimacy of the victims' claims.

2.2 Towards Common Legal Representatives

The prosecution of international crimes before the ICC will involve large numbers of victims, of whom a substantial number may wish to participate in the proceedings. The participation of individual victims or even small groups of victims would put considerable time, capacity and financial constraints on the ICC.[17] Therefore, the

[5] ICC-02/11-01/12.

[6] ICC-02/11-01/11.

[7] ICC-02/11-01/11.

[8] ICC-02/05-01/12.

[9] ICC-02/05-01/09.

[10] ICC-02/05-01-07.

[11] ICC-02/05-01/05.

[12] ICC-01/05-01/08.

[13] ICC-01/04-02/12.

[14] ICC-01/01-01/12.

[15] ICC-01/01-01/10.

[16] ICC-01/01-02/06.

[17] On the 30th June 2013, in the *Prosecutor* v. *Thomas Lubango Dyilo* the application of 120 victims were accepted, in the *Prosecutor* v. *Germain Katanga,* the application of 364 victims were accepted, in the *Prosecutor* v. *Jean-Pierre Bemba Gombo* the application of 5229 victims were accepted, in the *Prosecutor* v. *Ruto and Sang,* the application of 327 victims were accepted, in the *Prosecutor* v. *Uhuru Muigai Kenyatta*, the application of 233 victims were accepted and in the

ICC judges have had to gradually streamline legal representation of participating victims by appointing common legal representatives. However, there is a difference in representing one victim and more than one hundred victims. The challenge for the legal representative will be to put forward efficiently the views and concerns of an extensive group of victims of violent sexual or reproductive crimes without adverse effect on their well-being.

The Rome Statute[18] and the Rules of Procedure and Evidence (RPE)[19] do not require participating victims to appoint a legal representative. Rule 90(1), in particular states that "a victim shall be free to choose a legal representative". The Court has interpreted this set of provisions to mean that victims are free to choose one or not.[20] In other words, victim participation is not dependent on legal representation. However, the Court has also stated that it is in the interest of justice to provide victims with a legal representative.[21] Legal representation may well be the corollary of access to the full array of participatory rights, whereas lack of legal representation may result in victims only being granted the right to make opening and closing statements (McGonigle Leyh, 2011, p. 326).[22] Therefore victims may prefer to be represented by a lawyer.

In theory, the Registrar will either suggest a common legal representative or leave it up to the victims to choose their own common legal representative. In practice, the growing number of participating victims in each case has resulted in the ICC organising victim representation in a meaningful rather than symbolic manner.[23] To have one legal representative for each participating victim would hamper the Court's efficiency in conducting judicial proceedings. The ICC, in order to enable victim participation without compromising the judicial proceedings has gradually moved towards group representation. When the number of participating victims is high, judges have appointed one or two common legal representatives.[24] This has culminated in further rationalisation in the *Ruto and Sang* case in which 327 victims have been granted participatory rights.[25] The judge appointed one common legal

Prosecutor v. *Laurent Gbagbo*, the application of 199 victims were accepted. These figures were produced by Women's Initiatives for Gender Justice (2014) Gender Report Card 2013, available at http://www.iccwomen.org/news/docs/WI-GRC13_launch/GRC13_launch.html. Accessed 21 February 2020.

[18] Rome Statute, Article 68(3).

[19] RPE, Rules 89–93.

[20] *The Prosecutor* v. *Kony et al.*, n. ICC -02/04-01/05-134, 1 February 2007, paras. 2–12.

[21] *The Prosecutor* v. *Kony et al.*, ibid. at para 48.

[22] See *Situation in Uganda*, n. ICC-02/04-105, Pre-Trial Chamber II (Single Judge), 28 August 2007, pp. 4–5.

[23] *The Prosecutor* v. *Germain Katanga and Mathieu Ngudjolo*, ICC-01/04-01/07, Order on the Organisation of Common Legal Representation of Victims, 22 July 2009 at para 7.

[24] RPE, Rule 90(2) and Rule 22(1).

[25] *The Prosecutor* v. *William Samoei Ruto and Joshua Arap Sang*, ICC-01/09-01/11-267. This rationalisation has also been applied in the *Prosecutor* v. *Uhuru Muigai Kenyatta*, ICC-01/09-01/11.

representative who was subsequently replaced by a common legal representative based in Kenya, because this would ensure greater geographical proximity to the victims.[26] Victim participation should add to the establishment of the truth, but should not unduly hamper the effectiveness of the proceedings. The greater the number of legal representatives of victims the greater is the number of interventions in the judicial proceedings and the greater is the risk of delays. With the growing number of participating victims in each of the cases, the appointment of one or two common legal representatives per case will become the norm.

As a consequence legal representatives will have to deal with large numbers of victims without the resources necessary for common legal representation. In addition, representing victims of sexual or reproductive violence requires specific skills and experiences. These are challenges that, if acknowledged and explained to participating victims, may assist in effective representation that gives due regard to the victims' specific needs and dignity.

Firstly, the growing numbers of participating victims and the limited number of common legal representatives are a cause for concern. For example, in the *Bemba* trial there are more than 5229 participating victims, but the ICC did not see fit to appoint more than two common legal representatives.[27] This is *a priori* a concern that affects victims generally and requires that the legal representative clearly informs each victim of the consequences of common legal representation, including the number of victims represented and if necessary the range of harms covered, the advantages of a group effort, limited contact and ability to enforce individual objectives and priority of pursuing the group's interest. Moreover, it raises a specific issue for the relationship between the common legal representative and the victims of violent sexual and reproductive crimes. How can the mental and physical well-being of each individual victims be safeguarded when huge numbers of victims are represented? How can the representative build a trusting relationship with all victims, and in particular how meet with each victim located in different places away from the ICC and thereby represent victims effectively before the ICC? The ICC recognises the strain on common legal representation and provides some support by appointing team members to assist, such as a co-counsel and/or assistants and case managers. The common legal representative has always been able to seek assistance from the Office of Public Counsel for the Victims (OPVC). Cooperation between the OPVC and the common legal representative is particularly important, because the OPVC will have represented the victims up until their application to participate was granted and they receive assigned legal representation (Funk, 2010). The OPVC thus has prior knowledge of the victims. Recently, this cooperation was enhanced further. In the *Ruto* and *Sang* case, the trial chamber, in order to relieve some of the pressures on the common legal representative, has clarified the relationship with the OPVC. The OPVC, within the common legal representative system is the link between the common legal representative and the Chamber, attending

[26] *The Prosecutor* v. *William Samoei Ruto and Joshua Arap Sang*, ICC-01/09-01/11-460 para. 60.
[27] Women's Initiative for Gender Justice Report Card 2013, p. 181.

hearings, intervening on behalf of the common legal representative and assisting them in preparing written submissions.[28] The role of the common legal representative is that of point of contact for the victims and keeping them up-to-date with the judicial proceedings whilst also identifying their views and concerns as a group. However, this enhanced role puts further strain on the limited resources of the OPVC. The role of the common legal representative may be less strained, but the difficulty of forging trusting relationships with great numbers of victims within tight time constraints remains a worry. In particular, the chosen strategy of group representation may not always reflect the views and concerns of all victims, and this needs to be carefully managed by the common legal representative, particularly with regards to victims of violence sexual or reproductive crimes.

Secondly, the gender of the legal representative may prove important in cases in which female victims prefer liaising with a female legal representative. Therefore gender mainstreaming of legal representatives is critical and should be a priority. However, this may be quite a challenge. Funk argues that the requirements for legal representatives are extremely onerous and have prevented local lawyers from the country or region under investigation by the ICC from qualifying (Funk, 2010, p. 93). The Registrar has a list of qualifying lawyers from which victims may choose their common legal representatives. All included legal representatives must possess the same legal qualifications as legal council for the defence would.[29] The requirements include amongst others at least 10-year experience working as a criminal lawyer, judge or prosecutor and fluency in one of the Court's working languages. On the other hand, the Court's Strategy for Victims promotes victim's choice of legal representative or at the least one originating from their own country or region.[30] Cultural reasons may dictate that the legal representative is either from the region and/or speaks the language spoken by the group of victims. If this is not possible then, as is the case for legal counsel for the defence, they may be assisted by a professional person competent to breach the cultural gap.[31] Similarly, gender mainstreaming may be a challenge and thus female team members with experience in working with victims of violent sexual or reproductive crimes should assist the common legal representative.

Thirdly, and most importantly, in appointing a common legal representative, the ICC should give prominence to the harm suffered by the victims. In other words, victims of violent sexual or reproductive crimes should be grouped by harm. Representing victims who have suffered similar harms helps develop a better understanding of the context of the crimes and thus enables more pointed

[28] *The Prosecutor* v. *William Samoei Ruto and Joshua Arap Sang*, ICC-01/09-01/11-460, paras. 42–43. At the request of the Trial Chamber, the Registry and OPVC have prepared a joint proposal: 'OPVC's Proposal on the Division of Responsibilities and Effective Functioning of the Common Legal Representative System', 17 October 2013.

[29] RPE, Rule 90(6).

[30] ASP, Report of the Court on the strategy in relation to victims, ICC-ASP/8/45, 18–26 November 2009, p. 10.

[31] RPE, Rule 22(1).

contributions to the judicial proceedings that reflect the particularity of this group of victims (McGonigle Leyh, 2011, p. 328). This may help in establishing the truth, but also support a possible future award of reparations.[32] The ICC Statute stipulates this. According to Rule 90(4), the choice of common legal representatives must ensure common representation guided by the "distinct interests of the victims, particularly as provided in article 68, paragraph 1". Article 68(1) identifies victims of sexual violence as a category of individuals with a distinct interest to be taken into account and thus should be grouped to be represented by a common legal representative. This requirement should guide the number and desirable qualifications of the common legal representatives to be appointed. If, as Funk argues, it is extremely difficult for a local lawyer to qualify, this requirement may equally be challenging (Funk, 2010, p. 93). However the ICC subordinates sexual violence to geography. In the *Bemba* trial the ICC decided to group on the ground of geography, despite an explicit distinct interest requirement in the ICC Statute. In fact, it should be the other way around: similarity of harm should prevail, because to represent victims having suffered similar harms enables the formulation of a collective position and more systematic proof of harm. It is unfortunate that the ICC did not stipulate specific requirements for common legal representatives of victims of violent sexual or reproductive crimes, because the *Bemba* judgment demonstrates that the 'distinct interest of the victims of sexual violence' is not forceful enough to guide ICC judges.

As a consequence of the appointment of common legal representatives for large groups of victims of violence sexual or reproductive crimes, it is important that the common legal representative has acquired experience in working with victims of such mass crimes at the international level as well as experience in trauma counselling. Furthermore the common legal representative and supporting team supporting should include members of both genders and competent in gender-sensitive treatment. Such characteristics will promote efficient representation of this category of participating victims whilst protecting their right to safety, privacy and dignity and physical and psychological well-being.

The legal representative no longer represents a small number of participating victims, but large numbers. The role is thus to identify what the victims, as a group, wish to achieve and to carve out a strategy of how best to participate in the proceedings to represent the interests of the group of victims and the harms they have suffered. There is of course a risk that the strategy does not conform to the views and concerns of all the represented victims and thus the rationale for this needs to be explained. Therefore, the role of the legal representative is two-fold: identification of the issues that matter most to the group (19.3) and planning of a strategy that fits the likely outcomes of the trial (19.4).

[32] RPE, Rule 22(1).

3 Gathering Victims' Stories

The ICC Statute recognises that victims should be afforded a role during the judicial proceedings before the court.[33] In light of the number of participating victims and limited legal representatives, victims may have expectations that cannot be fulfilled by victim participation. Few participating victims will be given an active role during the judicial proceedings, but they are able to tell their story to the legal representative and this in turn will establish a historic record of the atrocities they suffered (Funk, 2010, p. 127). The primary tool to obtain the historical narrative surrounding the crimes is by interviewing. However, there are numerous possible pitfalls when interacting with a victim of sexual or reproductive violence. Victims of violent sexual or reproductive crimes have suffered horrendous pain. To describe the circumstances surrounding sexual or reproductive violence can be extremely painful and humiliating for the victims and thus special care must be taken that the interview is conducted in such a manner as to minimise further suffering. The legal representative must address the needs and concerns of victims through client-centred lawyering. Therefore, careful preparation, including training, specific knowledge and consideration may make the process a lot smoother. This can be achieved with a number of precautionary steps, but needs coordination with the Victims and Witness Unit (VWU), because the VWU has particular expertise in a variety of issues useful to dealing with victims of violent sexual or reproductive crimes.[34] A report produced by Office of the Prosecutor for the International Criminal Court for Rwanda particularly emphases that it has been their experience that coordination between the different organs of and parties to the Court is an essential element.[35]

3.1 Training

As mentioned above, it will be rare that the legal representative will have extensive experience in mass prosecutions, and more importantly of mass prosecutions of violent sexual or reproductive crimes. Legal representatives should receive regular training in how to handle and interact appropriately and sensitively with victims of sexual or reproductive violence. The VWU will make training "in issues of trauma, sexual violence, security and confidentiality" available.[36] Such training should be a continuing process.

---

[33] Rome Statute, Article 68(3).

[34] RPE, Rule 17.

[35] Office of the Prosecution for the International Criminal Tribunal for Rwanda, *Prosecution of Sexual Violence – Best Practices Manual for the Investigation and Prosecution of Sexual Violence Crimes in Post-Conflict Regions: Lessons Learned from the Office of the Prosecutor for the International Criminal Tribunal for Rwanda*, 30 January 2014.

[36] RPE, Rule 17(2)(a)(iv).

Firstly, training should be undertaken to help understand and consider the impact that this type of violence can have on an individual. It is an opportunity to address entrenched rape myths. The victim has gone through a traumatic experience and although the effects will differ for every individual and can be long lasting and variable over time, it is useful to be aware of the common effects including physical injuries, illness and psychological issues such as shock, anxiety and post-traumatic stress disorder as well as the impact such effects may have on individuals.

Secondly, training should be undertaken to minimize the effects of cultural and gender biases and attitudes to avoid inadvertently conveying these to victims. Training ensures an understanding of how to approach victims in a sensitive manner, but also to identify the signs of distress and to react appropriately.

Once initial training has been undertaken, the legal representative will meet with the victims. Before gathering all the relevant facts, the legal representative should check the victims' specific safety, physical and mental concerns.

3.2 Identification of Safety Concerns and Physical/ Mental Needs

Ensuring victims' safety is a priority for the ICC.[37] Victims may fear reprisals from the perpetrators, accused or associates against themselves, their family, friends and property. When victims are in increased danger of violence, this may lead to reticence to speak. Thus, safety should always be the primary factor in any decision made by the victim.

The legal representative should begin with a safety assessment to understand the particular situation of the victim, to discuss the safety ramifications of the decision to participate, to determine how best to ensure the safety of the victim and to provide support and advice for the safety needs of the victim. Most importantly, if necessary the legal representative should raise these issues with the Chamber and the Prosecutor. Legal representatives may request protective measures from the VWU, such as relocation or support measures.[38]

Once the safety issues are addressed, the legal representative should check the physical and mental health of the victim. For victims of violent sexual or reproductive crimes, it is beneficial that the legal aspects remain closely linked to the physical and mental needs of victims.[39]

Legal representatives should be familiar with the range of resources available to assist and support victims of sexual or reproductive violence. Medical and

[37] Rome Statute, Article 68(1).

[38] RPE, Rule 17(2)(a)(i) & (ii) and 16.

[39] World Health Organisation (2003) Guidelines for Medico-Legal Care for Victims of Sexual Violence, Geneva. https://www.who.int/violence_injury_prevention/publications/violence/med_leg_guidelines/en/. Accessed 25 March 2020.

psychological conditions that are left untreated can affect the victim's welfare and thus it is important to ensure that their needs are met. There are a number of organs of the ICC that will provide, fund or refer access to medical and psychological care and support specifically needed by victims of sexual or reproductive violence. The VWU and the Registry of the ICC will provide specialised medical and psychological care or have partnerships with qualified local organisations.[40] The Victim's Trust Fund may also have resources available. Similarly, legal representatives and their staff who work with the victims should be aware that to deal with victims who suffered sexual and reproductive violence is demanding and may result in secondary trauma. To ensure the well-being of staff and victims, it is thus important that the appropriate counselling services are in place. The ICC has acknowledged this by providing in-house counsellors for staff to talk to. Similarly to on-going training, legal representatives and their team should attend counselling sessions regularly to manage individual experiences of accounts of violent sexual or reproductive crimes.

3.3 *Understanding of the Conflict and Harms Suffered*

Legal representatives must be sensitive to the special circumstances of the harm suffered by the victims. This would include an understanding of the history and nature of the conflict, but also the extent to which these crimes of sexual or reproductive violence were committed during the conflict. He/she should have competent legal knowledge and understanding of the intersectional nature of crimes of sexual or reproductive violence in which the individual is targeted as a result of belonging to a group. This involves not only an understanding of the violence suffered and the related dynamics, but also a cultural awareness.

The legal representative should also be familiar with societal attitudes and the cultural implications of the crimes of sexual and reproductive violence for the victims and understand the stigma associated with being a victim of such crimes. These can silence survivors and prevent them from speaking out about their experience. If female sexuality is taboo, then the gender of the legal representative may be of great importance. For children who have suffered sexual or reproductive violence, the stigma may impact their future opportunities for education, marriage and other fundamental aspects of life. Some parents or legal representatives may be unwilling to assist the legal representative, because of the risks to the family. It is essential to treat their experience with compassion and sensitivity.

[40] RPE, Rule 17(2)(a)(iii).

3.4 Listening

The role of the legal representative is to gather all relevant facts regarding the nature of the crimes suffered, the identities of the alleged perpetrators, the significant events and other relevant information in order to identify types of patterns of behaviour. In addition to the victim's recollection of events, the legal representative should gather as much independent evidence as possible, such as (*inter alia*?) photographs, physical evidence and medical records. To create a record of victims' accounts of events, the legal representative will meet with the victims.

Legal representatives should acknowledge that the meeting may be a daunting prospect for victims. Legal representatives should create an appropriate environment in which to listen to the victims' stories, their concerns and needs, preferably without too much interruption. Although re-traumatisation is inevitable, it should be kept to the utmost bare minimum. It is thus useful to prepare for meetings carefully in order to lessen the amount of re-traumatisation. Some initial steps may assist in providing victims an open environment in which to tell their stories.

At the start of the meeting, legal representatives should explain the manner in which the meeting will be conducted, issues of confidentiality, who is present and in what capacity, and audio/visual devices used and for what purpose. The legal representative should also acknowledge that the subject matter of the interview might be uncomfortable, embarrassing, painful or difficult for the victim and reassure them that they will be able to take a break whenever necessary or ask question to clarify any issue. Legal representatives should also provide victims with all the necessary legal information about the legal process and the role of the legal representative of victims within this process, about the nature of victim participation, as well as about the procedures that will need to be followed and what the victims realistically may expect as possible outcomes. It is important the victim has access to all the information, options, the possible outcomes and legal risks in order to manage their own expectations of the process.

The choice of location should assist in making the victim comfortable. Meetings should take place in secure, quiet and welcoming environments in order to give the victims the space and time to tell their story. This may require putting in place childcare arrangements or the presence of a support person. Victims should be able to speak openly without fear of being overheard. A frank and open discussion may not take place if other people, such as family members, friends or neighbours are present.

Similarly, an understanding of cultural sensitivities should guide the legal representatives' choice in clothing and body language. Clothing that is considered inappropriate or unprofessional or body language that conveys arrogance or disinterest should be avoided.

Furthermore, prior to the meeting, legal representatives need to reflect on the questions to ask and how these questions should be phrased and to consider how to present appropriate, non-judgmental responses. It is best to keep the language and phrases as simple as possible, because this ensures that information is conveyed accurately, which in turn helps the victims to feel more confident.

During the meeting itself, there are a number of challenges that may arise. Victims of violent sexual or reproductive crimes may have greater difficulty speaking about their ordeal.

The well-being of the victims is a major concern. If during the meeting, it becomes apparent that the subject matter of the meeting becomes too painful or traumatic for the victim, the meeting must be stopped. Legal representatives must be aware of the verbal and non-verbal responses of the victim. There is a number of tell tale signs that informs the legal representative that the victim is no longer at ease with the subject matter: heightened tone of voice, facial expressions and nervous hand gestures may signal distress. If this is the case, a judgment call needs to be made to decide whether to take a short break, postpone or cancel the meeting.

Victims are not always able fully and accurately to remember all the necessary details. Memory can suffer. In order to establish as truthful an account as possible, it may be necessary to organise several meetings or put questions in a number of different ways.

It is important not to make assumptions or reinforce stereotypes and that the experiences of the victims are treated with compassion and sensitivity. Victims should be involved with the process and their contributions and perspectives respected.

If the legal representative does not speak the language of the victim, an interpreter may be necessary. Interpretation may become an concern because the interpretation may not be sufficiently precise or the introduction of an interpreter to the meeting is problematic for the victim. Interpreting must be accurate, sensitive and confidential. The interpreter's political or ethnic background should not cause any distress to the victims.

During the discussions, the legal representative should learn their victims' values, experiences and priorities through sensitive questioning, but more importantly through careful listening and attention to verbal and non-verbal clues. The goal is to leave the victims feeling empowered for having shared their story and not to feel re-victimised or exploited.

At the end of the meeting, the legal representative should thank the victim for their time, but also to explain the next steps, such as a follow-up meeting to clarify or expand.

The aim of the meetings with victims is to document a historical record of the harms suffered by the group of victims. A further aim is to identify what the victims wish to achieve by participating in the judicial proceedings. With this in mind, legal representatives must determine the manner in which victims can contribute efficiently.

4 Linking Victims' Stories to Crimes and Modes of Liability

Many victims of violent sexual or reproductive crimes will not have knowledge of the international legal system, but they need to gain an understanding of the legal elements of the crimes and the modes of liability applicable under the ICC Statute. The role of the legal representative is to establish whether the victims' harms are linked to the crimes the accused is charged with and to determine the victims' story that emerges of how the accused affected the particular victim of group of victims at a particular time and place. A first step will be to establish the facts surrounding the underlying crime that is the sexual or reproductive crime. A second step is to establish whether the sexual or reproductive violence crime was perpetrated as part of the substantive international crime of genocide, crimes against humanity or war crimes. A final step involves establishing the link between the person who physically committed the crime of sexual or reproductive violence on the ground to the accused. This background knowledge will guide them and their legal representative in determining the victims' legal case and what role they may be able to play meaningfully in the legal proceedings.

4.1 Legal Elements for Successful Prosecution

In the first instance, the focus is the identification of the specific violent sexual or reproductive crimes. This helps to establish a fuller picture of the events that took place and to identify trends and patterns. The ICC Statute contains a list of sexual violence or reproductive crimes and the Elements of Crimes (EOC) set out the contours of these crimes. However, this list is not exhaustive and there are numerous acts of sexual or reproductive violence that may not be covered by the ICC Statute. In particular, it should be noted that whereas the ICC Statute has incorporated the concept of crimes of sexual violence or indeed gender-based crimes, it refers only fleetingly to violent reproductive crimes. The relevant crimes that have been included in the ICC Statute and thus could be prosecuted are as follows:

The crime of rape involves "the perpetrator invading the body of a person by conduct resulting in penetration, however slight, of any part of the body of the victim or of the perpetrator with a sexual organ, or of the anal or genital opening of the victim with any object or any other part of the body. The invasion was committed by force, or by threat of force or coercion, such as that caused by fear of violence, duress, detention, psychological oppression or abuse of power, against such person or another person, or by taking advantage of a coercive environment, or the invasion was committed against a person incapable of giving genuine consent".[41]

The crime of sexual slavery involves "the perpetrator exercising any or all of the powers attached to the right of ownership over one or more persons, such as by

[41] Rome Statute and Elements of Crimes, Article 7(1)(g) -1.

purchasing, selling, lending or bartering such a person or persons, or by imposing on them a similar deprivation of liberty. Furthermore, the perpetrator caused such a person or persons to engage in one or more acts of a sexual nature".[42]

The crime of enforced prostitution involves "the perpetrator causing one or more persons to engage in one or more acts of a sexual nature by force, or by threat of force or coercion, such as that caused by fear of violence, duress, detention, psychological oppression or abuse of power, against such person or persons or another person, or by taking advantage of a coercive environment or such persons or persons incapacity to give genuine consent. The perpetrator or another person obtained or expected to obtain pecuniary or other advantage in exchange for or in connection with the acts of a sexual nature".[43]

The crime of forced pregnancy involves "the perpetrator confining one or more women forcibly made pregnant, with the intent of affecting the ethnic composition of any population or carrying out other grave violations of international law".[44]

The crime of enforced sterilization involves "the perpetrator depriving one or more persons of biological reproductive capacity. The conduct was neither justified by the medical or hospital treatment of the person or persons concerned nor carried out with their genuine consent".[45]

The crime of sexual violence involves "the perpetrator committing an act of a sexual nature against one or more persons or caused such person or persons to engage in an act of a sexual nature by force, or by threat of force or coercion, such as that caused by fear of violence, duress, detention, psychological oppression or abuse of power, against such person or persons or another person, or by taking advantage of a coercive environment or such persons or persons incapacity to give genuine consent".[46]

To establish that victims have suffered violent or reproductive crimes is not sufficient. It is also necessary to establish that the particular violent sexual or reproductive crime was part of, or associated to the international crime the accused is charged with: genocide, crimes against humanity and war crimes. Firstly, in order to support a conviction of genocide, it is important to establish that the act(s) of sexual or reproductive violence took place "in the context of a manifest pattern of similar conduct" against a particular national, ethnical, racial or religious group and that the accused had the intention to destroy or contribute to the destruction of the particular group, in whole or in part.[47] For instance, such destruction may be achieved by "causing serious bodily or mental harm to members of the group" or by "imposing measures intended to prevent births within the group".[48] Secondly, in

[42] Rome Statute and Elements of Crimes, Article 7(1)(g) - 2.
[43] Rome Statute and Elements of Crimes, Article 7(1)(g) -3.
[44] Rome Statute and Elements of Crimes, Article 7(1)(g) - 4.
[45] Rome Statute and Elements of Crimes, Article 7(1)(g) - 5.
[46] Rome Statute and Elements of Crimes, Article 7(1)(g) – 6.
[47] Rome Statute and Elements of Crime 6(a).
[48] Rome Statute and Elements of Crime, Article 6(b)(4) and 6(d)(5).

order to support a conviction of crimes against humanity, it is important to establish that the act(s) of sexual or reproductive violence were committed as part of a pattern of widespread or systematic attacks against a civilian population. "Rape, sexual slavery, enforced prostitution, forced pregnancy, enforced sterilization, or other forms of sexual violence of a comparable nature" may constitute a crime against humanity.[49] Furthermore they may also constitute persecution as a crime against humanity if the victim was perceived to be a member of a group defined on the basis of politics, race, nationality, ethnicity, culture, religion or gender and they were targeted because of this perception of affiliation to the particular group. Thirdly, in order to support a conviction of a war crime, the act(s) of sexual or reproductive violence must be shown to have been committed during an armed conflict and that the victims were not taking active part in the hostilities at the time of the alleged crime.[50]

The contribution of victims' testimony to the establishment of the crimes is but one part of the puzzle. It is also necessary to establish how the accused, who may not have personally committed the violent sexual or reproductive crimes, is linked to the persons who physically perpetrated the crimes.

4.2 Modes of Liability

The determination how the crimes are linked to the individual under investigation is not a straightforward task. The ICC targets the most senior leaders suspected of being most responsible for the large-scale atrocities committed. These high level accused may include senior government and military officials who may have taken part in the organisation of, planning of or inciting the commission of these crimes, but were not physically present at the time. They are not the ones who "soiled their hands with flesh and blood" (Schabas, 2007, p. 211). Victims of violent sexual or reproductive crimes may not have suffered at the hands of the accused; nonetheless they may be able to provide vital evidence that links the accused to the crimes under investigation.

The ICC provides for a number of different modes of liability that permits to establish a link between the leaders and the crimes as follows:

Command responsibility is specified in Article 28 of the ICC Statute and refers to criminal responsibility of a commander for offences committed by subordinates.

Individual responsibility is listed in Article 25 of the ICC Statute. It goes beyond the direct and individual commission or perpetration of the crimes by the alleged perpetrator. The ICC Statute also recognises the commission of the crime jointly with another or through another person. It furthermore recognises a number of behaviours as conducive to criminal liability. Ordering is when a person in a position

[49] Rome Statute, Article 7(1)(g).

[50] Rome Statute, Article 8(2)(b)(xxi) & (xxii), Article 8(2)(c)(ii), Article 8(2)(e)(vi).

of authority uses it to convince another to commit an offence. Instigating, alongside soliciting and inducing takes place when a person encourages another to commit a crime whereas incitement is linked solely to the crime of genocide and refers to public encouragement to commit a crime. Finally, the ICC Statute criminalises anyone who "for the purpose of facilitating the commission of such a crimes, aids and abets, or otherwise assists in its commission or its attempted commission, including providing the means for its commission".[51]

In order to convict the accused, the ICC must establish the involvement of the accused. This does not simply mean to prove that those who personally committed the crimes were criminally responsible for the crime. It involves proof of the relationship between the accused and actual perpetrators, proof that the accused knew the crimes were committed and proof that the accused failed to take action to prevent or punish the commission of the crime. If the accused was present then proof of orders, direct knowledge and facilitation of the crimes, such as transportation, leading directing, controlling, instructing or rewarding the perpetrators are useful elements to establish the truth. If the accused was not present, then evidence relating to the accused's position, the chain of command, the relationship with the perpetrators, attitude towards the commission of the crime are useful element to establish the truth.

5 Strategy for Meaningful Victim Participation

Having done the contextual work, the legal representative must establish the case of the victims. The legal representative must persuade the Court that the personal interests of the represented victims are affected, because they suffered the crimes charged. Furthermore, the legal representative must identify the modalities of victim participation that will assist victims to present their case.

5.1 The Victims' Case

For participating victims, any request to contribute to the proceedings must be supported by proof of her/his personal interest. As a consequence, the harms suffered by victims of violent sexual or reproductive crimes must fit the ones codified in the ICC Statute. The acts of sexual violence must be proven to have occurred, but it must also be demonstrated that those acts are linked to the precise events under investigation. In other words that the accused committed the crimes he/she has been charged with in a particular place at a particular time. For instance, the recent ICC judgment found Germain Katanga guilty of war crimes and crimes against humanity

[51] Rome Statute, Article 25(3)(c).

for his part as an accessory in the brutal attack on 24 February 2003 against civilians in Bogoro, a village in the Ituri district of eastern Democratic Republic of Congo. Yet, the ICC acquitted him of all responsibility for the charges of rape and sexual slavery, because the evidence linking Germain Katanga to the charges of rape and sexual violence were insufficient. The ICC did not believe these crimes formed part of the common purpose of the attack, a link that was proven for the other crimes of directing an attack against a civilian population, pillage, murder and destruction of property. In this case, 366 victims were given the right to participate in the trial. To receive permission, these victims will have had the additional burden to establish their personal interests that the accused, Germain Katanga harmed the victim directly or indirectly in the particular place and time.

5.2 Modalities of Victim Participation

Victims of violent sexual or reproductive crimes, through their legal representative, are able have some input in the ICC's judicial proceedings. It is thus necessary to give a brief outline of the possible modalities for victim participation, as this will guide the participatory strategy of legal representatives.

The rights of victims to participate are limited.[52] The judges will determine the extent of participation to suit the judicial proceedings of the particular case. In doing so, it will carefully balance the rights of the victims against the rights of the accused. Victims will be given a set of participatory rights that will not affect the Prosecutor's independence nor the smooth running of the judicial proceedings. However, participation will be conducted in gender-sensitive circumstances.[53]

In the first instance, for each application to participate judges will be guided by the personal interest of the victims in determining their participatory rights. The Appeals Chamber in the *Lubanga case* held that:

> "The Trial Chamber did not create an unfettered right for victims to lead or challenge evidence, instead victims are required to demonstrate why their interests are affected by the evidence on issue, upon which the Chamber will decide, on a case-by-case basis whether or not to allow such participation. For example, should a victim demonstrate that his personal interests would be negatively affected if a particular witness (who could attest to the harm suffered by the victim) was not called to testify or if a piece of evidence (which would have ramifications on the safety and security of the victim) were to be declared admissible, then the victim would be able to move the Chamber to exercise its

---

[52] *The Prosecutor* v. *Thomas Lubanga*, ICC-01/04-01/06, *Judgment on the Appeals of the Prosecution and the Defence against Trial Chamber I's Decision on Victims' Participation of 18 January 2008*, 11 July 2008, at 33.

[53] Rome Statute, Article 68(1) and RPE, Rule 16(1)(d).

powers under Article 69(3) to present the evidence or challenge admissibility of the evidence respectively".[54]

Therefore, the modalities of victims' participation will vary according to the personal interests of the victims. At the least, victims will be kept informed of decisions that affect their interests in the case. In particular, they have the right to be informed when the confirmation of charges against the accused will take place.[55] More importantly, participating victims are given a voice, because they or their legal representatives are granted the right to present their "views and concerns".[56] Judges have interpreted this right to mean that victims do not simply express their views and concerns in writing, but are present in court[57] and their participation "may include making opening and closing statements".[58] The opening statement is an important modality of victim participation. The legal representative is given the opportunity to persuade the Court of the important elements of the case from the victim's perspective. Victims may under some circumstances be allowed to give oral testimony.[59] The presentation of views and concerns are different from giving oral testimony, because the views and concerns of victims do not form part of the trial evidence. In order for participating victims to contribute to the evidence in the trial, it is necessary for them to give evidence under oath from the witness box.

Additionally, legal representatives have been allowed to: be present in the courtroom, make oral submissions, have access to all public evidence; provide and challenge evidence; question witnesses, provided such questioning does not prejudice the accused and that victim intervention assists in better understanding the cultural and social context of the case; question experts and the accused, provided it is limited to clarifying points at issue or completing the evidence; call new witnesses; present documentary evidence; and participate in the witness familiarization process.[60] They may also produce incriminating and exonerating evidence in order to help the establishment of the truth, as long as it does not prejudice the defense, and

---

[54] *The Prosecutor* v. *Thomas Lubanga*, ICC-01/04-01/06, *Judgment on the Appeals of the Prosecution and the Defence against Trial Chamber I's Decision on Victims' Participation of 18 January 2008*, 11 July 2008, at 33.

[55] RPE, Rule 92. in particular r. 92(3).

[56] Rome Statute, July 17, 1998, 2187 U.N.T.S, Article, art. 68(3).

[57] *The Prosecutor* v. *Bahar Idriss Abu Garda*, Case No. ICC-02/05-02/09-136 17–18; *Prosecutor v. Jean-Pierre Gombo Bemba,* Case No. ICC-01/05-01/08-320 101.

[58] See the *Prosecutor* v. *Thomas Lubanga Dyilo*, ICC-01/04-01/06-462-tEN 6 and ICC-01/04-01/06-1119, Trial Chamber I, 18 January 2008, par. 117; *Prosecutor* v. *Bahar Idriss Abu Garda*, at 19; *Prosecutor* v. *Germain Katanga and Mathieu Ngudjolo Chui*, ICC-01/04-01/07-1665, Trial Chamber II, 20 November 2009, p. 9; *Prosecutor* v. *Jean-Pierre Gombo Bemba*, at 102.

[59] *The Prosecutor* v. *Germain Katanga and Mathieu Ngudjolo Chui*, ICC-01/04-01/07-1665, Trial Chamber II, 20 November 2009, paras 19–30.

[60] *The Prosecutor* v. *Katanga & Ngudjolo Chui*, Case No. ICC-01/04-01/07, Decision on the Modalities of Victim Participation at Trial, paras 72, 74–75, 78–81, 94, 99 (Jan. 22, 2010). http://www.icc-cpi.int/iccdocs/doc/doc831030.pdf. Accessed 21 February 2020.

may file written motions and gain access to confidential documents and evidence in the case.[61]

The modalities of victim participation guide the relationship between the legal representative and the victim. The main objective of the legal representative is efficient representation of the victim. As Judge van den Wijngeart stated: "The Chamber considers it of utmost importance that there be a steady and reliable flow of information about the proceedings to the victims and that there is real involvement by the victims in terms of instructing the legal representatives on how their interest should be represented".[62]

Legal representatives will represent a number of victims. As a consequence, once the legal representative has gathered all the evidence, he/she should meet with the victims in order to decide on a case strategy. In doing so, the legal representative should collaborate with other local community based resources. The victim should be encouraged to reach out to these other professionals to help the client address the variety of needs including safety planning, economic independence, physical or mental health issues. Because of safety issues, it is even more important that the legal representative keeps the victim's information and statements confidential. The legal representative must ensure that no relevant personal information of the victim and/or children are divulged.

6 Conclusion

The representation of victims of violent sexual and reproductive crimes must be seen as part of the overall investigation and prosecution of these crimes. It is part of a coordinated effort.

Suggested Further Resources:

- OPVC, *Representing Victims before the International Criminal Court, A Manual for legal representatives*, ICC-OPCV-MLR-002/13, 5th edition, 2019, available at https://www.icc-cpi.int/Pages/item.aspx?name=pr1447. Accessed 25 March 2020.
- Office of the Prosecution, *Statement of the Prosecutor of the International Criminal Court, Fatou Bensouda, providing an update on the ICC-OTP Policy Paper on Sexual and Gender-Based Crimes,* 07 March 2014, available at https://www.icc-cpi.int/Pages/item.aspx?name=statement-otp-07-03-2014. Accessed 25 March 2020.
- OPCV's Proposal on the Division of Responsibilities and Effective Functioning of the Common Legal Representation System, *The Prosecutor,* v. *William*

[61] *The Prosecutor* v. *Katanga & Ngudjolo Chui*, Case No. ICC-01/04-01/07, Decision on the Modalities of Victim Participation at Trial, paras 81, 107, 121–22.

[62] *The Prosecutor* v. *Germain Katanga and Mathieu Ngudjolo Chui,* ICC-01/04-01/07-1665, at para 7.

Samoei Ruto and Joshua Arap Sang, ICC-01/09-01/11, 17 October 2012, available at https://www.icc-cpi.int/Pages/record.aspx?docNo=ICC-01/09-01/11-462. Accessed 25 March 2020.

References

Boesten, J., & Fisher, M. (2012). *Sexual violence and justice in postconflict Peru*, United States Institute for Peace Report, 2012. Retrieved February 21, 2020, from http://www.usip.org/publications/sexual-violence-and-justice-in-postconflict-peru

Funk, T. M. (2010). *Victim's rights and advocacy at the International Criminal Court*. OUP.

McGonigle Leyh, B. (2011). *Procedural justice? Victim participation in international criminal proceedings*. Intersentia.

Schabas, W. A. (2007). *An introduction to the International Criminal Court* (3rd ed.). Cambridge University Press.

Solange Mouthaan is an Associate Professor at the University of Warwick, School of Law. Her research interests focus on two defined fields related to the protection of people under international law: first, the legal protection of minorities, particularly linguistic minorities, and, second, the effective protection of individuals through the International Criminal Law. Her current research project falls in the realm of international criminal law with especial reference to the notion of gender, children and gendered aspects of armed conflict. She examines the developments of international criminal law through the workings of the ICC regarding the protection, voice and role given during the trials to victims of gender-based crimes, such as children. Her recent publications include 'Barefoot, pregnant and in the kitchen: am I a child soldier too?' Women's Studies International Forum, 51, 2015 and 'The ICC and victim participation for victims of gender-based crimes - a conflict of interest?' Cardozo Journal of International and Comparative Law, 21 (3) 2013. She obtained her degrees at the Université de Paris.

Representing Victims Who Are Children

Francesca Capone

1 Introduction

This Chapter focuses on a specific group of victims who have been enjoying very limited visibility and recognition in the international criminal law framework. Children's rights in international proceedings, in particular those established to bring to justice the authors of the most reprehensible crimes, have been often overlooked and neglected. In contexts where an international or internal armed conflict occurs, several observers have noted that the civilian population is often targeted by the parties involved, and that the commission of systematic atrocities is often the result of a rational strategy within current warfare (Kaldor, 1999). Children are no longer, and probably never have been, the passive bystanders of such atrocities. On the contrary, they tend to be deliberately victimised and in some cases even used as perpetrators (Capone, 2017). The establishment of the Special Court for Sierra Leone (SCSL), a hybrid court which dealt for the first time with the crime of recruitment, enlistment and use of child soldiers, and the entry into force of the Rome Statute of the International Criminal Court (ICC)[1] have contributed to draw attention to the issue of child victims of gross international humanitarian law and international human rights law violations.

The situation of children involved in judicial proceedings has been the subject of extensive studies conducted, *inter alia*, by the UN relevant agencies and bodies. In particular, in 2005 the UN Economic and Social Council (ECOSOC) adopted a set of guidelines on justice for child victims and witnesses of crime in which it was clearly stated that 'children who are victims and witnesses are particularly vulnerable and

[1] Rome Statute of the International Criminal Court (last amended 2010), 17 July 1998, 37 ILM 1002 (1998) 2187 UNTS 90 (Rome Statute).

F. Capone (✉)
Public International Law, Scuola Superiore Sant'Anna, Pisa, Italy
e-mail: f.capone@santannapisa.it

E. King et al. (eds.), *Victim Advocacy before the International Criminal Court*,
https://doi.org/10.1007/978-3-030-56733-0_13

need special assistance, protection and support, appropriate to their age, level of maturity and unique needs in order to prevent future hardship and trauma that may result from their participation in the criminal justice processes'.[2] In addition to children's peculiarities as particularly vulnerable subjects, the judicial system, both at the national and international level, should respect and implement the key principles enshrined in the Convention on the Rights of the Child (CRC),[3] especially the primary consideration of the child's best interests and the right of the child to participate in the proceedings affecting him or her. Ensuring child victims' rights represents at the same time a challenge and a priority which cannot be achieved without guaranteeing the accused's fair trial standards and without striking a balance between children's right to be active stakeholders and their right to be protected from harm. For instance, investigation and practices of judicial bodies should be adapted to afford greater protection to children and to respect children's rights without undermining the defendant's right to a fair trial.[4] Moreover, the existence of less strict rules on giving evidence such as absence of the requirement for oath or other similar declarations, or other child-friendly procedural measures, should not be perceived as a threat to the rights of the accused, but rather as actions to guarantee the exercise of children's rights.

The present Chapter is going to address all these issues and will particularly introduce and discuss the main challenges that representing children in international criminal proceedings entails. More in detail, this contribution will provide an overview of children's current situation within the international criminal justice framework, dwelling in particular on the experiences of the SCSL and of the ICC. With regard to the latter, which represents the paramount focus of this Chapter, it is important to note that the first judgment issued by the ICC against Mr Lubanga will be used as a recurring example to highlight the most crucial issues which emerged in the case and that, in the author's opinion, hindered the full exercise of children's rights and the respect of children's prerogatives as vulnerable victims.

A large number of provisions throughout the Rome Statute underline the important role of victims and guarantee the participation of their families or their representatives at every stage of the proceedings, from the initiation of investigations to

[2] UN Economic and Social Council (ECOSOC), UN Economic and Social Council 2005/20: Guidelines on Justice in Matters Involving Child Victims and Witnesses of Crime, 22 July 2005, E/RES/2005/20 (Guidelines on Justice in Matters Involving Child Victims and Witnesses of Crime).

[3] UN General Assembly, Convention on the Rights of the Child, 20 November 1989, United Nations, Treaty Series, vol. 1577, p. 3.

[4] The Guidelines on Action for Children in the Justice System in Africa, adopted at the Global Conference on Child Justice held in Kampala, Uganda, on 7–8 November, 2011. The Guidelines are available at: https://juvenilejusticecentre.org/resources/guidelines-on-action-for-children-in-the-justice-system-in-africa/. Accessed 20 May 2020. See also the Guidelines of the Committee of Ministers of the Council of Europe on Child Friendly Justice (Adopted by the Committee of Ministers on 17 November 2010 at the 1098th meeting of the Ministers' Deputies. Available at: http://www.coe.int/t/dghl/standardsetting/childjustice/Guidelines%20on%20childfriendly%20justice%20and%20their%20explanatory%20memorandum%20_4_.pdf. Accessed 4 March 2020.

post-conviction proceedings. Such provisions also discern the right of victims and their families to reparations, including compensation, restitution and rehabilitation.[5] In the case of child victims the provisions have not always been applied or implemented in accordance with the principles embedded in the CRC or, more in generally, in accordance with children's needs as vulnerable victims (Chamberlain, 2015).

The following sections, hence, will tackle four aspects that emerged in the Lubanga case and that will remain a key concern for the Court's present and future relationship with child victims, namely children's vulnerability, the special needs of children, in particular girls affected by sexual violence, the protective measures in place for children who participate in the proceedings as witnesses and finally the question of children and their right to reparation.

2 Child Victims' Best Interests and the Right to Express Their Views in International Criminal Proceedings

The first consideration in relation to children who come in contact with judicial procedures is to determine what is in their best interests.[6] Article 3, paragraph 1, of the CRC provides the child with the right to have his or her best interests assessed and taken into account as a primary concern in all actions or decisions that affect him or her, both in the public and private sphere (Zermatten, 2010). The concept of the 'child's best interests' is not new, but in fact it pre-dates the CRC and was already enshrined in the 1959 Declaration of the Rights of the Child,[7] the Convention on the Elimination of All Forms of Discrimination against Women (CEDAW),[8] as well as in regional instruments, many national legislations and international law.[9] Despite the broad use of this concept, the 'child's best interests' has been properly defined only through the adoption of the Committee on the Rights of the Child (CRC Committee or the Committee) General Comment 14, in 2013.

According to the Committee, the best interests of the child is a dynamic concept that encompasses various issues which are continuously evolving (Zermatten, 2015).

[5] Art 75(1) Rome Statute.

[6] Art. 3(1) of the UN Convention on the Rights of the Child. According to this provision: 'In all actions concerning children, whether undertaken by public or private social welfare institutions, courts of law, administrative authorities or legislative bodies, the best interests of the child shall be a primary consideration.'

[7] UN General Assembly, Declaration of the Rights of the Child, 20 November 1959, A/RES/1386 (XIV), at para 2.

[8] UN General Assembly, Convention on the Elimination of All Forms of Discrimination Against Women, 18 December 1979, United Nations, Treaty Series, vol. 1249, p. 13. Arts. 5 (b) and 16, para. 1 (d).

[9] Committee on the Rights of the Child, General Comment No. 14 (2013) on the right of the child to have his or her best interests taken as a primary consideration (Art. 3, para. 1), CRC/C/GC/14.

It should be read as a threefold concept, which entails a substantive right, a fundamental interpretative legal principle and a rule of procedure.[10] With regard to the first, the Committee explains that Article 3(1) creates an intrinsic obligation for States, which is directly applicable (self-executing) and can be invoked before a court. Moreover, as a substantive right it should be guaranteed that it will be implemented whenever a decision is to be made concerning a child, a group of identified or unidentified children or children in general. Secondly, the best interests of the child as a fundamental, interpretative legal principle implies that if a legal provision is open to more than one interpretation, the interpretation which most effectively serves the child's best interests should be chosen. Thirdly, as a rule of procedure, the best interests of the child requires that whenever a decision is to be made that will affect a specific child, an identified group of children or children in general, the decision-making process must include an evaluation of the possible impact (positive or negative) of the decision on the child or children concerned. In other words, the decision must be the result of the assessment and determination of what is the best interests of the child under the specific circumstances. Assessment and determination of the child's best interests are two fundamental steps. The 'best-interests assessment' consists of evaluating and balancing all the elements and factors necessary to make a decision in a specific situation for a specific individual child or group of children. It is carried out by the decision-maker, if possible assisted by a multidisciplinary team, and requires the direct and active participation of the child. The 'best-interests determination' describes the formal process with strict procedural safeguards designed to determine the child's best interests on the basis of the best-interests assessment.[11] In cases where a child finds him or herself in what the Committee defines as a 'situation of vulnerability' (e.g. children affected by disability, armed conflict, gender violence, children belonging to a minority group, refugees or asylum seekers, victims of abuse, street children etc...) authorities and decision-makers need to take into account the different kinds and degrees of vulnerability of each child, as each child is unique and each situation must be assessed according to the child's uniqueness.[12]

The notion of the 'child's best interests' is aimed at ensuring both the full and effective enjoyment of all the rights recognized in the CRC and the holistic development of the child, which shall embrace the child's physical, mental, spiritual, moral, psychological and social development.[13] In one of its General Comments, the Committee on the Rights of the Child has further explained that 'an adult's judgment

[10] Committee on the Rights of the Child, General Comment No. 14 (2013) on the right of the child to have his or her best interests taken as a primary consideration (Art. 3, para. 6), CRC/C/GC/14.

[11] Committee on the Rights of the Child, General Comment No. 14 (2013) on the right of the child to have his or her best interests taken as a primary consideration (Art. 3, para. 47), CRC/C/GC/14. See also UNHCR, Guidelines on Determining the Best Interests of the Child, May 2008, available at: http://www.unhcr.org/4566b16b2.pdf. Accessed 4 March 2020.

[12] Committee on the Rights of the Child, General comment No. 14, at para 76.

[13] Committee on the Rights of the Child, General Comment No. 5 (2003), General Measures of Implementation of the Convention on the Rights of the Child, CRC/GC/2003/5.

of a child's best interests cannot override the obligation to respect all the child's rights under the Convention'.[14] This means that since no hierarchy exists among the provisions enshrined in the CRC, all the rights provided for therein are in the 'child's best interests' and no right could be compromised by a negative interpretation of the child's best interests.[15] Significantly the Committee clarifies that the assessment of a child's best interests must include respect for the child's right to express his or her views as stated in Article 12 of the CRC. These two Articles, 3 and 12, appear to be intimately entwined and mutually reinforcing. In particular, Article 3(1) cannot be correctly applied if the requirements of Article 12 are not met. Similarly, by facilitating the essential role of children in all decisions affecting their lives, Article 3(1) is crucial for the implementation of Article 12.

Article 12 of the CRC is represented as one of the most innovative of the Convention and it is considered as a unique provision in human rights treaty law.[16] Its scope is to address the legal and social status of children, who, on the one hand lack the adults' full autonomy but, on the other hand, are recognized by the CRC as subjects of rights. Paragraph 1 assures to every child capable of forming his or her own views the right to express those views freely. Paragraph 2 states, in particular, that the child shall be afforded the right to be heard in any judicial or administrative proceedings affecting him or her.[17] Article 12 attributes the right to be heard not only to an individual child, but also to a group of children (e.g. the children in a neighbourhood, the children of a given country, children with disabilities, girls, and children associated with armed forces or groups). In both cases, i.e. views expressed individually or as a group, due weight should be given in accordance with age and maturity. Article 12 states very clearly that age alone cannot determine the significance of a child's views. In fact, children's levels of understanding are not uniformly linked to their biological age. Research has shown that many factors, such as information, experience, environment, social and cultural expectations and levels of support, contribute in different ways to the development of a child's capacities to form his or her view (UNICEF, 2012). For this reason, the views of the child have to be assessed on a case-by-case examination (Bradley & Corwyn, 2002). Maturity is mentioned in Article 12 as one of the key factors that shall be taken into account when determining the individual capacity of a child. Generally speaking maturity

---

[14] Committee on the Rights of the Child, General Comment No. 13 (2011), The right of the child to freedom from all forms of violence, CRC/C/GC/13, at para 61.

[15] Committee on the Rights of the Child, General comment No. 14 (2013) The right of the child to have his or her best interests taken as a primary consideration, CRC /C/GC/14, at para 4.

[16] Article 12 of the CRC establishes that: '1. States Parties shall assure to the child who is capable of forming his or her own views the right to express those views freely in all matters affecting the child, the views of the child being given due weight in accordance with the age and maturity of the child. 2. For this purpose the child shall in particular be provided the opportunity to be heard in any judicial and administrative proceedings affecting the child, either directly, or through a representative or an appropriate body, in a manner consistent with the procedural Rules of the national law'.

[17] The Committee on the Rights of the Child, General Comment No. 12 (2009) The right of the child to be heard, CRC/C/GC/12, at para.3.

refers to the ability to understand and assess the implications of a particular matter; in the context of Article 12 it can be defined as the capacity of a child to express, in a reasonable and independent manner, her or his views on various issues. As pointed out by the Committee, evaluating the views expressed by the child cannot disregard the impact of the matter on the child. In particular it shall be borne in mind that 'a child cannot be heard effectively where the environment is intimidating, hostile, insensitive or inappropriate for her or his age'.[18]

According to the principles embedded in the CRC, proceedings must be both accessible and child-appropriate. In particular it is necessary to pay attention to the provision and delivery of child-friendly information, adequate support for self-advocacy, appropriately trained staff, design of courtrooms, clothing of judges and lawyers, sight screens, and separate waiting rooms.[19] As stressed by the Committee, children are free to decide whether or not they wish to exercise their rights. Expressing views, for instance, must always remain a choice for the child, not an obligation, and this applies to all kinds of proceedings, i.e. administrative, civil or criminal. Clearly children can participate in criminal proceedings as offenders or as victims and witnesses. As the latter categories are the focus of this contribution, it is important to note that the principles embedded in the CRC are also affirmed in the ECOSOC Guidelines,[20] which remark that every possible effort has to be made to ensure that a child victim or/and witness is consulted on the relevant matters with regard to his or her involvement in the case under scrutiny.

Given the fact that the right enshrined in Article 12 needs to be implemented in accordance with the factors that characterise a specific situation, it is not possible to dictate in general terms how exactly the child's views should be heard. In its General Comment, the key findings of which have been highlighted above, the Committee sets out a number of general principles, according to which processes involving children must be: transparent and informative, voluntary, respectful, relevant, child-friendly, inclusive, supported by specific training, safe and sensitive to risk and accountable.[21] In line with the provisions embedded in Articles 3(1) and 12 of the CRC, investigations and trials, both at the national and at the international level, must take all possible steps to minimize the risk of harm to the child and ensure that his or her rights are fully respected and duly implemented. At the international level, however, according to the Office of the Special Representative of the Secretary General for Children and Armed conflict, the current situation before international

[18] The Committee on the Rights of the Child, General Comment No. 12 (2009) The right of the child to be heard, CRC/C/GC/12, at para. 34.

[19] The Committee on the Rights of the Child, General Comment No. 12 (2009) The right of the child to be heard, CRC/C/GC/12, at para. 34.

[20] Guidelines on Justice in Matters Involving Child Victims and Witnesses of Crime, ECOSOC Resolution 2005/20 of 22 July 2005, available at: https://www.un.org/en/ecosoc/docs/2005/resolution%202005-20.pdf. Accessed 20 May 2020.

[21] Guidelines on Justice in Matters Involving Child Victims and Witnesses of Crime, ECOSOC Resolution 2005/20 of 22 July 2005, at para 134, available at: https://www.un.org/en/ecosoc/docs/2005/resolution%202005-20.pdf. Accessed 20 May 2020.

and hybrid courts does not reflect the standards set in the CRC and in the ECOSOC Guidelines (Beresford, 2005). In fact

> at present time, all the international and hybrid courts require children to give evidence during the trial and to be subject to cross-examination. It is not possible for the child to give pre-recorded testimony, although many western legal systems now permit this. Neither does the ICC permit the use of intermediaries to rephrase questions in simpler language, enabling the child to give a clear and unambiguous response.[22]

Bearing in mind the fundamental provisions enshrined in Articles 3(1) and 12 of the CRC and the guidance offered by the Committee on the Rights of the Child in its General Comments, the following subsections will provide a concise overview of the current situation of child victims before international and hybrid courts and, in particular, of the extent to which child-friendly principles have been concretely implemented in the different settings.

3 An Overview of Provisions Governing Child Victims' Rights Within the Current International Criminal Justice Framework

Until the adoption of the Rome Statute, the rights of victims in international criminal law were to a large extent marginalised (Mouthaan, 2013). Before the ICC was set up, other international criminal tribunals, e.g. the International Criminal Tribunal for the former Yugoslavia (ICTY) and the International Criminal Tribunal for Rwanda (ICTR), did not provide victims with significant rights and were mainly concerned with bringing criminals to justice (Cohen, 2009; Zappalà, 2003; Shabas, 2011).

With regard in particular to child victims, it should be noted that the Statute and the RPE of both the ICTY and the ICTR failed to include any child-specific provisions. Moreover, even though the ad hoc tribunals have dealt with cases involving crimes committed against children, none of them is statutorily required to hire staff with proper expertise on child protection and children's rights. For the crimes of sexual violence that targeted also children and that have been addressed before the ICTY and the ICTR, the testimony of the adult witnesses were considered sufficient to corroborate the evidence, and minors have not been heard at all.[23] Generally speaking, so far only a few children have appeared as witnesses before international

[22] Office of the Special Representative of the Secretary General for Children and Armed conflict, Working Paper No 3, Children and Justice During and in the Aftermath of Armed Conflict, September 2011, at p. 16, available at: http://childrenandarmedconflict.un.org/publications/WorkingPaper-3_Children-and-Justice.pdf. (Children and Justice During and in the Aftermath of Armed Conflict) Accessed 20 May 2020.

[23] See, for instance, *Prosecutor v. Jean Paul Akayesu* (ICTR-96-4), 2 September 1998, at para 416 et ss. And also *Prosecutor v. Dragoljob Kunarac, Radomir Kovac and Zoran Vukovic* (Foča case, IT-96-23 and IT-96-23/1), 22 February 2001.

and hybrid tribunals. With regard to the latter typology of courts, it should be stressed that the Special Court for Sierra Leone distinguished itself in this field by adopting several procedures and measures to ensure protection for young people in order to avoid their re-traumatization. Notably, the SCSL recognises the participation of victims in the proceeding only as witnesses, however, some interesting features deserve to be highlighted and properly introduced in the following section.

3.1 Children Before the Special Court for Sierra Leone

As stated above, the issue of balancing the fair trial standards enshrined under human rights law with the need to give voice to child victims, who are often accused of giving tainted evidence and of being influenced by adults,[24] has emerged also with regard to the work of the Special Court for Sierra Leone. In the first place it is interesting to note that the Court confers to the notion of 'child' (witness) a broad significance in the sense that the prosecution's principal criteria to determine whether or not a witness can be regarded as a 'child witness' is his or her past as child soldier. More in detail, the Court focuses only on the witness' personal history and vulnerability; therefore the individual's actual age is not taken into account (Sanin & Stirnemann, 2006). During the SCSL's years of activities,[25] the Prosecutor called several child witnesses to give evidence and support the charges against the leading members of three armed groups accused of conscripting and enlisting child combatants.[26]

The prosecution teams decided to include a witness in the child witnesses' category (named category B) if one of the following conditions occurred: the witness him/herself claimed to know his/her age, the age was already determined during the demobilisation process, the legal guardian knew the alleged child witness age, or the person was a former child soldier. Once a witness was recognised as a child witness, he or she was entitled to benefit from the special measures set up by the SCSL. Article 16(4) of the Statute established the Witnesses and Victims Services Unit

---

[24] Office of the Special Representative of the Secretary General for Children and Armed conflict, Working Paper No 3, Children and Justice During and in the Aftermath of Armed Conflict, September 2011, at p. 15, available at: http://childrenandarmedconflict.un.org/publications/WorkingPaper-3_Children-and-Justice.pdf. Accessed 20 May 2020. 'There may be accusations that children may be more inclined to give the answers that they think the adult wants to hear, and [. . .] may learn their testimony as they go, taking their cue from the adults who interview or assist them.' Moreover, there is a risk that child witnesses may learn their testimony as they go, taking their cue from the adults who interview or assist them.

[25] The SCSL completed its mandate in 2013 and since then has transitioned to a residual mechanism.

[26] The Appeals Chamber of the SCSL on 23 September 2013 upheld the conviction of former Liberian President, Charles Ghankay Taylor, for a range of crimes under international law, including recruiting children under the age of 15 years and using them to participate actively in hostilities.

(WVSU) within the Registry and according to it the Unit was in charge of providing counselling and assistance to all the witnesses, including children. Rule 34 of the Rules of Procedure and Evidence (RPE) further states that the WVSU is in charge of developing both short and long-term plans for witnesses' protection and support. According to Rule 69(b), the Trial Chamber should consult the WVSU with regard to the protective measures that had to be taken during the trial, which may have encompassed the non-disclosure of a victim's identity and the testimony via video link from a different room.[27] As reported by the Office of the Special Representative of the Secretary General for Children and Armed Conflict, all child witnesses at the SCSL gave evidence seated outside the courtroom, using video conferencing.[28]

In order to accomplish child witnesses' protection the Special Court designed, relying on UNICEF's expertise, a set of guidelines able to promote children's participation without jeopardising the efforts to overcome the traumatic events experienced. In the first place the WVSU, the Office of the Prosecution (OTP) and the experts from UNICEF identified suitable child witnesses amongst those who were more resilient and already resettled within their families and communities. Secondly, UNICEF provided an intensive training to both prosecution and defence investigators in order to make them able to interrogate the child witnesses, taking into account their best interests and according to the guidelines developed.[29] As explained above, the exercise of children's right to participation, enshrined in Article 12 of the CRC, is subject to the full consent of the child, the parents or the legal guardian. Since many children were still displaced when the SCSL started its work and the first witnesses were selected, the consent was often given by the child or by the child protection agency (CPA) responsible for taking care of him/her during the process of demobilisation. Upon confirmation, child witnesses were brought to Freetown, where the Special Court was located. At this stage child witnesses were accommodated in the so-called 'safe houses', assigned also to the adult witnesses who, according to the SCLS investigators, were threatened by their own community (Horn et al., 2011). Immediately after their arrival, child witnesses were provided by the WVUS's qualified staff with psychosocial support and relevant information about the process and the procedures thereof. Children, just as adult witnesses, were entitled to an allowance for their service before the Court, an allowance

[27] See also Rule 75 and 85 of the SCSL' RPE, last amended May 2005. The option to testify in camera or via video link was available for all vulnerable witnesses, including children. Despite the fact that neither the Statute nor the RPE took into account children's vulnerability, the Trial Chambers ruled that child witnesses under 18 must always have the opportunity to testify using these methods, instead than appearing in the courtroom.

[28] Office of the Special Representative of the Secretary General for Children and Armed conflict, Working Paper No 3, Children and Justice During and in the Aftermath of Armed Conflict, September 2011, endnote 27, available at: http://childrenandarmedconflict.un.org/publications/WorkingPaper-3_Children-and-Justice.pdf. Accessed 20 May 2020.

[29] Office of the Special Representative of the Secretary General for Children and Armed conflict, Working Paper No 3, Children and Justice During and in the Aftermath of Armed Conflict, September 2011, endnote 27, available at: http://childrenandarmedconflict.un.org/publications/WorkingPaper-3_Children-and-Justice.pdf. Accessed 20 May 2020.

which corresponded to 16,000 Leones per day, the equivalent of 5.25 USD.[30] Notwithstanding the fact that the amount of the allowance was in line with the witness compensation scheme adopted at the ICTY and the ICTR, the payments made by the Special Court to its witnesses have attracted much criticism, mostly due to the 'chronic poverty' of the country and the huge gap existing between the allowance and the average salary received by workers of the public and private sectors. In particular with regard to children, one of the biggest concerns expressed by UNICEF pertained to the individualistic approach followed by the Court, which privileged the payment of benefits to each child witness rather than the development of a comprehensive strategic plan able to trigger the reintegration and rehabilitation of a larger number of children.

Another point raised by UNICEF was that the child witnesses after the trial appeared 'ill equipped for the reality of the life in Sierra Leone', as they normally came back to school with clothes and supplies that prompted the classmates to think that the child in question was a former child soldier who has been taking advantage of the national demobilisation efforts (Sanin & Stirnemann, 2006, p. 24; Drumbl, 2012).

4 Child Victims Before the International Criminal Court

The Preamble of the Rome Statute affirms that ensuring justice for victims represents one of the main goals of the International Criminal Court. In particular the drafters of the Rome Statute declare that for the sake of present and *future* generations, they undertook to establish the ICC 'mindful that during this century millions of children, women and men have been the victims of unimaginable atrocities that deeply shock the conscience of humanity'.[31] The central place of victims in the Statute has led to granting victims' rights *as victims,* rather than merely providing rights as witnesses (McCarthy, 2012). Participating in a proceeding, in fact, is different from serving as a witness: participation is voluntary and allows the victim to communicate his or her own views and concerns to the Court at various stages of the proceedings, whereas a witness serves the interest of the Court and is called by either the defense or the prosecution to testify at a specific time about specific facts or events (Mouthaan, 2013).

The ICC recognises two types of victims for the purposes of participation in its proceedings: individual persons who suffered harm as a result of one of the crimes listed in the Rome Statute; and organisations or institutions, when their property dedicated to certain purposes (religion, education, art, science or charitable and humanitarian purposes, or historic monuments or hospitals) is harmed as a result

[30] The allowance corresponds to the daily salary of a UN General Service 1, step 1 level employee in Sierra Leone.

[31] See the Preamble of the Rome Statute of the International Criminal Court.

of one of the ICC crimes.[32] Victims can be 'direct', namely persons against whom the illegal conduct is directed immediately, explicitly and deliberately, or indirect, i.e. the persons who do not suffer the illegal conduct in the same way (immediately, directly and deliberately), but who also see their own rights affected or violated from the impact on the so-called direct victim.[33] With regard specifically to child victims, the Rome Statute incorporates children's rights in different ways: firstly by including provisions which punish crimes committed against children; secondly requiring that judicial staff have expertise on children's issues, e.g. children's vulnerability; and finally, recognising that special measures are necessary to protect children as victims and witnesses during judicial proceedings.[34]

The Lubanga case,[35] the first judgment issued by the ICC,[36] provides an important record of the extent to which the 'new' course of international criminal law can be regarded as one that it is truly mindful of children's rights as embedded in the CRC. In the *Lubanga case* the Court recognised as direct victims the children enlisted, conscripted or used as soldiers and as indirect victims those persons with a close relationship with the child soldiers (such as their parents) and those who have suffered as a result of their attempts to prevent the recruitment of child soldiers.[37] The Court was called to deal with a number of challenges such as the special vulnerability of the children involved in the proceeding, the issues related to gender-based violence, the reliability of child witnesses and, finally, the thorny matter of the principles and procedures to be applied to reparations. All of them will be discussed in detail in the following sections to provide a comprehensive account of the key issues that child victims' participation in international criminal proceedings entails.

---

[32] Rule 85 of the ICC Rules of Procedure and Evidence (RPE).

[33] See the Judgement on the Appeal of The Prosecutor and the Defence against Trial Chamber I's Decision on Victims' Participation of 18 January 2008, ICC-01/04-01/06-1432. See also ICC-01/04-01/06-1119; ICC-01/04-01/06-1813. In defining direct and indirect victims the ICC has relied specifically on the jurisprudence of the Inter-American Court of Human Rights (IACtHR), for instance *Case of the Ituango Massacres v. Colombia*, (Preliminary Objections, Merits, Reparations and Costs) Ser.C, No 148, 1 July 2006, Separate Concurring Opinion of Judge S. Garcia Ramirez, at para 11.

[34] The International Criminal Court and Children's Rights, The American Non Governmental Organizations Coalition for the International Criminal Court, available at: http://www.iccnow.org/documents/FS-AMICC-ICCnChildRights.pdf. Accessed 4 March 2020.

[35] Thomas Lubanga Dyilo, founder of the Union des Patriots Congolais (UPC) and commander in-chief of its military wing, the Forces Patriotiques pour la Liberation du Congo (FPLC), was convicted of the war crime of conscripting and enlisting children under the age of 15 and using them to participate actively in hostilities in an armed conflict not of an international character, as set out in Art. 8(2)(e)(vii) of the Rome Statute.

[36] *Prosecutor v. Thomas Lubanga*, Case No. ICC-01/04-01/06, Judgment Pursuant to Article 74 of the Statute, 14 March 2012.

[37] Decision on victims' participation, 18 January 2008, ICC-01/04-01/06-1119; Judgment on the Appeal of The Prosecutor and the Defence against Trial Chamber I's Decision on Victims' Participation of 18 January 2008, 11 July 2008, ICC-01/04-01/06-1432; Redacted Version of Decision on 'indirect victims', 8 April 2009, ICC-01/04-01/06-1813, at para 48.

5 Crimes Against Children in the Rome Statute

From the outset some preliminary clarifications are needed. In the first place it is important to determine which wrongful conducts affecting children are criminalised under the Rome Statute. Generally speaking under international criminal law, crimes committed against children can be divided in three sub-categories: child-specific crimes, in which children are a material element of the crime (e.g. forced transfer of children and imposition of measures intended to prevent births in order to perpetrate genocide, enlistment, conscription and use of children to participate in hostilities); crimes which target children in a way that they are disproportionately victimised in comparison to the adult population (e.g. destruction of schools and hospitals, attacks to humanitarian missions); crimes with particularly serious effects on children, in which children, due to their age and development, face more difficulties to be rehabilitated than adult-victims (e.g. rape and sexual violence), (Capone, 2017).

The Rome Statute encompasses all the typologies of crimes against children introduced above. More in detail Article 6(e) criminalises as genocide the forcible transfer of children from a group to another with the intent to destroy, in whole or in part a national, ethnic, or racial group as such. Articles 7(1)(c) outlaws widespread or systematic enslavement, including trafficking in children, whilst Article 8(2)(b)(xxvi), (e)(vii) lists as war crimes the conscription, enlistment or use to actively participate in hostilities of child soldiers under the age of fifteen years, both in international and non-international armed conflicts. As for the second category of crimes, those which affect children disproportionately, the Rome Statute condemns intentional attacks against non-military objectives such as buildings dedicated to religion, education, art, science or charitable purposes, Article 8(2)(b)(xxiv), (e)(ii), and also attacks against personnel, installations, material, units or vehicles involved in a humanitarian assistance or UN peacekeeping missions, as stated in Article 8(2)(b)(iii), (e)(iii). Finally, the wrongful conducts which fall within the third category of crimes, are duly criminalised by Articles 7(1)(g), 8(2)(b)(xxii), (e)(vi), according to which rape, sexual slavery, enforced prostitution, forced pregnancy, enforced sterilization and other forms of sexual violence amount to both war crimes and crimes against humanity.

International criminal law's taxonomy of crimes affecting children matches the 'Six Grave Violations against Children' (during an armed conflict) identified by the UN Security Council.[38] Such crimes, singled out due to their especially egregious nature and severe impact on a child's wellbeing are: killing or maiming; recruitment or use of child soldiers; rape and other forms of sexual violence; abduction; attacks against schools or hospitals; and denial of humanitarian access. The classification by the UN of the worst crimes affecting children in armed conflict and the specular provisions enshrined in the Rome Statute shall be read as evidence of the fact that children's victimhood is characterised by unique features and that the international community is finally striving to acknowledge it.

[38] UNSC Res. 1612 (2005) and 1882 (2009).

6 Child Victims' Vulnerability

The urge to provide child victims with specific provisions stems from the assumption that children constitute a particularly vulnerable group of victims. Vulnerability can be generally defined as 'the exposure to uninsured risks leading to a socially unacceptable level of well-being' and it is measured according to physical and emotional development, ability to communicate needs, mobility, size and dependence' (Hoogeveen et al., 2005). From a legal point of view, even though the notion of vulnerability has not been clearly defined at either the national or international level, the necessity of special treatment of certain categories of victims is well established and acknowledged.[39] According to the Recommendation on Assistance to Crime Victims of the Council of Europe: '[S]tates should ensure that victims who are particularly vulnerable, either *through their personal characteristics or through circumstances of the crime*, can benefit from special measures best suited to their situation'.[40] Thus, 'vulnerable victims' are those victims who find it especially difficult to fully exercise their recognised rights due to cultural, physical or psychological reasons. Children's experiences of vulnerability have been described as 'multidimensional and different from those of adults'.[41] Besides child-specific factors, some authors have recognised also 'child-intensified vulnerabilities', which may affect the whole population, but have a stronger impact on children (Sabates-Wheeler et al., 2009) i.e. physical/biological vulnerabilities; dependency related vulnerabilities and institutionalized disadvantage. Furthermore, it has been argued that child-specific sources of vulnerability are related to (a) their multidimensionality; (b) their changing pattern over the life-cycle; (c) the relationship with their caregivers; and (d) their 'voicelessness', a category including the lack of proper legislative frameworks to allow children to participate in societal settings, including judicial proceedings (Jones, 2009). Moreover, according to Article 21(4) of the EU Directive establishing minimum standards on the rights, support

---

[39] See the Report 'Victims in Europe: Implementation of the EU Framework Decision on the standing of victims in the criminal proceedings in the Member States of the European Union', Jul 2009, at 39, available at: http://www.bkb.cz/files/uploaded/UserFiles/File/Project_Victims_Europe_Final_Report.pdf. Accessed 4 March 2020.

[40] Art 3.4 of the Recommendation Rec (2006) 8 of the Committee of Ministers to Member States on Assistance to Crime Victims (Adopted 14 June 2006), available at: https://wcd.coe.int/ViewDoc.jsp?id=1011109&Site=CM&BackColorInternet=9999CC&BackColorIntranet=FFBB55&BackColorLogged=FFAC75. Accessed 4 March 2020. See also Directive 2012/29/EU of the European Parliament and of the Council of 25 October 2012 establishing minimum standards on the rights, support and protection of victims of crime, and replacing Council Framework Decision 2001/220/JHA, which is available at: http://eur-lex.europa.eu/LexUriServ/LexUriServ.do?uri=OJ:L:2012:315:0057:0073:EN:PDF. (Directive establishing minimum standards on the rights, support and protection of victims of crime). Accessed 4 March 2020. According to Art: 21(4): 'For the purposes of this Directive, child victims shall be presumed to have specific protection needs due to their vulnerability to secondary and repeat victimisation, to intimidation and to retaliation.'

[41] UNICEF, Joint Statement on Advancing Child-Sensitive Social Protection, 2009, available at: http://www.unicef.org/aids/files/CSSP_joint_statement_10.16.09.pdf. Accessed 4 March 2020.

and protection of victims of crime, child victims shall be presumed to have specific protection needs due to their vulnerability to secondary and repeat victimisation, to intimidation and to retaliation.[42]

With regard to children affected by armed conflict, in her groundbreaking report, Graca Machel pointed out that children in war torn countries face higher risk than their peers in experiencing

> infant, child and adolescent mortality, low immunization, low access to health services, high malnutrition, high burden of disease, low school enrollment rates, high repetition rates, poor school performance and/or high drop-out rates; intra-household neglect; family and community abuse and maltreatment, in particular harassment and violence; economic and sexual exploitation, due to lack of care and protection.[43]

In her work Graca Machel identified the groups of children most affected by armed conflicts and therefore, most vulnerable: child soldiers, unaccompanied children, refugees and internally displaced children, children sexually abused or exploited, children injured by landmines and unexploded ordnance.[44] The Special Representative of the UN Secretary General on Children and Armed Conflict has further stressed the growing vulnerability of children and its relationship with the changing nature of the current armed conflicts

> Children have become more vulnerable due to new tactics of warfare, the absence of clear battlefields, the increasing number and diversification of parties to conflict that add to the complexity of conflicts and the deliberate targeting of traditional safe havens such as schools and hospitals. Moreover, the increasing use of terrorist and counter-terrorist activities sometimes blurs the line between what is legitimate and what is not in addressing security threats.[45]

Consistently with the primary principles enshrined in the CRC, which, as stressed in the previous sections, shall guide the participation of children in judicial proceedings, vulnerability represents a crucial factor that should definitely be taken into account to assess and determine the child's best interests and also to duly weigh his or her views.

---

[42] Directive establishing minimum standards on the rights, support and protection of victims of crime.

[43] UN Report on the Impact of Armed Conflict on Children, A/51/306, 1996.

[44] UN Report on the Impact of Armed Conflict on Children, A/51/306, 1996.

[45] See *Changing Nature of Conflict*, http://childrenandarmedconflict.un.org/effects-of-conflict/the-changing-nature-of-conflict/. Accessed 4 March 2020.

6.1 *Child Victims' Vulnerability in the ICC's Framework*

The ICC recognises as vulnerable: children, elderly persons, persons with disabilities and victims of sexual or gender violence.[46] More in detail, Article 68 of the Rome Statute specifies that

> The Court shall take appropriate measures to protect the safety, physical and psychological well-being, dignity and privacy of victims and witnesses. In so doing, the Court shall have regard to all relevant factors, including age, gender as defined in article 7(3),[47] and health, and the nature of the crime, in particular, but not limited to, where the crime involves sexual or gender violence or violence against children.

According to this provision, some factors, including victims' age and gender, need to be duly considered because, in line with the general definition of vulnerability reported above, they may lead to an overexposure to risks. Such risks can be both 'biological and environmental', the latter encompassing also the risk of being re-traumatised following the participation in a judicial proceeding (Hamzei, 2011). In particular, with regard to children affected by armed conflict, to use the words of Ms Schauer, a psychologist who served as expert witness in the Lubanga case

> Among a number of at risk populations, children of war and child soldiers are a particularly vulnerable group and often suffer from devastating long-term consequences of experienced or witnessed acts of violence. Child war survivors have to cope with repeated traumatic life events, exposure to combat, shelling and other life threatening events, acts of abuse such as torture or rape, violent death of a parent or friend, witnessing loved ones being tortured or injured, separation from family, being abducted or held in detention, insufficient adult care, lack of safe drinking water and food, inadequate shelter, explosive devices and dangerous building ruins in proximity, marching or being transported in crowded vehicles over long distances and spending months in transit camps.[48]

Moreover, the expert witness highlighted the fact that these experiences can hamper children's healthy development and their ability to 'function fully' even once the violence has ceased. In fact, children's experiences during armed conflict affect their recovery and also their capacity to participate in transitional justice processes, including criminal proceedings. As specified above, all children can be potentially affected by an armed conflict although of course not all of them suffer in the same way and to the same degree. For example, children who were direct victims of violence, associated with armed forces or groups, victims of sexual violence or who have very few support to rely on are particularly exposed to stigma and

---

[46] Art. 68 of the Statute and Rule 86 of the RPE.

[47] Art 7(3) of the Statute clarifies that: 'For the purpose of this Statute, it is understood that the term 'gender' refers to the two sexes, male and female, within the context of society. The term 'gender' does not indicate any meaning different from the above'.

[48] Expert Report of Ms Schauer (CHM-00001), The Psychological Impact of Child Soldiering, ICC-01/04-01/06-1729-Anxl (EVD-CHM-00001). (The Psychological Impact of Child Soldiering).

discrimination, which significantly increases the difficulties to achieve rehabilitation and reintegration. UNICEF, in its submission on the principles to be applied and the procedures to be followed with regard to reparations in the Lubanga case, has stressed that

> The fact the victims were children at the time of the commission of the offence should be given great weight by the Court in assessing the harm they endured because their vulnerability as children. The physical and psychological effects of crimes on children are extensively long lasting and harmful. The victims, in addition to suffering from violations of their fundamental rights, were also denied basic needs. The denial of their rights and needs can have enduring and sometimes lifelong repercussions, for example where children have lost access to education.[49]

Besides affecting the victims, it has been scientifically assessed that psychological exposure and suffering from trauma can 'cripple' individuals and families even into the next generations. For example, after having experienced armed conflict, organised violence and forced displacement, affected parents can leave an imprint in their grandchildren's generation.[50] In particular, violence and trauma at the time of parents' childhood may result in problematic attachment relationships that have long-term consequences for mental health and interpersonal relationships on the part of the children, setting in motion what can be described as an 'intergenerational cycle of dysfunction' (Yehuda et al., 2001).

6.2 Child Soldiers' Special Vulnerability

Given its jurisdiction *ratione materiae*, the International Criminal Court is expected to deal with a growing number of child victims of armed conflict. As noted by Graça Machel, 'war undermines the very foundations of children's lives, destroying their homes, splintering their communities and shattering their trust in adults' (Machel, 2001, p. 80). This is true for all the children affected by an armed conflict, especially those who experienced international human rights law and international humanitarian law violations, such as child soldiers illegally recruited and used to actively participate in hostilities. According to the latest working paper released by the Office of the UN Special Representative of the Secretary General for Children and Armed Conflict, 'while many children are affected by armed conflicts and some of them are direct victims of war crimes, a very small minority of children are also involved in committing crimes'.[51] The number of children unlawfully recruited to participate in

---

[49] See UNICEF, Submission on the Principles to be Applied and the Procedures to be Followed by the Chamber with regard to Reparations, ICC-01/04-01/06-2878 11-05-2012, at para 2.

[50] Expert Report of Ms Schauer (CHM-00001), The Psychological Impact of Child Soldiering, ICC-01/04-01/06-1729-Anxl (EVD-CHM-00001). (The Psychological Impact of Child Soldiering), at p. 25.

[51] Office of the Special Representative of the Secretary General for Children and Armed conflict, Working Paper No 3, Children and Justice During and in the Aftermath of Armed Conflict,

armed conflicts is certainly low if compared to the number of children affected by them, in particular those injured, sexually abused, orphaned and so on. Nevertheless, in the past two decades the use of children as soldiers who play a role in the actual combat, or perform ancillary tasks supporting the fighters, has increased, generating a widespread phenomenon, endemic in each context where an armed conflict arises (Drumbl, 2012; Capone, 2017).

The recruitment of children under the age of 15 is prohibited under the Rome Statute,[52] international treaties,[53] and international customary law,[54] regardless of whether this crime is committed in the context of an international or non-international armed conflict and regardless of the nature of the armed group or force that recruited the child. All these sources of law seek to protect children under the age of 15 from the multiple and different risks which they are subject to in the context of any armed conflict, such as ill treatment, sexual violence and forced marriages. As noted by Judge Odio Benito

> Children are protected from child recruitment not only because they can be at risk for being a potential target to the 'enemy' but also because they will be at risk from their 'own' armed group which has recruited them and will subject these children to brutal trainings, torture and ill-treatment, sexual violence and other activities and living conditions that are incompatible and in violation to these children's fundamental rights. The risk for children who are enlisted, conscripted or used by an armed group inevitably also comes from within the same armed group.[55]

As highlighted by Ms Radhika Coomaraswamy, former Special Representative for Children and Armed Conflict and expert witness in the Lubanga case, child recruitment is *per se* against the best interests of a child.[56] During her testimony, Ms Coomaraswamy described her experience with former child soldiers. In particular she stressed that all the victims of child recruitment, even those who had the resilience to come up and share their stories, tend to emphasise how their education and livelihood have been deeply damaged, and how they need some kind of psychosocial support. The witness went on saying that she had never met one child soldier, including the ones who have survived and tried to move on, who

September 2011, available at: http://childrenandarmedconflict.un.org/publications/WorkingPaper-3_Children-and-Justice.pdf. Accessed 20 May 2020.

[52] See Art 8(2)(b)(xxvi) and Art 8(2)(e)(vii) of the Rome Statute.

[53] Art 77(2), Protocol Additional to the Geneva Conventions of 12 August 1949 and Relating to the Protection of Victims of International Armed Conflicts, 1125 UNTS 3 (1977), Art 4(2)(c), Protocol Additional to the Geneva Conventions of 12 August 1949 and Relating to the Protection of Victims of Non-International Armed Conflicts, 1125 UNTS 609 (1977), Art 38 CRC.

[54] SCSL-2004-14-AR72(E), Hinga Norman, Decision of the SCSL Appeals Chamber, 31 May 2004.

[55] See *Prosecutor v. Thomas Lubanga Dyilo*, Separate and Dissenting Opinion Judge Elizabeth Odio Benito, ICC-01/04-01/06-2842 14-03-2012, at para 6.

[56] See Radhika Coomaraswamy, former United Nations Special Representative of the Secretary-General for Children and Armed Conflict, as expert evidence in: *Prosecutor v. Lubanga*, Situation in the Democratic Republic of the Congo, Case No. ICC-01/04-01/06, Transcript ICC-01/04-01/06-T-223-ENG.

would depict his or her experience as positive. In light of the previous considerations, the particular vulnerability of the child soldiers recognised as victims in the Lubanga case should have been a major concern of the Court from the inception till the end of the proceedings.

However, the Court has failed to take it into account and to act in accordance with the concept of 'best interests of the child' in two particular instances. In the first place, and this point will be further addressed in the relevant section, the child soldiers who participated in the trial both as witnesses and victims have been labeled as 'unreliable witnesses' and lost their victims' status. Secondly, the Court, i.e. the majority of the Trial Chamber, has overlooked the importance of legally defining the activities covered by Articles 8(2)(b)(xxvi) and 8(2)(e)(vii) of the Rome Statute, namely those that should be included within the legal definition of enlistment, conscription and 'use to participate actively in the hostilities'. In particular with regard to the latter, the judges disagreed on whether or not the term 'use to participate actively in hostilities' should actually be rendered precisely in the judgment.[57] Since neither the Statute nor the Elements of Crimes outline further these criminal conducts, the scope of the activities covered by Article 8(2)(e)(vii) of the Statute must have been determined in accordance with Articles 21 and 22(2) of the Statute, which compel the Chamber to interpret and apply the law consistently with internationally recognised human rights.[58] Nevertheless, the majority declined to provide a legal definition of the concept of 'use to participate actively in the hostilities', leaving it to a case-by-case determination, which is limited by the charges and evidence brought by the prosecution against the accused.[59]

The Trial Chamber also failed to clearly differentiate between 'use to participate actively in hostilities' and 'direct participation in hostilities', raising criticism because of the potentially dangerous consequences for the children concerned (Graf, 2012), which might result in a loss of protection under international humanitarian law (Urban, 2012). The majority found that 'active participation' under Article 8(2)(e)(vii) ICC Statute is a concept distinct from, and broader than, 'direct participation in hostilities,' whilst instead international humanitarian law treats the terms as synonymous.

The Court's focus on children as potential targets clearly reflects the desire to protect them from the danger and harm of armed conflicts, however, the lack of clarity in the use of the terms 'active participation', which Trial Chamber I equated to

[57] See *Prosecutor v. Thomas Lubanga Dyilo,* Separate and Dissenting Opinion Judge Elizabeth Odio Benito, at para 4.

[58] *Prosecutor v. Thomas Lubanga Dyilo*, Judgment Pursuant to Article 74 of the Statute, 14 March 2012, at para 600.

[59] *Prosecutor v. Thomas Lubanga Dyilo*, Judgment Pursuant to Article 74 of the Statute, 14 March 2012, at para 627 '[. . .] Given the different types of roles that may be performed by children used by armed groups, the Chamber's determination of whether a particular activity constitutes 'active participation" can only be made on a case-by-case basis.'

the expression 'children associated with armed groups/forces'[60] and the hasty approach on this sensitive issue could lead to unintended, but dangerous effects for the children concerned. The problems raised by the Trial Chamber's interpretation of 'active participation' were, at least in part, addressed in the judgment issued by the Appeals Chamber on 1 December 2014. The Appeals Chamber ultimately stressed that Trial Chamber I erred in law in finding that '[t]he decisive factor . . . in deciding if an "indirect" role is to be treated as active participation in hostilities is whether the support provided by the child to the combatants exposed him or her to real danger as a potential target'.[61] According to the Appeals Chamber, in assessing whether an activity or role falls within the scope of Article 8(2)(e)(vii) of the Statute, it is necessary instead to analyse the link between the activity for which the child is used and the combat in which the armed force or group of the perpetrator is engaged. Unfortunately, the Appeals Chamber did not consider it appropriate to give further guidance on the parameters of the notion of 'active participation in hostilities' in the abstract 'in view of the complex and unforeseeable scenarios presented by the rapidly changing face of warfare in the modern world'.[62] To justify the refusal to finally shed light on this issue the Appeals Chamber underlined that the determination as to whether a particular activity falls within this definition must be made, again, on a case-by-case basis.Concerning the possibility of a conflict between the Rome Statute and the law of armed conflict, the Appeals Chamber clarified that the difference, therefore, lies in the interpretation of the two terms, which must reflect the purposes of the provisions (and of the treaties) in which they are enshrined, rather than in their meaning, which is *de facto* identical. In other words not interpreting the term 'active participation' against the principle of distinction would allow the Court to overcome potential frictions with IHL and draw a line between the sets of values that the two regimes seek to protect.

In conclusion, the prohibition on conscripting, enlisting or using children under the age of 15 years to take part in hostilities is also embedded in the ICC Statute and it is framed as a war crime, regardless of whether it is committed in the context of an international or internal armed conflict. The important step of criminalising a course of conduct that was neglected by the Statutes of the previous international tribunals,

---

[60] The term 'children associated with armed forces or armed groups'—also known as CAAFAG—is used to include the girls and boys used for example as domestic servants, even if they never directly participate in hostilities. The definition can be found in the Paris Principles: 'A child associated with an armed force or armed group refers to any person below 18 years of age who is, or who has been, recruited or used by an armed force or armed group in any capacity, including but not limited to children, boys and girls, used as fighters, cooks, porters, spies or for sexual purposes. It does not only refer to a child who is taking, or has taken, a direct part in hostilities.' See the Paris Principles and Guidelines on Children Associated with Armed Forces or Armed Groups, UNICEF, February 2007, available at: http://www.unicef.org/emerg/files/ParisPrinciples310107English.pdf. Accessed 4 March 2020.

[61] See *Prosecutor v. Thomas Lubanga Dyilo*, Judgment on the appeal of Mr Thomas Lubanga Dyilo against his conviction, 1 December 2014, ICC, Case No. ICC-01/04-01/06-3121, at para. 236.

[62] *Prosecutor v. Thomas Lubanga Dyilo*, Judgment on the appeal of Mr Thomas Lubanga Dyilo against his conviction, 1 December 2014, ICC, Case No. ICC-01/04-01/06-3121, at para. 329.

risks, nonetheless, being overshadowed by two main issues, i.e. the decision to criminalise child soldiering keeping the age limit of 15 years and the adoption of the term 'active participation' without providing a decisive argument to fully explain and justify the ICC's departure from the traditional understanding of the concept of 'direct participation in hostilities' (Capone, 2017, p. 60).

7 Victims of Sexual and Gender-based Violence Before the ICC

The Rome Statute includes unique provisions compared to other international courts and tribunals, that require it to provide gender-inclusive justice. The Rome Statute not only includes gender-based crimes within the jurisdiction of the Court as war crimes, crimes against humanity and acts of genocide, but also contains specific provisions requiring the Court to apply and interpret law consistent with internationally recognised human rights and without any adverse distinction founded on grounds such as gender.[63] Furthermore, it should be noted that the RPE and the Regulations of the Court also provide specific provisions for women victims and survivors of gender-based crime.[64] Even though a specific legal framework exists, it should be noted that the discussion about the definition of the terms 'use to participate actively in hostilities' has also been fueled by the blatantly scant attention that the Court in the *Lubanga case* has paid to the large numbers of girls associated with armed forces/groups, who experienced sexual violence. As Ms Schauer, in her capacity as expert witness in the *Lubanga case*, has highlighted 'some 40 percent or 120,000 child soldiers are girls, whose plight is often unrecognized since international attention has largely focused on boy soldiers. Generally, when people speak of "child soldiers", the popular image is that of boys rather than the thousands of girls who comprise the less visible, 'shadow armies' in conflicts around the world.'[65]

Despite these significant numbers, girls' situation remains overlooked and neglected, including in international proceedings. As stated above, in the *Lubanga case* the prosecution focused its charges on the recruitment, enlistment and use of child soldiers to the detriment of other crimes; in particular, gender-based crimes, such as sexual violence or sexual slavery. As a consequence of the prosecutorial strategy, the Court closed the door to the participation of victims of gender-based crimes other than those who fulfilled the victim requirements of being a child under

[63] The Women's Initiative for Gender Justice, Gender Report Card on the International Criminal Court, 2012, available at: http://www.iccwomen.org/documents/Gender-Report-Card-on-the-ICC-2012.pdf. Accessed 4 March 2020.

[64] See The Women's Initiatives for Gender Justice, Observations of the Women's Initiatives for Gender Justice on Reparations, ICC-01/04-01/06-2876, at para 8.

[65] Expert Report of Ms Schauer (CHM-00001), The Psychological Impact of Child Soldiering, ICC-01/04-01/06-1729-Anxl (EVD-CHM-00001). (The Psychological Impact of Child Soldiering), p. 5.

the age of fifteen who was conscripted, enlisted, or used in the hostilities. Consistently with this approach the victims of gender-based crimes committed by the rebel forces, including those who suffered gender-based crimes at the hands of the child soldiers, could not participate because unable to demonstrate the necessary link between the harm they suffered and the crimes charged.[66] Although the Court was provided with evidence from witnesses and participating victims that, particularly for girl child soldiers, the suffering of gender-based crimes was an inherent part of 'using' child soldiers, the majority of the judges decided that the prosecution did not provide sufficient evidence to this effect. Notably, in May 2009, the legal representative of the victims filed a request before the Chamber in order to change the legal characterisation of the facts and include inhuman and cruel treatment and sexual slavery. The request was rejected by the Appeals Chamber on procedural grounds and, notwithstanding the strong evidence of sexual enslavement and other kinds of sexual abuses widely perpetrated by the members of the Forces Patriotiques pour la Liberation du Congo (FPLC) against the girls and the boys recruited in its armed forces, these crimes were not embedded in the charges. The lack of what can be called a 'proper legal justification', which would have allowed the Chamber to directly address the victims of gender-based and/or sexual violence, represents a limitation that openly contrasts with the principle of the best interests of the child and also with the right of the child to participate in the proceedings affecting him or her.

In the *Lubanga case,* thus, the Court failed to prosecute crimes of sexual violence both as distinct crimes that could have been evaluated separately by the Chamber if the Prosecutor would have presented charges against these specific conducts,[67] and as an element of the legal definition of the crimes of enlistment, conscription and use of children under the age of 15 to participate actively in hostilities. With regard to the former option, it is worth stressing that in the *Ntaganda case,* which is currently ongoing, the Appeals Chamber of the ICC has affirmed that the Court has jurisdiction over cases in which soldiers of an armed group commit war crimes against members of the same group, namely the alleged rape and sexual slavery of child soldiers.[68] More in detail, the Appeals judges noted that Article 8(2)(b)(xxii) and (2)(e)(vi) of the Rome Statute does not expressly provide that the victims of rape or

[66] See *Prosecutor v. Lubanga Dyilo,* Case No. ICC-01/04-01/06-172, Decision on the Applications for Participation in the Proceedings Submitted by VPRS 1 to VPRS 6, June 29, 2006, at para 6.

[67] The Prosecutor decided early in the case not charge Lubanga with any crimes of sexual violence because he was confident only about the evidence of child soldier crimes. Therefore, the OTP P failed to charge sexual enslavement and rape and even opposed the failed attempt at recharacterization on the grounds that the charges amounted to an addition, which if included could jeopardise the rights of the accused. See ICC-01/04-01/06-2055 Appeals Chamber Judgment on the appeals of Mr Lubanga Dilyo and the Prosecutor against the decision of the Pre-Trial Chamber I of 14 June 2009 entitled: 'Decision giving notice to the parties and participants that the legal characterisation of the facts may be subject to change in accordance with regulation 55(2) of the Regulations of the Court', 8 December 2009, at paras 109–112.

[68] *Prosecutor v. Bosco Ntaganda,* Judgment on the appeal of Mr Ntaganda against the 'Second decision on the Defence's challenge to the jurisdiction of the Court in respect of Counts 6 and 9',15 June 2017, ICC-01/04-02/06-1962, at paras 46–48.

sexual slavery must be 'protected persons' in terms of the Geneva Conventions or 'persons taking no active part in the hostilities'.[69] This means that members of an armed group, which in the case at stake belong to a particularly vulnerable category, are not categorically excluded from protection against the war crimes of rape and sexual slavery when committed by members of the same armed group. The Court, hence, has the mandate to try Mr Ntaganda and now it rests on the prosecution to prove that he is criminally responsible for the alleged rape and sexual enslavement of child soldiers by UPC members.

Whereas the ICC case law concerning sexual violence committed against children is still at an embryonic stage, research in this sensitive field is fast-growing. A groundbreaking study conducted in Sierra Leone by a group of researchers from the François-Xavier Bagnoud Center for Health and Human Rights at Harvard School of Public Health has shown that children formerly associated with armed forces or groups are labeled as different or untrustworthy and that this approach deepens their senses of solitude and alienation (Betancourt et al., 2010). Once they return to their home communities, they are normally blamed for the atrocities committed, e.g. for having destroyed lives, homes, and property. It was ascertained that those who are socially isolated are especially vulnerable to addictions and abusive relationships. With regard to girls in particular, the study pointed out that they face a compound burden since, in comparison with their male peers, they are more likely to suffer depression, anxiety, and post-traumatic stress disorder. Many girls illegally recruited or abducted by armed forces and armed groups have returned to their communities having had unwanted pregnancies during the time spent in captivity. Therefore, in addition to the stigma of having taken part in violence, which they share with the boys, they have to face the additional load of being seen as 'impure', regardless of what their experience was.

Notably, as reported by Human Rights Watch, a study carried out in the United States determined that approximately 95 percent of child victims of sexual violence are frightened to testify in court, and many of them have described the day they testified as the worst day of their lives. Moreover, the children involved in the study also explained that they feared 'retaliation by the perpetrator, being sent to jail, being punished for making a mistake, having to prove their innocence, crying on the witness stand, describing the details of the offense(s) in front of strangers, and not understanding the questions being asked' (Human Rights Watch, 2009). Nevertheless, depriving child victims who experienced sexual and gender-based violence of the possibility to participate in a judicial proceeding can never be regarded as a solution that respects and implements the key principles enshrined in the CRC.

[69] *Prosecutor v. Bosco Ntaganda,* Judgment on the appeal of Mr Ntaganda against the 'Second decision on the Defence's challenge to the jurisdiction of the Court in respect of Counts 6 and 9',15 June 2017, ICC-01/04-02/06-1962, at paras 49–50.

8 ICC's Protective and Special Measures for Child Victims and Witnesses

As stated in the Manual for Legal Representatives produced by the Office of Public Counsel for Victims (OPCV) of the ICC, victims who participate in the proceedings and witnesses are entitled to enjoy protective measures. These measures are of first importance in order to encourage them to communicate with the Court and to testify without endangering their security. However, these measures cannot be applied in a manner which is prejudicial to or inconsistent with the rights of the suspect or accused and a fair and impartial trial.[70] Article 43(6) of the Rome Statute provides for the creation of a Victims and Witnesses Unit within the Registry in order to assist and advise victims and witnesses, as well as Chambers and participants on protective measures and security arrangements.[71] The protection also extends to persons who are at risk on account of testimony given by a person, for example the family members of the witnesses; and generally to persons at risk because of their interaction with the Court. Concerning the protective and special measures, in line with the general principle enshrined in Rule 86 of the RPE, the Trial Chamber recognises that there are particular specials needs to be taken into account to the fullest extent possible for some categories of victims participating in the proceedings, namely children and elderly victims, victims with disabilities, and victims of sexual and gender violence.[72] As stated in Rule 88 of the RPE, the Chamber may order special measures to assist victims and witnesses, including measures to facilitate the testimony of a traumatized victim or witness, again children, the elderly, disabled persons and victims of sexual and gender violence.[73] In addition to internal structural arrangements to protect witnesses, the Court is mandated to apply 'in-court protective measures' to protect vulnerable witnesses under the Statute and RPE. Furthermore, according to Rule 88(5) of the RPE Judges may also apply 'special measures' to protect vulnerable witnesses including by 'vigilantly controlling the manner of questioning a witness or victim so as to avoid any harassment or intimidation'.[74] Such measures have been adopted, to different extents, in all ICC trials. As reported by the International Bar Association

> During the Lubanga trial for example, the Trial Chamber ordered a variety of protective measures including withholding witnesses' identities from the public; use of pseudonyms; and conducting parts of the proceedings in closed session. Face and voice distortion was in

[70] Representing Victims before the International Criminal Court: A Manual for Legal Representatives, The Office of Public Counsel for Victims, 2bd ed. 2012, (The Manual for Legal Representatives), p. 31.

[71] This Unit is the only one expressly mentioned in the Rome Statute with regard to protection.

[72] See No. ICC-01/04-01/07-361, Pre-Trial Chamber I (Single Judge), 3 April 2008, at para 35.

[73] Representing Victims before the International Criminal Court: A Manual for Legal Representatives, The Office of Public Counsel for Victims, 2bd ed. 2012: 31. (The Manual for Legal Representatives), p. 68.

[74] Rule 88(5).

> place for all alleged former child soldiers, and screens were used so that witnesses did not have to see the accused while testifying. Furthermore, testimony via electronic means was permitted, and the Chamber allowed some child witnesses to be accompanied during testimony by a family member, psychologist or legal representative.[75]

Notably, all these measures have been adopted after the first former child soldier who served as witness in the *Lubanga case* recanted his testimony, most likely due the fact that at the beginning of the trial he sat in clear view of Lubanga and was able to make eye contact with his persecutor. As a result, additional precautions have been put in place, in particular all child soldiers were shielded from Lubanga's direct view when providing testimony to the Court through the use of curtains pulled across the sides of the witness box (Lara, 2011).

Significantly, some of the former child soldiers who took part in the *Lubanga case* enjoyed a 'dual status' which entails that a victim may also be called as a witness by the Prosecution, the Defence or a Legal Representative.[76] In the case at stake, however, conferring the dual status has not produced the expected result of enhancing child victims' participation. On the contrary, it has demonstrated how little the children's special vulnerability and needs were taken into consideration. As explained in the Judgment pursuant to Article 74 of the Statute, due to inconsistencies within and between the accounts of the alleged former child soldiers, Trial Chamber I deemed their testimonies unreliable as regards the matters that were relevant to the charges in the *Lubanga case*.[77] In addition to discharging the testimonies, the majority of the Judges, given the Chamber's conclusions as to the reliability and accuracy of the witnesses,[78] decided that it was necessary to withdraw the victims' right to participate on the account that 'it would be unsustainable to

[75] See International Bar Association, Witnesses before the ICC: International Criminal Court Programme Report on the ICC's Efforts and Challenges to Protect, Support and Ensure the Rights of Witnesses, July 2013. The Report is available at: https://www.ibanet.org/Document/Default.aspx?DocumentUid=9C4F533D-1927-421B-8C12-D41768FFC11F. Accessed 20 May 2020. The Report also specifies that in the Katanga Ngudjolo trial the Court made use of pseudonyms, and facial and voice distortions. However, there were reportedly fewer closed sessions during that trial in comparison to the Lubanga case. Moreover, given its high numbers of victim-witnesses who allegedly suffered sexual violence, other vulnerable witnesses and high-profile defence witnesses, the Bemba trial has perhaps employed the most frequent use of in-court protective measures, mostly in the form of pseudonyms, face and voice distortion during testimony and closed-session hearings.

[76] *Prosecutor v. Thomas Lubanga Dyilo*, Decision on Certain Practicalities Regarding Individuals who have the Dual Status of Witness and Victims, 5 June 2008, see para. 52, principle b: 'The fact that an individual has dual status does not grant him or her rights in addition to those of someone who is only a victim or a witness'.

[77] *Prosecutor v. Thomas Lubanga*, Case No. ICC-01/04-01/06, Judgment Pursuant to Article 74 of the Statute, 14 March 2012, at para 478 et ss.

[78] *Prosecutor v. Thomas Lubanga*, Case No. ICC-01/04-01/06, Judgment Pursuant to Article 74 of the Statute, 14 March 2012, at para 499 et ss. For instance the Chamber in its conclusion on three victims who gave evidence has stated: 'The evidence of a/0225/06, a/0229/06, and a/0270/07 contains internal inconsistencies which undermine their credibility. [E.g.]a/0225/06's recollection of his abduction and military service lacked clarity, and he demonstrated uncertainty when questioned about the details of those events.'

allow victims to continue participating if a more detailed understanding of the evidence has demonstrated they no longer meet the relevant criteria'.[79] This episode sheds light on the fact that despite the crucial efforts made so far, the ICC is still far from striking a balance between the best interests of child victims and the implementation of fair trial standards.[80] In fact, as stressed by Judge Odio Benito in her separate and dissenting opinion

> These witnesses were subject to multiple interviews and strenuous examination and cross-examination, which took place on numerous occasions, during a period of time ranging from 2005 to 2009-2010. In all of these interviews and interrogatories they were asked to recall events that occurred between 2002 and 2003 [...] although I agree with the Majority of the Trial Chamber that the testimonies of these young individuals should not be used for the purposes of determining the individual criminal responsibility of Mr Lubanga, their victims' status should remain unaffected.[81]

In withdrawing the former child soldiers' right to participate in the proceedings as victims, the Trial Chamber has failed to consider the extent of the trauma suffered and its impact on the witnesses' capability to provide a lucid and precise account of their experiences. In particular, as stated by the expert witness Ms Elisabeth Schauer, recalling traumatic events entails extraordinary hurdles for the victims affected by posttraumatic stress disorder. In fact

> once posttraumatic stress disorder has developed, we see victims, including child soldiers, experience immense suffering due to involuntary sensory, visual or other recall of the most horrific moments of their lives, whereby their autobiographic memory is fragmented and their ability to willingly focus their mind and concentrate is reduced. Much of the daily and nightly energy is spent avoiding to get reminded, since remembering the traumatic experience brings up painful emotions and panic like physical arousal and distress. The severity of trauma symptoms and distress of talking about the event are tightly linked to each other. We have observed that with increasing severity of symptoms, the distress felt in people, when asked to disclose their traumatic scene increases.[82]

Moreover, it should be borne in mind that former child soldiers when called to testify relive their experiences both as victims and as perpetrators, meaning that although the Rome Statute clearly excludes from its jurisdiction *ratione personae* those who committed crimes while under the age of 18 years old, child soldiers can be influenced by the irrational, but understandable, fear that telling their stories in a courtroom can lead to unforeseen repercussions, such as being indicted or detained.

[79] *Prosecutor v. Thomas Lubanga*, Case No. ICC-01/04-01/06, Judgment Pursuant to Article 74 of the Statute, 14 March 2012, at para 484.

[80] The Preamble of the Guidelines on Justice in Matters Involving Child Victims and Witnesses of Crime, ECOSOC Resolution 2005/20 of 22 July 2005, available at: https://www.un.org/en/ecosoc/docs/2005/resolution%202005-20.pdf. Accessed 20 May 2020.

[81] *Prosecutor v. Thomas Lubanga Dyilo*, Separate and Dissenting Opinion Judge Elizabeth Odio Benito, at paras 30–34.

[82] This condition is known as 'speechless terror'; see Expert Report of Ms Schauer (CHM-00001), at p. 34.

9 Child Victims and Reparations

The last aspect that emerged in the *Lubanga case* and that is of great practical and scholarly interest is the issue of reparations for child victims. The key provision for the analysis of the right to reparation for children is Article 39 of the CRC. According to it

> State parties shall take all appropriate measures to promote physical and psychological recovery and social reintegration of a child victim of: any form of neglect, exploitation, or abuse; torture or any other form of cruel, inhuman or degrading treatment or punishment; or armed conflicts. Such recovery and reintegration shall take place in an environment which fosters the health, self-respect and dignity of the child.

Within the ICC's legal framework the right to reparation is is laid down in Articles 75 and 79 of the Rome Statute and it is further elaborated in Rules 94–99 of the Court's RPE (De Brouwer, 2007). According to Article 75: 'the Court shall establish principles relating to reparations or in respect of, victims, including restitution, compensation and rehabilitation. On this basis, in its decision the Court may, either upon request or on its own motion in exceptional circumstances, determine the scope and the extent of any damage, loss and injury to, or in respect of, victims and will state the principles on which is acting.' Subject to this Article the ICC can only order reparations, after conviction, either directly against the convicted person or through the Trust Fund for Victims. It is also clearly stated that the reparations claimable against the convicted person would be strictly related to the liability established at the trial. In this sense, the case 'built' by the prosecutor and the charges tried provide the framework for future reparations directly claimable against the convicted person.[83] It was already underlined how the limitation of the charges impacts, in a significant way, victims' participation before the Court and this also relates to the reparations phase (McCarthy, 2012; Evans, 2012). Moreover, Article 75 attributes to the ICC itself the challenging task to establish its own reparations principles and, therefore, to operate a significant change in the way international criminal law has been perceived so far, shifting from a purely retributive approach to a more victim-oriented one. Since Mr Lubanga's conviction, the ICC's first decision on reparations has been awaited with great expectations.

First and foremost it is important to remark that the Trial Chamber in illustrating the principles on reparations has extensively relied both on the submissions received by the Trust Fund for Victims, the Registrar, UNICEF, the International Center for Transitional Justice (ICTJ), Women's Initiatives and other NGOs and on the practice of the Inter-American Court of Human Rights, to which the Chamber has constantly

[83] In other words, the persons entitled to apply for the victims' status would be also the persons legitimated to claim for the reparations awarded directly against the perpetrator found liable of the crimes charged.

made references. It has been emphasised that the principles enunciated within the decision have been circumscribed to the specific case and therefore they do not necessarily represent the principles that will guide the future decisions of the Court on reparations. On the contrary, other Chambers could decide to adhere to different principles, triggering a potential lack of uniformity and coherence that has been strongly criticised by several experts.[84] With regard in particular to children, the Trial Chamber has underlined that the age of the victims is one of the key factors to be taken in due consideration, in particular

> In reparations decisions concerning children, the Court should be guided, inter alia, by the Convention on the Rights of the Child and the fundamental principle of the 'best interests of the child' that is enshrined therein. Further, the decisions in this context should reflect a gender-inclusive perspective.[85]

The Court also made explicit reference to Article 39 of the CRC, which, as stressed above, requires States Parties to promote the recovery and reintegration of child victims, including child victims of war, and, implicitly, recognize children's right to reparation. In the decision under consideration the Court also stressed the importance of taking into account the views of the child victims, as they necessarily 'are to be considered when decisions are made about individual or collective reparations that concern them, bearing in mind their circumstances, age and level of maturity'.[86] As for the procedural issues, which are dealt with in the second part of the decision, the Trial Chamber affirmed that reparations are an integral part of the overall trial process and, since the Rome Statute does not specify which body of the Court is in charge of monitoring and supervising the reparations order, the Chamber explained that such tasks fall within the responsibilities of the judiciary. The Trial Chamber also clarified that during the reparations proceedings new judges will be

---

[84] See for instance The Case-based Reparations Scheme at the International Criminal Court, Report by War Crimes Research Office, June 2010, which is available at: https://www.wcl.american.edu/impact/initiatives-programs/warcrimes/our-projects/icc-legal-analysis-and-education-project/reports/report-12-the-case-based-reparations-scheme-at-the-international-criminal-court/. Accessed 20 May 2020. According to the Report 'the absence of general guidance on a variety of issues related to the scheme, combined with the fact that the judges of the ICC hail from diverse backgrounds, may result in discrepancies in the approach to reparations across cases, which may in turn lead to perceptions that the overall scheme is unfair or arbitrary'. See Situation in the Democratic Republic of the Congo in the case of the Prosecutor v. Thomas Lubanga Dyilo, 'Decision establishing the principles and procedures to be applied to reparations', ICC-01/04-01/06-2904, 7 August 2012, at para 182 et ss.

[85] The Case-based Reparations Scheme at the International Criminal Court, Report by War Crimes Research Office, June 2010, at para 211, available at: https://www.wcl.american.edu/impact/initiatives-programs/warcrimes/our-projects/icc-legal-analysis-and-education-project/reports/report-12-the-case-based-reparations-scheme-at-the-international-criminal-court/. Accessed 20 May 2020.

[86] The Case-based Reparations Scheme at the International Criminal Court, Report by War Crimes Research Office, June 2010, at para 215, available at: https://www.wcl.american.edu/impact/initiatives-programs/warcrimes/our-projects/icc-legal-analysis-and-education-project/reports/report-12-the-case-based-reparations-scheme-at-the-international-criminal-court/. Accessed 20 May 2020.

appointed to substitute the current bench,[87] giving legitimate raise to the, unanswered, question of what impact the replacement of the judges will have on the victims.

The core of the decision lies, though, in the role assigned to the Trust Fund for Victims, which has been appointed by the Chamber as the designated body to deal with the overarching implementation of a five steps reparations plan. In fact, the indigence of the convicted person and his lack of private assets made the Court to draw on the logistical and financial resources of the TFV, in particular

> the Chamber is of the view that when the convicted person has no assets, if a reparations award is made 'through' the Trust Fund, the award is not limited to the funds and assets seized and deposited with the Trust Fund, but the award can, at least potentially, be supported by the Trust Fund's own resources. This interpretation is consistent with Rule 98(5) of the Rules and Regulation 56 of the Regulations of the TFV. Rule 98(5) of the Rules provides that the Trust Fund may use 'other resources' for the benefit of victims.[88]

Concerning the identification of the beneficiaries and the distribution of the benefits, the Chamber adopted a broader approach by affirming that reparations should be awarded to those who suffered personal harm as the result of the offences, *regardless whether they participated in the trial.*[89] Notably, the Court included also victims of gender violence amongst those who can have access to reparations,[90] showing that the decision went beyond the restricted notion of 'victim' inferred by the highly criticised prosecutorial strategy and the limited charges tried. In a nutshell, the difference in the Chamber's approach regarding the issue of sexual violence for purposes of sentencing and consideration of such evidence for purposes of a

---

[87] The Case-based Reparations Scheme at the International Criminal Court, Report by War Crimes Research Office, June 2010, at para 262-3, available at: https://www.wcl.american.edu/impact/initiatives-programs/warcrimes/our-projects/icc-legal-analysis-and-education-project/reports/report-12-the-case-based-reparations-scheme-at-the-international-criminal-court/. Accessed 20 May 2020.

[88] The Case-based Reparations Scheme at the International Criminal Court, Report by War Crimes Research Office, June 2010, at para 271, available at: https://www.wcl.american.edu/impact/initiatives-programs/warcrimes/our-projects/icc-legal-analysis-and-education-project/reports/report-12-the-case-based-reparations-scheme-at-the-international-criminal-court/. Accessed 20 May 2020.

[89] The Case-based Reparations Scheme at the International Criminal Court, Report by War Crimes Research Office, June 2010, at para 194, available at: https://www.wcl.american.edu/impact/initiatives-programs/warcrimes/our-projects/icc-legal-analysis-and-education-project/reports/report-12-the-case-based-reparations-scheme-at-the-international-criminal-court/. Accessed 20 May 2020. 'Pursuant to Rule 85 of the Rules, reparations may be granted to direct and indirect victims, including the family members of direct victims; anyone who attempted to prevent the commission of one or more of the crimes under consideration; and those who suffered personal harm as a result of these offences, regardless of whether they participated in the trial proceedings.'

[90] The Case-based Reparations Scheme at the International Criminal Court, Report by War Crimes Research Office, June 2010, at para 207 et ss, available at: https://www.wcl.american.edu/impact/initiatives-programs/warcrimes/our-projects/icc-legal-analysis-and-education-project/reports/report-12-the-case-based-reparations-scheme-at-the-international-criminal-court/. Accessed 20 May 2020.

reparations award can be explained by the fact that the standard of proof is different in each of these phases. In fact, while the prosecution must establish aggravating circumstances beyond a reasonable doubt for purposes of sentencing, a less exacting standard, 'the but for test', was used to determine the issue of causation in the reparation phase.

The Trial Chamber I decision on principles and procedures on reparations mainly outsourced the reparations regime to the TFV and left several questions unanswered, thus fuelling, instead of finally quelling, the discussion on whether the ICC can truly provide a forum to strike a balance between fair trial standards and victims' rights. Three years later, the Appeals Chamber significantly amended the decision by Trial Chamber I and issued a newly drafted Order for Reparations. Finally shedding light on what 'reparations' means in an international judicial setting, the Appeals Chamber has determined that:

> An order for reparations under Article 75 of the Statute must contain, at a minimum, five essential elements: 1) it must be directed against the convicted person; 2) it must establish and inform the convicted person of his or her liability with respect to the reparations awarded in the order; 3) it must specify, and provide reasons for, the type of reparations ordered, either collective, individual or both, pursuant to rules 97 (1) and 98 of the Rules of Procedure and Evidence; 4) it must Definethe harm caused to direct and indirect victims as a result of the crimes for which the person was convicted, as well as identify the modalities of reparations that the Trial Chamber considers appropriate based on the circumstances of the specific case before it; and 5) it must identify the victims eligible to benefit from the awards for reparations or set out the criteria of eligibility based on the link between the harm suffered by the victims and the crimes for which the person was convicted.[91]

These elements have, thus, been described as the cornerstone of every Order for Reparations and have been used by the Appeals Chamber to assess the decision issued by Trial Chamber I. The five elements must be kept separate from the principles, i.e. general concepts that can be formulated in light of the circumstances of a specific case, but nonetheless be applied, adapted, expanded upon, or added to by future Trial Chambers. It is not possible to elaborate in detail on the findings of the Appeals Chamber, however it is worth stressing that the judgment and the amended Order for Reparations have, at last, clarified a number of important points, including the relationship between the conviction and the reparations phase, the role of the TFV and its interplay with the ICC, the scope of reparations awarded in an international judicial setting and the practical hurdles that inevitably downsize the Court's ambition to act as a body able to successfully combine retributive and restorative justice (Capone, 2017).

Remarkably, since the case dealt with child victims, i.e. former child soldiers, the Appeals Chamber has clarified the importance of duly taking into account the age-related harm experience of the victims, in line with Article 68 of the Rome

---

[91] *Prosecutor v. Thomas Lubanga Dyilo*, Judgment of 3 March 2015 (Judgment on the appeals against the 'Decision establishing the principles and procedures to be applied to reparations' of 7 August 2012 with amended order for reparations (Annex A) and public annexes 1 and 2), (2015) ICC (Appeals Chamber), ICC- 01/04-01/06-3129-AnxA 03-03-2015, at para 35.

Statute, and of differentiating between the impact of the crimes on boys and girls. Furthermore the Appeals Chamber has referred to the key CRC principles that must guide and inform every reparations award for child victims, namely the best interests of the child; the promotion of children's recovery and reintegration; and children's right to participation.

10 Concluding Remarks

International criminal justice is still far from fully incorporating and implementing the principles enshrined in the CRC and many issues emerged in the first judgment delivered by the ICC which dealt with child victims. Remarkably, the victims identified in the *Lubanga case* were former child soldiers illegally enlisted, conscripted or used to actively participate in the hostilities. Therefore the Court had to deal with several challenges related to both child victims and witnesses who took part in the proceedings, and to those who were excluded. This contribution has constantly referred to the principle of the best interests of the child and the children's right to freely express their views, as paramount yardsticks to evaluate the ICC's interplay with four main aspects related to the involvement of children in international criminal proceedings. The four main aspects upon which the present Chapter has focused, namely child victims' specific vulnerability, the needs of child victims' of gender based and sexual violence, the special protection required by child witnesses and victims and finally the issue of reparations, were introduced and discussed to shed light on the shortcoming and the limitations of the existing framework, which does not fully recognise children's rights and prerogatives. Certainly, the fact that significant steps forward have been made since the entry into force of the Rome Statute cannot be denied or minimised. However, there is a strong need for clarity and coherence when it comes to identifying principles and measures to apply when dealing with child victims.

Examples of the Court's failures to provide clear-cut measures while coping with issues affecting child victims have been reported in the previous sections, showing the urge to promote a truly multidisciplinary approach able to achieve participation and protection without increasing the risk of re-traumatisation and stigmatisation. The views rendered in the *Lubanga case* by the expert witnesses, Ms Radhika Coomaraswamy and Ms Schauer, have not been taken into account to the fullest extent possible, undermining the importance of relying on psychological expertise other than legal knowledge. In particular, it is worth underlining that a courtroom or in any case a criminal proceeding will always represent a stressful environment for a child, especially when the trial is of an international character and takes place thousands of miles away from 'home'. However, there are measures and procedures meant to limit the impact and the damage that such experience can have on children, for instance the guidelines adopted by the SCSL to cope with child witnesses' vulnerability and the Guidelines on Action for Children in the Justice System in Africa. Moreover, it should be borne in mind that child victims' entitlement to take part in proceedings affecting them is not just a provision embedded in a legal document, but, whenever a child, freely and consciously, decides to exercise his or her right to participate, this could also be a way to provide empowerment and support in the long lasting process of overcoming the trauma suffered. In particular cases, for instance when sexual or gender-based violence occurred, the choice to participate in a judicial proceeding needs to be duly pondered by the child together with his or her family and legal representatives, as the experience might trigger secondary victimisation, intimidation and stigmatisation. The ICC's failure to recognise girls who suffered from sexual violence as victims in the Lubanga trial certainly deprived them of the opportunity to tell their stories, actively participate in the proceedings, e.g. by making observations, presenting their views and concerns and claiming for reparations, if they wished to do so. However, on the other hand it is undeniable that in such circumstances the decision to participate cannot disregard a thorough appraisal of the personal characteristics of the child victim, alongside the type, the nature and the circumstances of the crime (Human Rights Watch, 2009). Extremely important is, hence, the role of those assisting and guiding the child, who should provide him or her with all the necessary information to make the best choices as to the risks, progress and conduct of any proceedings, as stressed by the Guidelines of the Committee of Ministers of the Council of Europe on Child Friendly Justice. In conclusion:

- Within the broader group of child victims, the uniqueness of every child's experience should be given due consideration in accordance with the principles enshrined in the CRC, namely the best interests of the child and child's right to express her or his views in judicial proceedings;
- Child victims' vulnerability shall not be regarded as an abstract concept, but it needs to be effectively put in practice through the adoption of actions and the development of tools able to facilitate and promote child victims' access to justice; in particular, all professionals working with and for children should receive necessary interdisciplinary training on the rights and needs of children, taking into account the personal characteristics of the individual child victim such as his or her age, gender and gender identity or expression, ethnicity, race, religion, sexual orientation, health, disability, communication difficulties, relationship to or dependence on the offender, as well as on proceedings that are adapted to them;
- The ICC's first judgment on child soldiers provided a comprehensive overview of the challenges that representing child victims entails and, despite all the shortcomings identified and discussed in the present Chapter, it should be regarded as an unprecedented experience which, hopefully, will mark the pattern for a child friendly approach within the international criminal law framework. In particular, as stressed also in the EU Directive establishing minimum standards on the rights, support and protection of victims of crime,[92] a child-sensitive approach, taking

[92] Directive establishing minimum standards on the rights, support and protection of victims of crime.

due account of the child's age, maturity, views, needs and concerns, *should always prevail*. This means that the child and the holder of parental responsibility or *other legal representative*, if any, shall be informed of any measures or rights specifically focused on the child and actively promote their implementation. Moreover, since child victims shall be presumed to have specific protection needs due to their vulnerability to secondary and repeat victimisation, to intimidation and to retaliation, the ICC should carry out an individual assessment, covering both a 'best-interests assessment' and an assessment of the child's will and capability to participate in the trial,[93] to determine which are the measures of protection that effectively could match each child victim or witness's needs in the course of the criminal proceeding. Such individual assessment, as stressed by the Committee of Ministers of the Council of Europe in the guidelines on child friendly justice, should be crafted as a 'common assessment framework',[94] involving all the professionals working with or for children, (such as lawyers, psychologists, physicians, police, immigration officials, social workers and mediators), to provide any necessary support to those taking decisions and enable them to best serve children's interests in a given case. This multidisciplinary approach, which is encouraged at the national level, should also be promoted and implemented in international criminal settings.

References

Beresford, S. (2005). Child witnesses and the international criminal justice system: Does the International Criminal Court protect the most vulnerable? *Journal of International Criminal Justice, 3*(3), 721–748.

Betancourt, T. S., et al. (2010). Sierra Leone's former child soldiers: A follow-up study of psychosocial adjustment and community reintegration. *Child Development, 81*(4), 1077–1095.

Bradley, R. H., & Corwyn, R. F. (2002). Socioeconomic status and child development. *Annual Review of Psychology, 53*(1), 371–399.

Capone, F. (2017). *Reparations for child victims of armed conflict: State of the field and current challenges*. Intersentia.

Chamberlain, C. (2015). *Children and the International Criminal Court: Analysis of the Rome Statute through a children's rights perspective*. Intersentia.

Cohen, M. (2009). Victims' participation rights within the International Criminal Court: A critical overview. *Denver Journal of International Law and Policy, 37*(3), 351–377.

De Brouwer, A. (2007). Reparation to victims of sexual violence: Possibilities at the International Criminal Court and the trust fund for victims and their families. *Leiden Journal of International Law, 20*(1), 207–237.

Drumbl, M. (2012). *Reimagining child soldiers in international law and policy*. Oxford University Press.

[93] See the Committee on the Rights of the Child, General Comment No. 14 (2013) and General Comment No. 12 (2009).

[94] See Art 22 of the Directive establishing minimum standards on the rights, support and protection of victims of crime.

Evans, C. (2012). *The right to reparation in international law for victims of armed conflict*. Cambridge University Press.

Graf, R. (2012). The International Criminal Court and child soldiers: An appraisal of the Lubanga Judgment. *Journal of International Criminal Justice, 10*(4), 945–969.

Hamzei, H. (2011). Child victims before the International Criminal Court: Avenue to justice for the most vulnerable? In L. Hopkins et al. (Eds.), *Negotiating childhoods*. Inter-Disciplinary Press.

Hoogeveen, J.,Tesliuc, E., & Vakis, R. (2005). A guide to the analysis of risk, vulnerability and vulnerable groups, World Bank. Retrieved March 4, 2020, from http://siteresources.worldbank.org/INTSRM/Publications/20316319/RVA.pdf

Horn, R., Vahidy, S., & Charters, S. (2011). Testifying in the Special Court for Sierra Leone: Witness perceptions of safety and emotional welfare. *Psychology, Crime & Law, 17*(5), 435–455.

Human Rights Watch. (2009). Protecting child victims in sexual violence trials in the DR Congo: Suggestions for the way forward. Retrieved March 4, 2020, from https://www.hrw.org/news/2009/11/24/protecting-child-victims-sexual-violence-trials-dr-congo-suggestions-way-forward

Jones, N. (2009). *Promoting synergies between child protection and social protection: West and Central Africa, Regional Thematic Report 5 Study*. UNICEF WCARO and Overseas Development Institute.

Kaldor, M. (1999). *New and old wars: Organized violence in a global area*. Blackwell.

Lara, C. E. (2011). Child soldier testimony used in prosecuting war crimes in the International Criminal Court: Preventing further victimisation. *Southwestern Journal of International Law, 17*, 101–121.

Machel, G. (2001). *The impact of war on children: A review of progress since the 1996 United Nations Report on the impact of armed conflict on children*. Palgrave MacMillan.

McCarthy, C. (2012). *Reparations and victim support in the International Criminal Court*. Cambridge University Press.

Mouthaan, S. (2013). Victims participation at the ICC for victims of gender-based crimes - A conflict of interest? *Cardozo Journal of International and Comparative Law, 21*(3), 619–652.

Sabates-Wheeler, R., Devereux, S., & Hodges, A. (2009). Taking the long view: What does a child focus add to social protection? *IDS Bulletin, 40*(1), 109–119.

Sanin, K., & Stirnemann, A. (2006). Child witness at the Special Court for Sierra Leone, War Crimes Studies Center Berkeley. Retrieved May 20, 2020, from https://humanrights.stanford.edu/publications/child-witnesses-special-court-sierra-leone

Shabas, W. (2011). *An introduction to the International Criminal Court* (4th ed.). Cambridge University Press.

UNICEF. (2012). Inequities in early childhood development: What the data say: Evidence from the multiple indicator cluster surveys. Retrieved May 20, 2020, from https://www.unicef.org/publications/files/Inequities_in_Early_Childhood_Development_LoRes_PDF_EN_02082012.pdf

Urban, N. (2012). Direct and active participation in hostilities: The unintended consequences of the ICC's decision in Lubanga. EJIL:Talk! Blog of the European Journal of International Law. Retrieved May 20, 2020, from http://www.ejiltalk.org/direct-and-active-participation-in-hostilities-the-unintended-consequences-of-the-iccs-decision-in-lubanga/

Yehuda, R., Halligan, S. L., & Bierer, L. M. (2001). Relationship of parental trauma exposure and PTSD to PTSD, depressive and anxiety disorders in offspring. *Journal of Psychiatric Research, 35*(5), 261–270.

Zappalà, S. (2003). *Human rights in international criminal proceedings*. Oxford University Press.

Zermatten, J. (2015). Best interests of the child. In S. Mahmoudi, P. Leviner, A. Kaldal, & K. Lainpelto (Eds.), *Child-friendly justice: A quarter of a century of the UN Convention on the rights of the child (Stockholm studies in child law and children's rights)* (pp. 30–43). Brill-Nijhoff.

Zermatten, J. (2010). The best interests of the child principle, literal analysis and function. *International Journal of Children's Rights, 18*(4), 483–499.

Francesca Capone holds a Law Degree from the University of Naples Federico II and a Joint Ph. D. Degree from the Scuola Superiore Sant'Anna and Tilburg University. In 2012–2013 she worked as a research fellow at the British Institute of International and Comparative Law in London. She is Assistant Professor (tenure track position) of International Law at the Scuola Superiore Sant'Anna, where she serves also as a lecturer at both the undergraduate and postgraduate level. She has been a visiting fellow and a guest lecturer at several academic institutions across Europe, including Leiden University and the Max Planck Institute for Comparative Public Law and International Law. She has undertaken research on a wide range of topics, focussing in particular on children's rights and victims' right to a remedy and reparation. Her recent publications include Reparations for Child Victims of Armed Conflict: State of the Field and Current Challenges (Intersentia, 2017) and Foreign Fighters under International Law and Beyond, co-edited with Prof. Andrea de Guttry and Dr Christophe Paulussen (Springer/Asser Press, 2016).

Post-conflict Mental Health and the Role of Transitional Justice

Alvin Kuowei Tay and Zachary Steel

1 Introduction

The post-World War II era has seen a global shift in the nature of conflict with a reduction in the number of interstate and extrastate (colonial) conflicts but a rise in the number of intrastate conflicts (Mack et al., 2014; Themnér & Wallensteen, 2014) including those that have become internationalized with external states contributing troops to one of the warring sides. Notwithstanding evidence to suggest a general trend towards improved security internationally and a global reduction in armed conflict (Mack et al., 2014) recent decades have seen multiple countries and regions continue to be affected by periods of conflict. These have predominantly affected low-and-middle-income countries (Mack et al., 2014; Themnér & Wallensteen, 2014) and resulted in large sections of their civilian populations being exposed to mass conflict and gross human rights abuse.

The effects of mass violence are extensive and extend from the individual to the community and societal levels, resulting in severe destruction of vital institutions that collectively sustain a society such as economic, health and education systems; law and order, religious and cultural institutions; as well as the breakdown of social structures, networks, and relationships (Silove, 2004). At an individual level an extensive body of evidence has accumulated to show that populations exposed to endemic human rights abuse experience substantial mental health problems with depression and posttraumatic stress disorder (PTSD) being the most widely documented forms of mental disorder (Porter & Haslam, 2005; Reed et al., 2012; Steel et al., 2009b). A substantial proportion of those affected by post-conflict related mental disorders will continue to experience symptoms many years after the conflict period (Steel et al., 2009b).

A. K. Tay (✉) · Z. Steel
School of Psychiatry, University New South Wales, Sydney, NSW, Australia
e-mail: alvin.tay@unsw.edu.au; z.steel@unsw.edu.au

E. King et al. (eds.), *Victim Advocacy before the International Criminal Court*,
https://doi.org/10.1007/978-3-030-56733-0_14

The psychiatric diagnosis of PTSD came to prominence in the 1980s with the revision of the American Psychiatric diagnostic system (American Psychiatric Association, 1980). Although introduced primarily in response to the experiences of returning Vietnam veterans, the diagnosis has a long history prior to this period associated with periods of combat and mass disaster (Kinzie & Goetz, 1996; Wilson, 1994). The diagnosis is prototypically associated with distressing intrusive memories of traumatic incidents; nightmares and sleep disturbance; attempts to avoid reminders of traumatic incidents and heightened emotional reactivity when such reminders occur; persistent symptoms of hyperarousal and alterations in mood and cognition. PTSD is associated with high levels of comorbidity with other mental disorders such as major depressive disorder, alcohol and other substance abuse disorders and is associated with high levels of functional impairment and disability (American Psychiatric Association, 2013; Brunello et al., 2001). Within the post-conflict mental health field there has been a concern regarding the validity of PTSD across cultures and contexts. A number of critics have argued that PTSD may be a culture-bound construct of western societies that arose within a particular cultural context and noting in particular that there may be dangers regarding its uncritical extension to other settings (Bracken et al., 1995; Summerfield, 1999, 2001). Notwithstanding some important cautions noted by these commentators, accumulative evidence from a large number of qualitative and quantitative studies amongst conflict affected populations suggests that core symptoms of PTSD can be identified across a wide range of cultures and contexts (Hinton & Lewis-Fernández, 2011; Steel et al., 2009a, 2009b; Tay et al., 2015b).

There is increasing recognition that contextual factors such as lack of acknowledgement of past human rights violations, feelings of insecurity, and unresolved conflict in the homeland may influence the mental health and functioning outcomes of conflict-affected survivors (Silove, 1999; Silove & Steel, 2006). In particular, individual responses to experiences of persisting injustice (in relation to past and ongoing human rights violations) have been associated with several psychological problems following exposure to mass conflict and trauma (Başoğlu et al., 2005; Silove et al., 2014). For example, a growing body of studies have identified past experiences of injustice relating to gross human rights violations and persecution as one of the key factors in precipitating and perpetuating symptoms of posttraumatic stress disorder (PTSD) and chronic feelings of anger and resentment across a number of conflict-affected populations including in the Balkans (Başoğlu et al., 2005), amongst women residing in post-conflict Timor-Leste (Rees et al., 2013), and amongst West Papuan refugees settled in Australia (Rees & Silove, 2011; Tay et al., 2015a).

Post-conflict social reconstruction efforts by local authorities and the international community will necessarily focus on the crucial task of restoring social institutions supporting law enforcement and policing, investment and economic development, poverty reduction strategies including job creation and employment, re-establishing health care and education. Increasing evidence suggests that effective social reconstruction must also address establishing mechanisms to that can document the extent of and provide redress for the human rights abuses committed during the period of conflict (Cienfuegos & Monelli, 1983; Fletcher & Weinstein, 2002; Miller et al., 2008; Snyder & Vinjamuri, 2003; Vinck & Pham, 2008). Surveys of trauma survivors across multiple conflict settings where truth commissions have been undertaken including Argentina, Chile, El Salvador, Guatemala, South Africa, and Uganda have identified a significant demand by victims for justice in the aftermath of violent conflict (Backer, 2007; Wiebelhaus-Brahm, 2009).

2 Justice for Victims of Human Rights Abuse

Transitional justice refers to the set of judicial and quasi-judicial mechanisms that have been developed in post-conflict settings in response to mass atrocities and human rights abuses by acknowledging the impact of these experiences on individuals and communities through truth-telling, public apologies and other forms of reparation (Bell, 2009; Kritz, 2002), and by the establishment of judicial systems for holding perpetrators accountable for human rights violations under local or international law. Countries emerging from mass-conflict, autocratic rule and political instability face formidable challenges in developing the human resources, judicial processes, and political infrastructure required to implement legal mechanisms addressing the accountability of alleged perpetrators.

A major challenge that faces countries emerging from periods of prolonged conflict and mass-violence however has been the need to balance the right of victims for justice and the ongoing need for establishing a stable post-conflict society. Countries of Latin America that emerged from massive human rights violations in the 1970s and early 1980s such as Chile and El Salvador represent settings where truth telling and victims right to justice was placed second to nation building and stabilisation. The delay in justice did not reduce community demands that past abuses be examined but appears to have resulted in prolonged transitional justice procedures highlighting the critical importance of transitional justice as part of post-conflict peace building (Collins, 2008, 2010; Wiebelhaus-Brahm, 2009).

Perhaps in response to the persistence of political action around the inadequacy of mechanisms to address human rights abuse in the early aftermath of conflict in Latin America, the modern era has seen an expansion of models of transitional justice. The aim being to address the perceived need of establishing mechanism of redress for victims of violence and for holding accountable those who are directly or indirectly responsible for atrocities and other human rights abuses (Roht-Arriaza & Mariezcurrena, 2006; Teitel, 2003; Veale, 2010; Wiebelhaus-Brahm, 2009).

3 Contemporary Transitional Justice Models in Post-conflict Societies

It appears that three broad approaches to Transitional-Justice (TJ) can be identified: Those primarily involving the use of Truth and Justice Commissions, those that have mainly focused on punitive or retributive justice with the primary aim of holding trials and convicting perpetrators of human rights abuse, and models such as the International Criminal Court (ICC) which aim to provide an integrated form of truth telling, retributive and restorative justice. The value of each approach continues to be debated from multiple perspectives and within these debates it is important to understand what is known about the mental health impacts of these judicial and quasi-judicial procedures. There are compelling reasons to focus on the mental health effects of transitional justice models on survivors of war and persecution. Within the context of ICC for example, victims of war crimes appearing before the Court are typically subjected to legal procedures in which witnesses will be required to provide testimonial evidence and cross-examined in relation to their claims. Yet, little is known about the psychological effects of these procedures on individual survivors in the broader context of transitional justice. The purpose of this chapter is to describe and discuss the existing evidence with regards to mental health outcomes of different types of transitional justice approaches.

Countries emerging from decades-long autocratic rule often lack the necessary financial and human resources, judicial processes, and political infrastructure required to implement robust legal mechanisms for trying alleged perpetrators. Restorative justice programs such as truth commissions, reparation and amnesty programs emerged as alternative models as a consequence for enforcing accountability and justice in lieu of large-scale criminal proceedings (Roht-Arriaza & Mariezcurrena, 2006). These non-punitive measures give prominence to the needs of victims and have been incorporated into the broader agenda of restorative justice promotion at the international level as opposed to focusing on retributive justice (Braithwaite, 1989).

4 Mental Health of Victims of Human Rights Violations

Over recent years, there has been a burgeoning interest in the impacts of transitional justice initiatives on the long-term mental health outcomes of victims of human rights violations, in particular, whether these mechanisms have contributed to societal peace, communal stability, and individual recovery from the effects of trauma in post-conflict settings (Brounéus, 2008, 2010; Mendeloff, 2009; Pham et al. 2010; Silove et al., 2006). Specifically, critics have raised concern that community-oriented Truth and Justice initiatives aimed at promoting social reconciliation (for example through truth-telling, public apologies, or prosecution of perpetrators of war crimes) frequently occur against a backdrop of long-standing inter-ethnic and communal conflict (Pham et al., 2010). Within the context of clinical intervention, the focus is on the individual's intra-psychic processes and the impacts of extreme interpersonal violations (such as torture, rape, and abuse Foa, 1997, 2006). The tension between the imperative to bring about a sense of justice at the community level on the one hand, and the need to establish a therapeutic environment conducive to post-traumatic recovery at the individual level on the other, remains a critical issue to be addressed in contemporary models of transitional justice amongst victims of human rights abuses.

In considering these issues, we present a brief review of the extant body of research concerning the mental health impact of transitional justice programs including retributive (such as judicial tribunals) and restorative justice programs (such as truth and reconciliation commissions (TRC), drawing on studies undertaken in post-conflict South Africa, Rwanda, and the states of the Former Yugoslavia. Studies of TRC at the country level have examined the contributions of factors such as past conflict-related exposure, attitudes towards judicial responses, and openness to reconciliation, to mental health outcomes.

5 South Africa

In 1994, following the end of Apartheid, the newly elected democratic government of South Africa passed the *Promotion of National Unity and Reconciliation Act* 1995 (SA) that led to the creation of the TRC. According to the Act, the TRC was charged with the mandate of responding to mass atrocities committed by the Apartheid regime by providing reparations for victims and amnesty for perpetrators in exchange for the full disclosure of their criminality. The provisions were endorsed by the former and new governments with the chief aim of promoting truth-telling and forgiveness based on the model of restorative justice. Past studies that have examined the impact of the provisions of South African TRC on the mental health outcomes of individual victims have produced mixed results (Backer, 2007; Gibson, 2004; Heylen et al., 2010; Young, 2004).

Byrne (2004) in a study undertaken with thirty participants in the TRC found that only a small number of participants identified testifying before the commission as a positive experience, while the majority (80%) reported emotional distress and feelings of disempowerment following the commission. Hamber (2001) found that two out of twenty participants reported optimism and positive experiences in relation to their participation in the TRC, while the remainder participants reported feelings of ambivalence, discomfort, regret, and disappointment in the outcome. In a community-based study involving 400 participants, Backer (2007) found that half of the sample reported high levels of emotional distress while giving testimony. According to that study, participants showed wide variations in their reactions to the proceedings, ranging from low (64% reported testifying as a positive experience) to high levels of dissatisfaction.

Population-level mental health studies that have been undertaken in post-conflict countries have examined indices of victims' attitudes and reactions following their participation in TRC. In the largest study of the psychological impact of TRC to date, Stein et al. (2008) found that, while there was a general positive attitudes towards the TRC at a population level, those who had been involved directly in testifying before the TRC showed an increase in anger and distress and held negative views of the TRC. Those who reported anger appeared to be less likely to forgive perpetrators for their actions compared to those who did not (Stein et al., 2008).

A small set of studies show that the way in which TRC proceedings are conducted may impact on the mental health outcomes amongst victims. Allan and colleagues (Allan et al., 2006) following interviews with 134 survivors of torture and human rights abuse found that genuine remorse by the perpetrators was associated with higher feelings of forgiveness by victims. In a similar study into the impacts of forgiveness on past human rights violations (Kaminer et al., 2001) found no association between TRC participation and PTSD, depression, anxiety-related disorders, or attitudes towards forgiveness, suggesting that participants with PTSD show no symptomatic reduction from participating in the commission, and no evidence that they forgave the perpetrators as a result of their participation. One interpretation of these findings is that shortcomings in existing TRC procedures, whereby the absence of commensurate mechanisms to prosecute perpetrators for their crime, may have contributed to negative reactions by participants in relation to TRC.

Observations from mental health professionals in the Timor-Leste Commission for Reception, Truth and Reconciliation noted that the "failure to bring the main perpetrators to justice continued to generate widespread feelings of impotence and resentment amongst survivors and their families" (p. 197) particularly those identified as having the more severe histories of abuse and current difficulties (Le Touze et al., 2005). In a review of the South African TRC mental health literature, Mendeloff (Mendeloff, 2009) concludes that across multiple mental health studies, nearly all victims of human right abuse reported disappointment and ambivalence about the TRC. There was some evidence that those who provided testimony reported somewhat more favourable outcomes than those who did not, but any gain was very marginal. This stands in contrast to the broader community experience with the TRC which appears to have been more positive with evidence of the success of the process in promoting community reconciliation (Wiebelhaus-Brahm, 2009). For the most part, the empirical literature has tended to focus on the effects of TRC on individual experience, with relatively less attention paid to the broader community experience. Further research applying an ecological or community design is needed to evaluate the mental health effects of TRC at the individual and community levels.

6 The Republics of the Former Yugoslavia

The approach to TJ and redress for human rights abuse within the Republics of the former Yugoslavia applied a more traditional retributive justice model. The International Criminal Tribunal for the former Yugoslavia (ICTY), established following evidence of widespread ethnic cleansing in the Balkans, has been principal judicial mechanism designed to prosecute perpetrators of war crimes and crime against humanity committed during that period of time (Schabas, 2011). The few studies that have examined the mental health impacts of ICTY have depicted a complex and intricate relationship between participation in criminal proceedings, past human rights violations, and desire for justice and accountability, with contextual factors such as ongoing deprivations, perceived injustice playing an instrumental role in mediating that relationship., For example, in studies undertaken with 263 Croatian refugees and 300 Bosnian-Muslims located in Zagreb and Sarajevo respectively, Ivković (2001) found that, although participants reported in general positive experience about the ICTY, they expressed profound disappointment in its' outcome regarding the severity of punishment for the perpetrators. The research found no association between levels of trauma exposure and desire for vengeance. In accordance with these findings, a multiethnic study conducted with Serbian and Bosnian residents found that the former group reported negative feelings about the ICTY, while the latter were in favour of the Tribunal, these experiences were not associated with the impact of past trauma exposure (Biro et al., 2004). Other studies have found increase in hostility and violence between ethnic groups in Bosnia and Herzegovina following the issuance of arrest warrants and judgments by the ICTY (Meernik, 2005).

In an epidemiological survey of 1358 survivors of the Balkan wars reporting the relationship between individuals' perceptions of justice, accountability, and mental health outcomes, Başoğlu et al. (2005) found no association between reported desires for revenge or redress and symptoms of PTSD and depression. However, threats to safety and security and loss of control over life were associated with PTSD and depression. Consistent with previous research, the authors found that negative experience with the ICTY did not contribute to risk of traumatic stress or depression.

7 Truth Telling Before Transitional Justice Proceedings

There is a dearth of empirical studies into the effects of truth telling amongst victims of human rights violations before transitional justice proceedings. Mental health professionals have noted the psychological effects of trauma narration in which victims may experience a sense of "catharsis" after sharing their traumatic experiences. The legacy of testimonial therapy, a treatment approach pioneered by Chilean psychologists working with victims of the Pinochet Regime in 1970s (Cienfuegos & Monelli, 1983) has catalysed subsequent development of clinical modalities based on trauma narration. Adapted to and tested amongst refugees and post-conflict populations in transcultural settings, Narrative Exposure Therapy (NET) has shown effectiveness in reducing symptoms of posttraumatic stress and depression (Neuner et al., 2004). It is important to note however that such intervention models differ from contemporary models of transitional justice programs in which inquiries such as truth commissions are typically held in public arena with participants testifying in open settings before commissioners selected from a variety of backgrounds. Clinical interventions, however, conducted by an experienced therapist are based on a foundation of trust and respect, safety and security in which the victim is guided in sequential steps in narrating their traumatic experiences ("prolonged exposure therapy") with the ultimate aim of normalizing associated arousal and distress (Foa, 1997, 2000; Foa & Riggs, 1993).

Several mechanisms have been proposed by which truth telling in which victims provide testimonial accounts of past human rights violations before transitional justice proceedings may exert a positive influence on the mental health of participants. Specifically, proponents have postulated that the process of recounting traumatic experiences may reduce feelings of anger and desire for retaliation, which may, in turn, increase the likelihood of the individual engaging in reconciliation and non-violent actions, with the ultimate goal of achieving long-term peace and security (Mendeloff, 2009). An alternative theory is that the process of truth-telling may reduce the severity of trauma-related symptoms and distress, which may lead to tolerance and reconciliatory behaviour (Gibson, 2004). Conversely, lack of acknowledgement of past grievances and persecution are expected to exacerbate feelings of injustice and resentment, which may in turn contribute to a desire for vengeance, thereby increasing propensities for retributive justice and further episodes of violence (Gibson, 2004). Provisional data from past studies indicates that trauma survivors who reported a high level of psychiatric comorbidities were less likely to accept amnesty for perpetrators in Uganda and the Democratic Republic of Congo (DRC) (Pham et al., 2010). Similarly, a population level study undertaken with 2585 conflict survivors in Uganda found that symptoms of PTSD and depression were associated with propensities to engage in violent means to address ongoing conflict (Pham et al., 2010). Together, data from extant studies indicate that there is a complex relationship between past trauma, perceptions of justice, post-conflict attitudes in relation to reconciliation, ongoing political and social contexts, and mental health outcomes.

8 Rwanda

The 1994 Rwandan genocide resulted in deaths of over a million people as a result of ethnic violence perpetrated against the Tutsi minority and some Hutu moderates by the Hutu extremists (Melvern, 2000). To establish a judicial mechanism aimed at holding high office perpetrators accountable, the UN Security Council passed a resolution that led to the creation of the International Criminal Tribunal for Rwanda

(ICTR). Following the establishment of ICTR, gacaca courts, commonly presided over by lay 'judges' elected by members of the community, were established to complement the ICTR and the domestic Rwandan criminal justice system by trying perpetrators of less serious crimes through local judiciary processes and dispute resolution mechanisms. The proceedings were often held in classrooms or public settings across villages with numerous gacaca courts being utilised throughout the country (Pagnier, 2004).

Several studies have investigated the effects of gacaca participation on the mental health of victims. For example, in a multi-stage survey of 2074 participants of gacaca, Pham et al. (2004) reported that those who met criteria for PTSD were less likely to have positive attitudes towards local tribunals, belief in community, and interdependence with other ethnic groups. Whereas participants who reported exposure to multiple traumatic events were more likely to support the ICTR as opposed to gacaca trials, and less open towards reconciliation. In another study of 1200 gacaca participants, Brounéus (2010) found that witnesses testifying before gacaca trials reported higher levels of depression and PTSD compared to their non-witness counterparts, however, there was no association between higher levels of participation and psychiatric morbidity. In comparing the rates of PTSD and depression in the current study with that of the previous studies, the authors noted that mental health outcomes of participants of gacaca did not improve over time.

Qualitative data from in-depth interviews undertaken with sixteen female victims of sexual violence who testified before the gacaca revealed that virtually all women experienced retraumatization during and post-gacaca. The widely reported symptoms included re-experiencing, avoidance of reminders of traumatic experiences, and heightened physical reactions to environmental stimuli such as the sight of machetes and noises (Brounéus, 2008). Victims reported a wide range of physical problems related to sexual violations including severe headaches, genitourinary injury, sexually transmitted diseases, and HIV-AIDS. In addition, victims reported social ostracism from their community and associated feelings of shame and humiliation. Lack of security in the community placed women at direct risk of retaliation, threats, harassment, and further violence by perpetrators who continue to live the community (Brounéus, 2008).

In spite of the widespread implementation of transitional justice programs across post-conflict societies globally, there are limited data to support their effectiveness in assisting survivors recover from the effects of past trauma. Sound rigorous evaluations of these programs at the individual and community levels are needed to assist public health practitioners and policy makers involved in post-conflict development and stabilization.

Relatively little attention has been given to the mental health impacts of the process of truth-telling amongst victims of extreme human rights violations. A small body of studies undertaken in western countries with victims of sexual and other forms of gross human rights violations within the forensic and criminal justice contexts have highlighted the traumatizing effects of victim participation before criminal justice proceedings (Herman, 2003; Meffert et al., 2010).

9 Victim Testimony Before Criminal Justice Systems

There is a paucity of empirical data in relation to the mental health effects of complainer or victim participation in different forms of domestic legal intervention (Herman, 2003). In a study based on interviews with counsellors working with torture survivors involved in criminal and civil cases, O'Connell (2005) found that those who testified reported feelings of empowerment, acknowledgment, and disappointment. Those who were not directly involved in testifying reported negative experiences as a result of perceived disparity between severity of crimes and imposed punishments. Virtually all victims who participated in criminal trials as litigants reported negative experiences and fear of retraumatization.

An important factor in mediating the mental health effects of victim participation in legal intervention may be related to the quality of individuals' experience and interaction with the legal system. For example, in a study undertaken with rape victims, all participants interviewed who encountered complex challenges in interacting with the legal system reported higher levels of PTSD symptoms compared to those who did not report their rape (Campbell et al., 1999). In another study involving 93 survivors of childhood sexual abuse, participants who testified in court reported psychological distress and interpersonal disruptions (Campbell et al., 2001). Limitations in current research (such as lack of comparator groups, follow-up studies) however prevent definitive conclusions from being drawn. Further research based on experimental and longitudinal design and rigorous methodology is needed to shed light on these issues. Taken together, these findings are of particular relevance to victims appearing before the ICC who may be at substantial risk of PTSD and other mental disorders and who may be placed under similar circumstances involving testifying before alleged perpetrators and cross-examination over the course of the proceedings. It is therefore important for judicial, administrative personnel, or advocates for victims to be cognizant of the potentially traumatizing effects of the forms of legal intervention commonly applied in both domestic and international legal systems.

10 Conclusion

In spite of the widespread implementation of transitional justice programs across post-conflict societies globally, there is a paucity of empirical data to support the effects of these programs on the mental health and functioning outcomes of victims of extreme human rights violations. A key challenge confronted by policy makers and public health practitioners in post-conflict development efforts is to bring about a sense of justice and accountability at the individual and community levels, factors consistently identified as important by victims and their families (Backer, 2007; Wiebelhaus-Brahm, 2009). Most studies undertaken to date have focused largely on the mental health effects of victim participation before transition justice proceedings with comparatively less attention paid to the broader community experience and needs. Although reparation programs (for example, in the form of monetary compensation to the victim's family) have been used to supplement punitive measures to meet community demands for justice, evaluation of the effectiveness of these programs is needed. Data from extant studies from the diverse fields of psychiatric traumatology, public health, social sciences, forensic and criminal justice system have produced mixed results, suggesting that a wide range of factors, including victims' perception of justice, levels of exposure to past human rights violations, quality of individuals' experiences during transition justice proceedings, psychiatric morbidity, severity of imposed punishments for the perpetrator, attitudes in relation to reconciliation, ongoing political and social contexts interact in a complex manner in shaping the experience of victim participation (in the form of truth telling, narrating trauma histories) before transition justice proceedings. Our targeted review of the literature supports the need for further investigations into the mental health impact of transitional justice intervention on victims of mass human rights violations who are likely to face challenges in providing testimonial evidence before relevant decision makers given the high level of conflict-related psychiatric morbidity and impairment.

11 Recommendations

1. Advocates for victims appearing before the ICC must be sensitive to the pervasive effects of mass trauma and violence not only on the individual but also on the family and community where he or she resides.
2. Feelings of anger, resentment, grief, anxiety are common reaction patterns amongst survivors of extreme violence. These may be related to both historical (e.g., past human rights violations) and contemporary factors (e.g., gross deprivations, access to legal redress). Victim support services must include a focus on addressing these issues.
3. Post-traumatic reactions may manifest in a range of cognitive and behavioural symptoms (e.g., affect, expression, communication, and mannerism) in a manner that may impact on the capacity of the victim or complainer testifying before the ICC. Assessment of the credibility of witness testimony should be informed by a growing evidence base that traumatic injury can have a pervasive impact on the ability of affected witness to provide coherent testimonial evidence.
4. A multi-disciplinary approach drawing on the related fields of traumatology, psychiatry, social sciences, community mental health is needed to strengthen the existing mechanisms for supporting victims and witnesses appearing before the ICC.
5. Judicial and administrative personnel, advocates who work directly with alleged victims of war crimes should be encouraged to undertake training in the core areas identified above as a key component of ongoing professional development.

References

Allan, A., Allan, M. M., Kaminer, D., & Stein, D. J. (2006). Exploration of the association between apology and forgiveness amongst victims of human rights violations. *Behavioral Sciences & the Law, 24*(1), 87–102. https://doi.org/10.1002/bsl.689

American Psychiatric Association. (1980). *Diagnostic and Statistical Manual of Mental Disorders* (3rd ed.). American Psychiatric Association Press.

American Psychiatric Association. (2013). *Diagnostic and Statistical Manual of Mental Disorders* (5th ed.). American Psychiatric Association Press.

Backer, D. (2007). Victims' responses to truth commissions: Evidence from South Africa: When the wars end. In M. Ndulo (Ed.), *Security, reconstruction, and reconciliation: When the wars end* (pp. 165–196). University College London.

Başoğlu, M., Livanou, M., Crnobarić, C., Frančišković, T., Suljić, E., Durić, D., & Vranešić, M. (2005). Psychiatric and cognitive effects of war in former Yugoslavia association of lack of redress for trauma and posttraumatic stress reactions. *Journal of the American Medical Association, 294*(5), 580–590, e581–e582.

Bell, C. (2009). Transitional justice, interdisciplinarity and the state of the "field" or "non-field". *The International Journal of Transitional Justice, 3*(1), 5–27.

Biro, M., Ajdukovic, D., Corkalo, D., Djipa, D., Milin, P., & Weinstein, H. M. (2004). Attitudes toward justice and social reconstruction in Bosnia and Herzegovina and Croatia. In E. Stover & H. M. Weinstein (Eds.), *My neighbor, my enemy: Justice and community in the aftermath of mass atrocity* (pp. 183–205). Cambridge University Press.

Bracken, P. J., Giller, J. E., & Summerfield, D. (1995). Psychological responses to war and atrocity: The limitations of current concepts. *Social Science and Medicine, 40*(8), 1073–1082.

Braithwaite, J. (1989). *Crime, shame and reintegration*. Cambridge University Press.

Brounéus, K. (2008). Truth telling as talking cure? Insecurity and retraumatization in the Rwandan Gacaca courts. *Security Dialogue, 39*(1), 55–76.

Brounéus, K. (2010). The trauma of truth telling: Effects of witnessing in the Rwandan Gacaca courts on psychological health. *Journal of Conflict Resolution, 54*(3), 408–437.

Brunello, N., Davidson, J. R., Deahl, M., Kessler, R. C., Mendlewicz, J., Racagni, G., ... Zohar, J. (2001). Posttraumatic stress disorder: Diagnosis and epidemiology, comorbidity and social consequences, biology and treatment. *Neuropsychobiology, 43*(3), 150–162.

Byrne, C. C. (2004). Benefit or burden: Victims' reflections on TRC participation. *Peace and Conflict, 10*(3), 237–256.

Campbell, R., Sefl, T., Barnes, H. E., Ahrens, C. E., Wasco, S. M., & Zaragoza-Diesfeld, Y. (1999). Community services for rape survivors: Enhancing psychological well-being or increasing trauma? *Journal of Consulting and Clinical Psychology, 67*(6), 847–858.

Campbell, R., Wasco, S. M., Ahrens, C. E., Sefl, T., & Barnes, H. E. (2001). Preventing the "second rape" rape survivors' experiences with community service providers. *Journal of Interpersonal Violence, 16*(12), 1239–1259.

Cienfuegos, A. J., & Monelli, C. (1983). The testimony of political repression as a therapeutic instrument. *American Journal of Orthopsychiatry, 53*(1), 43–51.

Collins, C. (2008). State terror and the law: The (Re)judicialization of human rights accountability in Chile and El Salvador. *Latin American Perspectives, 35*(5), 20–37.

Collins, C. (2010). *Post-transitional justice: Human rights trials in Chile and El Salvador*. Penn State University Press.

Fletcher, L. E., & Weinstein, H. M. (2002). Violence and social repair: Rethinking the contribution of justice to reconciliation. *Human Rights Quarterly, 24*(3), 573–639.

Foa, E. B. (1997). Psychological processes related to recovery from a trauma and an effective treatment for PTSD. *Annals of New York Academy of Sciences, 821*, 410–424.

Foa, E. B. (2000). Psychosocial treatment of posttraumatic stress disorder. *Journal of Clinical Psychiatry, 61*(Suppl. 5), 43–51.

Foa, E. B. (2006). Psychosocial therapy for posttraumatic stress disorder. *Journal of Clinical Psychiatry, 67*(Suppl. 2), 40–45.
Foa, E. B., & Riggs, D. S. (1993). Post-traumatic stress disorder in rape victims. *American Psychiatric Press Review of Psychiatry, 12*, 273–303.
Gibson, J. L. (2004). Does truth lead to reconciliation? Testing the causal assumptions of the South African truth and reconciliation process. *American Journal of Political Science, 48*(2), 201–217.
Hamber, B. (2001). Does the truth heal? A psychological perspective on political strategies for dealing with the legacy of political violence. In N. Biggar (Ed.), *Burying the past: Making peace and doing justice after civil conflict* (pp. 131–148). Georgetown University Press.
Herman, J. L. (2003). The mental health of crime victims: Impact of legal intervention. *Journal of Traumatic Stress, 16*(2), 159–166.
Heylen, B., Parmentier, S., & Weitekamp, E. (2010). The emergence of "holistic reconciliation": Lessons learned from victims and offenders inside the South African truth and reconciliation commission. *International Perspectives on Victimology, 5*, 1–12.
Hinton, D. E., & Lewis-Fernández, R. (2011). The cross-cultural validity of posttraumatic stress disorder: Implications for DSM-5. *Depression and Anxiety, 28*(9), 783–801. https://doi.org/10.1002/da.20753
Ivković, S. K. (2001). Justice by the international criminal tribunal for the former Yugoslavia. *Stanford Journal of International Law, 37*(2), 255–334.
Kaminer, D., Stein, D. J., Mbanga, I., & Zungu-Dirwayi, N. (2001). The Truth and Reconciliation Commission in South Africa: Relation to psychiatric status and forgiveness among survivors of human rights abuses. *British Journal of Psychiatry, 178*, 373–377.
Kinzie, J. D., & Goetz, R. R. (1996). A century of controversy surrounding posttraumatic stress-spectrum syndromes: The impact on DSM-III and DSM-IV. *Journal of Traumatic Stress, 9*(2), 159–179.
Kritz, N. J. (2002). Progress and humility: The ongoing search for post-conflict justice. In M. C. Bassiouni (Ed.), *Post-conflict justice* (pp. 55–88). Martinus Nijhoff.
Le Touze, D., Silove, D., & Zwi, A. (2005). Can there be healing without justice? Lessons from the commission for reception, truth and reconciliation in East Timor. *Intervention, 3*(3), 192–202.
Mack, A., Merz, S., Bui, M., Cooper, T., Echlin, G., Gray, J. L., Harris, K., & Ridgway, L. (2014). *Human Security Report 2013*. Human Security Press.
Meernik, J. (2005). Justice and peace? How the international criminal tribunal affects societal peace in Bosnia. *Journal of Peace Research, 42*(3), 271–289.
Meffert, S. M., Musalo, K., McNiel, D. E., & Binder, R. L. (2010). The role of mental health professionals in political asylum processing. *Journal of the American Academy of Psychiatry and the Law, 38*(4), 479–489.
Melvern, L. (2000). *A people betrayed: The role of the west in Rwanda's genocide*. Zed Books.
Mendeloff, D. (2009). Trauma and vengeance: Assessing the psychological and emotional effects of post-conflict justice. *Human Rights Quarterly, 31*(3), 592–623.
Miller, K. E., Omidian, P., Rasmussen, A., Yaqubi, A., & Daudzai, H. (2008). Daily stressors, war experiences, and mental health in Afghanistan. *Transcultural Psychiatry, 45*(4), 611–638. https://doi.org/10.1177/1363461508100785
Neuner, F., Schauer, M., Klaschik, C., Karunakara, U., & Elbert, T. (2004). A comparison of narrative exposure therapy, supportive counseling, and psychoeducation for treating posttraumatic stress disorder in an African refugee settlement. *Journal of Consulting and Clinical Psychology, 72*(4), 579–587.
O'Connell, J. (2005). Gambling with the psyche: Does prosecuting human rights violators console their victims? *Harvard International Law Journal, 46*(2), 295–345.
Pagnier, J. (2004). *Gacaca tribunals: Justice and reconciliation in Rwanda?* Master's thesis. The Netherlands: University of Amsterdam.
Pham, P. N., Vinck, P., & Weinstein, H. M. (2010). Human rights, transitional justice, public health and social reconstruction. *Social Science and Medicine, 70*(1), 98–105.

Pham, P. N., Weinstein, H. M., & Longman, T. (2004). *Journal of the American Medical Association, 292*(5), 602–612.

Porter, M., & Haslam, N. (2005). Predisplacement and postdisplacement factors associated with mental health of refugees and internally displaced persons: A meta-analysis. *JAMA, 294*(5), 602–612.

Reed, R. V., Fazel, M., Jones, L., Panter-Brick, C., & Stein, A. (2012). Mental health of displaced and refugee children resettled in low-income and middle-income countries: Risk and protective factors. *The Lancet, 379*(9812), 250–265.

Rees, S., Silove, D., Verdial, T., Tam, N., Savio, E., Fonseca, Z., . . . Steel, Z. (2013). Intermittent explosive disorder amongst women in conflict affected Timor-Leste: Associations with human rights trauma, ongoing violence, poverty, and injustice. *PLoS One, 8*(8), e69207. https://doi.org/10.1371/journal.pone.0069207

Rees, & Silove, D. (2011). Sakit Hati: A state of chronic mental distress related to resentment and anger amongst West Papuan refugees exposed to persecution. *Social Science and Medicine, 73*(1), 103–110. https://doi.org/10.1016/j.socscimed.2011.05.004

Roht-Arriaza, N., & Mariezcurrena, J. (2006). *Transitional justice in the twenty-first century: Beyond truth versus justice*. Cambridge University Press.

Schabas, W. (2011). *An introduction to the International Criminal Court* (4th ed.). Cambridge University Press.

Silove, D. (1999). The psychosocial effects of torture, mass human rights violations, and refugee trauma: Toward an integrated conceptual framework. *Journal of Nervous and Mental Disease, 187*(4), 200–207.

Silove, D. (2004). The challenges facing mental health programs for post-conflict and refugee communities. *Prehospital and Disaster Medicine, 19*(1), 90–96.

Silove, D., Liddell, B., Rees, S., Chey, T., Nickerson, A., Tam, N., . . . Steel, Z. (2014). Effects of recurrent violence on post-traumatic stress disorder and severe distress in conflict-affected Timor-Leste: A 6-year longitudinal study. *Lancet Global Health, 2*(5), e293–e300. https://doi.org/10.1016/s2214-109x(14)70196-2

Silove, D., & Steel, Z. (2006). Understanding community psychosocial needs after disasters: Implications for mental health services. *Journal of Postgraduate Medicine, 52*(2), 121–125.

Silove, D., Zwi, A. B., & le Touze, D. (2006). Do truth commissions heal? The East Timor experience. *Lancet, 367*(9518), 1222–1224. https://doi.org/10.1016/S0140-6736(06)68519-X. S0140-6736(06)68519-X [pii].

Snyder, J., & Vinjamuri, L. (2003). Principle and pragmatism in strategies of international justice. *International Security, 28*(3), 5–44.

Steel, Z., Bateman Steel, C. R., & Silove, D. (2009a). Human rights and the trauma model: Genuine partners or uneasy allies? *Journal of Traumatic Stress, 22*(5), 358–365.

Steel, Z., Chey, T., Silove, D., Marnane, C., Bryant, R. A., & van Ommeren, M. (2009b). Association of torture and other potentially traumatic events with mental health outcomes among populations exposed to mass conflict and displacement: A systematic review and meta-analysis. *JAMA, 302*(5), 537–549.

Stein, D. J., Seedat, S., Kaminer, D., Moomal, H., Herman, A., Sonnega, J., & Williams, D. R. (2008). The impact of the truth and reconciliation commission on psychological distress and forgiveness in South Africa. *Social Psychiatry and Psychiatric Epidemiology, 43*(6), 462–468. https://doi.org/10.1007/s00127-008-0350-0

Summerfield, D. (1999). A critique of seven assumptions behind psychological trauma programmes in war-affected areas. *Social Science and Medicine, 48*(10), 1449–1462.

Summerfield, D. (2001). The invention of post-traumatic stress disorder and the social usefulness of a psychiatric category. *BMJ (Clinical Research Ed.), 322*(7278), 95–98. https://doi.org/10.1136/bmj.322.7278.95

Tay, A. K., Rees, S., Chen, J., Kareth, M., & Silove, D. (2015a). Examining the broader psychosocial effects of mass conflict on PTSD symptoms and functional impairment amongst West

Papuan refugees resettled in Papua New Guinea (PNG). *Social Science & Medicine, 132*, 70–78. https://doi.org/10.1016/j.socscimed.2015.03.020
Tay, A. K., Rees, S., Chen, J., Kareth, M., & Silove, D. (2015b). The structure of post-traumatic stress disorder and complex post-traumatic stress disorder amongst West Papuan refugees. *BMC Psychiatry*. https://doi.org/10.1186/s12888-015-0480-3
Teitel, R. G. (2003). Transitional justice genealogy. *Harvard Human Rights Journal, 16*(1), 69–94.
Themnér, L., & Wallensteen, P. (2014). Armed conflicts, 1946-2013. *Journal of Peace Research, 51*(4), 541–554.
Veale, A. (2010). Transitional justice, post-conflict agendas, and psychology. *Peace and Conflict: Journal of Peace Psychology, 16*(3), 323–326.
Vinck, P., & Pham, P. (2008). Ownership and participation in transitional justice mechanisms: A sustainable human development perspective from eastern Democratic Republic of Congo. *The International Journal of Transitional Justice, 2*(3), 398–411.
Wiebelhaus-Brahm, E. (2009). *Truth commissions and transitional societies: The impact on human rights and democracy*. Taylor and Francis Group.
Wilson, J. P. (1994). The historical evolution of PTSD diagnostic criteria: From Freud to DSM-IV. *Journal of Traumatic Stress, 7*(4), 681–698.
Young, S. (2004). Narrative and healing in the hearings of the South African Truth and Reconciliation Commission. *Biography - An Interdisciplinary Quarterly, 27*(1), 145–162.

Alvin Kuowei Tay is National Health and Medical Research Council (NHMRC) Clinical Fellow at the School of Psychiatry, UNSW, Sydney, Australia. He also a Visiting Scholar in the Department of Clinical Psychology, and the Global Mental Health Lab, at Teachers College, Columbia University, and an expert Advisor to the United Nations in New York. His research spans psychiatric epidemiology, global mental health psychological and psychosocial treatments across low-and-middle-income and high-income settings. He is an active member of the Australian Psychological Society, Singapore Psychological Society, and a fellow of the Hong Kong Psychological Society.

Zachary Steel is a Clinical Psychologist and holds the St John of God Chair of Trauma and Mental Health a partnership between St John of God Richmond Hospital, the School of Psychiatry UNSW and the Black Dog Institute. Professor Steel's research has focused on the wellbeing of people exposed to mass global conflicts. He has undertaken research and clinical work with communities in Australia including refugees, asylum seekers, aboriginal communities, veterans, police and emergency service workers and with trauma-affected populations in Indonesia, East Timor and Vietnam.

Effective Communication in Multilingual Judicial Proceedings

Andrew Constable

1 Introduction: Legal Basis of ICC Language Regime and Linguistic Responsibilities

The territorial jurisdiction of the International Criminal Court (ICC) has resulted in investigations in a large number of geographical areas in which the languages spoken are as numerous as they are diverse, giving the ICC a language regime unlike any other international organisation. The linguistic rights of the accused are set out in Article 67 of the Rome Statute, namely "(a) To be informed promptly and in detail of the nature, cause and content of the charge, in a language which the accused fully understands and speaks", and "(f) To have, free of any cost, the assistance of a competent interpreter and such translations as are necessary to meet the requirements of fairness, if any of the proceedings of or documents presented to the Court are not in a language which the accused fully understands and speaks".

In addition, several other provisions of the Rules of Procedure and Evidence have relevance to linguistic services at the Court, including Rule 76(1), which provides that the "statements of prosecution witnesses shall be made available in original and in a language which the accused fully understands and speaks". Finally, it should be noted that under Article 64(2) of the Rome Statute it is the Trial Chamber that is responsible for ensuring that a trial is fair, expeditious and "conducted with full respect for the rights of the accused".

Trials at the ICC are held in the working languages of the Court (English and French) and in the so-called situation languages, i.e. the language(s) of the accused

The views expressed herein are those of the author alone and cannot be taken as reflecting the views of the International Criminal Court.

A. Constable (✉)
The Hague, The Netherlands
e-mail: a.constable@aiic.net

E. King et al. (eds.), *Victim Advocacy before the International Criminal Court*,
https://doi.org/10.1007/978-3-030-56733-0_15

(there may be more than one accused in a particular trial) and the languages spoken by the witnesses called to testify at trial, with hearings to date held in up to four languages.

The Language Services Section (LSS) of the Registry is tasked with the provision of Court translation and interpreting services to meet the Court's commitments under the Rome Statute. It provides simultaneous interpreting in the working languages of the Court, the official languages of the Court, and in the situation languages of the Court, which have included languages of lesser diffusion (LLDs) such as Acholi, Congolese Swahili, Lingala, Sango and Zaghawa. Where no simultaneous interpreters can be found (which is frequently the case for LLDs) with the specific language combination required to interpret for the accused in a given case, LSS recruits and trains linguists with the requisite combination in simultaneous interpreting, a process that takes a minimum of six months (Constable, 1996, p. 73). However, for the interpretation of specific witnesses with languages for which no simultaneous interpreters can be found, LSS provides training in consecutive interpreting in a much shorter programme, with a mixture of consecutive and simultaneous interpreting being used at trial.

Alongside the interpreter training, LSS undertakes considerable terminological work with linguists and the trainee interpreters in the situation languages, for example in the area of legal terminology, where many of the concepts of common law, civil law and international criminal law may not exist in certain situation languages of lesser diffusion.

2 Simultaneous Interpretation in International Criminal Proceedings

> Quality in interpreting cannot be regarded as the sole responsibility of interpreters. All parties need to assume responsibility (Hale et al., 2009, p. 3).

> The Members of the Court do not necessarily follow the oral submissions in the language in which they are made but often listen to the simultaneous interpretation. This imposes certain constraints to which Counsel should, in their own interests, be attentive in order to ensure that what they say is perfectly understood by the Members of the Court. Counsel must therefore regard the interpreters as essential partners in the presentation of their argument (CJEC, 2009).

Simultaneous interpretation has been the modus operandi in international criminal tribunals since it was first implemented in response to the linguistic challenges of the Nuremberg tribunal, where trials had to be expeditious yet held in its four languages (Gaiba, 1998). This rationale is still valid today, with simultaneous interpretation having been the mode used in the hearings of the UN international criminal tribunals (ICTY, ICTR), the so-called hybrid or internationalised criminal tribunals (STL, ECCC, SCLC), as well as the ICC.

The quality of such interpretation, and thus the accuracy and reliability of any transcription thereof, is of fundamental importance in bilingual or multilingual trials. The requirement pertains to the primacy of the principle of orality in international criminal law (Klamberg, 2013, p. 417), namely that witness testimony should be given live, *viva voce* and under oath. Thus, the interpretation of oral proceedings and the transcripts thereof form an integral part of the court record. According to Trial Chamber I of the International Criminal Court (ICC) in the *Lubanga* case (2009), "[i] t is well arguable that the right to a fair trial includes access to a reliable record of the proceedings".

The following subsections are intended to give counsel an insight into the processes involved in simultaneous interpretation, explaining its inherent limitations compared to translation as well as associated "problem triggers" (Gile, 1995). With a view to making recommendations for counsel working with interpreters, focus is first placed on Gile's Effort Model and its notions of Short-term Memory Effort and Listening and Analysis Effort in simultaneous interpreting. This paper will then set out associated problem triggers before giving examples of best practice and recommendations.

2.1 Translation, Interpretation and Transcription

The fact that the court interpreter's output is transcribed and thereby converted into written form, taking on the allure of translation, gives rise to end-user expectations of accuracy and reliability on a par with those for written translation. Despite the very different production methods as well as quantitative and qualitative output of translation and interpretation, the transcription of simultaneous interpretation constitutes evidence in criminal proceedings. The levels of scrutiny that the interpretation is subject to in international criminal proceedings is therefore unlike many conference interpreting environments.

> Accuracy is central to the work of all interpreters. In a criminal trial it is essential. The interpreters' words become evidence, as they are recorded in transcripts that become the official trial record and are quoted in judgments. At the ICTY, the prosecution and defence are constantly scrutinising the transcript in court, ready to challenge any aspect of the interpretation that they consider incorrect, or prejudicial to their cause (Mackintosh, 2015, p. 192).

As much of the work of counsel requires reference to court translations, courtroom interpretation and transcripts of oral proceedings, it is important to understand the difference between them, as the nature of their respective sources and modes of production dictate both the nature and quality of the corresponding product.

Otto Kade (1968), a self-taught interpreter and translation scholar at the University of Leipzig, adopted the English word "Translation" as a German term to cover both translation (Übersetzen) and interpreting (Dolmetschen) (Pöchhacker, 2004, p. 10; Munday, 2009, p. 9). Interpreting in his definition is a translational activity distinctive for its immediacy, a special form of "Translation" (Pöchhacker, 2004, p. 9).

> As early as the 1960s, Otto Kade (1968) defined interpreting as a form of translation (in the wider sense) in which (a) the source-language text is presented only once and thus cannot be reviewed or replayed, and (b) the target-language text is produced under time pressure, with little chance for correction and revision.
>
> This far-sighted definition avoids the usual reference to spoken messages and elegantly accommodates also interpreting from, into or between signed languages, as well as such variants of interpreting as 'sight translation' and live subtitling. Foregrounding the aspect of immediacy, or real-time performance, interpreting could be described more succinctly as a translational activity in which a first and final rendition in another language is produced on the basis of a one-time presentation of an utterance (or text) in a source language (Pöchhacker, 2009, p. 133).

This definition of interpreting, with the focus on the "here and now" as opposed to the oral element is different from the common usage, where interpreting is equated with the 'oral rendering of spoken messages' (Pöchhacker, 2004, p. 10). Elena de Jongh's definition encapsulates the more commonly articulated dichotomy between oral interpreting and written translation as follows:

> *Translation* generally refers to the transfer of thoughts and ideas from one language (the source language) to another (the target language) by means of the written word. *Interpretation* refers to oral communication situations in which one person speaks in the source language, an interpreter processes this input and produces output in a second language, and another person (or persons) listen(s) to the interpreted target language version of the original speaker's message. The term "translation", therefore, refers to the processing of written language while "interpretation" refers to the processing of spoken language. Translation converts a written text into another written text, while interpretation converts an oral message into another oral message (de Jongh, 1992, p. 35).

Given that certain interpreting problem triggers commonly encountered in international courts have an oral source element, it is useful to adopt a definition that encompasses elements of both definitions above. Interpreting could be described as the immediate and real-time oral or signed rendition of a spoken or physical source language into a target language, and translation as the written rendition of source language text into a target language. Both are bilingual processes but translation lacks the immediacy and orality—at least in the case of a spoken source[1]—of interpreting.

Unlike translation or interpretation, *transcription* is a monolingual process. It is the conversion of spoken language into written language (Gibbons, 2003, p. 28). Transcription of oral judicial proceedings is performed live or *post facto* by court reporters (also known as stenographers, recorders, transcribers or keepers of the record (Elias-Bursać, 2015, p. 88)). In international criminal proceedings, live or real-time transcription is common, although not necessarily in all languages of the

[1] For example, sight translation—though spoken—has a written source and thereby lacks certain problem triggers of simultaneous interpreting.

proceedings.[2] At the ICC, real-time transcription is available in both French and English, the transcripts of which can be accessed during the proceedings via personal monitors in the courtroom and interpreter booths. The written transcript of the proceedings (including the transcription of the interpretation) is published after the hearing as the record of the oral proceedings.

> [A]ll public sessions of the ICTY are web-cast and all its proceedings, whether in public or closed session, are recorded and transcribed, which places additional burden on the interpreters who, unlike translators, work in real time. The level of accuracy expected of ICTY interpreters is quite a bit higher than in a typical conference setting and can be likened to the one required for translation (Pavetić, 2012; Elias-Bursać, 2015, p. 92).

Although courtroom transcripts of interpretation may appear to be a translation—at least in form (written)—they are not. They remain transcription of the interpretation due to the process involved in their production. The same is true if a text is read out in court and the interpretation thereof transcribed; although this constitutes the conversion of a written text in one language into a written text in another, no written translation process has actually occurred.

The filings in relation to Sreten Lukić' Submission Relative to Translation Verification of 31 August 2007 before the International Criminal Tribunal for the former Yugoslavia (ICTY) are instructive by way of example. In its application to the Chamber, the Lukić Defence advocates a literalist view of the interpreter's role as performing "verbatim translation" (Morris, 1995; Laster & Taylor, 1994, p. 112).

In the application, the Lukić Defence requested the Chamber to "take steps to ensure that the translation service is providing verbatim and accurate translation of the proceedings, so as to preserve the transcript record" as follows:

> For purposes of preserving a proper record of these proceedings, and more importantly, for purposes of preparing cross examination, it is essential for the transcript and record of proceedings, as much as possible, [to] provide an accurate, verbatim record of the sworn testimony of witnesses. Without such a record, the integrity of these proceedings is called into question... (ICTY, 2007, p. 1).

The Registry response highlights the importance of adequately delineating interpretation and translation in terms of their nature, purpose, means of production, notions of accuracy and qualitative expectations:

> The language services provided by the Registry during court proceedings at the Tribunal is interpretation and not translation. Interpretation is used for oral communication whereas translation deals with transcription of the written word....
>
> Simultaneous interpretation is the rendition of the speech in the target language as it is being delivered in the source language. Since interpreters, unlike translators, have to deal with fleeting messages in real time, synthesizing and editing are not only legitimate interpretation techniques but they are necessary to make it possible....

---

[2] Although the record of court proceedings at the International Criminal Tribunal for the former Yugoslavia (ICTY) was in English and French, real-time transcription was only provided in English (Elias-Bursać, 2015, p. 65). As was the practice at the ICTY and ICTR (International Criminal Tribunal for Rwanda) (Elias-Bursać, 2015, p. 66), ICC transcripts are provided in English and French only, not in other languages that may be spoken by the accused or witnesses appearing before the court.

> [T]he Registry notes that the level of accuracy and completeness of the simultaneous interpretation services provided for hearings meets the highest standards expected of the profession (Lukić Decision, 2007, pp. 2, 3, 4).

The example echoes Holly Mikkelsons's (1999:1) assertion that "it is clear that a verbatim interpretation of courtroom proceedings is meaningless, if not impossible": interpreters "must convey the meaning of the source-language message as precisely as they can within the limits of the target language's grammar and syntax". The Registry response furthermore underscores one of the key differences between translation and interpretation as the "real time" element of the latter, requiring interpreters to use certain legitimate interpreting techniques which would be inappropriate for written translation.

2.2 *Quantitative Output of Interpreters and Translators*

Translation can be measured both in terms of source language input or target language output, for example in the number of words (or standard pages) translated per day. Quantitative assessments of interpretation are generally not made in terms of interpreter output but in terms of the speed of source language input, which in interpretation studies literature is often quantified in words per minute (wpm).

A common question about source language input for interpreters is whether there is a maximum delivery rate to be adhered to by speakers (measured in wpm) for successful interpretation to take place, and if so, what it is. Experiments have been carried out to ascertain what input speeds (speed of delivery by the original speaker) result in a higher frequency of errors or omissions by the interpreter (omissions are mentioned separately here as they can both be accidental errors but also strategic omissions of redundant or repetitive items, for example, made deliberately to permit successful interpretation at higher delivery rates).

Kilian Seeber provides a succinct overview of interpreting studies literature on appropriate delivery rates for speakers who are being interpreted simultaneously, stating that the input rate recommended for simultaneous interpretation "ranges between 95 and 120 wpm (Gerver, 1976; Seleskovitch, 1978; Lederer, 1981). These recommendations seem warranted: research indicates that omissions, substitutions and pronunciation errors (Pio, 2003) increase with higher rates of input", making input rate a "major constraining factor" in simultaneous interpretation (Seeber, 2011, p. 186).

Translation rates are, as mentioned, usually measured in terms of the number of words per day. Assuming a translator works an 8-hour day and translates 1650 words per day,[3] the average hourly translation rate is 206 words, or approx. 100 words per half hour. On the other hand, a simultaneous interpreter working at the highest recommended input rate of 120 words per minute (i.e. two words per second) will

[3]The standard United Nations rate is 1650 words per day (UN A/57/289, 2002, p. 13) subject to revision, a process of quality-control by a senior translator.

interpret 3600 words in a 30-min turn (maximum recommended turn length for simultaneous interpreters). This then raises the question as to why organisations employ translators at all if simultaneous interpreters are capable of producing oral translation (which could then be transcribed) *of the same quality* at 36 times the translator rate?

2.3 Qualitative Output of Interpreters and Translators

Whereas simultaneous interpreters hear a spoken utterance once and have to formulate the message in another language within seconds (or even split-seconds), translators have the time to consult various resources, e.g. works of reference, terminology databases, corpuses of similar previously translated texts, etc., as well as to reread or read ahead in the written text to aid their understanding of the source material and to find the appropriate expression in the target language (Skaaden, 2013, p. 19). Given the constraints of simultaneous interpretation, it is clear that we cannot have the same qualitative expectations of interpretation as we have of translation.

This therefore raises the question as to whether, rather than relying on transcripts of interpretation, full verbatim written translations should be made of transcripts of original courtroom discourse to ensure the reliability and accuracy of the record of proceedings, with the simultaneous interpretation itself serving solely to facilitate communication live in the courtroom. There is indeed a precedent for this, given that it is the practice at the International Court of Justice. Furthermore, outside of the judicial environment, transcription of interpretation is by far the exception. Kalina describes the use of interpreter output as a basis for transcription as a "violation of the rule that interpretation products are intended only for the moment and to make people understand each other in a multilingual setting" (Kalina, 2010, p. 94).

However, hitherto international criminal courts and tribunals, which have lengthy oral proceedings, have chosen not to adopt this *modus operandi* due to the significant associated time and financial constraints. If we take a delivery rate of 120 words per minute, in a typical court day at the ICC of 270 min (four and a half hours excluding breaks), we come to a figure of 32,400 words, which at the above translation output rates would take approximately 20 days for one translator to produce, or 1 day for a team of 20 translators.

Here it should be said that the speed of translation is also dependent on many factors, including the use of footnotes, density of material etc. Given that much courtroom dialogue may be extemporaneous speech, it may be assumed that translation of courtroom speech could be performed at higher rates than the 1650 words per day rate quoted here. However, official court translations at the ICC must also be revised, which would limit the daily capacity to that of the reviser or team of revisers, which at the standard UN rate would be 3960 words per day (UN A/57/289, 2002, p. 13).

Where hearings are held on a daily basis, and in particular where concurrent hearings are held, the amount of translation required—and therefore the number of translators required to perform it—would grow exponentially, as would the costs and delays. This could potentially undermine the accused's right to expeditious proceedings, irrespective of the potentially negative budgetary impact on the institution concerned.

Given that this method has therefore not been adopted at international criminal courts and tribunals, there is a need to ensure that the quality and accuracy of the court record is as near to translation level as possible while the method of production remains transcription of the simultaneous interpretation. It is the contention of this paper that the court record can meet the levels of accuracy and reliability required for international criminal proceedings where best practice prevails and courtroom parties and participants work together to ensure effective multilingual communication.

2.4 The Process of "Simultaneous" Interpretation

In order for counsel to understand the inherent limitations of simultaneous interpretation, and how to work most effectively within them, it is useful to understand the cognitive processes involved in interpretation.

> Simultaneous interpreting is a highly complex cognitive activity (Gerver, 1974; Moser, 1978; Paradis, 1994) that requires the interpreter to simultaneously listen, analyze, comprehend, translate, edit and reproduce in real-time a speaker's utterance (Moser-Mercer et al., 1998, p. 47).

Interpretation is not instantaneous, as the word "simultaneous" is sometimes assumed to convey. The interpreter must comprehend a source language utterance before delivering it in the target language, something that creates a lag of a few seconds between the source language input and the target language output. Research has shown that the average lag, or ear-to-voice span (EVS) as it is known in interpretation literature, is around three seconds (Seeber, 2011, p. 185).[4]

[4] Although different to the ear-to-voice lag, the interpreting lag, namely the time from initial source utterance to final interpreter output will be cumulated in cases where relay interpretation is used, where the source language is interpreted into a first target language (the "pivot" language) which is then used as the source language for interpretation into a second (or more) target language(s) (i.e. the interpretation between two languages is not direct but passes through a third (pivot) language). Relay interpretation is used where the interpreters do not speak all the languages used in the courtroom but do share a common pivot language which can be used to provide the relay from and into those languages they do not speak. This mode of interpretation has been used at the ICC for simultaneous interpretation at proceedings with Acholi, Lingala, Sango, Swahili and Zaghawa.

2.5 Daniel Gile's Effort Model of Interpretation

Performing the tasks outlined above simultaneously requires intense mental energy and effort on the part of the interpreter. It is the concept that such energy is finite that underpins the "Effort Model" developed by Daniel Gile (1995) to analyse interpretation processes. His model is based on two ideas: that interpretation requires mental energy, a necessarily finite resource, and that where the act of interpretation requires greater mental energy than is available at any given time to the interpreter, this will result in cognitive overload and a deterioration in performance (Gile, 1995, p. 161). Although other models have been developed in the field of interpretation studies to describe the interpretation process, Gile's model is particularly useful when it comes to explaining "triggers" of interpretation problems and hence the recommendations that can be made to speakers to avoid them.

According to Gile's model, simultaneous interpretation consists of the following Efforts: a Listening and Analysis Effort, a Short-term Memory Effort, a Speech Production Effort and a Coordination Effort (Gile, 1995, p. 169).

The Listening and Analysis Effort consists of "all comprehension-oriented operations, from the analysis of the sound waves carrying the source-language speech which reach the interpreter's ears, through the identification of words, to the final decisions about the 'meaning' of the utterance" (Gile, 1995, p. 162). The Memory Effort refers to the short-term memory operations that continually occur in simultaneous interpretation, with an interpreter holding information in short-term memory before releasing it in speech production (Gile, 1995, p. 168). The Production Effort is what Gile describes as the "output part of interpretation", which includes firstly forming a mental representation of the message to be delivered, planning the speech and then delivering it (Gile, 1995, p. 165).

Monitoring and correcting speech delivery is an activity common to all speakers, not only interpreters (Skaaden, 2013, p. 72), a phenomenon described as "self-monitoring" and "self-repair" (Levelt, 1989). In all types of discourse, speakers monitor not only what they are saying but also how they are saying it, interrupting themselves to "make a repair" (error correction). Self-monitoring is not constant but context-sensitive, meaning that contextual factors, among others, will impact the degree of attention that a speaker gives to monitoring output as part of the speech production process at any given time (Levelt, 1989, p. 458).

Finally, the Coordination Effort is required to coordinate the other three (Gile, 1995, p. 169). Generally speaking, at any given time, the interpreter will be applying each Effort concurrently to a different speech segment and the specific processing capacity he or she requires for each Effort can fluctuate within a fraction of a second. Gile's model shows us that in order for interpretation to succeed not only does total available processing capacity have to meet the total requirement, but that the total capacity has to be distributed in such a way as to meet the requirements of each interpretation Effort. Any shortfall of capacity in a given Effort may result in failure. For example, if a specific problem trigger, e.g., an unfamiliar name or unexpected concept, forces an interpreter to suddenly redirect capacity from Production to

Listening and Analysis, it may result in a Production failure should the available capacity for Production drop below the requirement.

With a view to making recommendations for counsel working with interpreters, the next section will focus on the Short-term Memory Effort, the Listening and Analysis Effort, and their associated problem triggers.

2.5.1 Short-Term Memory Effort

The amount of information and the length of time for which information is held in short-term memory before it is released at the production stage will depend on several factors. One factor affecting this is structural differences between source and target language. Such differences may oblige the interpreter to hold information while waiting to hear a key source-language structural element before correctly rendering the meaning in the target language. An example of this would be an interpreter waiting for a source-language verb at the end of a sentence prior to delivering the message in the target language.

Another factor is contextual information: the meaning of an utterance is not immediately clear but gradually unfolds as more contextual information becomes available. The more contextual information the interpreter requires before embarking on production, the more of the speaker's utterance has to be held in short-term memory. On the one hand, due to short-term memory's limitations, if the interpreter waits too long before releasing information from short-term memory for production, some information will be lost. On the other hand, extremely slow speech can also represent a cognitive challenge for interpreters, as it may require the interpreter to hold information in short-term memory for too long whilst waiting for further structural or contextual information before production. The interpreter must therefore strike the right balance between on the one hand retaining information in short-term memory for comprehension and structural reformulation, and on the other, releasing information for production before the short-term memory capacity becomes overloaded.

Where a live transcript of the source language is available on a monitor in the booth, and provided the pace of transcription is close to that of the speaker, the interpreter can also use it as an additional short-term memory aid, for example for temporary retention of unfamiliar names or numbers, which can then be included in a segment being interpreted where they might otherwise have been lost.

2.5.2 Listening and Analysis Effort: Audiovisual Comprehension

Where Gile's Effort Model arguably falls short is that it appears to focus on auditory-verbal input as the sole source of information in simultaneous interpreting (Seeber, 2017: 464). Although Gile's description of the Listening Effort encompasses "all comprehension-oriented operations", mention is not made of visual input in his model and it is therefore unlikely that it is included, whereas there is wide consensus among interpreters of the importance of visual information (Seeber, 2017: 464). Where visual information is lacking, constructing meaning is more demanding and more error prone due to its ambiguity (Moser-Mercer, 2005; Skaaden, 2013, p. 54; Skaaden, 2018). Audiovisual information is said to be complementary when information provided on one channel can compensate for inadequacies (or resolve ambiguities) of information provided on another (Seeber, 2017: 463).

> Sensory systems have evolved to work in concert, and normally, different sensory cues that originate from the same event are concordant in both space and time. The products of this spatial and temporal coherence are synergistic intersensory interactions within the central nervous system, interactions that are presumed to enhance the salience of the initiating event. Thus, for example, seeing a speaker's face makes the spoken message far easier to understand (Sumby & Pollack, 1954) which is why conference interpreters insist on a direct view of the speaker and the meeting room. And rightly so, their insistence finds its justification in the special nature of our sensory systems (Moser-Mercer, 2005, p. 728).

Interpreters are of course not the only professionals for whom multiple sensory inputs are important. The same can certainly be said of counsel and judges, who have to assess the demeanour and credibility of witnesses, most often in person but increasingly via videolink.

By way of example, it was a concern about not being able to "effectively and accurately assess the testimony and demeanour" of a key witness via videolink that led the Trial Chamber of the International Criminal Tribunal for Rwanda (ICTR) to travel to The Netherlands to hear the witness testimony in the trial of Protais Zigiranyirazo,[5] rather than remain at the seat of the Tribunal in Arusha, Tanzania, and take the testimony via videolink from there.

The problem in this case was that when Zigiranyirazo was refused entry into The Netherlands, the Trial Chamber ruled that he should follow the hearings in Arusha via videolink. In order that he would not be disadvantaged by this arrangement, the Chamber ordered that one of the defence counsel for the accused should also attend the hearings in The Netherlands.

However, the Defence appealed the Decision, arguing that neither Zigiranyirazo nor his lead counsel, both of whom remained in Arusha connected by videolink, could observe either the judges or the witness continuously, but only when the camera was pointed on them, thereby denying them normal visual interaction with the proceedings. The Appeals Chamber, in its Decision on Interlocutory Appeal of 30 October 2006, decided to exclude all of the testimony that was taken via videolink on the grounds that the Trial Chamber had failed to accord the accused the right to be present at his own trial, adding: "although one of the Appellant's counsel was in the courtroom with the Judges and the witness, the Appellant himself was thousands of kilometres away, connected to the proceedings only by means of audio-visual

[5] *Zigiranyirazo (Protais) v Prosecutor* (Decision on interlocutory appeal, Case No ICTR-2001-73-AR73, ICL 979 (ICTR 2006), 30 October 2006), [4]. https://www.legal-tools.org/doc/6be72d/pdf/. Accessed on 30 May 2020.

equipment. The Appellant's sense of being wronged in such circumstances is well-understandable".[6]

While the "virtual" participation of the accused in international criminal proceedings continues to be controversial[7] and is indeed exceptional, videolink has nevertheless become common practice for witness appearances in international criminal proceedings, particularly for protected or vulnerable witnesses, the modalities of which are set out in Rule 67 of the Rules of Procedure and Evidence of the International Criminal Court[8]. Furthermore, the onset of the Covid pandemic also saw the remote participation of counsel and the judiciary via videolink in partially virtual hearings at the ICC, and it would seem likely that the possibility of remote participation for counsel in international criminal proceedings will continue in the future. However, remote participation in hearings can present challenges to effective communication in the multilingual courtroom as it introduces an additional element into the communicative process, namely the quality of the external audiovisual input provided to the courtroom parties, participants and interpreters.

2.5.3 Listening and Analysis Effort: Problem Triggers

High Speech Density and High Rates of Delivery

In addition to sensory aspects, other factors affect the interpreter's processing capacity at any given time. Gile (1995, p. 173) describes high speech density as "probably the most frequent source of interpretation problems". It increases processing capacity requirements because more information must be processed per unit of time. Numbers, names and acronyms represent high speech density elements as they are "more vulnerable than others to a momentary processing capacity shortage because of their short duration and low redundancy" (Gile, 1995, p. 174). However, high speech density is not only related to speech content but also speech structure and speed of delivery. The higher the delivery rate, the more information has to be processed per unit of time.

Given the nature of prepared speeches, which are generally more densely formulated with longer sentences than spontaneous speech (Skaaden, 2013, p. 73), a written

---

[6] *Zigiranyirazo (Protais) v Prosecutor* (Decision on interlocutory appeal, Case No ICTR-2001-73-AR73, ICL 979 (ICTR 2006), 30 October 2006), [21]. https://www.legal-tools.org/doc/6be72d/pdf/. Accessed on 30 May 2020.

[7] *Prosecutor v. Laurent Gbagbo and Charles Blé Goudé* (International Criminal Court, Defence of Mr Charles Blé Goudé, Case No. ICC-02/11-01/15, 6 May 2020) "Public Redacted Version of "Blé Goudé Defence Urgent Request for Postponement pursuant to Article 67 of the Statute". Retrieved January 17, 2021, from https://www.icc-cpi.int/CourtRecords/CR2020_01812.PDF

[8] "A Chamber may allow a witness to give viva voce (oral) testimony before the Chamber by means of audio or video technology, provided that such technology permits the witness to be examined by the Prosecutor, the defence, and by the Chamber itself, at the time that the witness so testifies", and that "the venue chosen for the conduct of the audio or video-link testimony is conducive to the giving of truthful and open testimony and to the safety, physical and psychological wellbeing, dignity and privacy of the witness".

text read at a slower speed could actually have a higher speech density than that of a faster speech containing little information. However, the delivery rate of written speeches is usually significantly faster than that of spontaneous speeches as they are "generally devoid of the hesitations, filled or unfilled, which characterize ad-libbed speech", thereby adding to the speech density in the delivery (Gile, 1995, p. 173).

The lack of spontaneous speech pausing patterns in prepared speech is further problematic in that they are important communicative elements of extemporaneous speech; they guide the listener as to where a unit of speech ends and another begins (like punctuation in written texts) and indicate where the speaker intends to introduce new information. Linguistic studies have shown spontaneous speech to be marked by pauses every five to six words, giving the speaker the opportunity to plan their speech prior to articulation (Kess, 1992, p. 58; cf. Skaaden, 2013, p. 73). Such pauses significantly aid interpreters.

In light of the abovementioned factors, the advice of most international organisations is therefore to avoid reading from texts when being interpreted and to moderate one's pace when speaking. In this regard, the advice given to counsel pleading before the Court of Justice of the European Communities (2009) is as follows:

> In the first place, it is highly inadvisable to read a text prepared in advance. The reason for this is that an address prepared in writing is generally made up of longer and more complicated sentences and is delivered at greater speed than one which is largely extemporaneous. It is preferable to speak on the basis of well-structured notes, using simple terms and short sentences.
>
> In cases where Counsel prefers to follow a text, the same advice applies: simple terms and short sentences should be used and the text should be read at normal talking speed.[9]

The European Civil Service Tribunal (2014) echoes these recommendations:

> D. Specific features of simultaneous interpretation
> 64. In cases in which simultaneous interpretation is required, parties' representatives are reminded that it is generally preferable to speak freely on the basis of notes rather than to read out a text. Likewise, a series of short sentences is preferable to a long, complicated construction.
> 65. If, however, oral submissions are prepared **in writing**, it is advisable when drafting the text to take account of the fact that it must be presented orally and should therefore resemble an oral address as closely as possible.[10]

[9] Notes for the Guidance of Counsel in Written and Oral Proceedings before the Court of Justice of the European Communities: http://www.lexnet.dk/law/download/procedur/Proc12-2.pdf. Accessed on 30 May 2020.

[10] Practice directions to parties on judicial proceedings before the European Union Civil Service Tribunal https://eur-lex.europa.eu/legal-content/EN/TXT/?uri=CELEX:32014Q0714(03), Accessed on 30 May 2020.

Poor Quality or Lack of Audiovisual Input

Whereas Gile (1995, p. 173) described high speech density as "probably the most frequent source of interpretation problems", since the onset of the Covid pandemic, with the systematic recourse to videoconferencing and the exponential rise in the interpretation thereof, arguably the most frequent source of interpretation problems is poor sound (from a spoken language source). Poor audio input, even where still intelligible to the "normal" listener, is an interpreting problem trigger, causing the interpreter to divert cognitive resources to the Listening and Analysis Effort, thereby depleting available resources needed for other areas such as Production.

Skaaden (2018) suggests from research on remote interpreting that interpreters are more vulnerable than the "normal" listener to audio disturbance, possibly because their memory is already under pressure, while the masking effect of the interpreter's voice over the audio input is another factor that distinguishes the interpreter from the "normal" listener. The fact that simultaneous interpreters produce sound themselves as they interpret means they have the challenge of listening in a noisy environment, given that simultaneous interpreters produce audio output in one language while having to listen to and process audio input in another (Seeber, 2017: 464).

> Speaking and listening at the same time is impossible for any normal person. It is only rigorous training together with the use of headphones separating to a large extent the input stream arriving at the interpreter's ears from the output stream (his/her voice), that makes simultaneous interpretation possible. Since speaking (formulating a coherent message) already commands considerable attention of the interpreter, just as is the case for any normal person, listening, auditory perception and comprehension must require only minimal effort; in the words of D. Seleskovitch (1968: 210) "l'interprète a besoin d'entendre sans écouter". Working under inferior sound conditions is like working from an imperfectly understood language: a large part of the interpreter's attention is diverted to reconstructing (or guessing) the original message with a consequent reduction in the quality of the output. (Mouzourakis, 1996).

Beyond comprehension issues, it increasingly appears that the poor sound that has become synonymous with videoconferencing since the onset of the Covid pandemic has given rise to major health impacts, and in particular auditory complaints, among conference interpreters. According to AIIC TFDI's (2022) Press Release on World Hearing Day, "the cause of such auditory health conditions increasingly appears to be the defective sound generated during such online videoconferences, for which there are multiple sources: first and foremost, the substandard equipment used by participants and the audio processing performed by the videoconferencing systems and platforms, in particular dynamic range compression and background noise suppression."[11] There is of course a question mark as to why this should be affecting conference interpreters to a far greater extent than "normal" listeners, but the answer may lie in the way that interpreters listen to the input. As

[11] For further information see AIIC's Technical Note on the Effects of Dynamic Range Compression and Other Forms of Digital Sound Processing on the Hearing of Conference Interpreters (AIIC, 2022).

they are trying to decipher the audio above their own voices, where the audio becomes unintelligible they may be tempted to increase the volume, thereby also increasing whatever non-signal elements are in the source and thereby maximising any negative effects. This does not mean that "normal" listeners are necessarily immune to this phenomenon however. Suffice to say that where video link or a videoconferencing platform is used, not only interpreters but all courtroom parties and participants require audiovisual input of high quality in order to perform their respective functions properly. Where remote participants connect to a hearing from their computers via a videoconferencing platform, it is essential that they have the requisite audiovisual peripherals (external ISO-compliant microphone[12] and camera), processing capacity, network connection stability and speed in order to provide optimal audiovisual input to the courtroom parties and participants.

The recognition of the importance of high quality audiovisual input for interpreters is underscored in Regulation 64 of the Regulations of the Registry[13], which provides that every effort shall be made to ensure optimal sound (broadcast quality) for the sake of accuracy and completeness. The ISO standards (ISO 2016a, 2016b, 2016c, 2017, 2019, 2020) provide the relevant requirements both for the quality and transmission of sound and image provided to interpreters and for the equipment needed in the booths.[14]

In addition to the use of a microphone of requisite quality, the network connection of each and every participant in the proceedings is another key factor in quality audio and video transmission, given that the system is only as strong as the weakest link in the chain, technically speaking. The AIIC Interpreter Checklist[15] (AIIC TFDI, 2020) recommends a wired Ethernet connection for all videoconference participants to ensure a stable connection. Other recommendations for remote speakers to prevent audible signal disturbance include turning off all sound notifications while attending virtual meetings, eliminating background noise and interference from the local environment and muting the microphone when not speaking. Further tips for remote speakers can be found in the document AIIC Covid-19 Distance Interpreting Recommendations for Institutions and DI Hubs (AIIC, 2020).[16]

[12] AIIC has tested microphones for ISO-compliance and performance for videoconferencing purposes which at the time of writing are to be listed on its website: www.aiic.org.

[13] International Criminal Court. (2018). Regulations of the Registry. Official documents of the International Criminal Court. https://www.icc-cpi.int/resource-library/Documents/RegulationsRegistryEng.pdf. Accessed on 31 May 2020.

[14] Regulation 61 (2) of the Regulations of the Registry.

[15] International Asssociation of Conference Interpretors. (2020). "AIIC Interpreter Checklist: Performing Remote Interpreting Assignments from Home *in extremis* during the Covid-19 Pandemic". https://aiic.org/document/4845/AIIC-Interpreter-Checklist.pdf. Accessed on 17 January 2021.

[16] International Association of Conference Interpreters (AIIC). (2020). "AIIC Covid-19 Distance Interpreting Recommendations for Institutions and DI Hubs". https://aiic.org/document/4839/AIIC%20Recommendations%20for%20Institutions_27.03.2020.pdf. Access on 17 January 2021.

Should the above measures prove insufficient to ensure the requisite audiovisual quality to enable effective multilingual communication in the virtual setting, the Checklist sets out a protocol for interpreter intervention: indicating poor audiovisual input where this is the case; stating "inaudible" or "not visible" where this is the case; pausing interpreting to allow for technical problems to be resolved (AIIC TFDI, 2020, p. 10).

Audiovisual materials presented at trial are frequently characterised by poor sound (overlapping speakers, excessive background noise, faint speech etc.) and high rates of speech delivery. This is hardly surprising as for the most part they constitute live recordings of events in the field rather than studio recordings made with professional equipment. As such it can take even the "normal" listener many attempts to discern the relevant speech, making it far more suitable for transcription than interpretation. However, once a transcript has been made of the relevant audio, it can be sight translated by the interpreters for the Courtroom parties and participants whilst the original video is played. This is the one exception to where interpreters can "check against delivery" on mic, as the quality of the original audio is usually too poor to allow the interpreter to check the transcript against the original audio whilst sight translating the text.

Occasionally audiovisual evidentiary materials are produced in a hearing that are not in a language spoken by the interpreters present, for example in a language of lesser diffusion. In such cases the interpreters may be asked to sight translate or read a translation of the original speech for the record whilst the recording is played. It goes without saying that the provision of accurate time stamps and line numbers is critical in such instances to ensure the correct passages are read. In such cases the interpreters should preface their intervention by stating for the record that they are not interpreting the language in question, but sight translating or reading a translation thereof. It should be noted that it is challenging for an interpreter to sight translate from text whilst simultaneously hearing incoming audio in a different language of which the interpreter has no understanding, meaning that they may well have to turn the audio down or off completely to do so. As such counsel should be mindful that the timing of the sight translation may therefore vary significantly from the original, and can finish well before or after the video excerpt in question has been played.

3 Interpretation Techniques

3.1 Reformulation

Trained conference interpreters have a range of strategies available to deal with various problem triggers. One such technique is reformulation: explaining, paraphrasing and deliberate omission (Gile, 1995, p. 197). For high speech density or rates of delivery, Jones recommends simplifying, generalizing, economy of expression, omission etc. in order to "convey as much as possible of the speaker's meaning in as few syllables as possible" (Jones, 2002, p. 102).

However, both the expectations and usage of court interpretation differ from that of conference interpretation. It is expected to be more complete, including speech elements such as hesitation, repetition and false starts that would normally be omitted in conference interpreting. This is because, unlike their counterparts in conference settings, courtroom users of interpretation need not only to understand what a speaker is saying but also—crucially—to assess their demeanour and credibility. Interpretation of a witness "must mirror the original utterance as closely as possible so that the triers of fact can assess the person's credibility" (Mikkelson, 2000, p. 71), an assessment backed up by Kate Mackintosh, Deputy Registrar at the ICTY.

> Interpreters in criminal trials... face the unique challenge of conveying the demeanour of witnesses without straying into the realm of partiality. A judge listening to five different witnesses over the course of a week in court will only hear the voice of the interpreter, who must reflect a positive cooperative tone, or reluctance, anger or sadness, all of which are important for a judge in evaluating a testimony. Accuracy in court interpretation is about more than the words, it enables judges to assess credibility (Mackintosh, 2015).

If court interpreters cannot make equal recourse to legitimate and necessary conference interpreting strategies for dealing with high rates of speech delivery, there is no other alternative than for speakers to simply slow down.

> Interpreter users – lawyers and judges – can assist the process of interpreted communication by being aware of the need to speak more clearly and slowly, pausing between sentences and paragraphs, and avoiding long sentences with numerous clauses (Stern, 2012, p. 28).

Given the parties and participants' reliance on live transcription during proceedings, an appropriate pace is also necessary to enable the transcribers to accurately perform their work as well.

> A multilingual courtroom that relies so completely on the interpreters and the on-screen transcript cannot function unless everyone speaks more slowly than they would in a monolingual courtroom (Elias-Bursać, 2015, p. 122).

However, there are other ways in which court parties and participants can contribute to the quality of interpretation in international criminal proceedings, namely by providing interpreters with advance documentation to aid in their preparation. This helps to develop their extralinguistic anticipation capabilities, thereby reducing the cognitive load on the interpreters during hearings.

3.2 Preparation and Anticipation

> By using documents and preparatory briefings in order to acquire knowledge about a conference, that is about names, ideas and terms likely to be used or referred to during the conference, interpreters increase their power of anticipation and therefore decrease their listening and analysis effort capacity requirements. By doing so, they increase the capacity left for the other two Efforts, and are likely to reduce the frequency of processing-capacity related problems (Gile, 1995, p. 178).

Interpreters reduce processing requirements through linguistic and extralinguistic anticipation. Linguistic anticipation is based on knowledge of the linguistic structures of a language which help anticipate upcoming speech segments, for instance typical colocations, grammatical imperatives, stock idioms and turns of phrase, etc., whereas extralinguistic anticipation is made possible by knowledge of the subject, context, situation and the speaker, enabling the interpreter to anticipate "the speaker's reacting or speaking in a particular way in a particular context or situation" (Gile, 1995, p. 178). Preparation is therefore a key element in extralinguistic anticipation.

> Preparation forms an essential component of competent interpreting – it forms an inherent part of interpreters' work in international courts (Stern, 2012, p. 19).

Even though staff interpreters and regular freelance interpreters working at a particular court will have extensive knowledge of the cases and be familiar with courtroom speakers (with the exception of new witnesses), they also need to prepare for each hearing thoroughly in order to perform optimally, the importance of which is underscored by Regulation 67 of the Regulations of the Registry.[17] Regulation 52 futhermore sets out that participants shall provide the evidence they intend to use at the hearing at least three full working days before the scheduled hearing, which is transmitted to the interpretation and translation service within the Registry under strict conditions of confidentiality.

Some counsel may mistakenly be deterred from submitting prepared speeches to interpreters in advance due to concerns about confidentiality. Here it should be noted that interpreters are professionals with a code of conduct. Confidentiality is sacrosanct for all interpretation services in international organisations, let alone international criminal tribunals, at which staff and freelance interpreters make a solemn undertaking to perform their duties faithfully, impartially and with full respect of confidentiality[18] prior to commencing their duties.[19]

---

[17] International Criminal Court. (2018). Regulations of the Registry. Official Document. https://www.icc-cpi.int/resource-library/Documents/RegulationsRegistryEng.pdf. Accessed on 31 May 2020.

[18] As set out for example in Rule 6 of the Rules of Procedure and Evidence at the ICC (2013). Rule 6: Solemn undertaking by the staff of the Office of the Prosecutor, the Registry, interpreters and translators 2. Before performing any duties, an interpreter or a translator shall make the following undertaking: "I solemnly declare that I will perform my duties faithfully, impartially and with full respect for the duty of confidentiality". The undertaking, signed by the person making it and witnessed by the President of the Court or his or her representative, shall be filed with the Registry and kept in the records of the Court. https://www.icc-cpi.int/iccdocs/pids/legal-texts/rulesprocedureevidenceeng.pdf. Accessed on 30 May 2020.

[19] Many interpreters are also members of professional associations such as AIIC (International Association of Conference Interpreters) and bound by their rules on confidentiality. Article 2 of AIIC's Code of Professional Ethics (2018): a) Members of the Association shall be bound by the strictest secrecy, which must be observed towards all persons and with regard to all information disclosed in the course of the practice of the profession at any gathering not open to the public. b) Members shall refrain from deriving any personal gain whatsoever from confidential information they may have acquired in the exercise of their duties as conference interpreters. https://aiic.net/page/6724/code-of-professional-ethics-2018-version/lang/1. Accessed on 30 May 2020.

The European Civil Service Tribunal (2014) requests counsel to actively contribute to ensuring the accurate interpretation of their submissions by providing documents, briefings, and speaking notes to the interpreting department well in advance. Whereas counsel may conceivably assume that only the "final version" of their prepared pleadings or speaking notes is of use to interpreters, in fact the knowledge that the interpreter builds up of the subject, the line of argument or questioning and the context of the hearing is crucial to facilitating anticipation. Furthermore, counsel can always submit later versions where necessary.

Interpretation services also have systems in place to ensure that any documentation provided in advance is only seen by the interpreters. Furthermore, interpretation services are quite willing to return hard copy documentation to counsel should they so wish. The norm in international criminal tribunals is for such documentation to be destroyed by the interpreters after any hearing.

Counsel should not be concerned that by submitting documentation in advance the interpreters will simply sight translate the written text provided to them. In the "Tips for Speakers" of the Directorate General for Interpretation of the European Commission (2006), speakers are asked to ensure that their prepared texts or statements are distributed beforehand to all the interpreters, adding that the documents will "of course be treated with the utmost confidentiality and checked against delivery". This technique of "checking against delivery" is a key element of what is known as simultaneous interpretation with text (Gile, 1995, p. 184).

The technique entails focusing on the oral speech rather than the written text, the reasons being:

- The fact that speakers often deviate from their text by skipping or changing some of its segments, and by adding comments. If interpreters focus on the text, they may miss parts of the speech.
- The importance for the delegates of the synchronicity between the speaker and the interpreter's voice (Gile, 1995, p. 206).

3.3 Interpreter Intervention

Even though preparation is an "essential component of competent interpreting" (Stern, 2012, p. 19), not all interpreting problems can be anticipated and prevented through pre-meeting preparations. The translation-like expectations of accuracy and completeness in courtroom settings, coupled with the different complexities of courtroom discourse, makes it a challenging environment. Whereas the court interpreter may not be able to access the full range of interpreting techniques available to their conference colleagues, they can and do nevertheless interact to a greater extent with meeting participants than their conference counterparts.

Gile (1995, p. 200) cites "informing delegates of an interpretation problem" as one of the "coping tactics in simultaneous interpretation" that is rarely used in a conference setting. However, interpreter intervention to ensure accuracy is a feature common not only to national courts and public service interpreting more generally, but also to international criminal proceedings. The National Register of Public Service Interpreting (NRPSI) Code of Professional Conduct (2016), for example, sets out specific conditions for interpreter intervention:

5.12 Practitioners shall not interrupt, pause or intervene except:

5.12.1 to ask for clarification;
5.12.2 to point out that one party may not have understood something which the interpreter has good reason to believe has been assumed by the other party;
5.12.3 to alert the parties to a possible missed cultural reference or inference; or
5.12.4 to signal a condition or factor which might impair the interpreting process (such as inadequate seating, poor sight-lines or audibility, inadequate breaks, etc.).

Where the input to the interpreters is such that it becomes a barrier to effective communication and thereby the accuracy and reliability of the court record, it is incumbent upon the interpreters to intervene. Such intervention can include requests for speakers to slow down, to repeat information where it has not been heard by the interpreters (for example where a witness is not speaking into a microphone or where speakers overlap), or generally to notify the parties and participants of issues that make accurate interpretation impossible. The following is an interpreter intervention on the quality of the audiovisual input: a video recording presented as evidence in a trial.

25 QUESTION FROM THE JOURNALIST: Can you confirm

1. that these planes were dropping off weapons to –
2. ANSWER: The truth is well-known. The inhabitants have greeted us here. The
3. planes, one is from the Cetraca and the –“
4. MESSAGE FROM THE INTERPRETERS: It is not possible to provide accurate interpretation
5. under these conditions.
6. (Viewing of the video excerpt)
7. PRESIDING JUDGE TRENDAFILOVA: Wasn’t the sound of the recent video
8. clearer?
9. THE INTERPRETER: Message from the interpreters: Usually we do not interpret
10. videos because of problems with sound and speed. In this occasion, we tried to do
11. our best, but it is not possible to provide an accurate interpretation under these

12. conditions.
13. PRESIDING JUDGE TRENDAFILOVA: Thank you so much. I think that we
14. shouldn't put too much pressure on the interpreters because they wouldn't like, as
15. far as I understand, to make inventions, because every single word uttered could be
16. extremely important. So I would -- just a moment.
17. I would like to suggest that we rely on what has been interpreted right now plus the
18. transcripts whereby you're going to make your comments, Mr Desalliers, and some
19. corrections if you find the interpretation that is provided by the Prosecutor's office at
20. some places inappropriate or imprecise.
21. MR DESALLIERS: (Interpretation) Yes, I would have liked to have shown the
22. footage and listened to the interpretation at the same time, but that seems to be very
23. difficult, so I would suggest that we show the videos and I could read out -- perhaps
24. I could pause and perhaps I could read out parts of the transcript that I think are of
25. relevance and I could make reference to the extracts that way. It wouldn't be
1. the -- quite the same thing. It would be me speaking, but I do understand the
2. difficulties that the interpreters are facing.
3. PRESIDING JUDGE TRENDAFILOVA: Mr Desalliers, I think that first and
4. foremost we have to pay tribute to the professionalism of the interpreters and that
5. they would like to adhere to the oath that -- under which they are doing their job.[20]

Although a reason for interpreters not intervening in a conference setting may be the concern that "the interpreter may lose credibility" (Gile, 1995, p. 200), the above example shows that in a court setting where judges are aware of the difficulties of ensuring the highest levels of accuracy and reliability in interpretation, such intervention is nevertheless appreciated.

Teamwork and effective booth partnering are intrinsic elements of conference interpreting, and are fundamental in interpreting international criminal proceedings

[20] *Prosecutor v. Bosco Ntaganda*. (Transcript) (Case No. ICC-01/04-02/06, 12 February 2014), pp. 57–58. https://www.icc-cpi.int/Pages/record.aspx?docNo=ICC-01/04-02/06-T-9-Red-ENG, https://www.legal-tools.org/doc/d3e5d2/pdf/. Accessed on 30 May 2020.

(Stern, 2012, p. 22). They are key to the quality of the interpreted output of a particular booth.

The off-mic ("passive") interpreter supports the on-mic ("active") interpreter[21] by noting numbers, acronyms, proper names, unfamiliar or technical terms; researching terminology and quotations; locating relevant passages of documentation; checking their booth partner's interpreted output against the floor delivery and noting any substantive errors for immediate (on-mic) or subsequent correction; as well as taking over from their booth partner should anything occur that would prevent the on-mic interpreter from continuing (e.g. coughing fit).

Here it should be noted that the onset of the Covid-19 pandemic has seen many conference interpreters having to work alone in the booth or even from their homes for the first time. Although it is possible to have a direct view of one's teammate in an adjacent booth and follow their interpreting, this is still well short of the immediate and effective teamwork that is the hallmark of conference interpreting. Nevertheless, it provides far greater possibilities for cooperation than where interpreters are dispersed at several different locations trying to communicate with each other e.g. via chat services, deprived of physical colocation with their booth partner (s) and needing to monitor different devices simultaneously whilst interpreting. This requires an additional mental effort from the interpreter, thereby increasing the cognitive load at any given time, potentially giving rise to overload and errors.

3.4 Error Correction

Even where interpreters are able to work closely together and with all courtroom parties and participants to ensure effective multilingual communication, given the nature of interpretation and the levels of reliability and accuracy required for the transcript, which constitutes evidence at trial, it is clear that substantive errors can occur nevertheless. In the event of "linguistic misunderstandings or errors of interpretation" Regulation 65 (2) provides that interpreters shall "endeavour to correct the misunderstanding or error immediately, during the hearing itself" (ICC RoR: 65 (2)).

As such, ICC interpreters frequently correct themselves (and thereby the transcript) on-mic, prefacing such corrections with the words "the interpreter corrects". Such immediate intervention to correct substantive errors can save the parties and participants valuable time during their examination of a witness.

The availability of a live transcript of the original language in the booth can be a great aid to the off-mic interpreter in monitoring the output of his/her colleague, and even to the on-mic interpreter, provided that the transcription speed is close to that of the original speaker. It can also enable courtroom participants to flag up errors and

[21] The author prefers the terms off-mic and on-mic to Gile's "passive" and "active interpreter" terminology (Gile, 1995, p. 193), due to the very active role played by the off-mic interpreter in the overall quality of the interpreted output from the booth.

have them resolved speedily, as can clear and established procedures for error correction:

> The transcript scrolling by on everyone's video monitors has vastly improved the expediency of error correction, and this, in turn, has meant that judges are less often misled by errors which might otherwise impede their deliberations. Hence a well-functioning translating institution is not one where errors never occur, but one where there are mechanisms for correcting them quickly so that they do not distort or otherwise impede the deliberations (Elias-Bursać, 2015, p. 140).

The following are some examples of live, on-mic error correction by ICC interpreters:

WITNESS: he replied to me, saying...

12 President Patassé - asked us to kill all the children over the age of two. So,

13 when I learnt his answer, I saw that my boys and myself were considered as dead,

14 and when I went back home I was completely sorrowful and I decided to get all my

15 children to leave, and I decided to stay.

16 THE INTERPRETER: The interpreter corrects, kill all the boys over the age of two

17 and not all the children.[22]

WITNESS

24 So they executed them in the village, and they took the village chief

25 who they presented to their leader and then they executed him as well. And when

1 they executed him, I was not there. And I would also inform you that when he was

2 executed, he was a -- he was cooked and they forced the mayor to eat the flesh. And

3 when we arrived in the morning, the mother --

[22] *Prosecutor v. Jean-Pierre Bemba Gombo* (Transcript) (Trial Chamber III, Case No ICC-01/05-01/08, 21 January 2011. https://www.icc-cpi.int/Pages/record.aspx?docNo=ICC-01/05-01/08-T-51-Red2-ENG, https://www.icc-cpi.int/Transcripts/CR2015_02808.PDF. Accessed on 31 May 2020.

4 THE INTERPRETER: The mayor, corrects the interpreter.[23]

Sometimes the interpreter will go so far as to alert the parties and participants to the exact place in the real-time transcript where an interpretation error was made:

THE INTERPRETER: And the interpreter corrects: Page 7, line 24, is only officials[24]

Further corrections can also be made to the transcript after the hearing using a formal procedure on the initiative of the interpreters themselves or at the request of the parties and participants to the proceedings. Procedures for post-hearing error correction are set out in Regulation 65 (3).[25]

4 Effective Communication in Multilingual Judicial Proceedings

4.1 Judges' Role in Managing Courtroom Proceedings

As mentioned, the judges are ultimately responsible for ensuring a fair trial, and judges at the various international criminal courts and tribunals have taken an active role in addressing linguistic issues arising in the cases they have adjudicated.

> Different judges have different styles for coordinating the work of the courtroom, but together they have, over the life of the Tribunal, established precedents not just for jurisprudence, but for how to steer translation and interpreting in a multilingual trial (Elias-Bursać, 2015, p. 241).

> The role of the presiding judge in monitoring and controlling courtroom communication can be crucial. ICTY judges have been known to intervene for linguistic reasons (for example, in cases of excessively long questions, or questions containing more than one question). Some of them were reported to repeat their statements for clarity of understanding, which benefits the interpreters, the defence and the witnesses. Judges from the continental legal system were reported to restrain allegedly aggressive counsel in order to remind them that their tactics were inappropriate in a bench trial – "Vous n'êtes pas devant le jury" (Stern, 2001, p. 272).

---

[23] *Prosecutor v. Jean-Pierre Bemba Gombo* (Transcript) (Trial Chamber III, Case No ICC-01/05-01/08, 30 May 2011, pp. 17–18. https://www.icc-cpi.int/Pages/record.aspx?docNo=ICC-01/05-01/08-T-119-Red2-ENG, https://www.icc-cpi.int/Transcripts/CR2015_02808.PDF. Accessed on 31 May 2020.

[24] *Prosecutor v. Jean-Pierre Bemba Gombo* (Transcript) (Trial Chamber III, Case No ICC-01/05-01/08, 07 May 2012. https://www.icc-cpi.int/Pages/record.aspx?docNo=ICC-01/05-01/08-T-51-Red2-ENG, https://www.icc-cpi.int/Transcripts/CR2015_02808.PDF. Accessed on 31 May 2020.

[25] *Prosecutor v. Thomas Lubanga Dyilo (Trial Chamber I, Case No ICC-O1/04-01/06, 18 June 2009) "Decision on discrepancies between the English and the FrenchTranscripts and related issues". https://www.icc-cpi.int/CourtRecords/CR2009_04635.PDF.Accessed on 17 January 2021*

During the Charles Taylor trial, for example, the judge drew the prosecutor's attention to the ineffective use of the double negative and requested rephrasing the questioning (Stern, 2012, p. 26).

4.2 Examples of Best Practice

If we now examine the guidelines issued by Presiding Judge Fulford in the *Lubanga* case (2009) regarding speed, we can see the awareness there is of the contribution of all parties to successful communication in multilingual proceedings:

> 43. All those speaking in court must ensure that their delivery enables the interpreters and court reporters to work at a reasonable and reliable speed. Counsel must constantly watch the relevant transcript screen (*viz.* that which shows the language being used by the interpreters), monitoring the progress of the questioning, and creating gaps whenever necessary. Particular attention should be paid to ensuring there is a pause between speakers (critically, two people should never speak at the same time), as well as to the marked problems that can exist when a witness speaks Swahili or Lingala, or a speaker has a strong accent.
>
> 44. Names should always be spelt into the record whenever they are first used, and care must be taken over dates and numbers. If one has not already been provided, a list of "usual" names, locations and acronyms is to be provided by the prosecution, in consultation with the parties, the participants and the court officer, within 10 days of the date of this Decision.
>
> 45. The Chamber will henceforth enforce a pace (e.g. the speed and manner of delivery) which is generally more measured.[26]
>
> PRESIDING JUDGE FULFORD:
>
> Finally, can I remind everyone about speed. It is very easy to forget that there are stenographers and interpreters. Rather than speaking in an unnaturally slow -- at an unnaturally slow pace, could you please try and build in very short gaps as you go through to give the interpreters and the stenographers an opportunity to catch up. If I feel it is running away and you see my hand going up and down, that is not an

[26] *Prosecutor v. Thomas Lubanga Dyilo* (Trial Chamber I, Case No ICC-O1/04-01/06, 18 June 2009) "Decision on discrepancies between the English and the French Transcripts and related issues". https://www.icc-cpi.int/CourtRecords/CR2009_04635.PDF. Accessed on 17 January 2021.

25 indication to speak more quietly. It's an indication to slow down.[27]

12 PRESIDING JUDGE MINDUA:[9:38:50] (Interpretation) Thank you. Thank you

13 very much

14 Now I have some issues to address of a practical nature. You must take into account

15 throughout your testimony that what is said in this courtroom is transcribed by

16 stenographers and it is simultaneously interpreted into several languages by

17 interpreters. And as such, it's important to speak into the microphone and to do so

18 clearly and slowly. Only speak when the person who has asked a question has

19 finished asking the question

20 When you are asked a question, please count up to three, not aloud, but to yourself

21 before answering. This pause is essential in order for us to be able to hear you

22 correctly and to ensure that your testimony is duly recorded[28]

4.3 Summary of Recommendations for Counsel

On the basis of the above, the following recommendations can be made for counsel for optimal communication in multilingual criminal proceedings:

Hearing Preparation

1. Provide the interpreters with any speaking notes or other documents you will rely on during the hearing. Be as specific as possible as to which pages or paragraphs of documents you intend to use during the hearing to enable the interpreters to prepare as effectively and thoroughly as possible.

[27] *Prosecutor v. Thomas Lubanga Dyilo* (Transcript) (Trial Chamber I, Case No ICC-01/04-01/06-T-107-ENG, 26 January 2009, p. 3. https://www.icc-cpi.int/Pages/record.aspx?docNo=ICC-01/04-01/06-T-107-ENG, https://www.icc-cpi.int/Transcripts/CR2009_00591.PDF. Accessed on 31 May 2020.

[28] *Prosecutor v. Al Hassan Ag Abdoul Aziz Ag Mohamed Ag Mahmoud* (Transcript) (Trial Chamber X, Case No ICC-01/12-01/18, 08 Nov 2020, p. 4. https://www.icc-cpi.int/Pages/record.aspx?docNo=ICC-01/12-01/18-T-019-Red-ENG, https://www.icc-cpi.int/Transcripts/CR2020_05182.PDF. Accessed on 17 January 2021.

Use of Audio Equipment

2. Take off your headphones or push them back off your ears when speaking in the courtroom—listening to yourself, or the interpreter's rendition of what you have said can be very distracting for you as a speaker.
3. Remember to speak into your microphone, and remind a witness to do the same if necessary. Switch the microphone off after speaking.
4. Use a wired Ethernet connection with ISO-compliant headset or headphone and microphone if participating in a hearing from a remote location.

Extemporaneous Speech

5. If possible, speak extemporaneously or from notes. Your speech will generally be slower and your speech patterns more natural if you do so.
6. Speak at a moderate pace, for the purposes of interpretation 95 to 120 wpm.

Reading from a Written Text and Quoting Sources

7. Although providing written texts in advance will aid interpreters in dealing with denser linguistic structures, the above caveats regarding speed above still apply. To become accustomed to them it may help to practice reading your prepared text aloud and timing yourself until such speeds come naturally.
8. When reading try to retain natural speech patterns that convey meaning such as pauses and variations in intonation. These are also hallmarks of good oratory, irrespective of the environment. By pausing at full stops, in addition to signalling natural breaks, you also allow the interpreters to catch up, thereby reducing the interpretation lag.
9. If quoting a specific documentary source (e.g. transcript, filing or evidentiary material), state the reference details and stipulate the language version the reference details relate to (page numbers will usually differ from one language version to another) prior to quoting or commenting on the substance. This is useful for all court participants, and particularly for interpreters to locate the exact passage concerned in real-time and then use the document as an aid to providing accurate and complete interpretation.

Three-Second Rule

10. Due to the lag in interpretation, which increases where there is use of relay interpretation, when taking the floor make sure to leave a 3–5 second pause to allow the interpretation of the previous speaker to finish. This will also prevent speakers from overlapping and is particularly important when examining a witness who speaks the same language. Counsel may also remind a witness to make a similar pause before answering each question put.

Proper Nouns, Acronyms and Numbers

11. Spell out names and acronyms the first time they are used. Acronyms should certainly be explained if they are not familiar to the parties and participants. It is also helpful, when quoting reference numbers, to give the numbers individually rather than provide a lengthy sequence; i.e. 498746 should be said as four-nine-eight-seven-four-six rather than four hundred and ninety-eight thousand, seven hundred and forty six.

12. If you have a list of names and acronyms that you will be using, please provide the interpreters and court reporters with a copy.

Presentation of Audio or Audiovisual Materials

13. If you intend to present recorded audio or audiovisual material in court, provide interpreters (and possibly other parties and participants in the courtroom) with a transcription thereof one or more days prior to its use.

Use of Appropriate Language

14. Remember in particular when talking to witnesses that they may come from very different cultures where certain legal concepts under common law, civil law or international criminal law may not exist and will have to be paraphrased by situation language interpreters. Similarly use of certain phrasing common in national courts such as double negation, highly idiomatic or legalistic language etc. may give rise to confusion when interpreted for witnesses into situation languages, in particular where there is the added element of relay

And Finally

15. Remember that the interpreters are there to help you communicate as effectively as possible!

5 Conclusion

Effective multilingual communication is at the heart of a fair trial, not only in international criminal proceedings but in all multilingual courtroom environments. Courtroom practice at the International Criminal Court shows that a multilingual court is not simply a monolingual environment with simultaneous interpretation, but a multilingual judicial environment in which each and every party and participant to the proceedings is aware of their responsibility for ensuring effective multilingual communication, with the presiding judge the ultimate arbiter thereof.

Despite the inherent limitations of simultaneous interpretation, where courtroom parties and participants work together, it is possible both to ensure accurate communication in the courtroom and to expeditiously produce a reliable written court record of interpreted oral proceedings. Although occasional linguistic errors can and do occur, effective review and correction strategies underpin the reliability of the final court record.

By way of conclusion, it is hoped that the insights provided into the process of simultaneous interpretation, the best practice at the ICC and other international courts and tribunals, and the recommendations made are sufficient to aid counsel communicate effectively not only in international criminal proceedings but also in other bilingual and multilingual environments.

References

Constable, A. (1996). Methodologies and techniques used in training simultaneous interpreters of languages of lesser diffusion at the international criminal court. In K. Balogh, H. Salaets, & D. Van Schoor (Eds.), *TraiLLD: Training in languages of lesser diffusion* (pp. 69–87).

Court of Justice of the European Communities (CJEC), (2009) Notes for the guidance of Counsel in written and oral proceedings before the Court of Justice of the European Communities. Retrieved August 6, 2015, from http://curia.europa.eu/jcms/upload/docs/application/pdf/2008-09/txt9_2008-09-25_17-37-52_275.pdf.

De Jongh, E. (1992). *An introduction to court interpreting: Theory & practice*. University Press of America.

Directorate General for Interpretation of the European Commission. (2006). "Tips for Speakers". Online Resource. Retrieved January 17, 2021, from https://op.europa.eu/s/n7hM

Elias-Bursać, E. (2015). *Translating evidence and interpreting testimony at a war crimes tribunal: Working in a tug-of-war*. Palgrave Macmillan.

European Civil Service Tribunal. (2014). Practice directions to parties on judicial proceedings before the European Union Civil Service Tribunal. Resource document. Retrieved January 17, 2021, from https://eur-lex.europa.eu/legal-content/EN/TXT/?uri=celex%3A32014Q0714%2803%29

Gaiba, F. (1998). *The origins of simultaneous interpretation: the Nuremberg Trial*. Ottawa University Press.

Gibbons, J. (2003). *Forensic linguistics: An introduction to language in the justice system*. Blackwell Publishers.

Gile, D. (1995). *Basic concepts and models for interpreter and translator training*. John Benjamins Pub. Co., Amsterdam.

Gerver, D. (1974). The effects of noise on the performance of simultaneous interpreters: Accuracy of performance. *Acta Psychologica, 38*, 159–167.

Gerver, D. (1976). Empirical studies of simultaneous interpretation: A review and a model. In R. W. Brislin (Ed.), *Translation: Applications and research*. Gardner Press.

Hale, S., Ozolins, U., & Stern, L. (Eds.). (2009). *The Critical Link 5: quality in interpreting : a shared responsibility*. John Benjamins Pub. Co., Amsterdam.

International Association of Conference Interpreters (AIIC). (2018). Code of Professional Ethics. Retrieved January 19, 2021, from https://aiic.org/document/6299/Code%20of%20professional%20ethics_ENG.pdf

International Association of Conference Interpreters (AIIC). (2020). AIIC Covid-19 Distance Interpreting Recommendations for Institutions and DI Hubs. Retrieved January 19, 2021, from https://aiic.org/document/4839/AIIC%20Recommendations%20for%20Institutions_27.03.2020.pdf

International Association of Conference Interpreters (AIIC) Taskforce on Distance Interpreting (TFDI). (2020). *AIIC interpreter checklist: Performing remote interpreting assignments from home in extremis during the Covid-19 pandemic*. Retrieved May 01, 2021, from https://aiic.org/document/4845/AIIC-Interpreter-Checklist.pdf

International Association of Conference Interpreters (AIIC) Taskforce on Distance Interpreting (TFDI), Technical and Health Committee (THC). (2020). *AIIC best practices for interpreters during the Covid-19 crisis*. Retrieved January 17, 2021, from https://aiic.org/document/4840/AIIC%20best%20practices%20for%20interpreters%20during%20the%20Covid-19%20crisis%20-%20ENG.pdf

International Association of Conference Interpreters (AIIC). (2022). *Technical note on the effects of dynamic range compression and other forms of digital sound processing on the hearing of conference interpreters*. Retrieved March 25, 2022, from https://aiic.org/uploaded/web/UN%20NegDel/Technical%20Note%20to%20the%20CEB.pdf

International Association of Conference Interpreters (AIIC) Taskforce on Distance Interpreting (TFDI), Press Release on World Hearing Day. (2022). Retrieved March 25, 2022, from https://

aiic.org/company/roster/companyRosterDetails.html?companyId=12892&companyRosterId=26
International Criminal Court. (2013). The rules of procedure and evidence. Resource document. Retrieved January 17, 2021, from https://www.icc-cpi.int/iccdocs/PIDS/legal-texts/RulesProcedureEvidenceEng.pdf
International Criminal Tribunal for the Former Yugoslavia (ICTY). (2007). Decision on Lukić Motion to Compel Registry to Provide Verbatim Transcript of Proceedings. Retrieved January 17, 2021, from https://www.icty.org/x/cases/milutinovic/tdec/en/070927b.pdf
ISO 20109 (2016) *Simultaneous interpreting — Equipment — Requirements*. Retrieved January 17, 2021, from https://www.iso.org/standard/67063.html
ISO 2603 (2016) *Simultaneous interpreting — Permanent booths — Requirements*. Retrieved January 17, 2021, from www.iso.org/standard/67065.html
ISO 4043 (2016) *Simultaneous interpreting — Mobile booths — Requirements*. Retrieved January 17, 2021, from www.iso.org/standard/67066.html
ISO 20108 (2017) *Simultaneous interpreting — Quality and transmission of sound and image input — Requirements*. Retrieved January 17, 2021, from www.iso.org/standard/67062.html
ISO 22259 (2019) *Conference systems — Equipment — Requirements*. Retrieved January 17, 2021, from www.iso.org/standard/72988.html
ISO 24019 (2020) *Simultaneous interpreting delivery platforms — Requirements and recommendations*. Retrieved January 17, 2021, from www.iso.org/standard/72988.html
Jones, R. (2002). *Conference interpreting explained*. St. Jerome Pub.
Kade, O. (1968). *Zufall und Gesetzmäßigkeit in der Übersetzung*. Verlag Enzyklopädie.
Kalina, S. (2010). New technologies in conference interpreting. In H. Lee-Jahnke & E. Prunč (Eds.), *Am Schnittpunkt von Philologie und Translationswissenschaft. Festschrift zu Ehren von Martin Forstner* (pp. 79–96). Peter Lang.
Kess, J. F. (1992). *Psycholinguistics. Psychology, linguistics, and the study of natural language*. John Benjamins Publishing Company.
Klamberg, M. (2013). *Evidence in International Criminal Trials: Confronting legal gaps and the reconstruction of disputed events*. Brill Publishers.
Laster, K., & Taylor, V. (1994). *Interpreters & the legal system*. The Federation Press.
Lederer, M. (1981). *La traduction simultanée: expérience et théorie*. Minard Lettres Modernes.
Levelt, W. J. M. (1989). *Speaking: From intention to articulation*. MIT Press.
Mackintosh, K. (2015). No justice without interpreters. *The Law Society Gazette*. Retrieved January 17, 2021, from http://www.lawgazette.co.uk/analysis/comment-and-opinion/no-justice-without-interpreters/5047270
Mikkelson, H. (2000). *Introduction to court interpreting*. St. Jerome.
Morris, R. (1995). The moral dilemmas of court interpreting. *The Translator, 1*, 25–46.
Moser, B. (1978). Simultaneous interpretation: A hypothetical model and its practical application. In D. Gerver & H. W. Sinaiko (Eds.), *Language interpretation and communication* (pp. 353–368). Plenum Press.
Moser-Mercer, B. (2005). Remote interpreting: Issues of multi-sensory integration in a multilingual task. *Meta, 50*(2), 727–738.
Moser-Mercer, B., Künzli, A., & Korac, M. (1998). Prolonged turns in interpreting: Effects on quality, physiological and psychological stress (pilot study). *Interpreting, 3*(1), 47–64.
Mouzourakis, P. (1996). Videoconferencing: Techniques and challenges. *Interpreting, 1*(1), 21–38.
Munday, J. (2009). *The Routledge companion to translation studies (rev. ed.)*. Routledge.
NRPSI (National Register of Public Service Interpreters). (2016). Code of professional conduct. Resource Document. Retrieved January 17, 2021, from www.nrpsi.org.uk/for-clients-of-interpreters/code-of-professional-conduct.html
Paradis, M. (1994). Toward a neurolinguistic theory of simultaneous translation: The framework. *International Journal of PsychoLinguistics, 9*(2), 133–145.
Pavetić, J. (2012). Interview with Greiss Lecturer Marijana Nikolić. *SlavFile: Newsletter of the Slavic Languages Division, 21*(4), 6–7, 9.

Pio, S. (2003). The relation between ST delivery rate and quality in simultaneous interpretation. *The Interpreters' Newsletter, 12*, 69–100.

Pöchhacker, F. (2004). *Introducing interpreting studies*. Routledge.

Pöchhacker, F. (2009). Issues in interpreting studies. In J. Munday (Ed.), *The Routledge companion to translation studies (rev. ed.)*. Routledge.

Prosecutor v. Germain Katanga (Transcript) (International Criminal Court, Trial Chamber II, Case No. ICC-01/04-01/07-T-163-Red-ENG, 30 June 2010, p. 31. Retrieved January 17, 2021, from https://www.icc-cpi.int/Pages/record.aspx?docNo=ICC-01/04-01/07-T-163-Red-ENG, https://www.icc-cpi.int/Transcripts/CR2010_05537.PDF

Prosecutor v. Jean-Pierre Bemba Gombo (Transcript) (International Criminal Court, Trial Chamber III, Case No. ICC-01/05-01/08-T-51-Red2-ENG, 21 January 2011. Retrieved January 17, 2021, from https://www.icc-cpi.int/Pages/record.aspx?docNo=ICC-01/05-01/08-T-51-Red2-ENG, https://www.icc-cpi.int/Transcripts/CR2015_02808.PDF

Prosecutor v. Jean-Pierre Bemba Gombo (Transcript) (International Criminal Court, Trial Chamber III, Case No. ICC-01/05-01/08-T-224-Red2-ENG, 07 May 2012, p. 7. Retrieved January 17, 2021, from https://www.icc-cpi.int/Pages/record.aspx?docNo=ICC-01/05-01/08-T-224-Red2-ENG, https://www.icc-cpi.int/Transcripts/CR2015_04202.PDF

Prosecutor v. Jean-Pierre Bemba Gombo (Transcript) (International Criminal Court, Trial Chamber III, Case No. ICC-01/05-01/08-T-119-Red2-ENG, 30 May 2011. Retrieved January 17, 2021, from https://www.icc-cpi.int/Pages/record.aspx?docNo=ICC-01/05-01/08-T-119-Red2-ENG, https://www.icc-cpi.int/Transcripts/CR2015_03835.PDF

Prosecutor v. Jean-Pierre Bemba Gombo (Transcript) (International Criminal Court, Trial Chamber III, Case No. ICC-01/05-01/08-T-276-Red2-ENG, 27 Nov 2012, p. 3. Retrieved January 17, 2021, from https://www.icc-cpi.int/Pages/record.aspx?docNo=ICC-01/05-01/08-T-276-Red2-ENG, https://www.icc-cpi.int/Transcripts/CR2015_05941.PDF

Prosecutor v. Laurent Gbagbo and Charles Blé Goudé (International Criminal Court, Defence of Mr Charles Blé Goudé, Case No. ICC-02/11-01/15-1340-Red 06-05-2020, 6 May 2020) "Public Redacted Version of "Blé Goudé Defence Urgent Request for Postponement pursuant to Article 67 of the Statute". Retrieved January 17, 2021, from https://www.icc-cpi.int/CourtRecords/CR2020_01812.PDF

Prosecutor v. Thomas Lubanga Dyilo (Transcript) (International Criminal Court, Trial Chamber I, Case No. ICC-01/04-01/06-T-107-ENG, 26 Jan 2009, p. 3. Retrieved January 17, 2021, from https://www.icc-cpi.int/Pages/record.aspx?docNo=ICC-01/04-01/06-T-107-ENG, https://www.icc-cpi.int/Transcripts/CR2009_00591.PDF

Prosecutor v. Thomas Lubanga Dyilo (International Criminal Court, Trial Chamber I, Case No. ICC-OV04-0V06, 18 June 2009) "Decision on discrepancies between the English and the French Transcripts and related issues". Retrieved January 17, 2021, from https://www.icc-cpi.int/CourtRecords/CR2009_04635.PDF

Seeber, K. (2011). Cognitive load in simultaneous interpreting: Existing theories - new models. *Interpreting, 13*(2), 176–204.

Seeber, K. (2017). Multimodal processing in simultaneous interpreting. In J. W. Schwieter & A. Ferreira (Eds.), *The handbook of translation and cognition*. Wiley.

Seleskovitch, D. (1968). *L'interprète dans les conférences internationales, problèmes de langage et de communication*. Minard Lettres Modernes.

Seleskovitch, D. (1978). *Interpreting for international conferences: Problems of language and communication*. Pen and Booth.

Skaaden, H. (2013). *Den Topartiske Tolken*. Universitetsforlaget.

Skaaden, H. (2018). Remote interpreting: Potential solutions to communication needs in the refugee crisis and beyond. *The European Legacy, 23*(7–8), 837–856. https://doi.org/10.1080/10848770.2018.1499474

Stern, L. (2001). At the junction of cultures: Interpreting at the international criminal Tribunal for the Former Yugoslavia in the light of other international interpreting practices. *Judicial Review, 5*(3), 255–274.

Stern, L. (2012). What can domestic courts learn from international courts and tribunals about good practice in interpreting? From the Australian war crimes prosecutions to the international criminal court. *T & I Review, 2*, 7–30.
Sumby, W. H., & Pollack, I. (1954). Visual contribution to speech intelligibility in noise. *Journal of the Acoustical Society of America, 26*, 212–215.
UN. Advisory Committee on Administrative and Budgetary Questions. (2002). Improving the Performance of the Department of General Assembly Affairs and Conference Services. Official Report. Retrieved January 17, 2021, from https://digitallibrary.un.org/record/476488
Zigiranyirazo (Protais) v Prosecutor (International Criminal Tribunal of Rwanda, Decision on Interlocutory Appeal, Case No ICTR-2001-73-AR73, ICL 979 (ICTR 2006), 30 October 2006). Retrieved January 17, 2021, from www.legal-tools.org/doc/6be72d/pdf/

Andrew Constable is a Court Interpreter at the International Criminal Court (ICC) in The Hague, the Netherlands, and former Vice-President of the International Association of Conference Interpreters (AIIC). He is a member of AIIC's Advisory Board (AB), AIIC's Executive Committee Advisor on Distance Interpreting, Coordinator of AIIC's Taskforce on Distance Interpreting (TFDI), Member and former Vice-Chair of AIIC's Staff Interpreters' Committee (CdP), Member of AIIC's ISO Group and ISO/TC 37/SC 5 expert (WG 2 & 3), and Member of AIIC's Technical and Health Committee (THC).

Andrew graduated from the University of Bradford with an MA in Interpreting and Translation in 1998, after which he was recruited by the European Institute of Public Administration in Maastricht, The Netherlands. It was at this time that he developed an interest in law, and was awarded a Postgraduate Certificate in EU Law in 2001.

He joined the ICC in 2004 and continued his legal studies, following the International Criminal Law module of the University of Bristol's LLM programme in 2005. His work at the Court has involved training simultaneous interpreters with languages of lesser diffusion (Acholi, Lingala, Sango and Zaghawa) for international criminal proceedings, for which he took a Master of Advanced Studies (MAS) in Interpreter Training at the University of Geneva in 2011.

He has also participated in a KU Leuven project funded by DG Justice of the European Commission on training interpreters with languages of lesser diffusion (TraiLLD), and is a member of the European Commission's DG Interpretation's Informal Working Group on Conference Technologies.

He continues to conduct research on new technologies, distance interpreting, court interpreting and interpreter training, supporting training and professional development initiatives for students, interpreters and interpreter trainers wherever possible.

Interview Dr Melinda McPherson: Considerations of Gender in Representing Victims Before the International Criminal Court

Melinda McPherson

Interviewee: Dr. Melinda McPherson

Interviewer: Elizabeth King

Interview date: 26th June, 2016

Location: Melbourne, Australia

Transcript of the interview (edited)

1. **You have written extensively on the theme of women and voice, and regularly engage with groups of women who might not have a voice. Why is this issue important to you?**

I have had a long term personal and professional interest in social justice, especially in the role education plays as a contributor to social justice. In my early teaching career I worked in an all girls' school, which influenced my interest in women's opportunities and women's rights. My research has focused on the link between education and improving women's lives, and the effects and impact education has in changing broader social attitudes and justice.

2. **Who are the main critical thinkers you have turned to in considering the question of women and voice?**

When I think about women and voice there have been a few authors who've had a significant impact on me; particularly in different areas of rights and engagement for women.

M. McPherson (✉)
Melbourne, VIC, Australia
e-mail: melinda.mcpherson@digitall.net.au

E. King et al. (eds.), *Victim Advocacy before the International Criminal Court*,
https://doi.org/10.1007/978-3-030-56733-0_16

In the field of education I have been heavily influenced by Paulo Freire, bell hooks, Elizabeth St Pierre, Mark Olssen and Georgina Tsolidis. Other feminist theorists that have impacted my thinking include Marilyn Waring, Gloria Steinem, Robin Morgan, Patricia Hill-Collins, Naomi Wolf, Judith Butler, and Margaret McLaren. In terms of voice, Michel Foucault has been a significant influence because of his views about marginality, power, knowledge, and the way that voice operates in dominant discourses.

Foucault talks about *discourses* that surround us; discourses are ways of thinking, being, and acting that are the dominant 'common senses'. In these dominant discourses, some subject positions—roles if you like—are privileged (for example psychiatrists in the mental health field) while others can be marginalised by the discourse (such as psychiatric patients). Social justice is concerned with identifying these dominant discourses and challenging the ways in which they marginalise some groups of people.

3. **If we consider the involvement of women who are constructed as *victims* in the ICC process—the investigative stage, the trial proper, or in a reparations phase seeking compensation—what immediately springs to your mind as being a valuable, critical framework that advocates can begin to think about? Knowing that they represent these women in that setting.**

The representation of refugee women is a topic I am deeply interested in, so much so I wrote a thesis and a book about it. I worked with refugee women and much of the research was exploring questions about subjectivity and agency. Historically, women have often been represented in development contexts and refugee contexts as *victims only* with little consideration for their agency. There is some fabulous writing on the topic of agency (MacKenzie & Stoljar, 2000) that has caused us to challenge those traditional constructs and the way we look at women.

One of the challenges when working in social justice with women is striking a balance between painting the negative material impact of women's circumstances and representing their agency. It is a critical thing to point out the terrible, debilitating, marginalising and inequitable circumstances that women face—the invisibility of women's experiences in the law and of women's experiences that have been misconstructed under the law. If you don't shine a light on that, you are not bringing women's experiences to the foreground. However, once you position women in relation to that kind of marginality, how do you then balance it with a notion of recognising those same women also have agency?

Refugee women are survivors who have a range of skills and experiences that inform their views about their lives and the world. Yet we struggle to represent the depth and complexity of their subjectivities; to recognise that within what are sometimes extraordinary constraints or debilitating circumstances, they bring knowledge, experience, critique, and strategy to their thinking and actions; that they are capable of reflection and decision making beyond the limitations of victimhood—they are survivors.

Another significant historical challenge in doing social justice work with women is ensuring our experiences are recognised as 'human' experiences. American scholar and activist Catharine MacKinnon jointly prosecuted the Kadzic case, which established rape and other forms of violence against women as war crimes; as crimes against humanity. One of MacKinnon's critical arguments has been that the law should regard women's experiences as human experiences rather than as some special annexure to the 'normal' human condition.

4. **So to extend the metaphor further, if an advocate is representing a woman (or women) who are categorised as *victims*, then they are operating within a very restrictive sets of parameters (within the court and the ICC system). Are you suggesting that an advocate can or should strive to find the subtleties within that paradigm to (at least) try and recognise a greater agency for the woman or women they represent?**

I believe so. In the field of social justice there has been an inclination to frame engagement with marginalised subjects in terms of how they can be 'helped'. It is a discourse of charity, in which privileged subjects who 'know best' (however well meaning) frame their efforts in relation to groups of individuals who need 'help.' As a simple example, royal families around the globe often contribute to 'charitable' works; their monies may go to 'helping' the poor. However these acts do nothing to challenge the privileged positions of royals nor the power structures that maintain their privilege and the marginalisation of others. In fact, some might argue that in many ways privileged acts of benevolence simply reinforce unequal relationships of power; would it not be unkind to critique the institution of royalty when it is doing such good work to 'help' others?

While caring and empathy are noble inclinations, there is no intrinsic politics or political will in a framework of charity to change the structure of privilege and its impacts. Australian writer Kathryn Choules does a fabulous analysis of discourses in social justice, beginning with the discourse of 'charity'—and how this discourse really only tinkers at the edges of changing relations of power. Charitable work may 'help' others but it does not really alter dominant relations of power. Choules also challenges us to reflect on the discourse of 'human rights' in advancing social justice. Part of the problem that has existed for human rights instruments is that their measures have usually been defined in relation to experiences of privileged subjects; for example, human experiences have usually been defined in relation to male subjectivities—women's experiences have been seen as ancillary.

International legal instruments and practices have often invisibilised the experiences of women. Choules challenges us to turn the lens on our own role in marginalisation—how do the privileged people represent groups we are 'helping.' How is it that dominant human rights experiences cannot 'see' women's experiences as human; how is it that our privileged eyes construct refugees, whom we are 'helping', as victims without agency.

I find Choules' lens very helpful for thinking about how we, as advocates, might frame our own thinking. First steps towards change should recognise the relationship between the advocate and the client and how the advocate conceives of the client. An understanding of diverse gendered experiences is important. This includes the advocate taking the time to familiarise themselves with some of the lived experiences of the women clients they are working with. Foucault was of the view that one could identify the operations of a dominant discourse by speaking to the very people who are marginalised by that discourse. Understanding and centring the experiences of victim-survivors provides a unique insight into the operation of dominant discourses around them; and the ways in which those discourses, in this case and especially legal ones, might silence or invisibilise client's experiences.

Thus, to my mind, having an understanding of the lived experiences of clients and being able to think about those experiences in a critical framework is really important to justice. There are many researchers, practitioners, and theorists who are progressing this 'thinking' work at the moment; reframing the ways in which we talk about refugees in dominant discourses of support and practice. By way of example, in the field of mental health, which has been heavily ensconced in the bio-medical model, there has been an historical pre-disposition to frame refugee survivors as patients in need of a cure. Patients are situated as 'ill', rather than as agents who have experienced extraordinary circumstances. Elzbieta Gozdziak and Jay Marlowe have both challenged the normative representation of refugees in relation to trauma (only). Gozdziak argues that many refugee women see their story telling not as therapeutic (only) but also as political acts, conceptualised as testimony in an exercise of agency.

It is important for the legal advocate to listen to client's perspectives, needs and aspirations as they collaborate in a litigation. At one level, the advocate's role is to be expert advisor, interpreter, and navigator of the discourse of the law—the 'legal system'; she or he is responsible for conveying to the client what is and isn't possible, the challenges that might confront them, how it is likely to make them feel, things they need to do to prepare. But it is also the role of the advocate to assist in articulating the lived experience of the client in a way that will render that experience visible to the court.

While the legal system can be limited in the way it recognises the rights of diverse communities, it is also the case that legal systems have been influenced, maneuvered and cajoled to change perspectives over time. The advocate's knowledge of the legal system means he or she is uniquely positioned to identify opportunities for advancing new and different ways of thinking; to persuade judges to new ways of understanding particular legal concepts. In this regard I'm reminded of Foucault's microphysics of power. Rather than conceiving of power as being 'top down' (in the traditional Marxist sense), Foucault conceived of power as a web. He did not reject the notion that inequitable relations of power sometimes become fixed or ossified, and radical actions such as revolution might occur, however his greater interest was in the small and medium acts and pathways of power—manoeuvers, readjustments, influences, reconceptualisations—that create change. Legal advocates engage in such micro acts of power when they use their legal expertise to identify fissures, gaps, and malleability in the system through which to effect change; this is precisely what MacKinnon and her colleagues did with and for their Bosnian clients.

5. **Do you have any particular thoughts on the experiences of women where they have been persecuted in some way or they have been victims of crimes?**

Examining structures and frameworks that have historically been (at times) gender blind; that have rendered invisible women's experiences within normative frameworks—is an important task.

Some of the early attempts to introduce women's experiences into research and literature were limited; as Sandra Harstock coined it, they took an 'add women and stir' approach. This means that even though greater attention was paid to including particular issues affecting women, the broader nature of a gendered system remained largely uninterrogated. It wasn't 'til the 1980s through the work of researchers such as Susan Martin or the edited collection of Doreen Indra that we begin to see and understand women's experiences of persecution and the refugee journey through a gendered lens.

I have turned to a range of theoretical frameworks for understanding how refugee women's invisibility is perpetuated. In her book *Are Women Human?* Catharine Mackinnon (2007) talks about the various ways in which women's experiences in the human rights context are rendered invisible. She argues that women's experiences of persecution or crimes are often positioned as 'normal' within a culture, and because they are normalised they are not seen as a crime or persecution. Arguments for cultural relativism inform these discourses. In a gendered context, cultural relativism is the argument that different cultures have different standards for the treatment of women and that critiquing those differences in a framework of western human rights standards is a form of colonialist and cultural elitism.

Hilary Charlesworth at Australian National University (ANU) has written quite a bit on gender and human rights, and has speculated that arguments about cultural relativism are conveniently trundled out in relation to gender more often than in relation to any other issue. I believe there are many feminist scholars, especially feminist legal scholars, who look at the kind of arguments that are put out there to sideline women's progress and women's visibility, and rightly feel skeptical about the way in which concepts like cultural relativism are used.

Yes, it is important to be mindful that people exist in different cultures and that they have experienced colonialism, westernism and also sometimes the legacy of white western feminism and its lack of inclusivity. However, it is very dangerous to step from that recognition to a judgment that we justify the mistreatment of women or we can justify the mistreatment of women on cultural grounds. There is a difference between the experiences of women around the globe and being mindful not to speak through colonial eyes.

Western countries themselves are not exempt from discourses that say violence against women is 'normal'; for example, many discourses around family violence position men's homes as their 'castles', and any actions within the home are 'private' matters. Recently I delivered a workshop to a group of early childhood educators and asked everyone in the room who thought that violence against women and children was a terrible thing—everyone put their hand up. However, when it came to the question of how and why family violence might come about, their views were far more disparate and heated.

Community attitudes that consider women deserve violent treatment in some circumstances are diminishing, although still firmly entrenched. The discourses that normalise violence these days are much more subtle. For example, when the topic of violence is raised, people are much more prepared to accept that there is a small core of 'bad men' out there who perpetrate violence, than to accept that discourses of gender inequity perpetuate the conditions for gender based violence generally. Most men will entertain a conversation about the evils of gender based violence if the blame can be located with a core of bad men; the 'bad apple' theory. It is much more difficult to persuade both men and women to the view that violence springs from gendered attitudes in the dominant discourse; that these attitudes can range from views about women's roles in society to judgments about women's sexualised behaviors.

While not all men action violence or agree with it, the system of patriarchy benefits from the perpetuation of violence, and is resistant to change; the 'bad apple' theory allows individuals to believe that 'something' is being done about violence, while simultaneously sidestepping the real reasons that violence is perpetuated. Acknowledging that a more pervasive set of attitudes about gender, even amongst the best and well intentioned of us, leads to violence is much harder to face. It is the existence of these attitudes in each of us, and our willingness to reflect, that is at the core of change.

In addition to theorising that women's experiences are invisiblised by virtue of normalisation, MacKinnon also argues they are invisibilised by virtue of being deemed abnormal; that such experiences are framed as infrequent or limited. 'If it's happening, it's not so bad; and if it's bad, it's not happening (Mackinnon, 2007).' The argument about abnormal acts is that even if they're happening, they're so rare or awful as to render them not attributable to gender; they are acts random to individuals or small groups. To my mind, the 'bad apple theory' is a strategy for 'abnormalising' violence; if it's a few men undertaking awful acts, the problem is not systemic, and locking them up will solve it. In the 'bad apple' discourse, violence is not situated across a spectrum of behaviours that arise from negative attitudes around gender. Until we challenge these discourses around gender and violence, it is always going to be very difficult to make visible women's experiences of violence on a larger scale.

6. **With all these elements at play (including invisibility, cultural relativism etc.) an advocate faces a difficult challenge—how do they present their client's story/experience with agency (as an individual) as well as drawing the court to consider the systemic or the broader picture?**

My mind turns to Deborah Wardley[1] who was the first female pilot in Australia to fly for a commercial airline. If I recall correctly, Wardley's was the first test case for

[1] Also known as Deborah Lawrie.

Victoria's Equal Opportunity Commission. The Commission selected this particular case because they believed it was strong and its principles would benefit the widest group of women. Wardley successfully completed her pilot training and tests, however at each step it appeared she was being put to a standard higher than the men. She finally met all of the requirements, however the airline still refused to employ her. Wardley had trumped each of the invisible hurdles; the airline was now cornered into stating its outrightly sexist perspective. Ansett is said to have argued that women were unsuitable to be pilots because of their menstrual cycles. It is an intriguing thing when unspoken prejudices must be outlined explicitly for the purposes of legal proceedings. The Commission's case was successful. It was a watershed moment in Australia.

I am mindful of advocates, especially in systems with high stakes such as the ICC, having to wait until they get a case that ticks so many of the right boxes before they can advance that case with the broader picture in mind. For every strong case that makes it to court there must be thousands of others which never do, and people for whom justice is not possible.

When an advocate is working to advance a case with systemic implications (especially when they are working with an individual) ethical considerations are important; these considerations have implications especially for client agency. Does the client have personal objectives only or do they understand where their case fits in a bigger picture. Do they understand what the trade-offs might be? When the advocate must consult with the client about tensions in a case, between the client's interests and bigger picture interests, how are these conversations facilitated?

I recall the famous *Roe v. Wade* case in the US, where advocates were fighting for women's right to choose to have an abortion. By the time the decision was made Roe had already borne her child. The outcome no longer had applicability to her personal circumstances. I often wonder what conversations were being had between advocates and client as time ticked by for this woman.

If the advocate sees the client as being part of a bigger picture of structural systemic change, then the client needs to understand (with the full support and guidance of the advocate) how that picture works and how they fit into it. Yes—advocates have an unequivocal obligation to make sure they are acting in the best interests of a client. However if there come points where there is a conflict between the 'bigger picture outcome' and the wellbeing of the client, difficult conversations within an ethical framework must be facilitated. Some clients may be accommodating of or even committed to bigger picture objectives that eventually surpass individual goals around their own needs.

I raise the topic of ethics because it is acutely illustrative of considerations about agency that the advocate must consider; an advocate should bring his or her knowledge and understanding of the limits and constrictions of the system—the failings and the strengths of the system—so that the client is always able to make an informed decision about how they wish to proceed.

7. **We have discussed previously the challenges of representing individual women victims, however on occasion an advocate might represent a group**

of victims in front of the ICC. What are some of the challenges representing a group of women who are said to be victims of, for example, great war crimes, and how can an advocate extract an minutiae voice or experience within a group?

I think there is an important interdependency between advancing collective rights and engaging with the minutiae in each case. When Catherine Mackinnon and her colleagues were working with their Bosnian clients, it wasn't simply a question of defending or supporting those individual women but also advancing a new argument—opening a door further—to make the experiences of these particular women, and other women, visible. By its very nature, advancing this 'new' argument required an engagement with the circumstances and the minutiae of the experiences of those particular women. Arguing that rape constitutes a war crime required drawing on the minutiae of individual client's experiences, in order to illustrate what those experiences mean in the bigger picture.

There is no such thing as a universal woman or a universal woman's experience, but there are experiences that women share in common because of our embodiment. Working in a gendered framework, it is the job of the advocate to show *both* that women can have diverse experiences which, at the same time, can be (commonly) gendered.

8. **What is your view on the 'universality' of human and/or women's rights in contrast to the question of cultural relativism? I believe the tension between the two becomes particularly pointed when we think of women being represented as victims before the ICC. Is it dangerous to over-universalise their experiences and conversely can it be dangerous to take such heed of cultural relativism that we find no common ground between experiences?**

The debate between sameness and difference has been an ongoing one in feminist philosophy and theory, and it plays out in very real ways in the application of international legal instruments, particularly under the United Nations (UN). It was only many decades after the Refugee Convention was introduced that its limitations as a protection mechanism for women became obvious. I think it is always important to acknowledge positive change and advancements for marginal groups, such as the introduction of programs and funding in the United Nations designed and directed specifically towards women and to benefit women. These were borne largely of the hard work of dedicated second wave feminists and their supporters. However after the 1995 Beijing Declaration and Platform for Action (hosted by the UN) there has been a push towards gender mainstreaming.

The mainstreaming approach has received mixed responses from women's groups. There is a strong feminist argument to be made that 'separate' programs and funding for women only tinkers at the edges of a larger mainstream problem; the historical exclusion of women as 'human' in general provisions. In other words, that gender should be an integral and an integrated part of the way one goes about defining human right issues. In theory this is the more progressive and necessary approach; that is, to be challenging the fundamental definitions of what it means to be 'human' and to have women's interests and needs integrated into core programs and funding. However in practice such a shift often removes the spotlight from critical issues affecting women, including funding dedicated to women's needs, without actually delivering on the mainstreaming promise.

9. **Do you have any views on how the advocate, who is acting on behalf of a woman or women victim(s), can render their role more *meaningful* in relation to reparations? And, how might an advocate navigate the process of both recognising cultural relativism within the common experience of the women involved as well as ensuring that they have an agency within their local community and the ongoing needs of that community into the future? This is especially relevant when there are already structural inequities existing within that community.**

These are challenging questions and the answers exist at many different levels.

Firstly, perhaps we might consider how reparations are informed and how they might be structured. Keeping in mind that the system itself only allows certain sorts of reparations ('you can do this, but you can't do that'; 'you can expect this, but you can't expect that')—you would hope that when initial conversations are happening, there is an engaged, collaborative, consultative process occurring which is making best efforts to include all voices (or as many voices as possible); whether that means participating in a discussion that is conducted within a community itself or individuals come to speak on behalf of that community to the advocate. Finding and establishing collaborative relationships with champions in a community will help advance that collaborative approach to reparations for the whole community.

Once a decision is made regarding what kind of reparations would be best for all parties, the next step is a little more complicated. How does the advocate have control or exercise influence in a set of circumstances that respect the independence of a community but also take into account values of inclusion and human rights?

If the advocate postpones pondering that question until after the reparations are settled, I believe it would be very difficult to reach a desired result for all. The advocate needs to have a holistic or a long-term view of how it would work from the beginning; illustrating through practice, illustrating through collaboration, ways of working that will hopefully continue on once reparations happen.

10. **Based on our discussions today, what are some key themes you would like to highlight for an advocate, and what are some key elements an advocate should be mindful of in their role?**

I would suggest that self reflection should be a critical element of the advocate's practice. Kathryn Choules' notion of turning the lens on privilege is central to this reflection. When working with a client or client groups the advocate should have the capacity to be able to think about and understand client experiences outside their own. Producing the best outcome for a client relies on an advocate bringing legal expertise but also the capacity to enter a place of deep understanding about experiences of the client. It is important to listen for what is said and what might not be said.

The advocate should also have the capacity to *understand* consent, engagement and a whole range of other things in relation to a client's needs and participation in the process. The advocate should understand that a client has a right to have full comprehension of what is happening around them, and to engage with them in the decision-making process. It is about bringing the advocate's expertise of the system and marrying it to the clients expertise about themselves.

If an advocate is working with *gender issues* and has little experience of them, it is always useful to develop some kind of basic knowledge or understanding of the constructs of gender in international law. Reading the work of pivotal feminist scholars, especially legal scholars, can be eye opening. It is important to be able to get a sense and an understanding of the core issues women face in life and the courtroom.

With respect to the way cases are conducted, we all know the stresses that exist going through the legal system, especially when one is talking about war crimes or personal experiences of such an acute nature. The advice that is normally given within a system of justice where the stakes may not be so high, apply more acutely in these circumstances; balancing the needs of the individual and the potentially bigger system outcomes is really important.

References

Mackenzie, C., & Stoljar, N. (2000). *Relational autonomy: Feminist perspectives on automony, agency, and the social self.* Oxford University Press.

MacKinnon, C. A. (2007). *Are women human?: And other international dialogues*. Harvard University Press, Cambridge, Mass.

Roe v Wade (No. 70-18), 410 U.S. 113. Argued: December 13, 1971. Decided: January 22, 1973. 314 F.Supp. 1217, affirmed in part and reversed in part.

Melinda McPherson is a social justice researcher and activist with an interest in gender, diversity, refugee issues, and education. Dr McPherson has completed a Master of Education in Women's Studies and Education from La Trobe University and a Doctor of Philosophy in Women's Studies and Education from Federation University. Her 2015 Routledge book 'Refugee Women, Representation and Education: Creating a discourse of self-authorship and potential', examined the ways in which negative representations in policy impact material outcomes for refugee women. Dr McPherson grew up in Melbourne's multicultural northern suburbs where she developed a lifelong interest in gender and cultural diversity. She trained originally as a cellist and music educator, but moved soon after into advocacy and education management. Her interests in social justice led to research and writing on negative representations of women in the media, gender and politics, women and the asylum process, and women and violence. Her research on gender, the law, and representation have led to articles on representations of women in crime reporting, the efficacy of Australia's approach to dealing with claims of gender based persecution, and consulting work on family violence projects.

Dr McPherson has worked for the past two decades as a consultant in strategic planning, policy, governance, and evaluation. She is a past board member of the Victorian Immigrant and Refugee Women's Coalition (VIRWC) and has undertaken work for the Centre for Multicultural Youth.

Part IV
Resources

This Part includes interviews with a range of practitioners and lists of resources, to provide practical guidance to victim advocates in representing their clients before the International Criminal Court. The interviews provide valuable insights and candid advice on victim advocacy from experts with experience in different parts of the Court's restorative justice framework. Interviewees include Jens Dieckmann, member of the List of Counsel who has appeared before the International Criminal Court as a victim advocate; Paolina Massidda, Principal Counsel of the Office of Public Counsel for Victims; Fiona McKay, former Chief of the Victims Participation and Reparations Section from 2004 to 2015; and Milê Glamcevski, an Australian Counselling Association accredited Clinical Counselor specialising in major trauma, on self-care for the victim advocacy practitioner. The final chapter in this Part, by Ronda Cress, provides a compilation of practical resources for ensuring that your client receives adequate non-legal professional support before, during and after the Court process.

The practical advice set out in this Part includes:

- First steps to take once you have been briefed as Counsel.
- Compiling a legal team.
- How to effectively utilise the support offered by different sections of the Court.
- Unique challenges of representing victims before the ICC and how to address them.
- How a legal representative can make victim participation as meaningful as possible.
- Practical steps legal representatives can take to bridge the gap of culture, language, geographical distance and experience with their clients.
- Common problems and mistakes when representing victims and how to avoid them.
- Legal and practical resources most helpful in their work as victim advocacy practitioners.
- How to recognise and protect yourself from vicarious trauma as a victim advocate.

Interview Jens Dieckmann: Member of the List of Counsel Who Has Appeared Before the International Criminal Court as a Victim Advocate

Jens Dieckmann

Interviewee: Jens Dieckmann

Interviewer: Erin Pobjie

Interview date: 20 November 2013

Location: Phone interview

Transcript of interview (edited)

1. **What experience do you have in international criminal law as Counsel for Defence and Counsel for victims?**

I am List Counsel at the ICTY, ICTR, ICC and the Special Tribunal for Lebanon. I am assigned continually in proceedings especially at the ICTY and the ICC. In 2006, I was assigned Co-Counsel in the case of *The Prosecutor v. Milan Lukić and Sredoje Lukić* at the ICTY. I defended Sredoje Lukić in Pre-Trial, Trial and Appeal and we requested re-consideration of the Appeal Judgment. In addition, I had some smaller assignments as the Duty Counsel in the initial appearance. I defended a client in contested proceedings in the Kosovo case of *The Prosecutor v. Astrid Haraqija & Bajrush Morina,* and in the contempt case of *Dragomir Pećanac.*

At the ICC, I was assigned *ad hoc* Counsel for the admissibility proceedings in the *Kony* case. The Pre-Trial Chamber initiated *proprio motu* admissibility proceedings. Uganda had referred the case to the ICC, and later on Uganda asked the

Editor's note: This interview reflects Mr. Dieckmann's experience and opinion in 2013, when he gave this interview. This documentation of his interview was not updated from him from his perspective in 2021.

J. Dieckmann (✉)
Becher&Dieckmann – Rechtsanwälte, Bonn, Germany

E. King et al. (eds.), *Victim Advocacy before the International Criminal Court*,
https://doi.org/10.1007/978-3-030-56733-0_17

Court to refer the case back to Uganda after Uganda established a High Court war crimes chamber and a special international criminal code. I represent the interest of the Defence in the procedure and the appeal. In 2011, I represented as a Co-Counsel 103 victims participating in the case of the *Prosecutor v. Abdallah Banda Abakaer Nourain*. It was the Darfur case regarding peacekeepers who survived an attack of the accused rebel leaders, and the widows and children of the dead peacekeeping soldiers.

2. **What first inspired you to work in international criminal law?**

I specialized in my law studies in Germany in public international law. At the time that I studied, international criminal law did not exist in this modern way, because I finished my university studies in 1993. This was a very decisive time because the ICTY and later the ICTR were founded in these years. My professor, Professor Tomuschat was the German representative in the United Nations International Law Commission at that time. He was part of the committee for drafting the idea of the International Criminal Court, and international criminal code, so during our studies, we followed the war in the Balkans and the war in Rwanda. When I finished my education, I decided to work as an asylum, refugee and immigration lawyer, because as a student I worked voluntarily for Amnesty International as a refugee consultant. During my practise as a lawyer, I worked on issues under the European Convention on Human Rights, the Geneva Convention for Refugees, and with international humanitarian law. And of course I worked as Criminal Defence Counsel. So I kept contact with these international human rights issues, even during my international law practice. And then in 2003, I discovered that at the ICTY there was an opening for List Counsel, so I applied to be included in the List of Counsel. I presented my application as a mix of human rights lawyer, refugee lawyer and as a criminal defence counsel of course, in combination with my background as a specialist in public international law. The ICTY decided that this mixture of different experience was sufficient to be included on the List of Counsel.

To sum it up, it's fascinating that in international criminal law, all aspects of my volunteer or professional activities come together. International criminal law practice has to do with public international law, international humanitarian law, with criminal law and with human rights aspects. This makes it so complex and so fascinating. I was always fascinated to work with clients—to assist people and to work together with them. It was difficult to imagine how to combine my interest in international law on the one hand and individual crimes on the other hand, there is such a small employment market. International criminal law is of course a small market, but it's a perfect combination to deal with all these fascinating international law issues and with clients, because you have individual proceedings, either from the victims' or the defence counsel perspective. For me, a student dream came true.

3. **So in the seven years of your domestic practice before you were admitted to the list of counsel at the ICTY, you worked on a mixture of national criminal defence work, refugee law, and human rights. Do you draw on any of those earlier skills now in your work in international criminal law?**

First of all, one of my advantages was that it was my daily practice to work with people from foreign countries. In my domestic practice, I represent people from more than 80 different countries, so I speak in my practice in French and English, my Associate also speaks Portuguese and Spanish, and we have assistants who speak Polish, Russian, Vietnamese, Chinese. So to work in a multi-cultural environment is a very helpful experience if you want to start at the international level. It is a very good experience to transfer the national legal system to your international clients—to translate for them, to explain to them what is the law expecting from them.

Secondly of course, also on the international level, a criminal case is a criminal case. You have an accused person in custody being confronted with long, complex proceedings, so all the skills to deal with evidence, to deal with the Prosecutor, to deal with the actors in the judicial system, to deal with the Registry, to deal with judges, all these elements are of course counting also at the international level. Since 2006 I'm a member of the ADC, The Association of Defence Counsel in the Yugoslavia Tribunal, and I'm in my second term as a member of the Membership Committee, so I review CVs and applications of candidates. For us, it's absolutely crucial that candidates have experience with clients and have experience in courtrooms. Because as a criminal defence Counsel, you must respond in a part of a second in the courtroom, you must respond to the Prosecution, you must jump up and raise your voice to protect the interests of your client, or your chance is gone. And for doing this, you need experience as an independent practitioner. So all this practice was very helpful and could be transferred to the international level.

A very important point dealing with victims: it was very helpful in my situation that I had experience working with refugees. Many refugees arriving in Europe or in Germany are escaping from war, so in my daily practice I am dealing with very traumatised people. The victims in the international proceedings are this kind of client as well, so it is very important that you have experience with communicating and dealing sensitively with people with such a background. I think this was a good point in my application when I applied to be selected as victims' Counsel at the ICC: this combination of courtroom experience in the ICTY on the one hand, and experience working with vulnerable persons.

4. **How did your experience in other international criminal law tribunals acting for the defence assist you with the victims' work that you're doing now at the ICC?**

There are some colleagues you say they are only Defence Counsel, and there are other colleagues who are saying that they can only represent victims. There are Counsel who say it's not possible to combine the two. I think it's wrong. If I now represent victims, I have to deal and respond to the Defence. It is absolutely important for the victims to understand the strategy of the Defence. If you represent victims, it's excellent if you have experience at international tribunals as a Defence Counsel, because you know what you are doing as Defence Counsel. You know how to provoke the Prosecution, you know how to make your point, and you can foresee the next step of the Defence. You know where the Defence wants to go by doing this. So you can on the one hand explain to victims the Defence activities, and you can respond very properly to the Defence if you know what the Defence is doing. I really appreciate my experience in six different assignments from 2006 up to now as Defence Counsel in my work for the victims. There is a transfer of experience, yes. To analyse and to foresee the Defence strategy—it is very helpful if you have this experience as Defence Counsel if you represent victims.

5. **The positions of the Defence and of victims are often considered to be completely opposed. Do you see any points where their interests may coincide?**

One important point is we are there to assist that justice is done in the end. Victim's Counsel are not there for conviction itself. This is to make the victims understand that our job is not only to work for conviction on all possibilities. Every part of the tribunal is assisting the ideal of justice, so we are doing our job and the Defence is doing their job. In the end, only if this balance is kept will justice be done. I can explain in more detail: I have spoken with so many refugees and victims of war crimes. Of course, some of them might feel that someone has to pay the bill. Their lives have been ruined. But on the other hand, if you represent victims in criminal proceedings you must make it very clear to your clients that in criminal proceedings, at the end of the day there could be an acquittal.

My experience when talking with victims is that victims want to have a serious procedure, and an unfair procedure or a procedure that's just a masquerade will never give victims a feeling that justice has been done. The example of Iraq, for instance, the procedure against Saddam Hussein, this was a complete disaster from the point of view of justice. This procedure was completely unjust, this procedure will never produce any positive effects for the victims in my opinion, because it was a farce. So this is the common interest: looking for justice, looking for truth.

The common element between the victim and the Prosecution of course is that the Prosecutor has a truth-finding mission. This is interesting at the ICC, since this is a civil-law element in an adversarial context. At the ICC, the Prosecution has the obligation to investigate the truth. This is completely different to the very much adversarial system at the ICTY and ICTR. You will never find the word 'truth' in the rules of the procedure and evidence at the ICTY. In fact, the idea at the ICC is that the Prosecutor has to investigate all aspects of the evidence, including exculpatory and incriminating evidence.

6. **From the Defence Counsel perspective, what do you think are the key things for victims' Counsel to consider?**

I think Defence Counsel can expect that victims' Counsel explain to their clients the nature of criminal procedure and that only a fair trial will bring justice to the victims. I think that is the most important point. And to respect that victims' Counsel are not co-Prosecutors. They have an independent role, or an additional role to the Prosecutor. They are not allowed to consider themselves as pure co-Prosecutor. Victims' Counsel can present evidence, this is allowed at the ICC under very limited circumstances, but we're not prosecuting. Our work is more complex than just prosecuting. And the second point is, from a Prosecutor's perspective, in fact the same. Victims' Counsel should be aware of this, they are not in competition to the Prosecutor, or assistants of the Prosecutor, they have an independent position.

7. **A List of Counsel member is briefed to appear for victims in a matter—what advice would you give them about where to start, what issues they should be mindful of and in what order they should address each of these issues?**

There is a two-fold answer, because victims have—in general—the right to choose their own Counsel. This right is in Rule 90, subparagraph 1 of the Rules of Procedure and Evidence. The right to Counsel for victims is not a statutory right set out in the Rome Statute. The Accused has a statutory, fundamental right to choose his own Defence Counsel. This is in Article 67 of the Rome Statute. For victims, it's restricted, so it's in the procedural law. In rule 90(2) of the Rules of Procedure and Evidence, you find regulations regarding the common legal representation. If you have for example 500 victims and they are in groups, each group with one lawyer, due to the system of the ICC, when the trial start comes nearer the Chamber will normally assign common legal representatives for the trial. It means that the Court is selecting victims' Counsel, and replacing the individual chosen Counsel. This is a delicate situation. If Common Legal Representatives are newly selected, they have as first point to establish a close and trustful relation with these victims even though they replaced their prior Counsel of choice.

The second thing, of course, is that you must know the case by heart. Like all other assignments you have, the starting point for your work for the victims is the case. So the case is material. You can only give advice to your clients if you know the case. This is a very stressful working period, because these proceedings have big databases and it takes a lot of time to get familiar with all the filings and all the material already disclosed to victims.

Thirdly, as a victims' Counsel, you have a right to a team. The team must be compatible with the structure of your client. We have cases at the ICC where you have victims from one village, or from one city, or children from one school living in one village. Then of course it will be essential that you have a field assistant as a kind of focal point in the area where the victims live, speaking their language, knowing their culture, keeping in contact with them. In other cases, where you represent victims from different countries, you do not have the resources to have field assistants in every country, so you have to develop an independent structure to communicate with the clients directly, via email, mobile, etc. This is a challenge to practically manage.

8. **Describe the process of compiling a legal team once briefed to act in a matter for victims. What are some key considerations in the formulation and management of such a team?**

To describe it from the common legal representatives' point of view, the Chamber makes an order following a report from the Registry. It is VPRS, the Victims' Participation and Reparations Section, making a report and a proposal for the Chamber about the selection of the common legal representative and the team structure. So the report said, since you have clients from different countries, English and French speaking, it would be preferable to have two full licensed Counsel, a Principal Counsel and an Associate Counsel, but not a legal assistant. We have a case manager, and we have an option to request assignment of additional assistance if we need it. So our team structure was ordered. We received a budget from the Court itself. And then we choose a case manager to keep our database in order and organize everything. Since Principal Counsel, Me. Hélène Cissé, is based in Senegal and I—as Associate Counsel—am based in Germany, it was essential that the case manager is based in the Hague. We found a case manager who was a case manager for victims in the *Lubanga* case for several years. The Principal Counsel is the Lead Counsel, who has overall responsibility and the responsibility for the team, representing the team with the Registrar, with the Court and victims. Associate Counsel is assisting and supporting the Lead Counsel in her mission in all aspects.

9. **What exactly does the case manager do?**

The case manager is a term you find at all international tribunals. It has simply to do with the mass of data. In 2011, I represented an accused in a terrorist case in Germany. More than 300,000 were papers disclosed, more than 320 binders of paper, 18 Gigabytes of material. The *Lukić* case was one of the smallest cases ever at the ICTY, only 70 Prosecution witnesses, it was one of the shortest and smallest cases ever. I had ca. 90 Gigabytes of material on my hard disc. For this, you need a case manager who organizes the masses of data. The second thing, and this is different to the national practice, in Germany for example, before the chamber decides if the trial can start and confirms the charges, disclosure has to be done. Normally, during the trial itself, the Prosecution is not coming up with new disclosure. At the international criminal tribunals, in the adversarial system, the Prosecution is continuing its investigation during trial and presenting sometimes every week, every month, new evidence. This was especially so in the *Lukić* case. It could happen that on Friday afternoon at 4 o'clock you received a DVD with 1500 pages of new material relevant for a Prosecution witness called next week. Then you need a case manager to organise this material effectively. Some teams have rather technical people as their case manager. In all teams I worked with, the case manager was a full licensed lawyer. It's absolutely essential since the case manager deals with evidence.

The second aspect is that the case manager should speak the language of the case, because the case manager is sometimes the first person to read the statements or the material. In the *Lukić* case for example, our case manager was a lawyer with a background from the Balkans, she could speak BCS, and she also had a Master of International Criminal Law from Utrecht, so she could read the statement and she could analyse it from a lawyers' perspective. Our current case manager is a full licensed lawyer at the Bar of Kinshasa in the Congo, she speaks French and English fluently, and she is perfect help.

10. **In the case that you're working on at the ICC, you're representing peacekeepers from several different countries. What practical advice can you give to a legal representative representing victims to manage the physical distance from their clients in terms of communication?**

You must find a way to reach every single client in short notice if necessary. This is the point for which you must find a practical solution. For example, if your client is living in rural areas, far away from a big city or a big village, and perhaps does not even have normal electricity. Then you must organize with them a kind of focus, it could be for example that there is an Internet cafe in the village five kilometres away.

11. **Given that your clients are a diverse group, how do you best manage to encapsulate a collective voice when representing them?**

They are from different countries but they suffered from the very same event. They share the same interests. Either they are soldiers who are traumatized or handicapped or widows of dead soldiers with their children. They are people from different nationalities, but they have common interests. So it's possible to speak on their behalf as a group, because they suffered from the same moment, it was one attack on 29 September 2007, it was one attack in the evening where everything happened, and so it's not a problem. They have a common position, even though they come from six different countries. The Chamber had confirmed it.

12. **Which sections of the court do you regularly deal, and in general terms what support do they offer to Counsel for victims?**

There are many. First of all, the CSS, the Counsel Support Section. They are helping us with very practical issues like travel and budget. We are dealing with them with our monthly bill, and if we want to travel we have to make a mission request, so they are deciding if we can meet in the Hague, if we can meet in the field or wherever. They are our contact point if we need an assistant, for all these team and resources issues. Second aspect, in the absence of a Bar of Counsel, the CSS is also a contact point if we have ethical issues to discuss.

Secondly, the Victims' Participation and Reparations Section[1]—very essential. VPRS is the first contact point for the victims themselves. It means for victims and their Counsel of choice, if they want to participate in the proceeding, that they contact VPRS, and VPRS is either coming to them in the country and assisting them to complete the 30 page form, and if the form is completed, then the VPRS is

[1]See interviews with Fiona McKay, former Chief of VPRS and Paolina Massidda, Principal Counsel at OPCV.

presenting a package of application forms and submitting it to the Chamber. So the participation and the question of right to participate has to do with VPRS.

We have OPCV, the Office of Public Counsel for Victims.* This is in fact a kind of legal resource. If we have some procedural law question for example. For all kind of legal aspects of our daily work we can contact OPCV. They are victims' lawyers, they can also independently represent victims for example in the procedure where applicants have a pending application, OPCV could represent them with the Chamber, with the Court. So it's the legal department.

Victims' Counsel has also contact with PIDS, the Public Information and Documentation Section, because they can assist Counsel with organising workshops with their clients in the field.

13. **Which resources, both legal and practical do you find the most helpful in your work?**

It's not the resources or the structure, it's the people. It's an experience I had at the ICTY as well. The resources at the ICC are under pressure, and there were budget cuts last year of more than ca. 20%. But the people are so excellent, so motivated at helping you. If you compare it with your national system where you spend days and weeks waiting for a simple answer, you cannot compare it. Here, the people are very proactive with assisting you, trying to find a solution under difficult circumstances. All sections, all offices are very much proactive and trying to do their best to assist you in the small and the big projects, so this attitude is the most helpful thing. The proactive attitude of the people working there is the best assistance you can imagine.

14. **Which stage of the proceedings do you think has the most legal impact, and also the most impact for your clients?**

From the victims' perspective of course the trial itself is the period with the most important juncture for the victims. All the hopes they put in the case, whether it was worth it or not to wait for justice. So the trial itself. The reparations phase in fact depends totally on the trial stage, if there's an acquittal then in the end there is no reparations stage.

15. **Do you find that the lack of a crystallised jurisprudence on the precise nature of victim representation is a fetter on your advocacy or an opportunity to be more creative? Can you give examples?**

This is a very important point, and I would really like to comment on this. We have two aspects to bear in mind. On the one hand, every case is different and the victim structure is different. Whether you have 3000 victims in the *Katanga* case, or if you have now 103 victims from different countries as in our case, it's natural that it should be dealt with in a different way. But it's really a big problem to foresee how the Chamber will respond. It's very difficult and it's not consistent. It's different than in your national system, as each Trial Chamber is completely independent. The Trial Chamber's judgment is not binding to any other. The Appeals Chamber decisions also could change completely. Of course, they have to analyse the prior Appeals Chamber decisions, but in fact they are free to decide differently. The third aspect is that if you see for example in Article 68 of the Rome Statute where the role and the position of the victims is defined, what does it really mean in practice? It is important to hear the voice of the victims in this context. It's very broad. Time and capacity from our side are taken by the attempts to get acceptance and permission to do something.

But on the other hand, this open legal framework is also a chance. What would be the alternative? The alternative would be a clear enumeration, of what victims can and cannot do. So then you have a chance or you don't have a chance. Now, we are in the position that we can fight, we can argue, we can fight on every motion from the Defence, every submission from the Defence, we can try to make our point and to try to be part of the submission of the argument. Well, it works sometimes, sometimes not. But we attempt with creativity and commitment we have every time again, sometimes the Prosecution supports us, sometimes the Prosecution is with the Defence. Yes, it's a struggle, but to put it in a positive way, since it's not always so absolutely clear in advance we have a chance to fight.

It's complicated, it's time consuming but at the end of the day it is always a chance to get your voice heard, but it took a lot of engagement, it took a lot of capacity and creativity. You must be creative.

16. **This raises the theme of the next question—what tone is most appropriate for a victims' advocate to adopt in ICC proceedings?**

Again, it depends on the case and on the structure of your victims. I don't know if you observed the opening statements of the victims of the Kenya cases. The opening and the closing statements are very important for the victims because you have to tell the story of your clients. Story-telling is a very important aspect of your work, because you always have to make clear why your submission is important, or why is it contributing to your mission to raise the voice of your clients. But on the other hand, you are presenting very detailed legal arguments which are different to submissions of the other parties in tone. The special aspect of the victims is that they have a special story to tell. This makes a difference because we are closer to the victims than the Prosecution is and so this is our chance, our mission to tell this story properly and at the right moment.

17. **Can an advocate can ever hope to transmit meaning when they tell the story of their clients within such a formal juridical framework?**

The key problem is that first of all, the victims' Counsel has to find a way to open the door to be listened to. It is a challenge. The Defence and the Prosecution have a constitutional right under the Rome Statute, they can always do something. They can make submissions when and wherever they want. From our point, we always have to find justifications. So it is limited but we have a legal framework to have an effect on the evidence, and all criminal proceedings are about evidence.

There are complex mechanisms to protect the Defence, for example in some Chambers, if the victims' Counsel wishes to question a Defence witness during trial, you must present the questions to the Chamber first, then the Chamber puts the question to the witness. This is one of the mechanisms to protect the fairness of the proceeding. But: you have the right to present your own witnesses! The mechanism is called 'Decision on the Modalities of Victims Participation'. In all cases at the ICC, sometime before the trial starts, the Chamber will render this kind of decision, and will give detailed information on how in this case, in this Chamber, the victims can effectively participate during trial.

18. **What has been your most challenging moment as a victims' advocate, and what moment are you most proud of?**

One of the first things you must get used to at the International Criminal Tribunals is that you have a limited time as Counsel to make oral submissions. I was aware from the ICTY that all Chambers, all courts have time limits. For example, if you make an appeal hearing, you have 20 min to respond to the Prosecution appeal etc. Even as a Defence Counsel you have time limits. But at the ICC as a victims' Counsel it's even more restricted. I will never forget the time that I made oral submissions on behalf of Principal Counsel in July 2012 in a status conference. It was a very important status conference because the Defence requested a temporary stay of proceedings because of the issue of defence investigations. The Defence said, as along as President Bashir in Sudan is not cooperating with the ICC and not allowing the Defence Counsel to enter the territory of Sudan, this proceeding has to be closed and terminated. But they asked only for a *temporary stay* of proceedings. I got the floor to make oral submissions, and I was prepared for 15 min or for 10 min. Then the Chamber told me before I started that I have 5 min.

And then, in effect, I put my notes aside and I started to tell the story of my clients. I said, 'I just want to address one point, and the point is this: what does it mean, 'a temporary stay of proceedings' from the victims' perspective? My clients are waiting since 2007, since more than 5 years now for the start of the trial. And the time is ticking away. The children do not go to school and they are growing up. The women do not have work and do not have any medical assurance. The soldiers are handicapped and they do not get a salary. What does it mean 'a temporary stay of proceedings'? When will Sudan change? In 5, 10, 15 years? Nobody knows, so the criteria are completely unclear when this termination of the case shall be lifted. Your Honour, from victim's perspective, a temporary stay is in fact a final stay of proceedings. From the victims' perspective it's final. And therefore there's no reason to decrease the criteria for a stay of proceedings just by saying it's only temporarily.'

This point was crucial for the Chamber. One of the judges took this point and talked with the Defence intensively about the meaning of 'temporary stay of proceedings', and if this is not just a trick to say it's temporary. So this was really something that meant a lot to me, because if you just have 5 min, you must be able to put your finger on the decisive point, you do not have any other chance. And then to become aware that your point is decisive, and then the Chamber can take it over, and they have all the time to do so. You see, you have limited resources, but you have a chance to make the best out of it. If you are able to identify the crucial point, you can have an effect even under these limited structures.

Jens Dieckmann is Founding Partner of Becher&Dieckmann in Bonn (Germany) and Associate Member of 9 Bedford Road Chambers in London. He has a varied national and international practice as Counsel in all areas of International Criminal Law and International Refugee Law. He is List Counsel at the ICTY/MICT, ICTR, ICC and STL. Since 2011, he is Common Legal Representative of Victims, Associate Counsel, for all participating victims in the Banda case (Darfur) before the International Criminal Court (ICC). In 2008, he was assigned as ad hoc Counsel in the interest of the Defence in the Kony et al. case (Uganda) before the ICC. He has also practiced as Defence Counsel before the International Criminal Tribunal for the former Yugoslavia (ICTY) in the cases against Milan Lukic & Sredoje Lukic, Sadri Selca, Astrid Haraqija & Bajrush Morina and Dragomir Pecanac.

From 2006 to present, I am elected member to the Board of the ADC-ICTY (membership-committee, amicus curiae committee, ad hoc committee for Post Tribunal Matters, 2014–2016 executive committee and Co Vice President of the ADC-ICTY, 2016–2017, 2017–2018 Chair of the disciplinary committee). From 2007 to 2019 I was Vice President of the International Criminal Defence Lawyer—ICDL—Germany e.V. I am Co-Founder of the International Criminal Court Bar Association—ICCBA. In 2015/2016, I was a member of the Drafters Committee and the Interim Board of the International Criminal Court Bar Association. 2016/17 I served as elected member to the ICCBA Executive Council as well as to the ICCBA Professional Standards Advisory Committee. In 2017/2018 and 2018/2019 I was re-elected member to the ICCBA Executive Council and elected ICCBA Vice- President for Victims and Chair of the ICCBA Victims Committee.

Entretien avec Jean-Louis Gilissen: les défis de la représentation des victimes de différentes cultures
Interview with Jean-Louis Gilissen: The Challenges of Representing Victims of Different Cultures

Jean-Louis Gilissen

Interviewé: Jean-Louis Gilissen

Interviewer: Elizabeth King

La date: Le 23 Mai 2017 - *23rd May 2017*

Emplacement: Entretien par email - *Email interveiw*

1 Introduction

Jean-Louis Gilissen exerce la profession d'avocat depuis 1983. Son activité est essentieiiement axée sur les concepts de la "gouvernementalité", sa pratique juridique concernant tant le droit international des droits de l'homme et le droit international humanitaire que le droit constitutionnel, le droit administratif et le droit pénal. Il a particulièrement développé des compétences reconnues en matière du droit de la peine et de la sanction (droit pénal et de la procédure pénale, droit disciplinaire et droit de "la peine déguisée"). Il est notamment intervenu dans plus de 70 affaires criminelles devant les Cour d'assises du Royaume de Belgique, il a été élu à quatre reprises au sein du Conseil de l'Ordre de son Barreau.

Parallèlement, Me Gilissen a développé une activité internationale qui l'a amené à intervenir notamment devant le Tribunal international pour le Rwanda où il a assumé la charge d'avocat de la Défense. Il a occupé la fonction de Procureur général adjoint en charge de la répression des crimes internationaux au sein de la Mission d'administration transitoire des Nations Unies au Timor oriental. Il a également

J.-L. Gilissen (✉)
Seraing, Cite of Leige, Belgium
e-mail: info@avocatgilissen.be

E. King et al. (eds.), *Victim Advocacy before the International Criminal Court*,
https://doi.org/10.1007/978-3-030-56733-0_18

défendu les intérêts des enfants soldats dans certains des premiers procès qui se sont déroulés devant ia Cour pénale internationale à La Haye. A plusieurs reprises, Me Gilissen a été invité à prendre la parole à l'Ecole nationale de magistrature de France et il a assuré sous la forme d'un séminaire un cours de Droit de ia procédure pénale internationale à l'Université de Liège. Il intervient régulièrement dans des colloques, en qualité de conférencier ou dans les médias en qualité d'expert. Me Gilissen est un des trois associés - gérants du Cabinet d'avocats Xharde-Gilissen.

Dans une brève interview, l'avocat belge Jean-Louis Gilissen réfléchit à certains des défis qu'il a rencontrés en représentant des victimes de différentes cultures à la Cour pénale internationale.

1. Introduction

Jean-Louis Gilissen has been practicing law since 1983. His activity is mainly focused on the concepts of "governmentality", with his legal practice engaging in both international human rights law and international humanitarian law as well as constitutional law, administrative law and criminal law. He has particularly recognised skills in the law of punishment (criminal law and criminal procedure, disciplinary law and the law of "disguised punishment"). Gilissen has intervened in more than 70 criminal cases before the Assize Courts of the Kingdom of Belgium, he has been elected four times to the Council of the Order of his Bar.

At the same time, Gilissen has worked on international cases, including the International Tribunal for Rwanda where he assumed the office of defense lawyer. He served as Deputy Prosecutor General in charge of the suppression of international crimes within the United Nations Transitional Administration Mission in East Timor. He also defended the interests of child soldiers in some of the first trials that took place before the International Criminal Court in The Hague. On several occasions, Gilissen has been invited to speak at the National School of Magistrates of France and he has provided, in the form of a seminar, a course in International Criminal Procedure Law at the University of Liège. He regularly attends conferences, as a speaker or in the media as an expert. Gilissen is one of the three partners - managers of the Xharde-Gilissen law firm.

In a brief interview, Belgian lawyer Jean-Louis Gilissen reflects on some of the challenges he has encountered in representing victims of different cultures at the International Criminal Court.

2 Quels sont les défis que vous avez rencontrés quand vous avec représenté un lien des clients des cultures différentes?

De manière générale, l'assistance ou la représentation de personnes devant des juridictions dans le cadre d'affaires pénales constitue un exercice complexe et sans aucun doute délicat.

En effet, il m'apparaît que l'avocat ne peut se concevoir comme le simple porte voix de ceux et celles qui lui font l'honneur de lui confier la défense de leurs intérêts.

Pour le professionnel du Barreau, il s'agit de tenter de prendre toute la mesure de la complexité et de la profondeur des intérêts qui lui sont confiés et d'arriver à rendre compte de ceux-ci auprès de Magistrats professionnels chargés d'appliquer la Loi.

Concrètement, il s'agit de parvenir à traduire la spécificité de ces intérêts dans des termes et des concepts qui rencontrent ceux repris dans les textes légaux tout en veillant à conserver la dimension humaine des personnes concenées et de leur vécu.

Le métier d'avocat m'apparaît donc nécessiter la recherche d'un équilibre entre une connaissance technique exigente et la capacité de capter et rendre compte des particularités plus humaines propres aux faits de la cause soumis à la juridiction compétente.

Cette réflexion élémentaire prend une dimension particulière lorsque l'avocat représente les intérêts de victimes ou de personnes qui prétendent l'avoir été.

Le besoin de reconnaissance d'un statut de victime constitue en effet une priorité pour les personnes qui se considèrent lésées et celles qui ont souffert d'un dommage.

La définition de l'ampleur du dommage et de son éventuelle réparation constitue en effet quasi invariablement une priorité secondaire à la reconnaissance d'une qualité de victime.

Il convient donc de comprendre que, outre le fait de la victimisation, la nature de celle-ci et des faits ayant causé le ou les dommages est d'une importance cruciale pour les personnes concernées.

Il s'agit donc pour l'avocat en charge de la défense des intérêts de victime d'y être particulièrement attentif et d'être capable de prendre toute la mesure de la victimisation de ceux et celles qui souhaitent faire entendre leur voix et reconnaître leur souffrance.

Ces difficultés sont donc particulièrement amplifiées lorsque vous représentez les intérêts de personnes provenant de cultures différentes.

Ainsi, outre les difficultés propres à l'usage de langues différentes, c'est toute la perception de ce qui est conçu et ressenti comme étant un dommage qui pose question.

A priori, chacun d'entre nous ne peut en effet concevoir et penser que comme l'on conçoit et l'on pense dans sa culture.

De même, il est particulièrement complexe de concevoir les choses autrement que comme ont le fait dans l'époque où l'on vit.

Dès lors, rendre compte de la réalité des faits, décrire ce que l'on considère être son dommage tant dans sa nature que dans toutes les dimensions de son étendue et de sa gravité constitue un exercice particulièrement difficile et douloureux pour une victime.

Dans la pratique, celle-ci rend d'ailleurs compte de sa vérité des faits et de ce qu'elle considère être son dommage.

Communiquer cette vérité à une personne parlant une autre langue que la vôtre et qui est issue d'une autre culture est d'autant plus ardu.

La vérité de la victime n'est en effet pas toujours fidèle à la réalité mais, de surcroît, il faut prendre toute la mesure de ce que la vérité de la victime ne ressemble pas toujours à ce qu'elle énonce au travers de schémas mentaux et de modes de communication propres à sa culture.

Le travail de l'avocat se doit dès lors d'être d'autant plus attentif et exigent.

Il s'agit bel et bien d'un défi majeur qui, pourtant, et paradoxalement, peut précisément trouver sa solution dans la prise de conscience et la connaissance de la nature de ce défi.

Concrètement, il s'agit donc pour l'avocat de tout mettre en œuvre pour posséder un maximum d'informations concernant les faits de la cause et la situation des hommes et des femmes concernés par ceux-ci.

Plus que jamais, l'avocat doit cultiver les outils nécessaires à lui permettre d'assurer son rôle de passeur.

Il s'agit pour lui de se doter des outils le rendant capable de reprérer la singularité des événements et de leurs conséquences dans la vie des victimes et dans le ressenti que celles-ci en ont.

Il convient de garder à l'esprit que devant la Cour Pénale Internationale les Juges qui ont à connaître d'un dossier sont eux-mêmes issus de cultures différentes et multiples.

Outre l'acquisition de connaissances particulières, l'avocat chargé de représenter les intérêts de victimes provenant d'une autre culture doit veiller à s'entourer de personnes aux compétences diverses dont, et plus particulièrement, de personnes issues de la même culture que les victimes concernées.

Il s'agit en effet de permettre de rendre compte de la subjectivité et du relativisme des faits ainsi que des ressentis via une translation en termes permettant un discours à la dimension universelle.

Ce faisant, il ne s'agit nullement de renoncer au pluralisme culturel mais d'en rendre compte dans une norme et des concepts communs à toutes les cultures, permettant au relatif d'atteindre une dimension universelle.

2. What Are Some of the Challenges You Have Encountered When Representing Clients from Different Cultures?

Generally speaking, assisting and representing people before courts in criminal matters is a complex and undoubtedly delicate exercise.

It is my opinion that the lawyer cannot be seen as a simple megaphone of those who do him the honor of entrusting him with the defense of their interests.

For the professional of the Bar, it is their duty to measure the complexity and the depth of the interests which are entrusted to them, and arrive to account for these before Magistrates charged with applying the Law. It is a question of translating the specificity of these interests into terms and concepts which meet those included in the legal texts while taking care to preserve the human dimension of the people concerned and their experiences.

Therefore, a lawyer, in my opinion, needs to search for balance between the demanded technical knowledge and the ability to capture and account for the more human particularities specific to the case.

This elementary reflection takes on a particular dimension when the lawyer represents the interests of victims or of people who claim to have been. The need to recognise victim status is indeed a priority for those who consider themselves injured and those who have suffered damage. defining the extent of the damage, and its possible reparation, is almost invariably a secondary priority to the recognition of the status of victim. It should therefore be understood that, in addition to the fact of victimisation, the nature of the victimisation and the facts which caused the damage(s) is of crucial importance for the persons concerned.

It is a matter for the lawyer in charge of defending the interests of victims to be particularly attentive to it, and to be able to understand to the greatest extent the victimisation of those who wish to make their voices heard.

These difficulties are therefore particularly heightened when you represent the interests of people from different cultures.

In addition to the predictable difficulties one encounters when working in different languages, it is important to try and understand what is conceived and felt as being a damage. Each of us can conceive and think only as we conceive and think in our culture.

Likewise, it is particularly difficult to conceive of things that have occurred in a different era to our own of which we have lived. Therefore, reporting on the reality of the facts, describing what is considered to be its damage (both in its nature and in all the dimensions of its extent and gravity), constitutes a particularly difficult and painful exercise for a victim.

In practice, the latter accounts for their truth of the facts and for what they consider to be damage. Communicating this truth to someone who speaks a language other than your own and who comes from another culture is all the more difficult.

The truth of the victim is not always true to reality and does not always resemble what it states through mental diagrams and culture-specific modes of communication, therefore the work of the lawyer is all the more demanding.

It is the responsibility of the lawyer to make every effort to have all the facts of the case and to understand the situation of the men and women affected by them. It is a matter of equipping oneself with the tools necessary to be able to fulfill their role as courier. They must be able to account for the subjectivity and the relativism of the facts as well as the feelings, via a translation, in turn allowing a discourse with universal dimensions. In doing so, it is not a question of renouncing cultural pluralism but accounting for it, relating concepts common to all cultures.

In addition to acquiring specific knowledge related to the case, the lawyer representing the victim(s) from another culture must take care to surround themselves with collegues that have diverse skills, particularly people from the same culture as the victim(s) concerned. It is also worthy noting that the judges that preside in the International Criminal Court are themselves from different and multiple cultures.

Jean-Louis Gilissen is Defense lawyer at the International Criminal Court and Lawyer at Xharde-Gilissen-Xharde.

Interview Paolina Massidda: Principal Counsel of the Office of Public Counsel for the Victims (OPCV)

Paolina Massidda

Interviewee: Paolina Massidda

Interviewer: Erin Pobjie

Date: 21 October 2013 (updated April 2016)

Location: Phone interview

Transcript of interview (edited)

1 What Is Your Role in the Court as the Principal Counsel of the Office of Public Counsel for Victims?

The Office of Public Counsel for Victims was established in September 2005. The legal basis for the creation of the Office is Regulation 81 of the Regulations of the Court. Regulation 81 was amended almost 2 years ago and has slightly expanded the role of the OPCV providing expressly the possibility for counsel of the Office to be appointed as legal representatives of victims throughout the proceedings.

P. Massidda (✉)
Office of Public Counsel for Victims, The Hague, The Netherlands
e-mail: Paolina.Massidda@icc-cpi.int

E. King et al. (eds.), *Victim Advocacy before the International Criminal Court*,
https://doi.org/10.1007/978-3-030-56733-0_19

1.1 Mandates

The Office has three main mandates. The first one is the possibility to represent victims as the legal representative or common legal representative in the proceedings before the Court. This means that counsel from the Office can be appointed by victims as their lawyer, or appointed by a Chamber to represent victims at any stage of the proceedings. At this point in time the Office is appointed for applicants in several cases, but also as common legal representative or as legal representative in other cases. The total number of people that Counsel from the Office represent as at April 2016 is over 6000 in all the different cases and situations. Representation of victims of a situation is probably 2 or 3% of our entire representation mandate. For the rest, it is mainly in active cases. Since the inception of the office in 2005 until the beginning of 2014 we had represented almost 35,000 people in all the different situations and cases.

The second mandate of the Office relates to the possibility for victims to choose their own lawyer, as long as said lawyer complies with the requirements under rule 22 of the Rules of Procedure and Evidence, meaning be on the List of Counsel and meet the criteria which descend from this. If a victim has his or her own lawyer, the Office has the mandate of assisting this external lawyer in providing him or her with legal advice and legal research.

The third mandate is the possibility to appear before Chambers in respect of specific issues which might affect the general interests of victims. This mandate can be triggered by the Office directly asking the Chamber to appear on specific issues; by the Chamber directly; by external lawyers; and by victims themselves. Until now, it has normally been triggered by Chambers, particularly at the trial stage, and by the Office.

This is the extent of the mandate of the Office of Public Counsel for Victims. At this point in time, Counsel of the Office are appointed as common legal representatives of victims in the proceedings at different stages. As a consequence, the task of providing support and assistance to external counsel has significantly decreased, while providing legal representation to victims is currently the main task performed by the staff of the Office. This implies daily presence in courtroom.

1.2 Experimentation with Forms of Legal Representation of Victims

The Court is still experimenting how legal representation of victims can be made more effective. In the *Laurent Gbagbo* case, the Counsel from the OPCV has been appointed as common legal representative so it means that I am the Lead Counsel, and the Chamber allowed me to have the assistance of a lawyer in Ivory Coast to help in maintaining frequent contact with victims, keeping them updated and collect their views and concerns. This system strengthens the effectiveness of the participation of victims, and addresses the needs of victims in an efficient manner.

The same system has been adopted in the *Ntaganda* and in the *Ongwen* cases and two Counsel from the Office are appointed as common legal representative. In the Kenya cases (*Ruto* and *Sang* case and the *Kenyatta* case), the Chamber adopted exactly the opposite system: an external lawyer was appointed as common legal representative and he has to be in Kenya and one OPCV staff was daily in courtroom on behalf of that lawyer. This system seems less effective because of difficulties in communication and decisions taking if the Lead Counsel is in the field and the member of the Office acts on behalf of the common legal representative in The Hague. There is also the problem of sharing of responsibilities, which is not so evident. The OPCV staff assigned to the external lawyer is still under the supervision of the Principal Counsel of the OPCV, in terms of performance appraisal and conduct as ICC staff, so the secondment of said person to an external lawyer, creates a double responsibility for the person concerned. Therefore, the position of the Office is that this system is less easily implementable.

The practice in the *Ruto and Sang* case shows that sometimes consultation between the external lawyer in the field and the OPCV staff at the hearing is difficult. Moreover the OPCV staff in the courtroom is not entitled to take decisions since this is the responsibility of the lead counsel. His or her role is still an advisory one and, like for any advisors, the person to whom you give the advice can take it or leave it. So you don't have any incidence on what could be said in the hearing if you don't have the okay from the appointed common legal representative. Moreover, there could be a problem in ensuring consistency of approaches to similar questions in different cases.

In conclusion what I think should really matter when deciding on the common legal representation system to be adopted is making sure that victims have a voice and have the most effective legal representation possible.

2 What Would You Say the Unique Challenges Are of Representing Victims Before the ICC?

2.1 Interpretation of Legal Texts

First of all there is the issue of interpreting the legal texts of the Court. Now, there is only one paragraph in one article in the Rome Statute in relation to the participation of victims, which is Article 68(3). All terms in said article require interpretation. This is already a problem because it means that your right to be heard always depends on an interpretation from judges which could differ and still differs between different situations and cases.

2.2 Coordination and Strategy

I strongly think that legal representatives can make a difference if they advocate the same way on issues which are important to everybody.

This could be achieved, for instance, by trying to have more coordination and more communication between the different legal representatives' teams.

2.3 Place of Victims' Counsel in the Proceedings

There is also the challenge of finding your place as legal representative in the proceedings, which is also not so evident because very often, the role of the legal representative is confused with or assimilated to the role of the Prosecution. After all these years, if there is one thing that I am convinced of, it is that the interests of the victims are in most of the cases, absolutely not coincident with the interests of the Prosecution. It's true that victims have an interest in finding someone—who they think is responsible for what happened to them—guilty. But the way in which victims would like this to happen is to some extent very different from the way in which the Prosecution conceives the responsibility of the suspect/accused. For instance, very often victims considered the charges brought by the Prosecution against a suspect not to be coincident with what really happened to them and the extent of their victimisation. This is the reason why it is very important for victims that their lawyer is able to understand the context in which they live and the way in which the events happened and were suffered from by them.

2.4 Allowing Victims to Tell Their Story

It's very important for a legal representative to go in the field to meet the victims possibly where they reside, to speak with them and to understand them. What I ask my client is to tell his/her story. What matters to me is to understand what the story is, what are the concerns of the person, why they are talking to me. When we meet our clients we normally ask why they want to participate, or why they don't. Normally they say, 'Because I want justice.' I say, well, the Office of the Prosecutor is also helping you in having justice. And they reply, 'Well, it might be true, but when I speak with someone from the Office of the Prosecutor, they will take from my story what is useful for their case. That's not necessarily what I want to be told.'

Considering what happened to them, victims are very reasonable people, and they are very smart in what they want. For them, the issue of justice is crucial. Ninety-nine per cent of the victims will tell you, 'I want my story to be told. I want someone in the courtroom who is really speaking for me'. For the victims is also a matter of reconstructing their lives via the telling of their individual stories. Because the perspective of victims, it's always individual. Even if you represent them in a group, you represent them also individually. And this is the richness, I would say of the entire process, being able to understand what victims want and try to convey their stories and expectations in terms of justice.

2.5 *Language and Communication*

[There is also] the issue of the distance of victims from The Hague, the place where proceedings are conducted. There is always a need to maintain regular contact with them and in a language that they can understand, which is another challenge. In this regard, it is important to make some efforts to understand their language to some extent, which is much better than passing through an interpreter. It's a matter of building trust. What happened to me for instance in DRC when I was appointed to represent some former child soldiers in the *Lubanga* case, they wanted to speak with me in Swahili or Lingala. After several times we met, they started speaking to me in French. And I knew it. When I was speaking French, I was sure that the person in front of me was able to understand French, it was just a matter of not trusting enough. And this happened also in other situations, which makes you understand how it's important for the victims that you empathise with them. It's very important. It seems evident to some extent. It's not.

2.6 *Keeping Victims Informed*

And finally also, the need of keeping victims regularly informed of what is happening in the proceedings. Victims have to feel that someone is there at the Court for them. And this is already very important. For instance, very often when you meet with someone at the beginning and the application of this person is not yet decided by the Chamber, you have to explain to them, that it could take months before having news about the process. They understand it. And then you need to find ways to communicate with them from time to time, even if nothing is happening in the proceedings so they understand that you are still working for them. The fact that justice takes so long; it's a very complicated and difficult concept to digest for victims.

3 What Are the Practical Things That Legal Representatives Can Do in Order to Bridge the Gap of Culture, Language and Experience with Their Clients?

3.1 Understand the Historical, Political, Geographic and Legal Context

I am speaking from my own experience of course. Now, this experience could be different for someone who comes for instance from the country where the victim is. For us, as Office, what we normally do is, first of all, to have a very good understanding of what happened in the country: from an historical point of view, from a political point of view, from a geographical point of view, because sometimes the origins of a conflict are historical but also geographical because of a partition for instance of some lands. It's also important to read as much as possible from local newspapers, reports from NGOs, anything that you can find about the country. NGOs, civil society, are a very good source to understand the civil dynamic within the country and also problems in relation to human rights, criminal proceedings, etc. Another important thing is to understand the legal context in the country, so which kind of crimes are prosecuted. Are these crimes within the scheme of the Rome Statute or not? Which level of evolution of the legal texts do you have in the national system, which remedies are available or not for victims? How the national judicial systhem works? These are issues which are important for instance for any matters relating to the admissibility of a case.

3.2 Understand the Social and Cultural Context

Second, try to understand the social and cultural context. Why? The way in which you approach people, particularly in the African culture, is different depending on the different tribes, or social or economic group. So it's also very important to understand the way in which you have to approach someone. For instance, sometimes in order to meet someone in a village you have first to pay a visit to the head of the village. And you have sometimes to make a choice: Do I want to meet the head of the village or not? Because maybe I might expose the other people I will meet in the village. So you have to balance all these issues. Another example, in Ivory Coast, during a meeting with the Malian Community, I had the older ones in front of me, and the young people behind. They will not speak to you if they don't have the authorisation of the older ones. So when I went to meet the Malian Community, I knew about that. And it was clear that the young people had questions to pose, but felt they could not ask. So I approached the oldest, and I asked them if the youngest could pose questions in order to solve the issue and have the young people expressing themselves.

3.3 *Language*

It also helps to know a little bit of the language of the person you meet. You can maybe greet the person in his/her own language. It immediately triggers a different reaction in people, immediately you can see it, because people understand that you are making an effort to approach them.

4 If You Were to Describe the Ideal Legal Representative of a Victim, in Addition to the Qualities That You Just Named, What Other Qualities Would They Have?

4.1 *Personal Qualities*

I don't know if there is an ideal one. I tend to think that we are all human and so the ideal is probably for a next life if you think that there is another one! But I would say that you need some empathy, you need to be a good listener, particularly at the beginning because normally the legal representative is the first person to whom the victim can speak freely, like having a conversation with someone in the family.

4.2 *Legal Knowledge and Skills*

Victim advocates must find the time to understand the legal texts of the Court very well. This is very important. Try to also be to some extent creative in interpreting the law, as a lot still needs to be defined/interpreted in the domain of victims' rights. I think a good lawyer is also someone who can find arguments which are maybe not so evident to enhance his clients' rights. As long as you can legally sustain an argument, even if you are the minority but if it's for the benefit of your clients you should go for it.

4.3 *Strategy*

And then, I think you should be trained in seeing when you can push and when you cannot in proceedings. You know the judges, you know the other parties, so you should calibrate your strategy also towards the person that you have in front of you. To some extent, you should try to understand when you have chances to win and when not. You cannot fight just for the sake of fighting, because if you have a negative precedent, that is a negative precedent also for other cases. But sometimes, you have to try because this is the only way in which you can advance the rights of victims. The point is that in my opinion the rights that are enshrined in the Rome Statute have not at this point in time been taken into account sufficiently before Chambers.

4.4 Advocacy

I do not think that the issue of participation of victims is necessarily a priority for the judges. They have a lot of issues to deal with in relation to matters involving the parties, redactions, disclosure of information, so maybe the participation of victims is almost at the end of the list, if you are lucky in the middle of the list. This is where legal representatives may have a role—they *should* have a role to make the judges understand, that the participation of victims is important and that can be efficiently approached with good organisation and strong legal representation. So advocacy is also important to advance the rights of victims.

5 Given the Potentially Vast Numbers of Victims Who Will Participate in the Proceedings, How Can a Legal Representative Make the Participation as Meaningful as Possible?

A lot depends on the way in which you organise your work. A huge component of successful work in this matter is organisation. First of all, when you are appointed as a lawyer, the first step in any case is to meet with your client individually. Why? Because it is important to understand the story of each of your clients and victims may not be comfortable in meeting in a group to explain what happened to them. Sometimes members of the same family are unaware of what happened to other members of their family (i.e. in case of rape or gender based crimes). If the number of victims you represent is huge, sometimes it is also important to meet victims in a group provided that you do not expose them to security concerns.

5.1 Contact Points

Coming back to the way in which you can represent them: the first issue when appointed is to try to meet with them individually to understand if they are members of the same family, because this is also important to find a way of contact, because for instance in some countries not everybody will have a mobile phone. If the family agrees, sometimes it's also a good idea to have only one focal point. This will facilitate your interaction, organising it. This method can also be used for other categories of victims.

5.2 *Organising Victims by Types of Crime and Age*

Another step is to understand the types of crimes suffered from by the victims, in order to be able to represent the interest of the victims also by type of crimes. An example: if you are a woman and you have suffered from sexual violence, your interest in justice is different from someone who has suffered from pillage; also on the level of reparations, for instance. If you ask someone whose house has been pillaged which kind of reparations he or she wants, the person will immediately say, I want back my house, horses, cows, whatever was lost. But if you ask a victim of gender crimes, or to a former child soldier, he or she will say to you, my life was ruined, I'm incapable of thinking of anything which could give me some reparations, some restoration for what happened to me. So the way in which you pass this message before the judges has to be different, it cannot be the same message. It is useful to group the people by type of crime, and within the type of crime by age. Because the way in which a young lady will approach the issue of rape is not the same as an old one. Or a very young child soldier and others abducted at the age of 14, it's different. Then, if they are a minor, you have always to meet with someone who is an adult who is acting on his or her behalf.

5.3 *Common Interests*

The way in which you organise the legal representation will allow you to always be able to have the views and concerns, not only of the person individually but also of the group of people that you represent. Even if you represent someone individually, normally victims have common interests in the proceedings. So it's important as a lawyer to find out which are the common interests that you can put forward in the proceedings.

6 For an External Legal Representative, Is There Anything Your Office Can Do to Support Them Representing These Kinds of Clients?

What we can do is to provide legal advice and legal researches. In the majority of the cases we are requested to provide legal advice, something related specifically to the proceedings. Sometimes, we are also requested to provide advice in a specific situation within a specific case. Rarely we have been asked to provide advice on how to find victims, how to approach victims, how to interview them.

7 You Spoke Before About the Need for Legal Representatives of Victims to Be Aware of Common Interests of Victims and Coordinate Their Strategy. Do You Have Any Suggestions for Increasing the Sense of Collegiality within the Profession?

I would love to have coordination on general issues pertaining to the participation of victims and having a common understanding of what may render more effective legal representation of victims. How this can be achieved? I think that the Office could be the initiator of these kinds of discussions, because we are in a privileged position since we are involved in all the situations and cases.

8 In Terms of Systemic Issues or Challenges, What Would You Change If You Could Change Anything About the Current System for Victim Participation?

I think that a standardised approach to participation and legal representation should be adopted in the future.

9 How Do You Imagine That the Role of Victim Representation Will Play Out in the Next Five Years?

It's very difficult to tell. It is clear that the system of application needs some adjustments since it is now very cumbersome.

Then I hope that the practice will be uniform on several issues pertaining to the participation itself, mainly on modalities of participation and I hope that more progress will be made for reparations.

9.1 *You May Not Want Bureaucracy to Shape What Should Be Seen as a Fundamental Right*

Exactly. At the beginning when I started at the Office, I had the impression that there was a fear of the unknown. It was difficult to predict how participation of victims would be handled, particularly in terms of a huge number of potential victims. So a huge number is automatically equated with problems. This is not the case. This is the reason why I was trying to say that organisation is a part of the way in which you can effectively provide victims with a voice in the Court's proceedings.

I think there is a need to change to some extent the mentality – a need to be more creative, more proactive. As I see it, there is no need to change the rules or regulations of the Court for this to occur. If the legal texts of the Court are interpreted in a less restrictive way, for victims it will be more than enough.

10 Which Stage Do You Feel There Is the Greatest Potency or Power for a Victims' Involvement: Representations Made Initially, the Views and Concerns, or the Reparations? Where Do You Think the Power Lies?

10.1 *Investigation*

For me, I think at least three. First of all, the investigation, because victims really value when they are asked what they want in the context of a criminal proceedings in which they pursue justice. Because they realise that in the beginning, the mode of liability, or the type of crimes, or the type of events, that the Prosecutions may choose matter to them.

10.2 *Admissibility*

The second one, is the admissibility proceeding. It's very important for victims—the possibility for victims to have a say in whether they want a case to be prosecuted by the ICC, or not.

10.3 Trial

The third one for me would be the trial stage. Because at this stage victims can present evidence going to the guilt or the innocence of the accused, not only to reparations; as well as the possibility to appear in person before the Judges. This triggers in the victims, the sense of being really involved in the claim for justice and truth.

10.4 Reparations

I'm not saying reparations at this point in time, because there reparations proceedings are still to some extent to be shaped.

Paolina Massidda is a member of the Genoa Bar (Italy) since 1994. She is specialised in human rights and international humanitarian law and she holds a master on international criminal law. In her over 20 years of experience, she practised before national and international tribunals, representing accused and victims.

Since September 2005, she is the Principal Counsel of the independent Office of Public Counsel for Victims at the International Criminal Court. In this capacity she has represented victims in the proceedings before the Court in almost all situations and cases, gaining a specific experience in gender crimes, victims' rights and in handling cases with high numbers of victims involved. She is currently the common legal representative of victims in the Ongwen, Yekatom and Ngaissona and Abd-Al-Rahman cases. She also represents victims in the Lubanga and Katanga reparations proceedings, as well as in the Gaddafi, Kony and Simone Gbagbo cases, Palestine and Afghanistan situations.

She has published extensively on matters related to international criminal law and the rights of victims. She regularly trains and gives lectures in international criminal law.

Interview Fiona McKay: Former Chief of the Victims Participation and Reparations Section (VPRS)

Fiona McKay

Interviewee: Fiona McKay

Interviewer: Erin Pobjie

Interview date: Tuesday 22 October 2013

Location: The Hague, The Netherlands

Transcript of interview (edited)

1. **Firstly, could you describe your role as the Chief of the Victims Participation and Reparations Section?**

My role is to manage the Victims Participation and Reparations Section (VPRS), which is a specialised unit within the ICC's Registry that is concerned with the participation of victims in the proceedings and reparations. The role of the Section is to facilitate access of victims to the Court so that they can exercise the possibility they have to apply to participate in the proceedings. We also manage the records relating to victims' applications and respond to various judicial orders that might arise relating to participating victims during proceedings. The Section also selects common legal representatives of victims when ordered to do so by a Chamber. As regards reparations, the role of the Section would depend on how a particular Trial Chamber decides to deal with reparations.

This interview took place whilst Fiona McKay was still occupying the position of Chief of Victims Participation and Reparations Section and thus her answers are responded to in the present tense. Her role in this position extended from 2004 to 2015.

F. McKay (✉)
The Hague, The Netherlands
e-mail: fiona.mckay@opensocietyfoundations.org

E. King et al. (eds.), *Victim Advocacy before the International Criminal Court*,
https://doi.org/10.1007/978-3-030-56733-0_20

There are differing approaches within the Court to organising victim participation, but in general, what happens is that Judges decide which victims are linked to a particular case and are entitled to participate in the proceedings. We map out on the ground who might be victims linked to a particular case, enable those people to make their applications if there is an application system, follow up on incomplete applications and organise the information received from the victims for the Judges so that they can decide on victims' status based on the relevant information. Some Judges want us to make *prima facie* assessments as to whether or not individual victims or groups of victims qualify or not to be considered victims. Our role varies according to the directions that a particular Judge or Chamber might give in a particular case.

2. **How has your experience at the Court shaped your view on the role of victims at the ICC?**

Victims had not had the same role in previous international criminal courts and tribunals. That indeed has been the biggest challenge—working under the direction of Judges to try to shape victim participation and make it work, because there wasn't the experience of other tribunals to draw on, so it was a question of creating from scratch the structure and the procedural frameworks. My experience has convinced me that it is possible to organise victim participation in international criminal proceedings effectively, even when there are large numbers of victims, and despite the very real challenges involved.

3. **In your experiences, what do victims value most when they seek to participate in the proceedings?**

That is one of the most difficult questions, because there is not one single answer. One of the things I have learned is that you cannot make assumptions about what victims think, about what they think is important, or what they want. There are anecdotes that could be conveyed, but something that we are trying to do now is to more scientifically get a sense of what is important to victims.

A study is being conducted by the University of California at Berkley—a team that has done population-based surveys in different places including in some of the ICC situation countries, to put questions to victims who have already participated in proceedings, or victims who have applied to participate, or victims who maybe decided not to apply to participate, to get a proper sense of what elements are important to victims. I hear a lot of things from my staff, from people on the ground and from NGOs, but it is so wide and differing that I certainly would not presume to say, well, victims think 'this'.

We do see some consistency in the responses when we ask victims what is important in a legal representative. Often we are not asking them which specific individual they want to be their legal representative, because there are a large number of victims so it would be impossible to take everybody's selection into account, and often they do not personally know any lawyers. But if you ask them, 'What do you want from your legal representative?', then you get fairly consistent responses to that question. For example: Somebody who understands my context, somebody who will communicate with me, somebody who is competent at their job.

4. **What are some key considerations for representing victims that are often missed by legal representatives, or mistaken assumptions that legal representatives make about the needs of their clients?**

When a lawyer is appointed to represent victims for the first time, what I observe is not so much mistaken assumptions as uncertainty caused by a lack of a clear framework for what it means to represent victims specifically. We have a Code of Professional Conduct for Counsel, which contains the elements that you would expect about diligence and ethics etc. But it is quite general, and I think that there is a genuine problem that when lawyers are appointed to represent victims before the ICC, that they do not necessarily know exactly what is expected of them.

The lack of clarity is not surprising, because most lawyers on the Court's List of Counsel will not in their normal practice, whether at the national or international level, have experience representing large numbers of clients in one case, or dealing with victims who have suffered from the types of crimes within the Court's jurisdiction. So I don't think we can expect them to automatically know how to deal with this.

Because victim participation in international criminal proceedings is an innovation of the ICC, the Court's law and practice is already different to what they might have experienced before even if they have practiced before other international courts and tribunals.

5. **Do you have any advice on how lawyers can prepare themselves for dealing with victims of the crimes within the jurisdiction of the Court?**

A lawyer thinking of representing victims before the Court would obviously need to familiarise themselves with the law and procedure of the Court in general, and specifically that relating to the participation of victims. They might also try to gain an understanding of what it means to manage a case involving large numbers of clients and what techniques could be used in such cases.

Counsel might need to be a bit humble and realise that they might not have all the skills that are needed. Somebody composing a team to represent victims should think about what different qualities and skills they need in their team, which probably includes people from the local community who know how to communicate directly and effectively with the victims linked to the case.

Another aspect for new victims' legal representatives to bear in mind is the fact that they will not only be dealing with large numbers of people, but also people who may have gone through very traumatic experiences that have marked them and may affect the way they interact. So they have to think about how to deal with a situation where they are with a victim or a room full of victims, and somebody is breaking down because they are talking about what happened to them.

6. **Does your office provide any support for lawyers who are representing victims who have suffered trauma?**

The Registry does not have the means to provide direct support for this, but we do have quite a lot of interaction with the lawyers who are representing victims and try to help them find ways to support their work, including sharing information about the local context and intermediaries who may be able to provide such support. In some instances we have organised training of legal representatives and their teams on how to interact with victims including vulnerable victims.

7. **What kinds of contact would your office have with Counsel for victims?**

We would expect to have quite a lot of contact in the beginning when they are first appointed, in order to transfer information to them, including extracts from our database regarding the victims they represent. After that we generally encourage some ongoing interaction, in order to share information about how things are on the ground, pass on any concerns and support their work in any way we can, such as for example providing them with key messages and outreach materials developed by the Court relating to the proceedings that they could use to keep victims informed

Sometimes we do play some part in communicating with victims, alongside the lawyers. Obviously we are not going to intervene in the lawyer/client relationship, but sometimes we work collaboratively with the lawyers, especially when there are large numbers of victims, to convey information to the victims. In the Kenya proceedings for example, when the common legal representatives were first appointed, we met with the victims and introduced the new lawyers, explained what their role was, and what they could expect from them.

8. **Given that your office has a lot of contact with victims, and communicates with victims, can you give any advice from that experience to Counsel for victims that would help them to connect with their clients or improve their communication with clients?**

Sometimes we notice that the information a lawyer is providing to victims has a tendency to be rather too technical. Where we are involved in selecting legal representatives, one of the things that we look for is strong communication skills, or at least a recognition that such skills must be obtained for the team, because as I said you can't expect to find all the skills that are needed in the one person.

9. **Can you describe some common problems and how they can be avoided?**

One of the most common things that we hear is that victims are not satisfied because they do not see their lawyer enough. That can be a problem in instances where, for example, there is a trial going on and the lawyer is in the Hague, so they cannot be regularly on the ground meeting with the victims. Victims may have unrealistic expectations, and think that they will see their lawyer regularly, whereas this is not realistic especially where the lawyer might be representing thousands of victims. There are instances certainly where we think that the lawyers are not doing enough to ensure that their team keeps in contact with the victims. Sometimes it is a question of moderating the expectations, and other times, there is a problem and we try to work with the legal representative to resolve it.

If we receive information, whether complaints or comments about how victims are experiencing their legal representation, then we pass it on to the Counsel. Obviously if it's something that's very serious we would take further steps, but at the very least we try to provide the information and make suggestions to the Counsel on how to resolve the matter.

10. **When your Office is making a list of Counsel for victims because you've been directed to do so by the Chamber, what do you look for?**

If a Chamber requests the VPRS to select a common legal representative of victims, we start by drawing up criteria based on any instructions from the Chamber, the knowledge and experience they have to have in order to be on the Court's List of Counsel etcetera. But we also include some criteria which are to do with qualities specially needed for representing victims, such as the ability to communicate, empathic qualities, and the ability to manage the file where you have many victims.

There are also some criteria that we leave open case by case, that are identified as a result of consultation with victims. Or if the case were to be mostly or completely about one particular type of crime, such as sexual violence, or recruitment of child soldiers, then we would look for particular experience and expertise in that area.

11. **What do you think are desirable personal qualities in a legal representative for victims?**

I think communication skills are important, and the recognition that if the legal representative does not have those skills themselves, that they have to make sure that they are present in their team. We find that victims think it very important to have some contact with their lawyer. And they have to be able to organise and manage the file, those kinds of case management skills are important as well.

12. **Given the cultural divide that there may be between Counsel for the victims, as well as other differences like language and geographic distance, what suggestions do you have for how Counsel for victims can connect with their clients?**

This will vary a lot case by case. For example, in some places it's perfectly feasible for you to fill a hall full of people and meet with hundreds or tens of people at once. In other places that is simply not possible, either for security reasons, or because the nature of the crimes means that people are not comfortable in that kind of context. You have be adaptable. It also makes a difference how the victims are distributed geographically; you have to think differently if your clients are scattered around not only a large area, but areas that are very difficult to access. So you have to think of other ways to contact people. This will depend on the communication means available, whether the victims have ready access to telephones, internet, etc.

I think it could be useful for legal representatives of victims to have more opportunities to share their experience with others, on matters such as how to go about keeping in contact with their clients and manage the conveying of information and taking of instructions; what works and what doesn't work in different circumstances.

In the Registry, since it is also our job to work out how to contact victims and enable them to make their applications, we have similar kinds of questions. For example, where is it safe to meet people.

13. **Given that a lot of victims might be very marginalised within their society, or in very remote places, or have suffered from sexual violence, how do you reach those kinds of victims, or even become aware of where they are, and how many there are?**

Normally we identify and reach victims through local counterparts—intermediaries is the general term that we use—who already have, or are best placed to develop, the trust and confidence of victims. So for instance, if there were charges of sexual violence in a case, then we would be looking for local women's organisations. These may not normally be concerned with legal matters, but may enable us to become aware of and reach victims, and ensure that these victims' interaction with the Court does not cause them further harm.

14. **Once Counsel is briefed, what do you think are the very first things they should be doing?**

The lawyer will have to be asking: What have I got to do next? Where are we in the proceedings, and what do I need to do in order to represent my clients effectively at this procedural stage? If I've got to make an opening statement in the trial next week, that's one thing. If I have to make submissions about whether the Accused should be released or not, it's a different matter. They would also have to immediately think about how to compose their team.

Secondly, they would need to organise the information about the victims, whether they represent a few or many victims. They will need to be ready to identify where their clients' interests are affected by what is happening in the proceedings.

Thirdly, they should find the most effective way to communicate with the victims they represent.

Sometimes these things have to be done with not very much time. Sometimes you have several months, and sometimes it's next week that you have to appear in Court for the first time, or write submissions.

15. **Is there much coordination between different legal representatives for victims in a single case?**

In the Registry, we normally don't recommend having more than one team of common legal representatives in any given case unless there's a conflict of interest between different groups of victims linked to the case (such as in the *Katanga and Ngudjolo* case where you had child soldiers on the one hand, and victims of attacks allegedly committed by those child soldiers on the other hand). Given that there are limited resources, we have found that it is more effective to use those resources to have one well resourced team than to have several different legal representatives in a case, and that this provides a better quality representation to the victims.

16. **Within such a context where one legal representative or a team represents many victims in a single case, what can that legal representative or team do to make the participation of those victims as meaningful as possible?**

All the things that I have already mentioned. At the same time, in the Registry we have been looking at the impact of way we do our work so it is as meaningful as possible for victims. Is it meaningful to victims to tell their story through filling in a form, or is an application just a means to an end and it doesn't really matter? How important is it to victims that their lawyer will actually take time to listen to each one of them, and what do you do about that when you've got 2000 clients?

17. **If you could change anything about the current system for victim participation in the proceedings, what would it be?**

I think it would be helpful to have a greater degree of predictability and certainty in the system. That will enable the whole system to stabilise and for people to have a basis on which to decide whether or not to come forward to participate in the proceedings. How can a victim decide whether or not to come forward and try to participate if they don't have much idea what's going to happen?

18. **Do you have a point of view of which phase has the most potency or power for victim representation, or does it vary?**

What we do find is that more victims tend to come forward at the trial stage. One reason is that there is not always enough time at the early stages to reach everybody. Sometimes we get the sense that people are waiting to see if there is really going to be a trial. The trial is the most visible stage, especially in countries where there is coverage in the media or where the Court's Outreach teams are able to reach the affected communities and show video summaries of the trial.

Some might consider the most important part of proceedings to be the early stages, because this is when the scope of a case is shaped.

An appeal proceeding is very difficult, because it takes time, and the victims do not necessarily visibly see much going on, as so much is on paper.

We know that reparation is of huge interest to victims, especially because in most of our cases, you're talking about people who have lost a lot, whether loved ones, their physical or mental health, or material goods through pillage.

Fiona McKay is an international lawyer and human rights practitioner with extensive experience in international criminal justice. Her expertise includes victim participation and reparations in criminal justice, claims processes, international human rights advocacy and access to justice initiatives, and managing field programmes and capacity building project. She is currently Senior Managing Legal Officer at the Open Society Justice Initiative, based in London. Prior that, from 2004 to 2015 McKay was Chief of the Victim Participation and Reparations Section at the International Criminal Court in The Hague. A common theme throughout her career has been creating and shaping new projects to bring justice to victims, including providing legal services to victims seeking remedies for serious violations of human rights and international humanitarian law.

Interview Milê Glamcevski: Vicarious Trauma and Self Care for the Victim Advocate

Milê Glamcevski

Interviewee: Milê Glamcevski, ACA accredited Clinical Counselor specialising in Major Trauma

Interviewer: Elizabeth King

Interview date: 27th April, 2014

Location: Melbourne, Australia

Transcript of the interview (edited)

1 Vicarious Trauma

1.1 Could You Describe What Vicarious Trauma Is?

There are usually two explanations I give for this question. The most straightforward one is a person taking on trauma that somebody else has experienced. The more technical definition is that when you are empathetically connecting with somebody the trauma that that person's describing and relating will have an impact on how you will feel. Perhaps not to the full degree of the person who has directly experienced the trauma, but at least partially.

M. Glamcevski (✉)
Royal University Phnom Penh, Melbourne, VIC, Australia

E. King et al. (eds.), *Victim Advocacy before the International Criminal Court*,
https://doi.org/10.1007/978-3-030-56733-0_21

1.2 Does a Person Experiencing Vicarious Trauma Feel It as If They'd Experienced It, or Is It a Muted Experience?

It's the same but different. An example that I use to explain this is that when a friend describes to you something bad that has happened to them, and you get emotional about it, you actually feel their emotions. It is not exactly the same as directly experiencing them but it is on the same continuum and a similar style of exposure.

Having a predisposition or a trigger will affect you more.

1.3 How Long Has Vicarious Trauma Been a Recognised Condition?

The concept itself has been around for approximately 100 years, with psychotherapists in the 1920s and 1930s having an awareness of the effect of a persons trauma on another, however the term "vicarious trauma" has only been around for the last 20 years. I believe McCann and Pearlman (1990) coined the phrase back the 1990s and it was slowly perpetuated through literature in the mental health and community service sphere. Eventually it came into our working lexicon in the early 2000s.

Compassion fatigue, which is a part (and a pre-term) of vicarious trauma has been around since the 1960s.

1.4 Does This Mean There Is Something in the Contemporary Term "Vicarious Trauma" That Wasn't Carried with the Term "Compassion Fatigue"? Is There a Newer or Fresher Understanding?

Compassion fatigue put the emphasis on the individual not coping, so there is something deficient in *you*. However, vicarious trauma identified and accentuated that you were taking on *another persons* trauma. I feel it's a term that takes the blame off the individual and creates more understanding.

1.5 What Kind of Professionals Might Suffer from Vicarious Trauma?

Anyone who deals with anyone who has trauma is susceptible. So your classic examples are:

- psychologist/counsellors
- social workers
- emergency service workers
- law enforcement
- legal professionals
- etc...

1.6 In What Circumstances Could a Professional Develop It?

Vicarious trauma in my experience is rarely an isolated incident—it is accumulative. The more exposure you have to it, the more likely you are to suffer from it. There are many factors that also fuel it, such as isolation, reduced resilience, work place stress, multiple and frequency of exposure, etc...

1.7 How Does It Happen? Does the Thinking Behind Vicarious Trauma Flow from the Same Thinking That Informs Trauma?

Very much so. It is still trauma. It's not a trauma that the person has directly experienced but is being experienced through (secondary exposure). We are just realising now in the field of psychology (and other fields such as social work and law enforcement) that you can be quite removed from the trauma, but still suffer symptoms.

Firstly you can have the client who faced the trauma, then there is the person that works with them around that initial trauma, and then that person has a supervisor or manager. An individual that is three-persons removed from the initial incident can experience vicarious trauma. So it's not necessarily how directly related you are to it, although the closer you are to the trauma the more likely you are to be affected.

1.8 Does Everyone Get It? Are Some More Susceptible to It Than Others?

If you are pre-disposed to empathise with another and have an oversensitivity to care, then you would be more susceptible than others. The occupations discussed previously usually possess these traits. A person who is *drawn* to a specific area of law (i.e humanitarian law) will, most likely, have more developed empathy than the average lawyer. There is a fine line between being empathetic enough to be connected with somebody and maintaining appropriate clinical distance.

If an occupation exposes a person regularly to very detailed material (e.g a lawyer representing victims of genocide and war crimes) then once again, they will be more susceptible.

In addition the more guilt and shame you feel in life, which might arise from being on a level of privilege, power and wealth, the more predisposed the person is to developing vicarious trauma.

1.9 What Are the Symptoms of a Person Suffering from Vicarious Trauma?

The symptoms are very similar to the trauma experienced by the primary person.

In addition, a person suffering from vicarious trauma will or could:

- feel tired
- feel unhappy
- be very emotional
- be struggling with personal relationships
- have difficulty sleeping
- have difficulty eating
- be relying on poor coping mechanisms (i.e drug and alcohol)
- be unsatisfied with life
- have a blunted range of emotions
- be struggling with self-regulation
- have more interpersonal conflict

1.10 Is It a form of Depression or Different?

Depression can result from it and it's often associated with it, however it is different. Trauma is more anxiety based were as depression is a clinical disorder which is more mood based.

On the other end of the spectrum, some people who experience vicarious trauma just shut down and not accept the trauma they have been exposed to.

1.11 How Does That Look and Feel for Those Affected?

Once again blunted emotions, being poorly connected with society, often poor quality relationships with close family members, and overall feeling unsatisfied with life.

People who are closed off often question 'why they are so clever', believing that they have successfully blocked themselves off from the trauma. Its a protection mechanism. They compartmentalise their life and put up barriers.

Both types of reactions aren't good for the person experiencing vicarious trauma. You can find that the pendulum can swing both ways in their careers and in their lifetime.

1.12 How Long Would an Inflicted Person Have Vicarious Trauma?

It's a complicated question. Once you have accumulated a certain amount of trauma there needs to be some time to release it. When someone has become dysfunctional from vicarious trauma, I often see them facing a recovery process of minimal 12 months; recovery meaning to restore the affected person back to a functional state.

1.13 Is the Inflicted Person Aware of It at Its Onset?

If you are in isolation and have been accumulating trauma over many years it is very difficult to notice. There is usually a crisis point that differentiates yesterday from today which motivates people to seek help. Usually others (such as family and colleagues) notice the symptoms and attempt to convince the individual to seek help.

1.14 Could You Give an Illustrative (De-Identified) Case Study of a Vicarious Trauma Case?

When I was 24 I lived and worked in Cambodia for a couple of years as a psychologist, during that time I saw a lot of trauma. Everyday I heard horrific and traumatic stories about mothers, fathers, and brothers being killed. In addition I was also exposed to quite a few instances of direct trauma. Just to note, at this point in my career I was very much into the neuroscience side of psychology and mental health. I believed that the brain determined behaviour and that people were just attached to that.

So one day, a 65-year-old blind woman was brought to me. She had been through all the medical tests and there was no biological reason for her blindness. I questioned why she brought to me. 15 years ago soldiers came into her village and beheaded her husband in front of her. At this stage she had nine children. They then proceeded to tell me that over the next 15 years each of her nine children were murdered in front of her and that she just decided to stop seeing. In psychology we call this *Somatoform disorder.*[1] They brought her to me in the hope I could do something for this woman. There wasn't much I could do for her at this point; the amount of trauma she has seen and her age, in combination with the number of other people I needed to see. So they asked "what could I do to help this woman?" and I said "well, I can take out my pistol, shoot her in the head and put her out of her misery", as it seemed the most humane thing I could do for her at the time.

She ended up being taken away and I never saw her again. Over the next couple of years I was faced with a number of patients with Somatoform disorders and I took all that trauma on board. I had both good and poor coping mechanisms which, of course, I developed into better ones over time.

Then I began supervising and seeing other psychologists who were coming to me with their issues. In the beginning I believed that my experience in this field would prepare me for taking the trauma onboard . However, overtime it started to affect me.

I ended up tracing it back to the Cambodian blind woman. She was my trigger. I felt really guilty for being quite flippant in my comments at the time; "we can shoot this woman, if that would help." This was my trigger. A direct trauma.

1.15 So Did You Identify Vicarious Trauma in Yourself?

Yes, it only took 13 years.

[1]*Somatoform disorder* which is now labeled as "Somatic symptom disorder" (SSD) is a form of mental illness that causes one or more bodily symptoms, including pain. The symptoms may or may not be traceable to a physical cause including general medical conditions, other mental illnesses, or substance abuse. People with SSD are not faking their symptoms. The distress they experience from pain and other problems they experience are real, regardless of whether or not a physical explanation can be found. http://www.webmd.com/mental-health/somatoform-disorders-symptoms-types-treatment. Accessed 6 May 2020.

2 The Victim Advocate and Vicarious Trauma

2.1 If I Were to Ask You to Consider the Sorts of Cases That a Victim Advocate Will Be Acting in: Cases Concerning War Crimes, Genocide, Crimes Against Humanity, Violent Acts, Innocent Lives—What Practical Measures Should an Individual Take and at What Point?

From the very beginning an advocate should undergo preparation in order to protect themselves. By being aware of individual triggers and understanding themselves within the system, the individual will have a better chance of dealing with trauma.

I recommend an advocate establish and develop their *professional skills*, through:

- training,
- continuous professional development,
- mentoring,
- supervision,
- debriefing,
- formal and informal conversations with colleagues, and
- research literature.

Personal skills the individual can focus on are:

- eating well
- sleeping well
- exercise,
- establishing realistic expectations,
- maintaining a balanced lifestyle, and
- being aware of emerging feelings of guilt and obligation, which in turn could overwhelm the individual.

2.2 How Do You Address the Challenge of People Denying That They Are Having Difficulty Coping?

Our whole society is still geared towards denying and hiding what we see as 'weakness'. How many people say "I have been exposed to a large amount of traumatic events, I am very emotional and I need to see someone about it?" This usually doesn't happen. We either need to change culture or policy within the workplace.

2.3 *By Definition, a Person Who Is Acting in a Victims Matter in Front of the ICC Would Have 10 Years Domestic Experience, of Which During Those Years Have Had Criminal Law Experience Undertaking Cases That Involve Sexual Abuse or Assault. Other Than These Professional Minimal Requirements, There Is for No Uniform Person Who Is a Victims Advocate for the ICC. What Things Could We Systematically Change (if any) to Help Prevent Vicarious Trauma Inflicting Future Advocates Representing Victims in the ICC?*

Given the culture we are facing, systemic change would be the most effective in protecting future advocates.

The military is a good example. Before they deploy somebody, they do a psychological briefing. When they come back, they are once again required to debrief with a psychologist.

So a possible situation could be if you are to be placed on the list to advocate for victims at the ICC, you are required to do a psychologically natured session. It would be built into the regulation to remove the personal challenge of electing to get help.

You can change policy to change culture. Or change culture to change policy.

In this situation it would be a much easier scenario to change policy.

Milê Glamcevski Since the early 1990's, Milê has had an intertwined career, working in health science and mental health fields. He has post graduate qualifications in mental health, medicine and education and has spent over 15 years working on community disaster or community development projects, often from an educational base, in developing nations such as Cambodia, Malaysia, East Timor and Turkey.

Ensuring That Your Client Receives Adequate Non-Legal Professional Support Before, During and After the Court Process

Ronda Cress

1 Introduction

Providing effective representation and advocacy to victims before the ICC can be a daunting task to advocates given the myriad number of issues to consider including, oftentimes, the accompanying financial and other resource constraints. The purpose of this chapter is to equip the victim's advocate with readily available resources on the issues most likely to be encountered by the advocate. Accordingly, the following list of resources is not intended to be exhaustive. Rather, it is a compilation of those resources viewed by the author as containing the most comprehensive, practical and easily accessible information relevant to the work of the victim's advocate.

The chapter is organized in a manner to present the most specific and relevant information first and then moving to more general, broad-based information. Thus, the chapter commences with International Criminal Law resources and the abundance of pertinent information available on the ICC's own website, and moves on to human rights resources and victimology resources. These resources provide both practical information, as well as the theoretical and legal background for victims' rights and reparations. The chapter then shifts into resources having a largely practical application, such as the sections on Working with Trauma Victims (including specifically with children), Interdisciplinary resources, and Advocacy Skills resources. Finally, the chapter concludes with sections on Best Practices resources, Useful Membership Organizations and recommended websites and scholarship for Further Reading.

R. Cress (✉)
Ohio Department of Medicaid, Columbus, OH, USA

E. King et al. (eds.), *Victim Advocacy before the International Criminal Court*,
https://doi.org/10.1007/978-3-030-56733-0_22

2 International Criminal Law Resources

2.1 Courts and Tribunals

2.1.1 International Criminal Court (ICC)[1]

The ICC's 'Resource Library' section under the 'Documents' tab contains direct links to the Rome Statute, the Rules of Procedure and Evidence, the Elements of Crimes, the Regulations of the Court, the Office of the Prosecutor and the Registry Regulations, the Code of Professional Conduct for legal counsel, the Code of Judicial Ethics, and the Court's Official Journal, among others.

Additionally, it may not be well known to legal advocates that the ICC has its own online, searchable Legal Tools Database.[2] The Database is a comprehensive repository of key Court documents, international legal instruments and international criminal law resources. The Database has robust filtering capability to aid in finding specific items.

Within the ICC, the Office of Public Counsel for Victims (OPCV) has published a Manual for Legal Representatives[3] appearing before the Court to represent victims. This Manual is extensive and is highly recommended to victims' advocates. It contains a wealth of information, including a general introduction to the ICC and to the role of victims in proceedings before the Court, synopses of the Court's most important decisions regarding victims, analyses of practical issues relevant to representing victims before the Court, and recommended resources.

Advocates may also wish to look at the information available on the ICC's website about the Victims[4] and Witness units,[5] the Trust Fund for Victims,[6] and "A guide for the Participation of Victims in the proceedings of the court"[7] published by the ICC's Victims Participation and Reparation Section.

---

[1] More information and further discussed documents can be found at the International Criminal Court website. https://www.icc-cpi.int/. Accessed 10 September 2021.

[2] https://www.legal-tools.org/. Accessed 10 September 2021.

[3] OPCV, International Criminal Court (January 2021). 'Representing Victims before the International Criminal Court: A Manual for legal representatives'. Resource document. https://www.icc-cpi.int/iccdocs/opcv/2021.03.01-ENG-5th-Rev-Rev.pdf Accessed 10 September 2021.

[4] OPCV, International Criminal Court (2014). 'Representing Victims before the International Criminal Court: A Manual for legal representatives'. Resource document. https://www.icc-cpi.int/iccdocs/opcv/OPCVManual-4-Eng.pdf. https://www.icc-cpi.int/about/victim Accessed 10 September 2021 .

[5] https://www.icc-cpi.int/about/witnesses. Accessed 10 September 2021.

[6] https://www.icc-cpi.int/tfv. Accessed 10 September 2021.

[7] International Criminal Court. "Victims before the International Criminal Court – A Guide for the Participation of Victims in the Proceedings of the Court". https://www.icc-cpi.int/NR/rdonlyres/8FF91A2C-5274-4DCB-9CCE-37273C5E9AB4/282477/160910VPRSBookletEnglish.pdf. Resource document. Accessed 10 September 2021.

The Assembly of States Parties Official Records[8] for each session are available. Notably, in response to a request by the Assembly of States Parties, the Court published its 'Revised strategy in relation to victims'[9] in November 2012 on how it will work to better ensure the realization and actualization of the rights of victims. In November 2013, the Court issued a report evaluating its implementation of the strategy.[10]

The ICC's Counsel Support Section of the Registry may be contacted for inquiries regarding the application process to join the List of Counsel or Assistants to Counsel via email at: css.lists@icc-cpi.int or by phone at: +31-(0)705158787. Candidates must submit applications by postal mail to:

ICC – Counsel Support Section

P.O. Box 19519

2500 CM, The Hague

The Netherlands

Applicants should review the Court's Guide for Applicants available on its website at https://www.icc-cpi.int/iccdocs/PIDS/docs/ICC_GuideForApplicants_ENG.pdf.

2.1.2 Other International Criminal Law Tribunals

International Criminal Tribunal for the former Yugoslavia (ICTY): http://www.icty.org
International Criminal Tribunal for Rwanda (ICTR): http://unictr.unmict.org
Special Court for Sierra Leone (SCSL): http://www.rscsl.org
Special Tribunal for Lebanon (STL): http://www.stl-tsl.org
Extraordinary Chambers in the Courts of Cambodia (ECCC): http://www.eccc.gov.kh/en
Extraordinary African Chambers within the Courts of Senegal: http://www.chambresafricaines.org/

[8] https://asp.icc-cpi.int/en_menus/asp/sessions/official%20records/pages/official%20records.aspx. Accessed 10 September 2021.

[9] International Criminal Court (2012). Assembly of States Parties—Court's Revised strategy in relation to victims. Resource document ICC-ASP/11/38. https://asp.icc-cpi.int/iccdocs/asp_docs/ASP11/ICC-ASP-11-38-ENG.pdf. Accessed 10 September 2021.

[10] International Criminal Court (2013), Assembly of States Parties – Report of the Court on the implementation in 2013 of the revised strategy in relation to victims. Resource document ICC-ASP/12/41. https://asp.icc-cpi.int/iccdocs/asp_docs/ASP12/ICC-ASP-12-41-ENG.pdf. Accessed 10 September 2021.

War Crimes Chamber (WCC), Court of Bosnia and Herzegovina: http://www.sudbih.gov.ba/

Special Panels for Serious Crimes (SPSC) – Timor Leste: http://www.worldlii.org/tp/cases/TPSPSC/

Supreme Iraqi Criminal Court (Iraqi High Tribunal): http://gjpi.org/2009/09/13/iraqi-high-tribunal/

2.2 *Organizations*

2.2.1 Coalition for the International Criminal Court (CICC)[11]

The CICC is a conglomeration of civil society organizations from 150 different countries working together to strengthen and advance justice to victims. It is the primary NGO provider of online ICC material, including extensive resources under the 'Library' tab at the bottom of the home page—from the CICC's own publications, factsheets, manuals and checklists, government documents, NGO statements, articles and reports, to links to external websites, resources and tools. The 'Explore the ICC System' tab from the main menu contains updates and developments about the Court, information on current ICC cases and situations, the structure of the Court, and the Assembly of States Parties. It is possible to subscribe by email to receive weekly global justice and civil society news by simply scrolling to the bottom of the website.

2.2.2 American Society of International Law (ASIL)[12]

ASIL's Electronic Resource Guide (ERG) page lists ERGs on a number of international law topics. The international criminal law ERG[13] contains links to relevant online resources, including: Research Guides, Books and Information Networks; international and regional criminal law Treaties, Conventions and Agreements; Courts, Tribunals & Other Adjudicatory Bodies; Crime Prevention, Prosecution & Criminal Justice; information on Specific Crimes; Statistical Sources; and, Information Clearinghouses and Related Sources.

[11] More information and further discussed documents can be found at the Coalition for the International Criminal Court website. http://www.coalitionfortheicc.org/. Accessed 10 September 2021.

[12] https://www.asil.org/

[13] Partin, G. International Criminal Law (2015). Resource document. *American Society of International Law*. https://www.asil.org/sites/default/files/ERG_CRIM.pdf?v=1. Accessed 10 September 2021.

2.2.3 Peace Palace Library[14]

The Peace Palace Library Research Guides section includes a research guide on international criminal law, which features links to a Bibliography, New Titles, Librarian's Choice, Databases, Blogs, and other online resources.

2.2.4 Commentary on the Law of the International Criminal Court (CLICC)[15]

Also known as the 'Klamberg Commentary'[16] this resource is a free, searchable database on the interpretation of the statutory texts and case law of the ICC. Notably, it provides a 'provision-by-provision analysis' of the Rome Statute and other instruments, including the Rules of Procedure and Evidence. The website also has a link to the Case Matrix Network, which has a variety of free online tools (including The Commentary) and information related to international criminal law.

3 Human Rights Resources

3.1 U.N. Office of the High Commissioner for Human Rights[17]

This website is a one-stop resource for database links to all of the core international human rights instruments and their monitoring bodies, as well as to the universal international human rights instruments. Under the 'Publications and resources' tab, users can select 'publications' for access to the OHCHR's facts sheets, special issue materials, reference materials, training and education materials, and policy and methodological materials on a number of human rights issues. There is also a 'Library' option linking to the OHCHR's searchable library collections.

[14] More information and further discussed documents can be found at the Peace Palace Website. https://peacepalacelibrary.nl/research-guide
Accessed 10 September 2021.

[15] https://cilrap-lexsitus.org/clicc. Accessed 10 September 2021.

[16] For the chief editor, Prof. Mark Klamberg.

[17] More information and further discussed documents can be found at the U.N. Office of the High Commissioner for Human Rights website. https://www.ohchr.org/EN/pages/home.aspx. Accessed 10 September 2021.

3.2 REDRESS[18]

REDRESS performs legal and advocacy activities primarily regarding torture victims, but it includes very useful material regarding reparations in general. The 'Reparations' section under 'Our Work' describes the organization's current work on the issue and contains links to projects. The 'Resources' section contains a variety of publications. Searching for "reparations" pulls up REDRESS reports and projects on reparations in specific contexts. There's also a 'Casework database' section with a searchable database of active REDRESS cases.

3.3 Amnesty International[19]

Amnesty International is a human rights NGO that has a wealth of human rights information and publications on its website. Because there are multiple pages of information under each thematic topic, probably the easiest way to find information is by searching the 'Research' section for specific information or looking for information on a specific country.

3.4 International Federation for Human Rights (FIDH)[20]

FIDH is a federation of 192 member organizations from 177 countries. The 'News' section is searchable by topic area, region, and document type. The International Justice topic contains a number of items related to victims rights and issues.

3.5 The International Bar Association, Human Rights Institute (IBAHRI)[21]

IBAHRI has a series of publications and training manuals for lawyers. Worth exploring is its 'Publications' and 'Digital Content' sections for reports, training manuals, guides, news analysis, etc.

---

[18] More information and further discussed documents can be found at the Redress website. https://redress.org/. Accessed 10 September 2021.

[19] More information and further discussed documents can be found at the Amnesty International website. https://www.amnesty.org/en/. Accessed 10 September 2021.

[20] More information and further discussed documents can be found at the International Federation for Human Rights website. http://www.fidh.org/en/. Accessed 10 September 2021.

[21] More information and further discussed documents can be found at The International Bar Association, Human Rights Institute website. https://www.ibanet.org/IBAHRI. Accessed 10 September 2021.

3.6 University of Minnesota Human Rights Library[22]

Developed and operated by the University of Minnesota Human Rights Center,[23] the library is a comprehensive collection of international instruments, U.N. documents, regional materials, refugee and asylum resources, and links to thousands of human rights related resources.

4 Victimology Resources

4.1 World Society of Victimology[24]

World Society of Victimology (WSV) is an NGO that has Special Category consultative status with the U.N. Economic and Social Council. It engages heavily in research and program development on victims, assistance to victims and victim rights. The 'Publications' tab (under Resources) includes links to U.N. reports and documents, WSV collaborative reports and documents, policy statements, and archived copies of WSV's quarterly newsletter, "The Victimologist." The 'About Us' tab includes a listing of WSV affiliated organizations, and a listing of National Societies of Victimology websites is included under the Resources heading.

4.2 The International Rehabilitation Council for Torture Victims (IRCT)[25]

The IRCT is a health-based umbrella organization that supports the rehabilitation of torture victims and the worldwide prevention of torture, including sexual torture. The 'Media and Resources' tab contains useful publications for both torture survivors and organizations, especially in the Thematic Reports section.

[22] http://hrlibrary.umn.edu/. Accessed 10 September 2021.

[23] https://www.law.umn.edu/human-rights-center. Accessed 10 September 2021.

[24] More information and further discussed documents can be found at the World Society of Victimology website.
http://www.worldsocietyofvictimology.org/. Accessed 10 September 2021.

[25] More information and further discussed documents can be found at the The International Rehabilitation Council for Torture Victims website. https://irct.org/. Accessed 10 September 2021.

4.3 Victims' Rights Working Group

This group is a network of hundreds of national and international civil society groups and experts focused on ensuring the protection and respect of victims' rights throughout the ICC's judicial process. Unfortunately, its website is no longer active and it's unclear whether the organization still exists. The Working Group was facilitated by REDRESS, and publications are still available on the REDRESS website by searching for 'Victims' Rights Working Group'.[26]

4.4 The Handbook on Justice for Victims[27]

This handbook was created in 1999 by the U.N. Office for Drug Control (UNODC) and Crime Prevention's Centre for International Crime Prevention[28] and focuses on the use and application of the Declaration of Basic Principles of Justice for Victims of Crime and Abuse of Power. The UNODC website has a number of publications regarding Victims under its Crime Prevention and Criminal Justice Reform section that readers may find useful.

4.5 Office for Victims of Crime[29]

The U.S. Department of Justice's Office for Victims of Crime has a 'Help for Victims' section that includes a variety of information relevant to victim services.

4.6 International Review of Victimology[30]

This Review contains journal articles on a variety of victimology topics. Although abstracts of each Issue are available online back to 1989, viewing of the full articles requires a subscription. Simply searching the journal for 'International Criminal Court' pulls up a number of articles specific to the ICC and victims.

---

[26] https://redress.org/. Accessed 10 September 2021.

[27] UN ODCCP (1999) https://www.unodc.org/pdf/criminal_justice/UNODC_Handbook_on_Justice_for_victims.pdf. Resource document. Accessed 10 September 2021.

[28] https://www.unodc.org/unodc/commissions/CCPCJ/. Accessed 10 September 2021.

[29] https://ovc.ojp.gov/help-for-victims/overview. Accessed 10 September 2021.

[30] *International Review of Victimology*. https://journals.sagepub.com/home/irv. Accessed 10 September 2021.

4.7 *International Handbook of Victimology*

Shlomo Giora Shoham, Paul Knepper and Martin Kett (CRC Press 2010). The book is not free, but it is available in eBook form and can be accessed for free for those with valid university library subscriptions. It's a very in-depth volume on the theoretical and historical framework of victimology and justice, restorative justice issues, how social divisions impact victims (e.g. gender, disability). A viewable Table of Contents[31] for the book is available.

5 Working with Trauma Victims

5.1 *International Society for Traumatic Stress Studies (ISTSS)*[32]

The ISTSS focuses on the advancement and exchange of knowledge about traumatic stress. It previously held. Special Consultative Status with the U.N. Economic and Social Council (ECOSOC). The website has information and resources for treating, assessing and researching trauma, including best practices. The 'Clinical Resources' section includes material specific to assessing adults and to assessing children and adolescents.

5.2 *The Center for Victims of Torture*[33]

The Center's 'Resources' section has a number of items specific to torture survivors, health care providers and human rights defenders. The Center developed an interviewing manual for NGO's that may have some useful application: Manual on Brief Ethnographic Interviewing: Understanding an Issue, Problem or Idea from a Local Perspective.[34]

[31] *International Handbook of Victimology* table of contents. https://www.crcpress.com/International-Handbook-of-Victimology/Shoham-Knepper-Kett/p/book/9781420085471. Accessed 10 September 2021.

[32] More information and further discussed documents can be found at the International Society for Traumatic Stress Studies website. https://istss.org/home. Accessed 10 September 2021.

[33] https://www.cvt.org/. Accessed 10 September 2021.

[34] Hubbard, J. https://www.cvt.org/sites/default/files/attachments/u8/downloads/Brief%20Ethnographic%20Interviewing%20Manual.pdf. Resource document. Accessed 10 September 2021

The *International Rehabilitation Council for Torture Victims (IRCT)*[35] has a number of reports relevant to organizations and individuals interviewing and assisting victims of torture, including manuals for evidence gathering and engaging with human rights mechanisms.

The *Human Rights Center - UC Berkeley School of Law*[36] *(University of California)* has some useful resources, especially with respect to survivors of sexual violence in its Sexual Violence Program, found under the 'Programs and Projects' tab.

5.3 Children-Specific Resources

Attorneys for Children Guide to Interviewing Clients: Integrating Trauma Informed Care and Solution Focused Strategies.[37] This is a guide developed by the New York Courts to assist interviewers of children who have been traumatized.

The Child Rights International Network[38] has some great resources and legal assistance toolkits available under its Guides section. For instance, there are a number of guides and toolkits available for legal, advocacy and other professionals who may work with children who have been traumatized.

5.3.1 Ethical Research Involving Children (ERIC)[39]

This organization and website is largely focused on dealing with children in a research context, but there is some useful information with general applicability in its Resources section.

ICRC's 'Children in War'[40] information kit is more legal-based and descriptive of ICRC's work in specific community programs, but it gives a very good overview of

[35] More information and further discussed documents can be found at The International Rehabilitation Council for Torture Victims website. https://irct.org/. Accessed 10 September 2021.

[36] More information and further discussed documents can be found at the Human Rights Centre – UC Berkeley School of Law website. https://humanrights.berkeley.edu/. Accessed 10 September 2021.

[37] Reitma, K.A (Ed) (2011). "Attorneys for Children Guide to Interviewing Clients: Integrating Trauma Informed Care and Solution Focused Strategies" http://ww2.nycourts.gov/sites/default/files/document/files/2018-10/attorneyGuide.pdf. Resource document. Accessed 10 September 2021.

[38] More information and further discussed documents can be found at the Child Rights International Network website. https://archive.crin.org/. Accessed 10 September 2021.

[39] More information and further discussed documents can be found at the Ethical Research Involving Children website. https://www.childethics.com/. Accessed 10 September 2021.

[40] International Committee of the Red Cross (2004). https://www.icrc.org/en/doc/assets/files/other/icrc_002_0577k_children_in_war_kit.pdf. The 2020 version is available at: https://shop.icrc.org/children-in-war-pdf-en Resource documents. Accessed 10 September 2021.

the international and regional legal instruments applicable to assisting children who have experienced war. There's also a more recent version available for free in pdf. format.

Interagency Panel on Juvenile Justice's (IPJJ)

Save the Children[41] has Practice Standards in Children's Participation,[42] as well as Guidelines for working with child soldiers and children associated with fighting forces.[43]

The Special Representative of the U.N. Secretary-General for Violence Against Children[44] has a number of useful links to reports, data and international standards pertaining to children's rights, restorative justice and effective treatment mechanisms.

Although it does not have material specific to treating or representing children who have experienced trauma, the Office of the Special Representative of the U.N. Secretary-General for Children and Armed Conflict has some useful background information worth looking into on its website,[45] particularly its Publications pages (under the 'Library' tab).

6 Interdisciplinary

6.1 Women's Initiatives for Gender Justice[46]

This organization is an international women's human rights organization that focuses primarily on women impacted by situations under investigation by the ICC. The organization advocates for gender justice through the ICC as well as domestic mechanisms. The website's 'Research and Publications' tab contains links to a good mix of both academic and practical publications and reports, resources, and blogs relevant to gender justice and the ICC. Members of the public can view on the website the organization's eLetters series, *Legal Eye on the ICC* and *Women's Voices*. The 'Resources' section at the bottom of the home page has a lot of

[41] https://resourcecentre.savethechildren.net/. Accessed 10 September 2021.

[42] Save the Children UK (2005). "Practice Standards in Children's Participation". Resource document. https://resourcecentre.savethechildren.net/node/3017/pdf/3017.pdf. Accessed 10 September 2021.

[43] Save the Children UK (2010). "Children not soldiers – Guidelines for working with child soldiers and children associated with fighting forces." Resource document. https://resourcecentre.savethechildren.net/node/1567/pdf/1567.pdf. Accessed 10 September 2021.

[44] https://violenceagainstchildren.un.org/content/homepage. Accessed 10 September 2021.

[45] More information and further discussed documents can be found at the Office of the Special Representative of the U.N. Secretary-General for Children and Armed Conflict website. https://childrenandarmedconflict.un.org/. Accessed 10 September 2021.

[46] More information and further discussed documents can be found at the Women's Initiatives for Gender Justice website. https://4genderjustice.org/. Accessed 10 September 2021.

relevant information, including: Overview of Sexual Violence and the International Criminal Court; Gender Training Handbook; Information Card Series: Rights and the Rome Statute; Gender Integration in the Rome Statute; and Provisions for Victims and Witnesses in the ICC.

6.2 *Women's Refugee Commission*[47]

This organization works to improve the lives and protect the rights of women and children displaced by conflict and crisis. The Commission's work also includes work on disability issues. Links to research and resources specific to each program area of work focused on by the WRC are available in each area under the 'Focus Areas' tab. Additionally, useful reports, news updates, and journal articles are available through the 'Research and Resources Library' and 'Media Center' tabs. Publications include materials on groups particularly susceptible to war and conflict, such as persons with disabilities, children and youth, and women (both in regards to gender-based violence and to peace and security).

6.3 *International Committee of the Red Cross (ICRC)*[48]

ICRC is the leading international humanitarian organization and is mandated essentially from the 1949 Geneva Conventions. Under its 'Resource centre' tab, you can search publications specific to vulnerable groups in times of war and conflict, including women, children, refugees and internally displaced persons and persons with disabilities.

6.4 *U.N. High Commissioner for Refugees (UNHCR)*[49]

UNHCR's website provides a wealth information specific to vulnerable refugee groups under its 'Who We Help' section under the 'About Us' tab. This includes information relevant to asylum seekers, internally displaced persons and refugees, returnees, and stateless persons.

---

[47] More information and further discussed documents can be found at the Women's Refugee Commission. https://www.womensrefugeecommission.org/. Accessed 10 September 2021

[48] More information and further discussed documents can be found at the International Committee of the Red Cross website. https://www.icrc.org/en. Accessed 10 September 2021.

[49] More information and further discussed documents can be found at the U.N High Commissioner for Refugees website. https://www.unhcr.org/cgi-bin/texis/vtx/home. Accessed 10 September 2021.

7 Advocacy Skills Resources

7.1 War Crimes Research Office (WCRO)[50]

The WCRO of American University's Washington College of Law publishes a series of reports on the ICC through its ICC Legal Analysis and Education Project. The reports contain very useful and practical information about such topics victim participation, witnesses, admissibility, cumulative charging, reparations, modes of liability, expedited proceedings, and the rights of the accused. This website is highly recommended.

7.2 International Justice Resource Center (IJRC)[51]

The IJRC's stated mission is to provide "advocates, civil society organizations, and victims of human rights abuses with the information and resources they need to effectively use international legal protections – including advocacy before human rights monitoring bodies and complaints before international and domestic courts – to bring about justice and accountability for human rights violations." IJRC has an online resource hub located under the 'What We Do' tab with links to information about human rights mechanisms, international criminal law, humanitarian law and refugee law, and to International Advocacy Guides and Research Aids.

7.3 Sierra Leone Special Courts

The *Special Court for Sierra Leone (SCSL)* and the *Residual Special Court for Sierra Leone (RSCSL)*[52] website has 'Best-Practice Recommendations for the Protection & Support of Witnesses' who are testifying before war crimes tribunals. While the document is specific to the situation of victims and witnesses before the SCSL, some of the practices and recommendations may be adaptable to the ICC context. The recommendations can be found under the 'Documents' section of the Special Court for Sierra Leone.

---

[50] More information and further discussed documents can be found at the War Crimes Research Office website. https://www.wcl.american.edu/impact/initiatives-programs/warcrimes/. Accessed 10 September 2021.

[51] More information and further discussed documents can be found at the International Justice Resource Centre website. https://ijrcenter.org/. Accessed 10 September 2021

[52] More information and further discussed documents can be found at the Special Court of Sierra Leone website. http://www.rscsl.org. Accessed 10 September 2021.

7.4 International Federation of Human Rights (FIDH)

The International Federation of Human Rights' (FIDH) guide on victims' rights and victim advocacy before the ICC was published 23/04/2007 and is available under the 'International Justice' Issue. Select the 'Reports' box and 'International Criminal Court' option to find it and numerous other helpful information.

7.5 Australian Advocacy Institute

Australian Advocacy Institute,[53] *The Complete Guide to Persuasive Advocacy*, George Hampel, Elizabeth Brimer, Randal Kune.

7.6 Advocacy Before the ICC

'Victims' Rights and Advocacy at the International Criminal Court', 2d ed., T. Markus Funk (OUP, 2015). Unfortunately, this is not available for free unless one has access to ebooks through a university library account or other online subscription. It is a valuable tool for those representing or wishing to represent victims before the ICC. It is a comprehensive analysis of the ICC and includes information on the theoretical underpinnings of international justice theory and victim rights, the development, structure and operation of the ICC, a detailed explanation of the ICC's rules of procedure and evidence, including how to become a victim representative before the Court, in-depth discussion of evidentiary hearings, pre-trial and trial proceedings, and sentencing, as well as tips for understanding victims' interests and managing their expectations.

8 Resources on Best Practices

International Bar Association publication, 'Principles on Conduct for the Legal Profession (2011)' updated in October 2018 and approved by the IBA in May 2019.

The International Association of Legal Ethics' Resources and Links[54] page contains links to international legal ethics materials, regional materials, legal ethics codes for specific countries, and issue-specific resources.

---

[53] http://www.advocacy.com.au/. Accessed 10 September 2021.

[54] More information and discussed documents can be found at the International Association of Legal Ethics' website. https://iaole.org/resources-links/. Accessed 10 September 2021.

International Criminal Tribunal for Rwanda (ICTR) publication, 'Best Practices Manual for the Investigation and Prosecution of Sexual Violence Crimes in Post-Conflict Regions: Lessons Learned from the Office of the Prosecutor for the International Criminal Tribunal for Rwanda'.[55] Though this manual is geared toward prosecutors, it contains a wealth of useful information to victims' advocates and representatives about interviewing, liability and evidentiary issues, other practice-based manuals, diversity and gender parity, and counselling services both for victims and staff members. The annexes provide an Investigative Work Plan, Interview Checklist, and Sources and Further Reading. Relatedly, see Amnesty International's publication, 'Rape and Sexual Violence: Human Rights Law and Standards in the International Criminal Court'.[56]

The Women's Initiatives for Gender Justice (see above) also has some useful legal resources, such as the 'Expert Paper on Modes of Liability: A review of the International Criminal Court's current jurisprudence and practice',[57] which includes illustrative charts of each mode of liability and summaries of the judicial interpretations and changes to the modes of liability.

9 Useful Membership Organizations

9.1 International Bar Association[58]

The International Bar Association's ICC Programme engages in monitoring and reporting on developments at the ICC. The Programme focuses heavily on fair trial monitoring, but also monitors and reports on issues relevant to lawyers. The website provides links to the ICC Code of Conduct for lawyers, IBA Reports, and the ICC Female Lawyers Campaign. Additionally, individual and group memberships are available, which provide access to the IBA online legal resources library.

[55] International Criminal Tribunal for Rwanda (2014) "Best Practices Manual for the Investigation and Prosecution of Sexual Violence Crimes in Post-Conflict Regions: Lessons Learned from the Office of the Prosecutor for the International Criminal Tribunal for Rwanda". https://unictr.irmct.org/sites/unictr.org/files/legal-library/140130_prosecution_of_sexual_violence.pdf. Resource Document. Accessed 10 September 2021.

[56] Amnesty International (2008). "Rape and Sexual Violence: Human Rights Law and Standards in the International Criminal Court". https://www.amnesty.org/en/documents/IOR53/001/2011/en/. Resource Document. Accessed 10 September 2021.

[57] Women's Initiatives for Gender Justice (2013). "'Expert Paper on Modes of Liability: A review of the International Criminal Court's current jurisprudence and practice". http://iccwomen.org/documents/Modes-of-Liability.pdf. Resource Document. Accessed 10 September 2021

[58] More information and discussed documents can be found at the International Bar Association website. https://www.ibanet.org/. Accessed 10 September 2021.

9.2 *International Criminal Court Bar Association (ICCBA)*[59]

The ICCBA is a representative association of ICC List Counsel and Support Staff. It advocates on behalf of its member, provides support services, and acts as a forum for discussion regarding ICC issues. For more information or to submit inquiries, see the 'About Us' section on the website.

9.3 *International Criminal Law Society (ICLS)*[60]

The ICLS is a non-profit public interest association that is a member of the Coalition for the International Criminal Court. Membership information, including a link to the application form, is available under the 'Membership' tab on the left-hand side of the website.

Further Reading

Web-based

International Committee of the Red Cross[61]
International Center for Transitional Justice[62]
International Criminal Law Sources, Peace Palace Library[63]
Inter-university Consortium for Political and Social Research (ICPSR)[64] at University of Michigan – free search engine
Directory of Open Access Journals (DOAJ)[65] – "online directory that indexes and provides access to quality open access, peer-reviewed journals"
JSTOR[66] – free online access to over 1300 journals with registration of individual account

---

[59] https://www.iccba-abcpi.org/. Accessed 10 September 2021.

[60] More information and discussed documents can be found at the International Criminal Law Society website. http://www.icls.de/. Accessed 10 September 2021.

[61] https://www.icrc.org/en. Accessed 10 September 2021.

[62] https://www.ictj.org/. Accessed 10 September 2021.

[63] https://peacepalacelibrary.nl/research-guide/international-criminal-law. Accessed 10 September 2021.

[64] https://www.icpsr.umich.edu/icpsrweb/. Accessed 10 September 2021.

[65] https://doaj.org/. Accessed 10 September 2021.

[66] https://about.jstor.org/. Accessed 10 September 2021.

Scholarship

Bassiouni, M. C. (2012). *Introduction to international criminal law*. Martinus Nijhoff.
Boyd Webb, N. (Ed.). (2004). *Mass Trauma and violence: Helping families and children cope*. Guilford.
Cassesse, A., Gaeta, P., & Jones, J. R. W. (Eds.). (2002). *The Rome Statute of the international criminal court: A commentary*. Oxford University Press.
Cryer, R. (2010). *Prosecuting international crimes: Selectivity and the international criminal law regime*. Cambridge University Press.
Jones, J. R. W., & Powles, S. (2003). *International criminal practice* (3rd ed.). Oxford University Press.
Lee, R. S. (Ed.). (1999). *The international criminal court: The making of the Rome Statute*. Kluwer Law International.
Lee, R. S. (Ed.). (2001). *The international criminal court: Elements of crimes and rules of procedure and evidence*. Transnational Publishers.
Mettraux, G. (2005). *International crimes and the Ad Hoc tribunals*. Oxford University Press.
Nathanson, R., & Crank, J. (2004). Interviewing children with disabilities. In *Children's Law Manual Series*. National Association of Counsel for Children (NACC)).
Politi, M., & Nesi, G. (Eds.). (2017). *The international criminal court and the crime of aggression*. Routledge.
Schabas, W. A. (2009). *Genocide in international law: The crime of crimes* (2nd ed.). Cambridge University Press.
Schabas, W. A. (2016). *The international criminal court: A commentary on the Rome Statute* (2nd ed.). Oxford University Press.
Schabas, W. A. (2017). *An introduction to the international criminal court* (5th ed.). Cambridge University Press.
Triffterer, O. (Ed.). (2015). *Commentary on the Rome Statute of the international criminal court: Observers' notes, Article by Article* (3rd ed.). Hart Publishing.
Zwiers, M. L., & Morrissette, P. J. (1999). *Effective interviewing of children: A comprehensive guide for counselors and human service workers*. Taylor and Francis. (eBook).

Ronda Cress is Senior Legal Counsel at the Ohio Department of Medicaid and has been a practicing lawyer for over a decade, with an emphasis in health law and disability rights. Ronda earned an LL.M. in International Human Rights Law from the University of Essex in 2013. Her studies focused on the right to health, disability rights, transitional justice and the rule of law. She also participated as an Associate with the Human Rights in Iran Unit. She currently works in state government as in-house counsel for the agency administering the Medicaid program, which is the U.S.'s public health insurance program for the poor, elderly and people with disabilities.

Appendix A: Summary of Advocacy Fundamentals

This appendix summerises advocacy fundamentals. Appendix B in this work then tests these fundamentals through hypothetical case studies. Material in this appendix has been drawn from victim advocacy training workshops delivered to List of Counsel members. This training was facilitated by the Counsel Support Section of the International Criminal Court in 2012 and 2013 at The Hague and was developed and delivered by the Australian Advocacy Institute and Faculty of Law, Monash University. For more detailed information on advocacy fundamentals and techniques, please read the related chapters in this work, particularly those authored by George Hampel.

1 Communication as an Essential Part of Persuasion

This involves building a relationship with the decision maker by:

- involving the decision maker,
- speaking with apparent conviction and commitment,
- using a conversational style,
- using simple, expressive language—avoiding jargon and legalese,
- speaking in an audible, varied voice,
- keeping a slow/punctuated pace,
- maintaining good eye contact,
- minimizing or avoiding the use of notes,
- using appropriate body language,
- avoiding distracting mannerisms and verbal habits, and
- being tactful and empathetic with witnesses and the decision maker.

E. King et al. (eds.), *Victim Advocacy before the International Criminal Court*,
https://doi.org/10.1007/978-3-030-56733-0

2 The Approach to the Trial Process

A trial is not an inquiry or an investigation. It is a purposive exercise by each side to achieve its desired result, based on its case theory.

In performance preparation of each task:

- the *final address* (Argument) must be prepared first based on the case theory and the arguments to support it;
- *evidence in chief* must be prepared next because it is usually the foundation for the case theory;
- *cross examination* is prepared next to discredit, accredit or emphasise;
- *re-examination* is next to the extent to which it is possible to anticipate cross-examination; and
- the *opening* is prepared last when all above steps have been prepared and the course of the trial is set.

3 Summaries of Specific Advocacy Tasks

3.1 Opening

An Opening is:

- a short outline of the case,
- told as a simple persuasive story,
- in narrative not argumentative form,
- painting pictures of places, people and events,
- well structured,
- not over detailed,
- presented with the use of visual aids, and
- related to the charges.

A Defence Opening should:

- identify the issues,
- outline the Defence story in relation to the contested issues,
- be in narrative not argumentative form,
- be positive, not defensive; and
- avoid repetition of the prosecution/plaintiff story.

3.2 *Examination in Chief and Re-Examination*

Examination in Chief:

- develops in detail of the story as opened,
- is organized and structured,
- sets the scenes before the action,
- is controlled by the advocate,
- is told by the witness in answer to non-leading questions on contested issues,
- establishes facts not conclusions,
- is assisted by visual aids (and tendering exhibits),
- involves the tribunal, and
- with expert witnesses—qualifies the witness and leads the opinion.

Re-Examination is:

- limited to that which arises in cross examination,
- elicited by non-leading questions, and
- used sparingly and only when necessary.

3.3 *Cross Examination*

Cross Examination is:

- a foundation for the final argument;
- organised, structured and controlled by the advocate;
- designed to discredit or accredit the evidence and/or the witness;
- consistent with the case theory;
- conducted by a series of leading propositions;
- not argumentative;
- conducted without repetition of evidence in chief;
- organised with appropriate 'gate closing';
- not unnecessarily aggressive or confrontational;
- compliant with Professor Irving Younger's "10 Commandments of Cross Examination"; and
- compliant with the rule in *Browne v Dunn*. (please see footnote no. 2, under heading "1. Rules of Evidence" in chapter titled "Leading Evidence in Chief" in this work).

3.4 Argument

Argument is:

- logical, credible, empathetic (Aristotle);
- a series of structured arguments;
- presented as a series of conclusions supported by facts or inferences;
- designed to persuade the tribunal;
- directed towards the desired result;
- consistent with the case theory;
- consistent with the onus of proof;
- balanced—deals with weaknesses;
- presented in a conversational style;
- prepared to be ready with answers to anticipated questions from the tribunal; and
- presented as appellate argument—based on the grounds of appeal and in compliance with appellate principles.

Appendix B: Advocacy Case Studies and Exercises

This appendix contains practical exercises to assist the reader in developing their advocacy skills in the context of victims and the International Criminal Court.

Before undertaking the exercises, it would be beneficial to reflect on the content and tips discussed in this book, especially *Part II Essential Advocacy Techniques; advocacy skills for the victim advocate.*

The fictitious case study is set out in two parts. Part A encourages the victim advocate to prepare a legal argument based on the case facts provided. Part B provides additional statements and reports that have been introduced during a hypothetical trial setting, consequently shaping your ongoing case theory and advocacy choices. Part B also canvasses the issue of victim reparations.

The original material in this appendix has been drawn from two victim advocacy workshops facilitated by the Australian Advocacy Institute and Monash University (Australia) in October 2012 and 2013. The workshops were delivered to ICC List of Counsel members, at the List of Counsel Seminars of 2012 and 2013, The Hague. They were organised and supported by the Counsel Support Section of the International Criminal Court.

1 Case Study—Part A

Exercise #1 for Case Study—Part A

As victim advocate, consider **how you would approach this case and prepare your presentation of argument.**

Several aspects to consider are your legal argument, examination in chief, cross-examination and opening address (see also Part II Appendix 1 for summaries of these specific advocacy skills).

E. King et al. (eds.), *Victim Advocacy before the International Criminal Court*,
https://doi.org/10.1007/978-3-030-56733-0

1.1 Background

The Petan Nation is a small country that is land locked by three other nations. Petan is a state signatory to, and has ratified, the Rome Statute.

In modern times it has been a country that has survived on a modest agrarian model of small scale farming. It has enjoyed a modest but vibrant domestic commerce based on the trade of essential products such as food, tools, livestock and building materials.

Petan is a developing nation and many of its inhabitants live in extreme economic hardship, particularly the inhabitants of the smaller regional villages. Most children in Petan have had access to some education although this is compromised by their work at home for their families. It has previously been recognised by the world community that the girl-children of Petan require particular attention in respect to socio-economic disadvantage.

Petan had enjoyed relative peace for many years although that has changed in recent times. Six years ago mineral deposits were discovered near the small rural village of Nuorm.

These mineral deposits represent a potential for vast wealth.

Five years ago, political agitations escalated over access to the mineral deposits. This agitation was between the governing military regime of Petan, known as the *Vento* and a breakaway politicised rebel militia known as the *Pana*. Civil War broke out shortly thereafter.

As part of its stratagem, the *Vento* began a fierce military campaign against all civilians who were perceived to be in sympathy with the *Pana*. Warfare methods included the deliberate targeting of civilian populations, wilful killing, sexual violence, looting, destruction of civilian infrastructure and the destruction of homes.

Captain Mayne was a key figure in devising the *Vento* military stategym, and was responsible for the infamous Nuorm civilian campaign. Nuorm was chosen as a target by the *Vento* for two reasons.

The first was because of its proximity to the mineral deposits.

The second was that one of Nuorm's residents, Vole Ventig, was an underground member of the *Pana*. Vole Ventig is reported to have engaged in the *Pana's* notorious interrogation tactics of torture. This disturbing practice was corroborated by contemporary eye witness accounts and reports of respected human rights NGO organisations. It is said that the attack on Nuorm was in part revenge for Vole Ventig's interrogation methods.

Nuorm was attacked in late 2007 by a military force under Captain Mayne's command.

Following a period of extreme destabilisation, peace resumed in Petan following the successful installation of a democratically elected government. This current government has stated its commitment to democratic principles, human rights and the rule of law. It referred the situation concerning Captain Mayne and the attack on Nuorm to the International Criminal Court.

Following the necessary investigations, Captain Mayne faced trial on charges of command responsibility for the commission of War Crimes and Crimes against Humanity under the relevant provisions of Articles 7 and 8 of the Rome Statute. He was found guilty of these crimes.

Vole Ventig remains missing and it is assumed that he is in hiding somewhere in the hills near Nuorm. Dissident *Vento* and *Pana* elements remain in the Petan population although the current government feels that these are adequately controlled.

1.2 STATEMENT of Aya Vinteg

I. I am eleven years old and I am the oldest of three children. I have two younger brothers. Their names are Alouin and Sabam. They are eight and six years old. Sabam died when the fighting in my village (called Nurom) happened last year. I feel sad. He was my brother and I took a lot of care of him. I loved him.

II. I have my mother but I do not know where my father is now. He joined one of the fighting groups to fight last year and we don't know where he is. I miss him. I think he went up, away from where we live, up towards the Dia border, but I don't know. I ask my mother where he is but she says that it is better for us not to worry about it. If he comes back to us then we will know. But he might not come back.

III. Before all the fighting, my father owned a sewing shop in our community, in Nurom. He would make things for people. From new material. They would choose the material. And he would fix the things that they brought in to him. Sometimes I would help him in the shop. He also sold small tools to people in our community, hammers and small axes and sometimes water buckets. He would get the things from the men on the boats on the river, coming from the city in Lin. I would help him collect from the boats and then help sell those things in the shop. The people who bought things gave him money and we had enough to eat for our family. For all of us. I would have liked more food but I wasn't hungry then the way I sometimes am now.

IV. When my father owned the shop I went to school with my brothers. It was a long walk to get there. We would walk up the hill near where we lived and then a long the river for a very long way. I would hold Sabam's hand while we walked and sometimes I would carry him. We went to school only sometimes, not every day. I liked school. I don't go there now. My teacher was funny and we learnt things on the blackboard. We learnt numbers, and writing. We also sang songs together and we had pencils and paper there.

V. I was good at my maths and sometimes I was good at the reading. I can't remember the names of the books but sometimes I was good at reading.

VI. When my mother and father would keep us home we would help. We would help my mother with her work getting the water and keeping the house and cooking and we would help my father with collecting things from the river men from Lin and the shop.

VII. My father closed the shop and left it to join the fighting group. Not the "Vento". Against the "Vento"—the "Pana". He left to join the fighting before the time that the "Vento" came to our village.

VIII. The *Vento* took our houses. When they came to our village shouting, they pushed the doors and they took things inside. I was sleeping when they came to my home. There were three men but I didn't know them. I didn't recognise them. They were *Vento* though. They were shouting and they had guns. They took my mother to a room and she was screaming and later, afterward, she was shaking and crying. I hid under my blanket with Alouin. We were quiet. I was scared that I would not be able to be quiet. The men shouted a lot and kicked things inside. They took our objects, our things. They took our tools and some fabric and they smashed things apart before they left.

IX. Other houses in my village were burned to the ground. The *Vento* set them on fire. People died in Nurom. They were shot with the guns, or burnt. Sabam was shot. He lived in my Aunt's house and that night he was shot.

X. After the fighting we were frightened that the *Vento* might come back. We left Nuorm and went walking for a lot of days afterward—my mother, Alouin and me. We walked along the river and saw all the bridges down. All the roads were torn up and there were no boats on the river. We passed my school. The *Vento* had locked it up and sprayed messages to keep out all over the front. We walked for a long time, for days and nights. We became sick from no food.

XI. When we came back, we had to move into my Aunt's house. Our house had been ruined while we were away walking.

XII. Our shop was no good. All the things inside it had been taken. The walls and the door were kicked in. There was no sewing machine anymore.

XIII. The *Vento* left a lot of damage in my village. A lot of broken things. There are some things that I would like, that I would like to see happen at the Court in The Hague. I think the *Vento* are bad and should be caught. They should go to jail. I would like to get my father's sewing machine back or a new one. I want to make some money for my family because my mother is too sick to work. I would like something to remind me of Sabam and I think I want to go back to school.

XIV. I am glad that the people from the Court came to talk with me to see how I felt. It felt good to talk about everything.

XV. My mother does not mind if I have a lawyer for the Court but she doesn't want to be part of anything. She says that it has already been enough.

1.3 STATEMENT of Witness Dav Phaid

I. I am 63 years old. I farm land. I have lived in the village of Nuorm for all of my life. The young girl Aya Ventig is known to me. Also her father and mother and brothers and cousins. I am a little older than Aya Ventig's father. His name is Vole Ventig. He is the tailor in our village of Nuorm.

II. Also for a long time now he has been a member of the *Pana*. They are the group that have been fighting against the *Vento*. He was very powerful in the *Pana*. Very high up. Before the *Vento* came to our village, he had already fled to the hills to help lead the *Pana*. A lot of people in Nuorm think that the *Vento* came because he lived here. The things that he had been messed up in were cruel to others. To the families of the *Vento*. So they came to our village for revenge.

III. I think that Aya is a good young girl. But a lot of people in Nuorm think that a member of Vole Ventig's family should not get reparations from the Court. All of the people in Nuorm are in need and Vole Ventig invited our troubles.

1.4 A Multidisciplinary Expert Team Organised by the Trust Fund for Victims[1] Reports That:

I. Aya is a child who has witnessed catastrophic events that have resulted in post traumatic shock and high mental anguish for her. These events include the invasion and looting of her home, her apprehension that her life was in danger, the loss of her brother Sabam, her disconnection from her home during a period of itinerancy and the partial witnessing (although not complete comprehension of) her mother's sexual assault at the hands of three members of the *Vento* militia.

II. Aya is a child whose physical development and health have been permanently compromised by the malnutrition that she has suffered over the past twelve months. Most particularly stemming from the period in which she and her family were itinerant following the attack on her village.

III. Aya's family are now living in extreme poverty.

IV. Aya is a highly intelligent girl-child who faces few educational or vocational prospects at this point. This will inevitably impact upon her capacity to enjoy a gender parity in respect to socio economic opportunity vis-a-vis her male peers within her community.

[1] The synthesised findings contained in this report reflect the expertise of child development psychologists (one of whom has consulted with Aya directly), paediatricians, historians, anthropologists, political scientists, post traumatic shock experts and those program officers of the Trust Fund for Victims who have been working on the ground in the village of Nuorm for the past twelve months.

V. Aya has no real knowledge of the level of her father, Vole Ventig's, role in the *Pana*, nor the inferences made by some leading members of her community that he (and by extension her) bear a moral culpability for the attack on Nuorm.

VI. Aya has no real knowledge of the ongoing level of physical disability and mental disorder that her mother now suffers as a result of having been the victim of extreme sexual violence at the hands of three militia.

VII. Sadly whilst the events that Aya has experienced are extreme and horrendous, in Nuorm they are not unique. Many members of her community, young and old, have also had traumatic experiences. She has been affected by the combination of seeing her mother harmed and the death of her brother.

VIII. The Trust Fund for Victims have already been successful in establishing an *Outreach Program* in Nuorm. It has successfully charted the rehabilitative needs of the youth community and has identified and made initial contact with those regional service providers who will be able to assist in providing rehabilitive counselling services. It is anticipated that many residents of Nuorm would benefit from such a service.

IX. There is a distinct possibility that an individual award of reparations for Aya could create some division in Aya's community. This could potentially flow from resentment that she has received an individual recognition, coupled with the associations of the Ventig family name.

X. Were Aya to be awarded a symbolic or transformative form of reparations, a monument to Sabam, noting the attack perpetrated by the *Vento*, would certainly accord with her wishes. Such a monument could potentially agitate *Pana* elements in her country more broadly and would need to be managed very carefully.

2 General Instructions for Victim Advocates

- Aya Vinteg's involvement with the International Criminal Court has commenced following the conviction of Captain Mayne for Crimes Against Humanity and War Crimes under the relevant provisions of Articles 7 and 8 of the Rome Statute.
- Namely, command responsibility for crimes relating to the perpetration of sexual violence, looting, wilful killing, the attacking of an undefended civilian population, attack on civilian objects, and the destruction of civilian infrastructure.
- This satisfies the requirement that for the purposes of reparations, a person claiming victim status must be a victim of a crime that was under prosecution before the court and that has resulted in a conviction.
- Trial Chamber 1 in the recent 'Decision establishing the principles and procedures to be applied to reparations'[2] devolved a number of reparations related

[2] 'Decision establishing the principles and procedures to be applied to reparations' situation in the Democratic Republic of the Congo in the case of the *Prosecutor v Thomas Lubanga Dylio,* Trial Chamber 1, No. ICC-01/04-01/06, 7 August 2012. For further contemporary analysis, case law and

functions to the Trust Fund for Victims (refer to *The Trust Fund for Victims: inter-cultural and collective perspectives* for more information on their role). For the purposes of this exercise, each of the arguments that you are preparing to make are being made before the Trial Chamber itself. This is in response to a request by the Court to be addressed on specific matters requiring legal argument. Namely:

- Should Aya Ventig be recognised as a victim for these proceedings and be represented individually? and
- In the event that Aya Ventig is recognised as a victim with individual standing, what modality and scope of reparations are most appropriate for her?

– The multidisciplinary team report provided by the Trust Fund for Victims (included above) was requested by the Court. It represents a consultative and multidisciplinary approach with input from a number of experts and outreach program workers who are familiar with the Nuorm region.
– There was no consultation with the defence in the selection of experts for this multidisciplinary team.
– Two of the report's authors, the child psychologist Professor Ella Ceta and the cultural historian, Dr Alan Wesley have stated commitment to the rehabilitation of the victimised people of Nuorm. They have previously authored a joint academic article decrying the impacts on children rendered by the *Vento* military strategy.
– Somewhat unusually, Captain Mayne has some limited (at this stage unquantified) funds. In the event that reparations are awarded he will be liable for any financial payments.
– The Child Rights International organisation (CRI) has been granted leave by the Court to address it on Aya Ventig's application for reparations.
– The CRI is an internationally recognised and respected NGO organisation dedicated to the promotion of the rights of the child. It is most particularly active in advocating for the rights of those children who are the victims of armed conflict. The CRI has often been consulted by the UN Committee on the Rights of the Child.

---

commentary on victims and reparations in international criminal law, see the ICC Legal Tools resource portal at https://www.legal-tools.org/ (Accessed 01/12/2021). See also chapter titled "A Brief Overview of the Crimes Prosecuted by the ICC, Defences to These Crimes, and the Scope of Liability for These Crimes" by Sam Garkawe in this work.

3 Case Study—Part B

Exercise #1 for Case Study—Part B
The advocate is requested to read all the materials below and understand the case for each side—both in the prosecution of Ms April Delphi and in the subsequent victim reparations claim.

3.1 The Prosecutor v. April Delphi

3.1.1 The Trial of Ms April Delphi: The Alleged Meeting of the 30th May

This part of the materials contains:

- General guidelines
- Instructions to Counsel from the accused, Ms April Delphi
- Statement of prosecution witness 1 (P1), Senior Assistant Officer Ang Long
- Record of interview of Senior Assistant Officer Ang Long and Ms April Delphi
- Written Statement of the Accused Ms April Delphi
- Report of prosecution witness 2 (P2), Xavier Stamford
- Report of defence witness 1 (D1), Dr Constance Sultan
- Agreed Statements of Fact of Ms Rema Chalk, Mr Herbert Till and Mr Frank Ng

3.1.2 General Guidelines for Participating Counsel

Charge:
The accused, Ms April Delphi, has been charged under Article 25(3) (a) of the Rome Statute, as individually criminally responsible as an indirect co-perpetrator for the following war crime:

> Intentionally directing an attack against a building dedicated to religion, education, art, science or charitable purposes, historic monuments, hospitals and places where the sick and wounded are collected, the building in question not being a military objective (pursuant to Article 8(2)(e)(iv)).

Particulars:
The prosecution alleges that:

I. It *was* Ms April Delphi who attended the meeting on the 30th May and gave orders to the *Vento* militia for the destruction of civilian property, particularly primary schools, throughout the South of Petan. This includes giving a specific directive to destroy the Nuorm Village School and assisting in the destruction of the school.

II. The fire at the Nuorm School was *deliberately* lit *by* the *Vento* militia with the intention to destroy it, pursuant to Ms Delphi's orders and with her assistance.

III. The Nuorm Village School was destroyed by fire.

Factual Background:

A non-international armed conflict was found to have taken place in the nation of Petan three years ago. That armed conflict is now over and Petan is currently governed by an interim government that maintains a commitment to peace, the rule of law and the community repair of Petan.

The parties to the conflict were the formally elected government of Petan (an oppressive regime that did not enjoy wide spread popular support and ultimately dissolved) and rebel forces calling for greater rights for Petan citizens and equitable access to resource wealth in Petan.

A splinter group of the rebel force was known as the *Pana* militia. The *Pana* tactics were notoriously extreme and their strategy was to target civilians and civilian infrastructure in order to destabilise the governing regime.

The *Pana* were initially concentrated in the hills of Petan. The incidents described in these materials immediately precede a swift infiltration of civilian village areas throughout Southern Petan by the *Vento* and the accelerated death of civilians and destruction of civilian property over a period of two months.

Instructions of Ms April Delphi:

April Delphi instructs that what she said in her written statement provided to Senior Assistant Officer Ang Long is correct.

She also confirms that, as far as she can recall, the record of interview is correct.

When she was asked in Q.7 if she knew Tanko, she became frightened but shortly after conceded that she knew him.

3.1.3 STATEMENT of Senior Assistant Officer Ang Long

1. I am a Senior Assistant Officer of the Petan Police. I am stationed with the Southern Region to maintain law and order throughout the area. The armed conflict that recently shook Petan made this task even more important but also more difficult. During the conflict, part of my job became to conduct surveillance of any suspicious meetings and arrangements that might involve the *Vento* militia and plans to hurt civilians or civilian property. My job was to then pass on any relevant information to members of the Petan Military Police for action.
2. Three years ago on 30th May I received information about a likely *Vento* meeting in Sera St, Nuorm in the Old Town Café. The meeting was to discuss and arrange a planned civilian property attack for very early the next day. Key figures of the informal *Vento* militia structure would be there, including one local woman said to be central to the *Vento* strategic planning and command. Accordingly I went to Sera Street, Nuorm, on surveillance at about 11.00 pm.

3. I parked my unmarked car opposite the Old Town Café building. I alighted from the car, walked north and took up a position opposite the telephone box which was on the other side of the street.
4. The traffic was medium density (there were bikes, mopeds, carts and an occasional car) and there were a few people moving about on the footpath.
5. At about 1.00 am on 1st June, I saw a person I now know to be April Delphi come out of the Old Town Café.
6. I had a good clear view of her and noticed that she was wearing a black cotton shirt dress, long black socks and flat ankle boots. She was about 170 cms tall, of medium build and had short ochre red tipped hair.
7. She walked north along the footpath. She then entered the phone box and closed the door. It was a glass sided phone box so I had a clear view of her. She looked around furtively, reached into her large floral patterned bag and withdrew a magazine and placed it on the shelf underneath the phone. She then left the phone box.
8. She crossed Sera Street diagonally to where my car was and then walked south down Sera Street. As she was crossing the road I noticed that her hair was spiked on top, she wore large hooped earrings and red-framed glasses. She was carrying the floral bag in her left hand. I then lost sight of her.
9. I continued my surveillance and at 1.10 am I saw a yellow moped stop beside the telephone box. It was ridden by a person I now know to be a *Vento* militia operative, Tem Tanko. He was wearing the scarf of the *Vento* militia. He went into the telephone box and appeared to remove the magazine. He got back on his moped and headed out on the road to the rural outskirts of Nuorm.
10. I immediately contacted a military police colleague by radio and informed him of what I had seen. I asked him to track Tanko as I had suspicions that he was about to perform an attack on civilians or civilian property. It was not my role to seek to apprehend Tanko.
11. Seven hours later I was called by my military police colleague. I was advised that they had lost sight of Tanko near the Nuorm Village School. That school had been burnt down at about 5.30 am. I was then told that Tem Tanko had later been apprehended at 7 am, along with fifteen or so other *Vento* Milita. They had been taking the road that leads out of Nuorm. Apparently a magazine with a photo of the Nuorm Village School inside its front cover was found in Tanko's jacket pocket. Tanko was arrested but later escaped.
12. At about mid-morning I went back to the Old Town Café. Once inside I noticed a woman behind the counter who I now know to be April Delphi. I recognised her as the woman I had seen on the previous night. She had changed her hair style, it was no longer spiked. I heard her speak to a man standing next to her. She said "Tanko was arrested earlier this morning". That's all I heard her say. I then went through the door at the back of the café and noticed a large room at the back with a table and chairs arranged around it.
13. I then walked back onto the street outside and quickly prepared a sketch plan of the street area and its buildings. [Fig. 1]

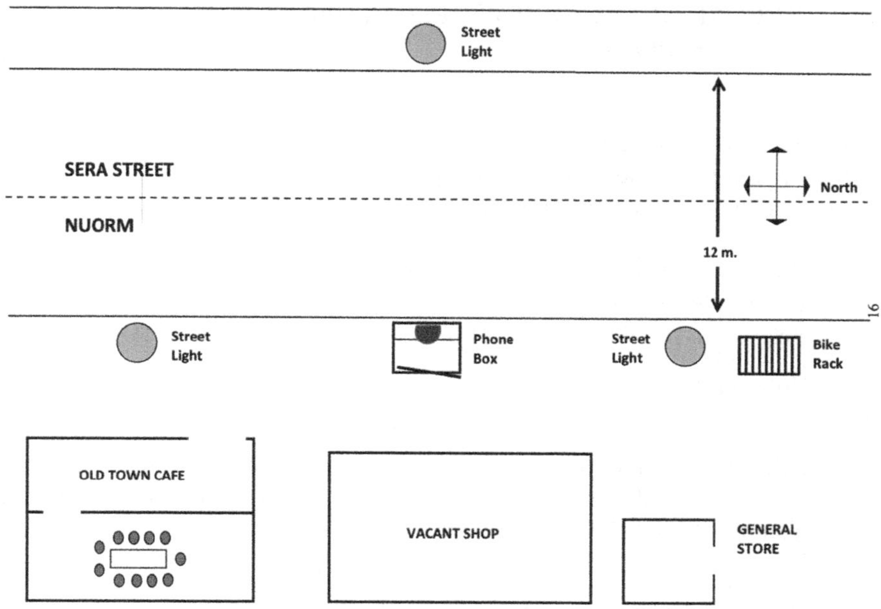

Fig. 1 Sketch plan of the street area and its buildings around Old Time Café—drawn and produced by Senior Assistant Officer Ang Long © COPYRIGHT 2013—Australian Advocacy Institute

14. I immediately went back to the police station where I looked up a list of known associates of Tem Tanko's. On his file I found an old photograph of April Delphi. In this photograph she was wearing large hooped earrings and her hair was spiked on top.
15. I then returned to the cafe and spoke to April Delphi. After I confirmed who she was, I said "It is alleged that you were involved with Tem Tanko and that you planned and gave orders for the destruction of the Nuorm Village School by *Vento* militia." She said "You've got the wrong woman."
16. I asked her to come with me to Nuorm's police station, where I conducted a formal interview which was tape-recorded.
17. I produced a transcript of that interview.
18. Later on the evening of 1st June, Ms Delphi came to the Police Station and handed me a written document. [see "Record of Interview" in this chapter, Sect. 3.1.4] She said to me "I thought I'd better tell you the whole story of what happened".

Signed: Senior Assistant Officer Ang Long
10.00 am, 2 June

3.1.4 RECORD OF INTERVIEW: Senior Assistant Officer Long and Ms April Delphi

Conducted on 1st June (three years ago).
Interview commenced at 4.00 pm
Senior Assistant Officer Long asking questions.
The interview was tape-recorded.

Q1 Your full name is April Delphi and you work as a manager at the Nuorm Old Town Café. Is that right?
A Yes.

Q2 How old are you?
A 37.

Q3 I wish to interview you in relation to the planning and the execution of that plan to target the primary schools of Southern Petan and particularly the Nuorm Village School. Do you understand that?
A No.

Q4 Do you understand why you are here today?
A You asked me to come, I don't know why.

Q5 It is alleged that you conspired with Tem Tanko of the *Vento* militia to target and set alight the Nuorm Village School. What do you say to that?
A I had nothing to do with it.

Q6 At 1.00 am on 1st June I saw you leave the Old Town Café and enter the nearest phone box where you deposited a magazine on a shelf under the phone.
A You didn't see me. You've got the wrong woman.

Q7 Do you know Tem Tanko?
A Never heard of him. No wait, I think I know who you mean. I think he might sometimes be a customer at the café—but I don't know him. I have had nothing to do with him.

Q8 I heard you tell a man at the café that you knew that Tanko was arrested this morning.
A OK, I might have been set up.

Q9 What did you do after you left the Old Town Cafe at about 1.00 am?
A I walked past the telephone box and got on my bike and rode home.

Q10 Do you own a black cotton shirt dress?
A Yes I do. I just got it. As a matter of fact, as I walked past the phone box I saw another woman in a shirt dress with buttons just like mine, near the door of the phone box. It struck me because I thought that mine was the only one with the coloured buttons.

< Senior Assistant Officer Long shows the file photo to Ms Delphi >

Q11 Is this a photo of you?
A Yes, but I haven't looked like that for a long time! Not since March, when I was away sick.

Q12 What do you mean?
A Well I was away sick and after that I didn't wear hooped earrings anymore. I changed my hairdo when I returned to work and I gave my hooped earrings away.

Q13 Do you wear glasses?
A Only for reading and sunglasses.

Q14 Do you have a floral bag?
A No. Only this brown leather hand bag.

Q15 I noticed that there was a meeting room at the back of the café. It is alleged that on the night I saw you, you were involved in a meeting with the *Vento* there.
A I don't have anything to do with the meetings there. I don't think there was a meeting there last night.

Q16 Tell me why you happened to be at the phone box just before Tanko turned up?
A I am not answering any more questions. I've told you all I want to say.

Interview terminated 4.40 pm.

3.1.5 STATEMENT of April Delphi

I thought I would write out what really happened in detail just in case I'm charged.

I am the manager of the Old Town Café. On the night of 30th May I remember leaving the café at about 1 am just before closing time. I walked north up Sera Street to pick up my bike which I leave locked at the bike rack outside the general store. As I passed the phone box just before the general store, I noticed that there was a woman standing near the door of the phone box.

There were other people about but I remember her because she was about my own height and wearing a black cotton shirt dress just like mine. Even the buttons were just like mine. I did not go into the phone box or leave any magazine or photo there. I continued past her and reached for my bike. I unlocked it and rode home.

I know a man called Tem Tanko. He has been to the café many times in the last couple of months. He has bought me a few drinks and he has asked me out but I have never been out with him. In the morning there was a rumour that he had been arrested.

I was afraid to tell the police more about me and Tanko because I don't really know whose side he is on. There are whispers about him and the *Vento* and I don't want to have anything to do with them.

I have no previous convictions. I have never been charged with anything. I deny that I was in any way involved with him or anything to do with the burning down of the Nuorm Village school.

As I told the police today, I have not worn my hair spiked since I was sick in March. I gave my earrings away and I've never owned a floral bag.

Signed: April Delphi

1st June, 9.00 pm

3.2 The Trial of Ms April Delphi: The Burning of the Nuorm Village School

3.2.1 Accepted Statement of Facts: Ms Rema Chalk

Former teacher at the Nuorm Village School and current Nuorm resident.

I worked as a teacher at the Nuorm Village School when the school burnt down.

The school was certainly a strange old building. There was a lot of exposed wood and there were long wooden eaves running the whole length of its roof. It had a rickety central passageway and several rooms. There was a staff room to the right as you walked in and then a sleep room for students to the left (many needed to sleep because they would work long hours for their families). Then further down the passageway there was a storage room again on the right (for mops and cleaning products) and then to the left again was the school class room. At the very back of the building was an archive room. It was used by *The Petan Quality Teaching Association* to store paper files.

In the front staff room there were two old fabric chairs to sit in with cushions and a small table. There was also an electric water jug on the table. It was very old and it sometimes gave off sparks at the electrical power point. It was always connected to the power point. We used the jug to make hot water to pour into a basin so that we could then wash our hands at the start and end of each day. We were told to pull the cord out after we used the jug but sometimes it was left in overnight. I was told this was because there were "power surges" but I didn't know what was meant by that.

Right next to the electric jug on the table we kept a pile of folded blankets. We kept these to put over the children when they wanted to go to sleep in the sleep room.

What has happened is so sad.

I have given all this information to the expert fire investigators.

3.2.2 STATEMENT of Mr Herbert Till, Accepted Statement of Facts

Farmer and resident of the village of Nuorm.

As is well known, Nuorm has had some shocking troubles in recent times. I have lived in Nuorm all of my life. My children went to the Nuorm Village School.

I was the one who discovered that the school was burning.

I woke very early on 1st June, three years ago. I went on a long walk at about 6 am. I was planning to purchase supplies at our neighbouring village. It was risky because there were whispers that the *Vento* were about.

As I walked up the Nuorm main hill I passed a group of about fifteen or twenty *Vento* militia laughing and shouting. They were walking away from the general direction of the school and punching their arms up into the air. I made sure that I didn't look at them straight in the eye. I did recognise their uniform. I also recognised the young man heading the group—I know him as "Tem Tanko". He comes from a village near Nuorm and is a local grocer. He sometimes runs a stall at the Nuorm produce market.

They were all carrying various items: boxes, food, large tins, carry cans and things like that.

Then I smelt smoke and in the distance I saw flames coming from the front part of the school where the staff room was. I ran closer, realised there was a problem and then ran to the nearest farm to get help. Then I rushed back to the school. As I approached the front entrance there was a large whoosh of air and flames. It forced me back into the school's front garden.

A lot of people turned up soon afterward with buckets of water but it was no use. Volunteer fire fighters were called but the fire was very strong and in the end the school was ruined.

3.2.3 Reported Observations of Local Volunteer Fire-fighter, Mr Frank Ng

Volunteer fire fighter Mr Frank Ng attended the fire scene immediately and reported the following observations to both Mr Xavier Stamford and Dr Constance Sultan:

a. The spread of the fire was greatly assisted by the eaves of the school that were unlined and which caused great draughts of air to be sucked in, fanning the fire.
b. The front staff room appeared to be the worst hit and the probable source of the fire.
c. There were two other seats of fire, that is to say, where there was intense charring of burning right through the floorboards. One in the hallway outside, what appeared to be the class room, and one in the archive room at the rear of the school.
d. There were no remains in the immediate vicinity of these areas which could have caused intense heat and burning. The sort of things one would expect to find would include household containers, flammable liquids such as methylated spirits, gas bottles and the like.
e. On return to the fire scene the next day, it appeared that the remains had been disturbed overnight, perhaps by looters.

3.2.4 REPORT by Expert Witness Called by the Prosecution, Mr Xavier Stamford

I am a fire investigator. I was employed by the Metropolitan Fire Brigade of New York for six years. During that time I investigated domestic fires and industrial, electrical and chemical fires. I have attended numerous extra courses in fire prevention, control, protection, detection and investigation. More recently I have worked as an independent consultant and have based my consultancy a short flight from Petan and its neighbours.

Three years ago, on the 1st June, I went to the Nuorm Village School to investigate the scene of a fire that had occurred there. I was called to urgently investigate by a not for profit organisation called *The Petan Quality Teaching Association*. They were very concerned about the targeting and burning of schools during the armed conflict there. Despite the unrest in Petan I agreed to attend the scene. I am familiar with the observations made by the volunteer fire fighter who first attended the scene, Mr Frank Ng. I have also read the agreed statement of facts of Ms Rema Chalk.

The site was a level rectangular acre block. Upon the block there were the remains of what had clearly been a double-fronted building of regular rectangular shape with a pitched roof. The school was old and built of timber. The inner walls and ceiling were lined with timber and plaster. The floors were timber. The ceiling was of galvanized iron. The eaves were not lined.

The fire was of comparatively recent origin, although all of the heat had gone out of the remains.

Upon investigation I saw three separate seats of fire. I was told by a local fire fighter that it was thought that an electric water jug, which was faulty, had malfunctioned. I did not find any jug but I did find the remains of a short length of flex in the staff room which was consistent with one used in an appliance such as an electric jug.

There were splash marks emanating from the first and largest seat of the fire in the staff room and down towards the second seat, which was in the hallway just outside the classroom. By splash or spread marks I mean areas of intense charring travelling down from the first large seat of fire towards the second seat.

The second seat was a circular charred area about eight inches in diameter where once again the floorboards had been burnt completely through. Upon investigation of the area of ground underneath that hole, I was unable to find the remains of any item that could have been standing in that area and which could have burnt so intensely. There were splash marks emanating again from that second seat of fire down the hallway and into the archive room at the rear of the school.

In the archive room there was a third large hole approximately 18 inches in diameter. Here again the floorboards had completely burnt through and upon investigation of the ground beneath I could find no traces of any object that may have been standing on that area.

It is my conclusion then that the fire was deliberately lit because of:

- the presence of three separate seats of fire;
- the absence from the first and largest seat of fire of the remains of any electric jug that may have been there; and
- the splash marks between each of the three seats of fire. These indicated a spreading or sprinkling of an inflammable liquid or fire accelerant along the floor. Another reason why the fire spread so rapidly (apart from my view that it was ignited in three separate areas and flammable liquids splashed around between those areas) was due to the age and condition of the building.

When the fire started in the front staff room, it spread rapidly throughout the rest of the school and consumed everything inside rapidly because the uncovered eaves enabled fresh air to be sucked in from outside and accelerated the spread of fire.

Another factor that leads me to believe the fire was deliberately lit was that I have been told by neighbours that a local farmer, Mr Herbert Till, saw militia acting suspiciously in the area not far from the school when it was first burning.

3.2.5 REPORT by Expert Witness Called by the Defence, Dr Constance Sultan

I am a freelance fire and safety consultant. I have a BSc and PhD on the topic of identifying causes of fire from the Sciences Faculty, New York University. I have had extensive experience both in domestic and industrial fires. For three years I ran the Fire Investigation Training School for the Metropolitan Fire Brigade in New York. In my time with the Metropolitan Fire Brigade I attended and investigated many fires. When I left the Metropolitan Fire Brigade I set up my own international consultancy business. I have written many expert reports for legal proceedings in relation to the cause of fires. Proceedings in which I have provided expert opinion include criminal matters, coronial proceedings and civil claims throughout Europe and America.

I was asked to express an opinion about the fire at the Nuorm Village School by the defence team for Ms April Delphi after a warrant for her arrest was issued by the Pre-Trial Chamber of the ICC.

I am familiar with the observations made by the volunteer fire fighter who first attended the scene, Mr Frank Ng. I have also read the agreed statement of facts of Ms Rema Chalk.

I have been shown a copy of the report of Mr Xavier Stamford relating to the fire at the site of the Nuorm Village School. I came across young Xavier Stamford as a trainee in the MFB. I would say he had potential but was somewhat sloppy and did not follow through the recommended instruction procedures. For example here he did not take photographs of the scene and particularly of the splash marks. Splash marks can be of different types, sizes and cause.

In my view the conclusions that the fire was deliberately lit cannot stand for the following reasons:

- It is not suspicious in itself to have three separate seats of fire. A seat of fire is nothing more than an area of more intense burning or charring than the surrounding area.
- A seat of fire can be, but is not necessarily, the source or commencement of the fire. It can be, and quite often is, simply an area where the fire was more intense than any other area because of the presence of a more flammable material than in the surrounding area.

As mentioned, unfortunately there doesn't appear to be any photographs of the scene after the fire. I have not been to the site of the Nuorm Village School. It would be of no use my going there now in any event because one can only properly investigate and draw conclusions from an examination of the scenes of a fire, when the fire is of recent origin. The school was demolished by the time I was consulted.

It is not unusual for fires that occur near soft furnishings (here cushions and fabric chairs and folded blankets) to have an intense area of burning in and around the area of the soft furnishings. That is because fabric is more flammable than many other objects in a room. The fabric can catch alight very quickly and cause deep and intense burning in the furnishings themselves and, if they are low to the floor, the floor beneath them.

It is not uncommon where an electric appliance has caused a fire for very intense heat to be generated before the fire breaks out.

The other seats of fire described in the reports are smaller. They are both consistent with the storage of domestic solvents or other products which are highly flammable. Unfortunately many such flammable liquids are sold and stored in thin plastic which ignites and burns very quickly leaving very little residue. It is not uncommon for the residue not to be detected by fire investigators. It is possible that some inflammable materials had earlier been spilt on the floor.

I have spoken to former teaching staff of the school who confirm that there was an electric water jug on a small wooden table in the front staffroom. I was also told that the electric jug was usually left on at the wall switch, and just turned on and off from the switch control. I was told that this appliance had been faulty for some time.

I asked former teaching staff whether they stored anything in the hallway area near the classroom. They said that they used the hallway cupboard and some cupboards in the classroom as storage. Modest painting work had recently commenced at the school and a number of containers of mineral turpentine, paints, oils and brushes were stored in these cupboards, in various states of use. Additionally various cleaning products were stored in plastic bottles alongside a mop and broom in the general storage room.

The splash or spread marks between the seat of fire in the staffroom down to the one in the hallway, and from the hallway down to the archive room, whilst consistent with the deliberate spreading around of flammable material, are not necessarily indicative of a deliberate act. They are just as consistent with several explosions or intense burning causing the splashing of inflammable materials and more intense areas of burning. Much of the interpretation of these would depend on the timing and number of explosions caused by the flammable material, and would also depend on when and to what extent the door and the class room wall were burnt. It is not uncommon in intense small building fires for flammable liquids to explode and spray around the floor. Such an explosion, caused by the already raging fire can also cause splash or spread marks of the type described by Mr Stamford.

I should also add that I asked teaching staff about the seat of fire in the archive room at the rear of the school. They denied that they kept any flammable liquids in the rear of the school but they did mention that they kept a waste paper bin in that room. The day before the fire they had thrown a large quantity of paper files and other rubbish into it. They told me that they were cleaning up old files to make room. That could have caused an area of more intense burning.

4 Victims' Reparations

This part of the materials contains:

- General guidelines
- Instructions to Counsel from the victim, *The Petan Quality Teaching Association* ("The Organisation")
- Statement of victim witness 1 (V1), Mr Daniel Caine
- Statement of victim witness 2 (V2), Associate Professor Ms Karima Dolma

4.1 General Guidelines for Participating Counsel

You are to assume that the prosecution of Ms April Delphi has already taken place and the following was established to the satisfaction of the Court:

- That it *was* Ms April Delphi who attended the meeting of 30th May and gave orders to the *Vento* militia for the destruction of civilian property, particularly primary schools, throughout the South of Petan. That these orders included a specific directive to destroy the Nuorm Village School.
- That the fire at the Nuorm School was *deliberately* lit *by* the *Vento* militia with the intention to destroy it, pursuant to Ms Delphi's orders.
- That the Nuorm Village School was destroyed.

Accordingly the Court found that:

Under Article 25(3) (a) of the Rome Statute, Ms April Delphi is individually criminally responsible as an indirect co-perpetrator for the following war crime:

> Intentionally directing an attack against a building dedicated to religion, education, art, science or charitable purposes, historic monuments, hospitals and places

where the sick and wounded are collected, the building in question not being a military objective (pursuant to Article 8(2)(e)(iv)).

You are further advised that:

> The convicted person, Ms. April Delphi is *not* indigent. Ms Delphi's personal funds of three million dollars (US) were frozen in good time and remain available for reparations payment should the Court so order.

Exercise #2 for Case Study—Part B
Please read the client instructions and both of the victim witness statements (below).

Please read all materials and consider and prepare an examination and cross-examination of both witnesses.

4.2 Victims Reparations: Instructions

Relevant Rule:

Noting that the ICC's *Rules of Procedure and Evidence* provides under Rule 85 that for the purposes of the operation of the Rome Statute, a "victim" may include:

> organisations or institutions that have sustained direct harm to any of their property which is dedicated to religion, education, art or science or charitable purposes, and to their historic monuments, hospitals and other places and objects for humanitarian purposes.

You are to assume that the client (the *Petan Quality Teaching Association*) has already been granted standing to appear in the Reparation's Proceeding as an "organisation or institution", pursuant to the above Rule and following its application in writing to the Registrar outlining a description of the direct harm suffered, pursuant to Regulation 86(2)(c).

4.3 Instructions from The Petan Quality Teaching Association ("The Organisation")

The *Petan Quality Teaching Association* ("The Organisation") is a not for profit, non-governmental organisation representing the primary school educational sector in Petan. The Organisation is seeking reparations for the property damage that was inflicted on the Nuorm Village School. The Organisation owns all school buildings and school land throughout Petan on trust. It also acts as an informal employee union for Petan's school teachers.

The Organisation additionally claims that its teaching members have suffered individually from psychological harm—their morale has been completely shattered and many are devastated at the violent destruction of their places of work.

Some teachers have suffered from post-traumatic stress (reported effects include sleeplessness, nightmares and mood swings). They are reluctant to return to work. They are deeply fearful that the schools at which they teach will be targeted again.

The forms of harm that The Organisation claims have been suffered are:

- psychological harm, by which a person's mind has been affected by what he or she has experienced or witnessed (i.e. the psychological harm of many of The Organisation's constituent member teachers working in the Nuorm region), and
- material harm, by which goods or property have been damaged or lost (here the building known as "the Nuorm Village School").

The Organisation argues that because the attack on the Nuorm Village School was calculated and conducted with a complete disregard for the rights of children to access education—the reparations order should include not just a property restitutional element but an additional compensatory element. The reparations order should help create a new (and far better) state of the art contemporary learning facility.

This architect designed facility will house laptop computers and a complex IT learning network. It is to be built predominantly for the children of Nuorm but it will also enable adults to access books and learning tools.

Additionally, The Organisation seeks compensation for: the destroyed educational materials; the cost of reinstituting an archival record system to replace the lost records that were burnt down (staff and resources to affect a fresh census); the cost of sourcing and paying new teaching staff and the psychological rehabilitation of previous staff members.

Indicative costing for this project is approx. 3.8 million dollars US overall

4.4 Victims Witness One: Mr Daniel Caine

Consultant to *The Petan Quality Teaching Association* ("The Organisation")

Board member of The Organisation and part of the team providing instructions to Victim's Counsel.

1. I have undergraduate qualifications in history and biology. I also have a graduate diploma in primary teaching pedagogy. I received these qualifications from the University of Frend (located in our neighbour nation).
2. I have worked in education in Petan for the past thirty years. For the first ten years I was a primary school teacher. After my teaching work I co-established The Organisation and moved into supporting the teaching profession and primary education as a whole.

3. I have sat on the board of The Organisation for the past twenty years. The Organisation is a very noble enterprise. It is not tangled up in politics—it just wants what is best for the community—for young children particularly.
4. I regularly visit Petan's schools and talk with students and teachers. I also seek funding from the NGO sector. As far as financing goes—it all depends. At the moment, post conflict, nearly all NGO funding is geared to housing, food and water supply.
5. I have previously visited The Nuorm School. It was a very typical Petan Primary School—a basic wooden building, wooden desks and chairs, some modest materials and quite a lot of garden to play in. There was never the funding to purchase computers, library texts or even very much stationary. The real success of the typical Petan learning environment has always been the warmth of the regional student-teacher relationships.
6. We had stored archival material at the Nuorm Village School—regional details of students as well as teachers. All that's been burnt to the ground.
7. It saddens me deeply to think of the traumatized teachers throughout Petan. I've had to deal with the teacher upset and concern about safety. They're all quite terrified about going back to work.
8. I had a conversation with a former Nuorm teacher the other month. He said that he couldn't sleep. He has nightmares about the school being burnt down whilst he is teaching inside. His moods are up and down. It is definitely a mental health problem for him. He didn't want his name identified in this proceeding.
9. The learning facility architectural plans proposed for Nuorm were commissioned by us. The facility will provide an optimum learning environment for the most vulnerable of Nuorm's civilian population. It will also serve a number of village communities in the region. I think the sign of a sophisticated society is the environment it offers its children. The cost to build the facility would be 3.5 million (US).
10. If we were to wait for the completion of the four phases suggested by the current interim government, then the children who live in Nuorm right now—those who have borne direct witness to the conflict will be the very ones who are too old to enjoy educational opportunity. We need to help our future generation of thinkers right now.

4.5 Victims Witness Two: Associate Professor, Ms Karima Dolma

Interim government Spokeswoman, qualified economist and senior public servant. Working as a member of the interim peace regime for the Petan nation.

1. I hold a Bachelor of Economics from the Geneva institute of Economics. My study covered both micro and macroeconomics and included elective units in

community development and public health. I additionally hold a MSc in Finance and Economics from the London School of Economics.

2. Since graduating, I have worked for the NGO and governmental sector in Petan for eight years. I have been responsible for community development and government expenditure. I have advised on public health and sanitation. I currently advise the interim regime's Minister for Capacity Building. The Minister is a member of the Petan People's Party ("the PPP"), as am I.
3. The impact of the recent conflict on local village communities throughout Petan has been devastating. Many thousands of people have been left without proper homes. It is true that schools appeared to have been targeted quite specifically but that shouldn't overshadow the other damage.
4. Over the past six months all of our energies have been dedicated to providing shelter and rebuilding homes for the people of Petan. We initially provided tenting and tarpaulin's throughout the South. We describe this as 'Phase One' of our rebuilding efforts. It is a very slow process I'm afraid. There were some initial distribution problems. We have to wonder where some of the money and the equipment went. We haven't managed to reach everyone just yet.
5. 'Phase Two' of our plan is to rebuild basic accommodation for villagers—this takes time, not to mention builders, willingness and materials. The process will take another two years, perhaps more. It would be very unfortunate if the available labour force in Nuorm was distracted from this.
6. I do have a connection to Nuorm—so I understand its people. My great uncle lives there. He says the water and sanitation systems are out of control—he says if it goes on, more people will end up dying. He says, roughly 11 people died in Nuorm over the last year from contaminated water. That's a terrible thing.
7. We have tentatively costed a centralised water plant for all of South Petan. It would be about 2.8 million (US). It would stop the water situation developing into a critical public health issue. This is Phase Three of our planning.
8. Prior to the conflict, Petan schools were established in a chaotic and decentralised fashion, with no real consideration of where they should be located to do the most good.
9. The PPP wants to change that—we want to move to a situation where there are urban centralised places of learning. This will be more efficient. This approach hasn't been voted on just yet—we won't be having democratic elections for another year or more.
10. We're also hoping to develop a university. Schools at the primary level will need to be built in the right location so as to offer the right pathways to tertiary opportunities. Planning this will take time too. This would be Phase Four.
11. I want to make it clear that I am very much in favour of education for young people. The problem is we have bigger things of concern just now. The timing isn't right. Awarding reparations to The Organisation will be a distraction.

The manufacturer's authorised representative in the EU is Springer Nature Customer Service Centre GmbH, Europaplatz 3, 69115 Heidelberg, Germany. If you have any concerns regarding our products, please contact ProductSafety@springernature.com

Printed and bound by CPI Group (UK) Ltd, Croydon, CR0 4YY
30/09/2026
02225490-0019